Get the eBook FREE!

(PDF, ePub, Kindle, and liveBook all included)

We believe that once you buy a book from us, you should be able to read it in any format we have available. To get electronic versions of this book at no additional cost to you, purchase and then register this book at the Manning website.

Go to https://www.manning.com/freebook and follow the instructions to complete your pBook registration.

That's it!
Thanks from Manning!

100 SQL Server Mistakes and How to Avoid Them

100 SQL Server Mistakes and How to Avoid Them

PETER A. CARTER

MANNING
SHELTER ISLAND

For online information and ordering of this and other Manning books, please visit www.manning.com. The publisher offers discounts on this book when ordered in quantity.

For more information, please contact

Special Sales Department
Manning Publications Co.
20 Baldwin Road
PO Box 761
Shelter Island, NY 11964
Email: orders@manning.com

Manning Publications Co.
20 Baldwin Road
PO Box 761
Shelter Island, NY 11964

Development editor: Connor O'Brien
Technical editor: Grant Fritchey
Review editor: Dunja Nikitović
Production editor: Andy Marinkovich
Copy editor: Kari Lucke
Proofreader: Katie Tennant
Technical proofreader: Mike Shepard
Typesetter: Tamara Švelić Sabljić
Cover designer: Marija Tudor

ISBN 9781633437401
Printed in the United States of America

For Terri, my rock. Thank you.

brief contents

contents

preface

SQL Server is an incredibly rich and powerful toolset that can be used to store, retrieve, manipulate, and transform data. Over the years, a vast array of enhancements and auxiliary features have been added to the product, making it a very large subject to learn and master.

It is designed to be easy to use, but this combination of ease and flexibility makes SQL Server a product that is very easy to do badly and challenging to do well. Because data is so important for all organizations, if we do SQL Server badly, then it can open our organizations to many risks. These risks range from reduced productivity caused by poor performance to security risks. Organizations can even fall foul of regulatory compliance if data is lost, becomes unavailable, or even becomes available to people who should not be able to see it.

I have worked with SQL Server for two decades. In that time, I was lucky enough to be involved in some of the largest and most complex SQL Server projects in London. I have worked as a T-SQL developer, a business intelligence developer, a database administrator, a platform engineer, and an architect. I also really enjoyed working as a SQL Server trainer, which gave me the opportunity to work across Europe and meet some incredible people.

For the last 10 years, I have been privileged to write technical books on SQL Server. These books have spanned topics that include administration, automation, security, AlwaysOn, and advanced data types. In fact, *100 SQL Server Mistakes and How to Avoid Them* is my 11th book project.

Because I have worked in multiple SQL Server disciplines for a variety of FTSE 100 organizations, I have seen a multitude of mistakes that are made when people find themselves working, sometimes unexpectedly and often without formal training, as

SQL Server professionals. This is the inspiration for this book. I wanted to compile the most common mistakes that I have encountered, or sometimes made myself, into a single volume and help others to avoid falling into the same pitfalls.

Many technical books are "happy path." They teach readers how SQL Server is configured to work "when all is well," or they demonstrate how to engineer code to meet a specific requirement. This book is different. It highlights common misconceptions and misconfigurations and explains why they are problematic. It then describes what we can do differently to avoid the issues.

acknowledgments

Writing books is hard. It takes a vast amount of time. It can be a stressful and unsociable activity. For this reason, writing impacts not only the author but also their family. Therefore, I would especially like to thank my partner, Terri, for both her endless patience and the endless cups of coffee that arrived on my desk.

Writing is also a team sport, and this book would not be nearly as good as it is without the efforts of Connor O'Brien, the development editor for this project, and Grant Fritchey, the technical editor, who is also a Microsoft Data Platform MVP and AWS Community Builder, and who currently works as Product Advocate at Red Gate Software. A big thank you to both of you for all your efforts.

Additionally, to all the reviewers who provided their valuable feedback: Adam Wan, Alexander Makeev, Amol Gote, Andrew Briers, Andrew Judd, Ankit Virmani, Ben McNamara, Christian Leverenz, Dave Corun, Edward Pollack, Eli Rabinovitz, Esref Durna, Evan Benjamin, Grant Colley, Ian Stirk, Ivan A. Fernandez, João Marcelo Borovina Josko, Jonathan Reeves, José Alberto Reyes Quevedo, Josephine Bush, Mary Anne Thygesen, Meghal Gandhi, Mick Wilson, Mihaela Barbu, Nadir Doctor, Naga Santhosh Reddy Vootukuri, Peter A Schott, Praveen Raju, Prithvi Shivashankar, Regina Obe, Richard Jepps, Ruben Vandeginste, Scott Ling, Stephen Viljoen, Tania Lincoln, Wenyu Shi, and Wondi Wolde—your suggestions helped make this a better book.

about this book

100 SQL Server Mistakes and How to Avoid Them guides accidental database administrators (DBAs) through the minefield of SQL Server, helping them to avoid the common pitfalls that database professionals can fall into across a range of topics, including administration, development, and security.

Who should read this book?

This book is meant for accidental DBAs, junior SQL Server professionals, application developers who need to work with SQL Server, and even senior SQL Server professionals who do not have experience with recent versions of the product.

How this book is organized: A roadmap

This book consists of 14 chapters:

- Chapter 1 introduces SQL Server and the learning methods that are used in this book. It also discusses "mistake #0," which explores the root of all other mistakes—the misconceptions that SQL Server is "just a database."
- Chapter 2 discusses the topic of coding standards. It explores the impact of stylistic choices as well as technical issues caused by using the wrong standards. We also look at naming conventions and their impact on maintainability.
- Chapter 3 explores data types in SQL Server. In this chapter, we look at the impacts of using inappropriate data types. We also explore advanced data types and evaluate the consequences of not using them.
- Chapter 4 looks at database design. With a strong focus on normalization, we learn why a good database design is so important. We also examine the use of keys and the consequences of making poor choices in this area.

- Chapter 5 gets down to the nitty-gritty of T-SQL. We explore a range of mistakes that can cause unpredictable results and poor performance. We also dive into loops in T-SQL and explore alternatives.
- Chapter 6 exposes some common mistakes that are made when using SQL Server Integration Services (SSIS). We look at common mistakes, including losing bad data, not optimizing data loads, and using SSIS purely as an orchestration tool.
- Chapter 7 discusses error handling, testing, source control, and deployment. In this chapter, you will learn how to handle errors in T-SQL and troubleshoot code. We also discuss the benefits of testing and of using modern deployment mechanisms.
- Chapter 8 moves us into administration, where we explore mistakes that are made when installing SQL Server. These mistakes include using an inappropriate operating system and using an inappropriate SQL Server edition. We also discuss automating installation and when we should choose cloud-native offerings.
- Chapter 9 explores instance and database management. We discuss the consequences of not addressing capacity planning and not patching. We also look at database corruption and administrative scripting.
- Chapter 10 focuses on optimization. In this chapter, we explore optimizations at the levels of the instance, tables, queries, and transactions. We also discuss the mistake of throwing more hardware at a problem.
- Chapter 11 looks at the mistakes and misconceptions relating to indexes. We explore index fragmentation, index maintenance, and how indexes interact with extract, transform, load (ETL) processes.
- Chapter 12 explores database backups. In this chapter, we discuss a multitude of mistakes around this very important topic. These mistakes range from not aligning our backup strategy with the organization's recovery requirements to not considering the security implications of our backup strategy.
- Chapter 13 discusses high availability. We take a look at the differences between high availability and disaster recovery, ensuring our availability strategy meets requirements and technical considerations such as overloaded clusters and when availability groups are not the correct technology choice.
- Chapter 14 is a deep dive into security mistakes. We explore a range of issues, from service account granularity to `xp_cmdshell`. We also explore some common forms of attack, such as whole-value substitution attacks and SQL injection attacks, and we discuss how to protect against them.

About the code

This book contains many code examples, both in numbered listings and embedded within the text. In all cases, code uses `this font` to help you identify it. Some code listings have annotations to help you follow what actions are being performed by complex code.

You can get executable snippets of code from the liveBook (online) version of this book at https://mng.bz/4pWR. The complete code for the examples in the book is available for download from the Manning website at www.manning.com, and from GitHub at https://github.com/100SQLServerMistakes/SourceCode.

liveBook discussion forum

Purchase of *100 SQL Server Mistakes and How to Avoid Them* includes free access to liveBook, Manning's online reading platform. Using liveBook's exclusive discussion features, you can attach comments to the book globally or to specific sections or paragraphs. It's a snap to make notes for yourself, ask and answer technical questions, and receive help from the author and other users. To access the forum, go to https://mng.bz/QVK6. You can also learn more about Manning's forums and the rules of conduct at https://livebook.manning.com/discussion.

Manning's commitment to our readers is to provide a venue where a meaningful dialogue between individual readers and between readers and the author can take place. It is not a commitment to any specific amount of participation on the part of the author, whose contribution to the forum remains voluntary (and unpaid). We suggest you try asking the author some challenging questions lest their interest stray! The forum and the archives of previous discussions will be accessible from the publisher's website for as long as the book is in print.

about the author

Peter A. Carter has two decades of experience as a SQL Server developer, administrator, architect, trainer, and author. He currently looks after a team of platform engineers for a well-known brand in London. He has an understanding of SQL Server that is both broad and deep. He has published multiple SQL Server books, covering subjects ranging from administration and security to automation and advanced data types.

about the cover illustration

The figure on the cover of *100 SQL Server Mistakes and How to Avoid Them* is captioned "Tzorbadji, ou Colonel des Jannissaires," or "Tzorbadji, colonel of the Janissaries," from the George Arents Collection and The New York Public Library Digital Collections. The Janissaries were a standing army of elite infantry units that served the Ottoman sultan from the fourteenth through nineteenth centuries.

In those days, it was easy to identify where people lived and what their trade or station in life was just by their dress. Manning celebrates the inventiveness and initiative of the computer business with book covers based on the rich diversity of regional culture centuries ago, brought back to life by pictures from collections such as this one.

1 Introducing SQL Server

This chapter covers

- What you should know about this book
- The SQL Server index mistake (mistake #0)
- The C4 model
- SQL Server's components, protocols, and platforms
- The importance of SQL Server skills

Over recent years, *DBA* has become a catchall term to describe anybody who works with databases. I always feel that this is doing something of a disservice to both the technology and the professionals who work with it. SQL Server is a massive product, and complex data-tier applications require teams to have a range of competencies to harness its full power. Therefore, when we refer to DBA in this book, we will be referring specifically to database administrators.

We will cover topics relevant to people with the following roles:

- Database administrators (DBAs)
- Database developers
- Extract, transform, load (ETL) engineers

This book may also be of interest to members of the following communities if they have overlapping responsibilities:

- Database architects
- Data warehouse developers
- Testers
- Data scientists
- Cyber security engineers
- Business intelligence developers

1.1 The SQL Server index mistake (mistake #0)

The modern SQL Server ecosystem is large and complex, which leads me nicely to mistake #0—terminology that I have borrowed from virology, where the index case (or case 0) describes the first patient to contract a virus and infect other people. In this context, it is the root of all other SQL Server mistakes. This mistake is not usually made by database professionals. Instead, it is generally made by solution architects, delivery managers, program managers, and business analysts. It can be summed up in a single quote—a quote that I wish I had a dollar for every time I heard it: "But it's just a database, right?"

This assumption of simplicity leads to an incredible number of projects not budgeting for the resources to develop a suitable data-tier application or factoring in enough time to sufficiently develop such an application. It leads to due consideration not being given to the postproject operational support of the environment, and it leads to the term *DBA* being used to describe anybody who works with databases, regardless of their competencies.

How are these problems addressed? Welcome the "accidental DBA," a person who has a limited amount of experience in SQL Server, often because they are an application developer who has created some small databases as a backend data store in the past. Suddenly, this person is responsible for the development, optimization, administration, and security posture of all things SQL Server related.

Does this scenario sound familiar? If so, then it is certainly worth reading on, as this book will explore the common mistakes made by database professionals who are finding their feet, many of whom fall into the accidental DBA camp.

In this book, we will discuss mistakes that are made by people performing tasks related to development, administration, high availability (HA), disaster recovery (DR), and security.

1.2 An overview of SQL Server

SQL Server is a leading *relational database management system (RDBMS)* produced by Microsoft. In its simplest form, it provides a platform for hosting and managing databases. It also has many other features that allow for advanced activities, such as reporting, data transformation, and master data management.

To understand the breadth of SQL Server a little better, let's imagine the use case of a confectionary company called MagicChoc. It has a website, hosted in the public cloud, which sells its chocolatey goodness. It also has a small data center in its factory, which hosts its manufacturing application, stock control application, and reporting solution. This is illustrated in the system landscape diagram in figure 1.1.

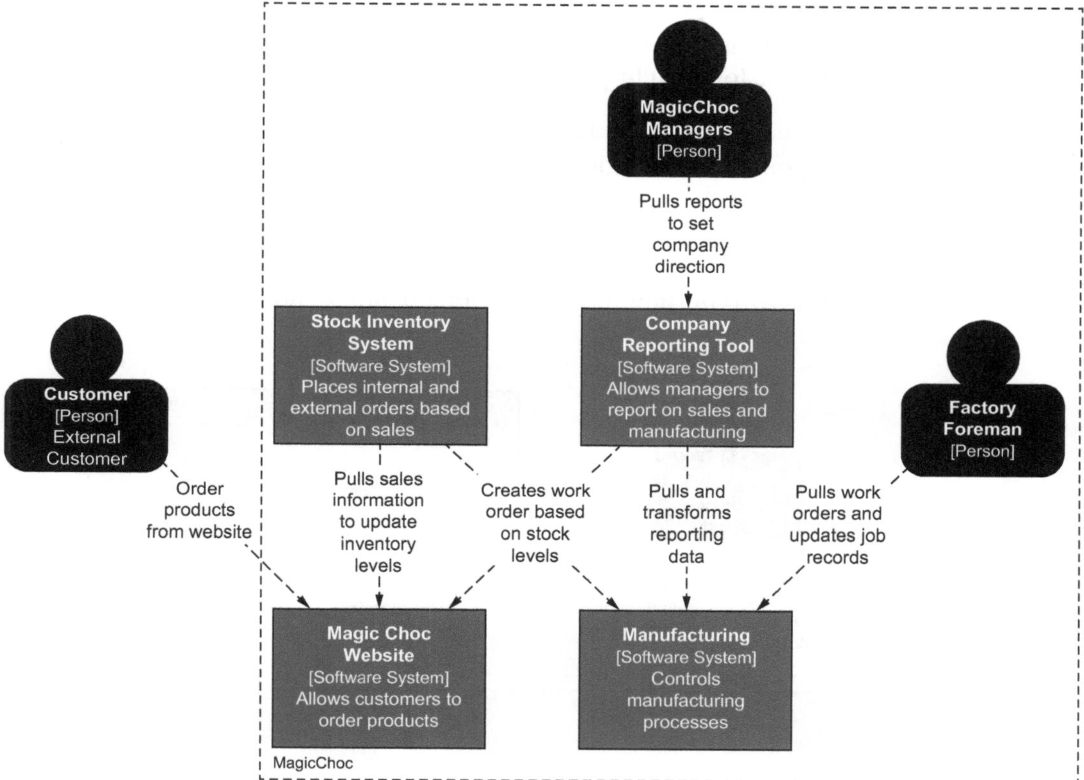

Figure 1.1 MagicChoc system landscape diagram

> ### C4 model
>
> In addition to technical diagrams in this book, we will also make use of the C4 model, where appropriate. The C4 model is a set of architectural standard diagrams. At its core, C4 contains four standard diagrams: a system context diagram, a container diagram, a component diagram, and a code diagram. The system context diagram is at the highest level, illustrating an application's interfaces with users and other applications. Each subsequent level drills through a specific area of the application, providing ever more granular detail. The lowest level of granularity is the code diagram at the bottom.

> ***(continued)***
>
> The model also contains side diagrams: a system landscape diagram, which illustrates how a portfolio of applications interacts; a dynamic diagram, which illustrates how static elements work together at run time to form a feature; and a final diagram, which is a deployment diagram and illustrates the platform that an application is deployed on.

TIP While a full discussion of C4 is beyond the scope of this book, a full description can be found at https://c4model.com.

The interesting part of this system landscape is that all four of the applications have a SQL Server component. The MagicChoc website is hosted in Azure and has an Azure SQL Database storing information in the backend. The stock inventory system and the manufacturing application both have SQL Server databases, and these databases are hosted on the same SQL Server instance, which runs on a virtual machine in the data center. The company reporting tool consists of a data warehouse, hosted in the data

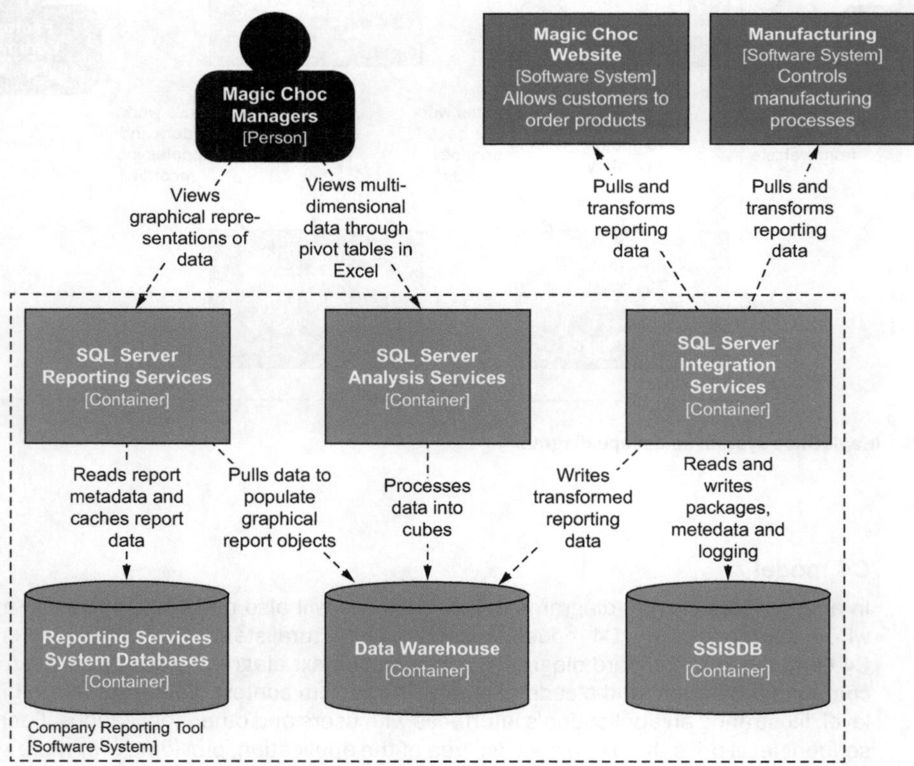

Figure 1.2 Reporting application container diagram

center, but it also uses SQL Server Reporting Services (SSRS) as the front end and SQL Server Analysis Services (SSAS) to produce multidimensional data models. It also uses SQL Server Integration Services (SSIS) to pull data from the other applications and transform it into a denormalized structure, optimized for reporting.

Let's zoom in and examine a container diagram that focuses on the reporting application. This diagram is shown in figure 1.2 and allows us to start seeing the breadth of the SQL Server stack.

> **NOTE** C4 diagrams should always be used appropriately, and you should pick and mix the most appropriate diagrams for any given scenario. In this chapter, the system landscape diagram and the container diagram are the most appropriate to illustrate the scenario, but we will be using other C4 diagrams throughout the book.

You can see how the reporting application actually uses multiple SQL Server components to serve the business requirements, as well as databases that sit alongside the data warehouse and enable the functionality of those components. A full list of the major components of SQL Server 2022 is given in table 1.1.

Table 1.1 SQL server major components

Component	Description
Analysis Services (SSAS)	Allows for the creation and hosting of multidimensional data models and tabular data models that can be used for advanced reporting
Azure Connected Services	Supports tight integration between Azure and SQL Server hosted on-premises. This includes the ability to easily integrate on-premises hosted SQL Server instances with Azure features such as Synapse, Purview, and Microsoft Defender. Additionally, the simple Azure Arc connection can be configured during instance installation. This allows a single view of SQL Server installations across multicloud and on-premises, and fully automated technical assessments.
Database Engine	The core database management service, which allows for relational databases to be built and hosted. It includes second-tier operating system components for managing memory and processor resources. It also incorporates data security, high-availability technologies, data replication, integrations with heterogeneous data sources, and support for semistructured data, such as XML and JSON.
Data Quality Services (DQS)	A data quality solution that provides a knowledge base to support critical data quality tasks, such as standardization and deduplication. The DQS Server component comprises data quality functionality and storage, while the Data Quality Client component provides a graphical user interface that can be used by data domain experts.
Data Virtualization with PolyBase	Allows developers to use T-SQL to query external data sources, such as Azure Blob, Delta Tables (the default table format in Azure Databricks), Hadoop, MongoDB, Oracle, S3, and Teradata
Integration Services (SSIS)	Provides versatile ETL operations. Often used to pull data from heterogeneous sources, denormalize the data, and populate data warehouses. Also used to integrate data from external sources, such as web services and FTP sites, into SQL Server databases.
Machine Learning Services (In-Database)	Allows developers to use R and Python scripts inside databases. These scripts can be used to prepare data for machine learning or to train, evaluate, and deploy machine learning models.

Table 1.1 SQL server major components (*continued*)

Component	Description
Master Data Services (MDS)	A Master Data Management (MDM) solution that allows data stewards to manage a company's master data. Stewards can create data models and rules. Master data can also be exported so that it can be easily shared with business stakeholders.
Reporting Services (SSRS)	Provides users with a graphical reporting tool. Reports can contain tabular data, as well as charts, maps, and other graphical elements. The reports can be complex, and there is support for parameters, variables, linked reports, and report caching.

As you can see, SQL Server is a vast and complex product, which can and does span many volumes. Therefore, in this book, we will focus mainly on the Database Engine, although we will also touch on cloud integration and SSIS. Therefore, let's dive a little deeper into the Database Engine.

1.2.1 Overview of the Database Engine

To explain the Database Engine, let's explore the journey a query takes when it is executed by a user. Let's imagine that a MagicChoc customer is exploring the website and decides to look more closely at the LushBar chocolate bar. The website runs the following query, which reads the `dbo.Products` table and returns the name and description of the product, alongside the product image. The `CASE` statement is used to return an appropriate response, depending on the quantity of the product in stock. If there are more than 10 in stock, it will return the text "In Stock." If there are 0, then it will return the text "Out of stock." If there are between 1 and 10 of the product in stock, it will build a string that informs the user of exactly how many are in stock:

```
SELECT
      ProductName
    , ProductDescription AS Description
    , CASE
        WHEN StockQty >= 10
            THEN N'In Stock'
        WHEN StockQty > 0 AND StockQty < 10
            THEN CAST(StockQty AS NVARCHAR) + ' left in stock'
        ELSE 'Out of stock'
      END
    , ProductImage
FROM dbo.Products WITH (NOLOCK)
WHERE ProductID = @ProductID
```

NOTE Using `NOLOCK` in this context is a mistake that we will discuss in chapter 5.

The journey of this query is depicted in figure 1.3. In this diagram, notice that the user interacts with SQL Server using the Tabular Data Streams application layer protocol. SQL Server receives this data via SNI, which is part of SQL Server's protocol layer. The protocol layer then sends the request to the relational engine.

Here, the query is parsed. If you have made a mistake in the syntax of your query, the parser is the component that will cause an error to be thrown. This process not only

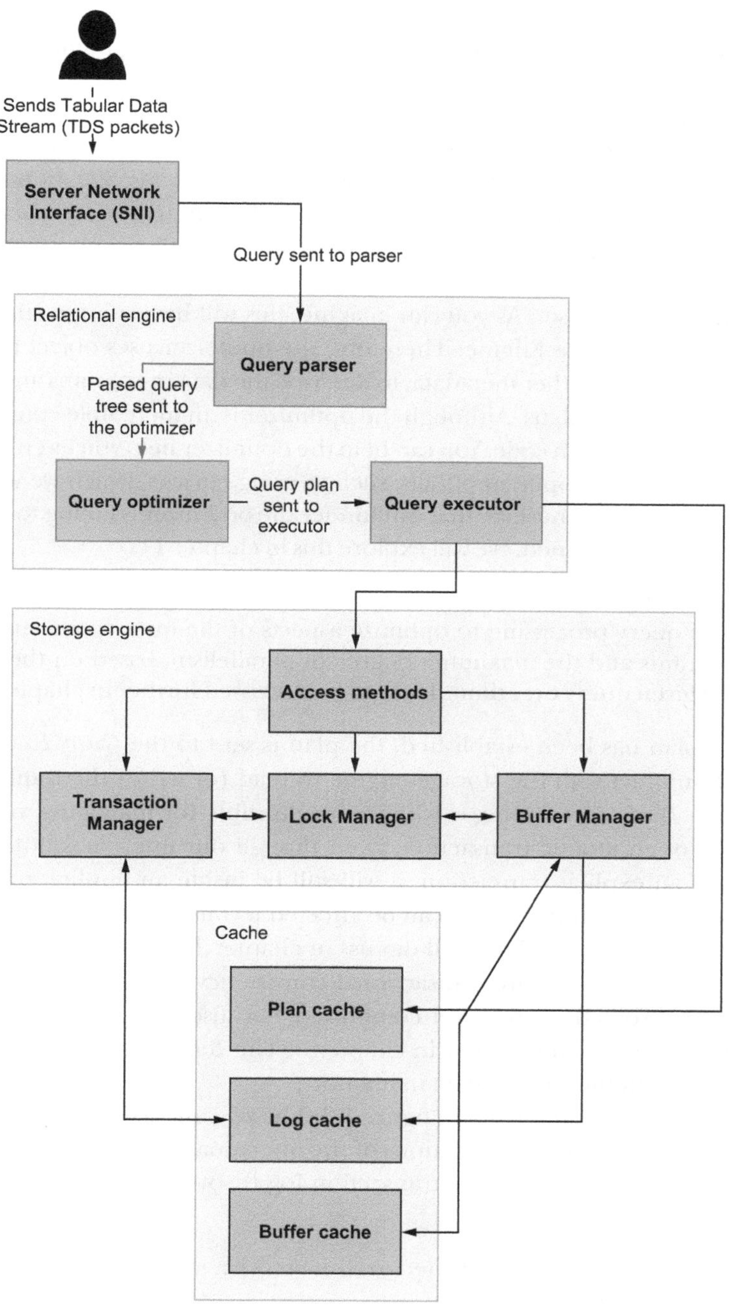

Figure 1.3 The flow of a query through the Database Engine

checks the validity of query syntax but also includes algebraization, a process that converts object names into object IDs. This results in the creation of a highly normalized query tree, which is passed to the Query Optimizer.

The Query Optimizer is a highly sophisticated process that sits right at the heart of the SQL Server. The difference between SQL and many other languages, such as C or BASIC, is that SQL is a descriptive language, rather than a prescriptive language. In prescriptive languages, a developer specifies exactly what they want the language to do. In a descriptive language like SQL, however, the developer simply describes the results that they want to return. The Query Optimizer is responsible for determining the most efficient way of returning the desired result set. As you can imagine, this will have a huge effect on the performance of the Database Engine. Therefore, the optimizer uses object types, data types, and statistics, among other metadata, to describe the data in columns and indexes, to assess the cost of various plans. Although the optimizer is an incredible component, it is no substitute for well-written code. You can help the optimizer help you by ensuring you do not fall into T-SQL development pitfalls, such as using cursors, which we will discuss in chapters 5 and 9. Another mistake that can hinder the optimizer is failing to keep your statistics and indexes maintained. We will explore this in chapter 11.

TIP SQL Server 2022 can also use *optimizer feedback*. This uses the Query Store and intelligent query processing to optimize aspects of the query plan, such as the memory grants and the maximum degree of parallelism, based on the performance of a given query over time. This will be discussed further in chapter 10.

Once a suitable plan has been established, the plan is sent to the *Query Executor*. This component will interact with the storage engine to read (or write) the required data. This involves the *Transaction Manager*, which is responsible for managing and distributing the results of an atomic transaction. Even though our query has not been run in the context of an explicit transaction, it will still be inside an implicit transaction. The performance of your transactions can be affected if you have chosen a suboptimal transaction isolation level, which we will discuss in chapter 10. *Lock Manager* is responsible for locking objects to ensure transactional consistency. In the case of our query, it is possible to read rows that are never committed, because we have used the `NOLOCK` query hint. We will discuss this further in chapter 5. The *Buffer Manager* is the component that interacts with the cached data in memory.

Three areas of cache are depicted in figure 1.3. The *plan cache* stores complex query plans, meaning that subsequent invocations of the query may be able to avoid the optimization process. The *log cache* caches transaction log records before they are flushed to disk.

TIP The log records are always flushed to disk before a transaction is committed unless delayed durability is used.

The *buffer cache* stores data pages that have been read from a disk. It is important to note that a query is always satisfied from the cache and never directly from data stored on disk. Even if the required data pages do not reside in cache, they will be read from the disk into the cache, and then the query will be satisfied from the cached data. A common mistake is to return more data in a query than you need. If you do this, then the buffer cache will fill up quicker than it needs to. This will result in older data being released from the cache sooner. In turn, this can lead to poor performance, as data needs to be read from disk more often. We will discuss this more in chapter 4.

1.2.2 Heterogeneous platforms

It is important to remember that SQL Server is no longer just "a database on Windows." Instead, it is supported on a veritable smorgasbord of platforms. First, let us consider the operating systems on which SQL Server 2022 is supported. These operating systems are laid out in figure 1.4.

NOTE SQL Server Express edition and Standard edition can also be installed on Windows 10 and Windows 11.

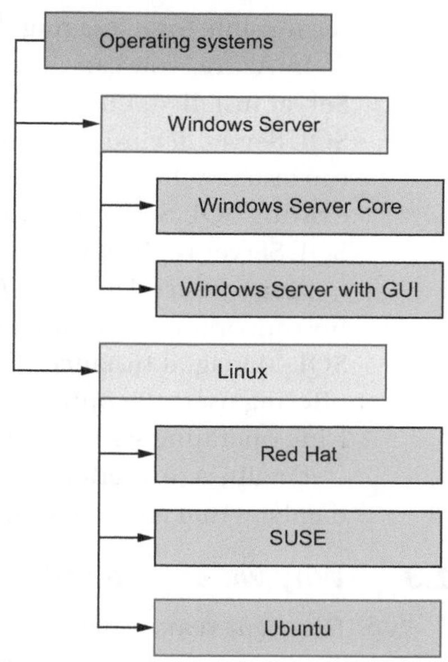

Figure 1.4 Operating systems supported by SQL Server

You will notice that not only can SQL Server be installed on *Windows Server Core*, which is a PowerShell-only version of Windows that does not have a GUI, but it can also be installed on three different flavors of Linux. This means that there is potential for a database professional to work not only with the GUI but also with PowerShell and Bash.

It is also worth discussing the hosts that SQL Server 2022 can be installed on, which are depicted in figure 1.5.

Official support for SQL Server on VMware has been around for some time. What may be more surprising is that recent versions of SQL Server are also supported on containers. This means that some database professionals may need to be familiar with technologies such as Docker and Kubernetes.

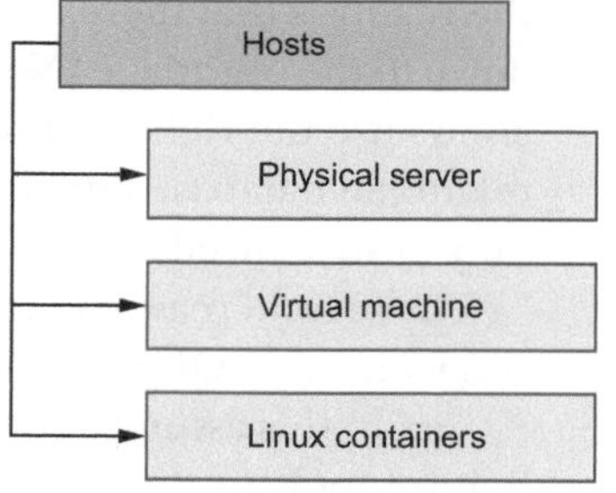

Figure 1.5 Hosts supported by SQL Server

NOTE At the time of writing, SQL Server is only supported on Linux containers. SQL Server on Windows containers was available in beta, but this program has since been canceled. There is nothing stopping you from creating your own Windows containers hosting SQL Server, based on a vanilla Windows Core container image. Just note that as it is unsupported, you should never do this in a production environment.

We should also consider cloud support for SQL Server. SQL Server is supported on Infrastructure as a Service (IaaS) virtual machines in the cloud. These are called Azure Virtual Machines in Azure and GCP or EC2 instances in AWS. There are also PaaS offerings from these vendors, however.

In AWS, Application Machine Images (AMIs) are available that have SQL Server installed. Depending on the AMI used, you can purchase SQL Server with the EC2 instance on a Service Provider License Agreement (SPLA). In this model, the license is included in the hourly cost of the EC2 instance. Alternatively, you can bring your own license (provided that this is within the terms of your license agreement with Microsoft).

There is also an option to use RDS, which is a Database as a Service (DBaaS) offering. The underlying server and SQL Server instance are managed by AWS, and you are only responsible for managing the databases hosted within it.

In Azure, you can create SQL Server VMs from Azure VM images that have SQL Server installed. Like AWS, you can use a license-included model, where the cost of the SQL Server license is included in the cost of the VM, allowing you to pay as you go. You can also use the Azure Hybrid Benefit (AHB) license model, which allows you to use an existing SQL Server license. Finally, in Azure, an HA/DR license can be used to host a SQL Server replica that is used exclusively for HA or DR purposes.

Azure offers *Azure SQL Database*, which is a DBaaS offering, similar to the AWS RDS hosting option. Additionally, there is a SQL Instance as a Service offering called Azure SQL Managed Instance. This option provides a balance between a VM and a DBaaS by offering users the option of managing their own SQL Server instance, while the underlying operating system and virtual machine are managed by Azure.

Finally, Azure offers Azure SQL Edge, which provides an Internet of Things (IoT) database that includes data streaming and data processing.

1.3 Why we should still care about SQL Server

In recent years, I have heard people question if we should still care about SQL Server. This is usually for one of two reasons. The first is because of an assumption that relational databases are not really required anymore because everything uses NoSQL.

This assumption is not really correct. While NoSQL has certainly grown massively over the last decade and is the correct choice for many use cases around data analytics, the reality is that there is still very much a place for relational databases. It simply boils down to the old adage "Never put a square peg in a round hole!" Simply put, you should always use the right tool for the job. Trying to force a dataset that is a natural fit for a relational database into an unstructured environment is as bad as trying to force naturally unstructured data into a SQL Server database.

The second reason is an assumption that DBaaS means that you simply don't need to run your own SQL Servers anymore; hence, there is no need for SQL Server skills.

Again, this assumption is not really correct. DBaaS and managed instances are very helpful tools in the toolbelt of any database professional. They do not eliminate the need for SQL Server skills, however. This is for two reasons. The first reason is that even databases hosted in DBaaS need to be developed and have their code optimized to avoid poor performance. The second reason is that DBaaS or even managed instances are not always a good choice. Sometimes they are not even feasible for a given workload. While there are several reasons for this, one common reason is cost. You are paying your cloud provider to host, patch, secure, and optimize all layers of the stack below the database. This comes at a premium. If you move every single database to an RDS or Azure SQL Database, then you may be able to offset this cost against the cost of your physical DBA team. If there are reasons why you cannot move all of your databases to a DBaaS offering, however, then you will end up double paying.

> **Physical DBAs vs. logical DBAs**
>
> *Physical DBA* is a term used to describe DBAs who have good knowledge of managing SQL Server instances but are not skilled in the database tier. This is opposed to logical DBAs, who are skilled at developing and tuning databases but do not have experience with managing instances.
>
> I have seen companies structure their database teams in this way when they have an infrastructure-managed service provider who builds and supports SQL Server instances and ensures they are available. Often, they then hand over responsibility for the databases to an in-house application support team who are responsible for the support and optimization of database-level constructs.

In my experience, it is almost always the case that you simply cannot move all of your databases to a DBaaS offering. One reason for this is vendor support. If you run a commercial off-the-shelf product that has a SQL Server backend, then you are at the mercy of the vendor agreeing to support the product if the backend is moved to a DBaaS.

Another reason is that many companies have large, complex data-tier applications, sometimes with hundreds of thousands of lines of code embedded in components such as SQL Server Integration Services. These can often not simply be *lifted and shifted*, which is a term used to describe migrating a data-tier application as is, without any transformation or modernization. Instead, they require re-architecture—and that means a significant investment of both time and expenditure, which often cannot be justified.

1.4 Why getting SQL Server right matters

In my youth, I used to play a board game called Othello. The tag line for the game was "A minute to learn, a lifetime to master." SQL Server always reminds me of this. One of the advantages of SQL Server over some of its rivals is that it is very easy to implement. It is, however, very difficult to implement well.

This matters because a poorly implemented SQL Server instance can lead to problems, including

- Poor performance
- Data theft
- Ransomware attacks
- Noncompliance with regulation

- Loss of data in the event of a disaster
- Prolonged outage in the event of a disaster

Poorly implemented database code can lead to

- Poor performance
- Security breaches
- Unhandled failures
- Code that can't be maintained

These problems can lead to companies experiencing vast expenses, loss of revenue, loss of reputation, increased staff turnover, or even prosecution. Therefore, getting SQL Server right really does matter.

Summary

- The root of SQL Server mistakes is an assumption that databases are simple and easy.
- SQL Server is a popular relational database management system.
- SQL Server has a large, complex ecosystem with multiple major components.
- The core component of SQL Server is the Database Engine.
- The Database Engine contains components, including the relational engine and the storage engine.
- SQL Server is supported on Windows and Linux operating systems.
- SQL Server is supported on physical servers, virtual machines, and Linux containers.
- In the public cloud, SQL Server is available on IaaS or as PaaS offerings.
- It is important to implement SQL Server well to avoid problems such as poor performance, loss of data, and security breaches.

2 Development standards

This chapter covers

- An introduction to development standards
- Naming standards
- Coding standards

In this chapter, we will explore why having (and following!) development standards is so important. So let's start by defining exactly what we mean when we talk about development standards in the context of building data-tier applications with SQL Server. Development standards cover the following areas:

- Naming conventions
- Coding standards
  - Stylistic
  - Technical

Specifically, we will look at the common mistakes that database professionals make and discuss how you can avoid the same pitfalls.

2.1 An example mistake

Imagine the topology depicted in figure 2.1. Suppose you get a call from the application team that looks after an application called TimeChewer. They report that some of their queries are running slowly and ask you to take a look. They advise that the application's database is hosted on the server called `sql-shared-app-server`.

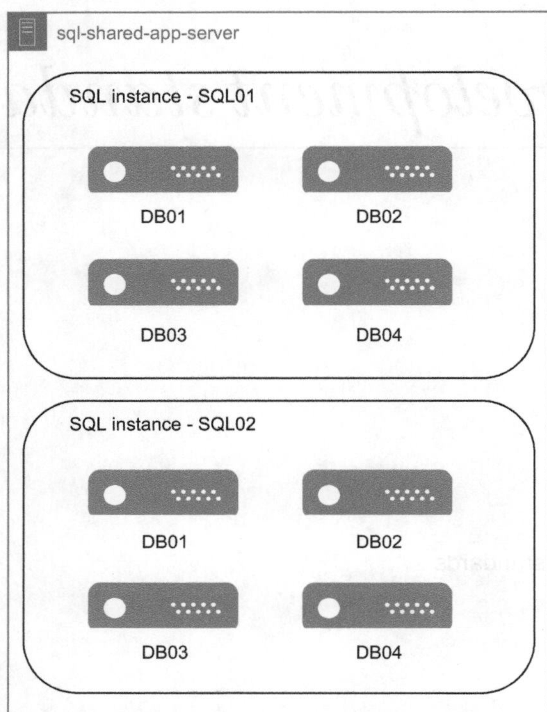

Figure 2.1 A SQL Server topology with poor naming conventions

You connect to the server, and your heart immediately sinks. The instances are called SQL01 and SQL02. This gives you no indication of which instance may host the application's database. So you connect to each instance in turn, hoping to find a database with a name like "TimeChewer." Unfortunately, you are greeted with database names DB01, DB02, DB03, and DB04.

Now you must contact the application team and ask them to find the connection string and work out which database and which instance the application is connecting to. Finally, they respond and let you know that TimeChewer is connecting to DB03 on SQL01. So you decide to have a look at one of the stored procedures that they have mentioned is performing badly and script out the stored procedure definition. The definition of this procedure is

```
ALTER PROCEDURE dbo.proc01
AS
BEGIN
;with t3 as (select col1, col2, col3 from tbl03) select t1.col1, t2.col2,
t1.col2, t1.col3, t3.col1, t3.col2 from dbo.tbl01 t1 inner join tbl02 t2 on
t1.col1 = t2.col1 and t1.col3 < 55 inner join t3 on t3.col1 = t1.col1 union
select col1, col2, col3, NULL, NULL, '0' from dbo.tbl04 ;
END
```

I imagine you have just been squinting at the stored procedure, trying to work out what on earth it's doing. In short, after spending 30 minutes trying to work out which database has the problem, you are now going to have to spend another 15 minutes reformatting the code into something legible and trying to work out what this very simple stored procedure is doing. That's 45 minutes wasted, before you even start to investigate the problem.

While this is an extreme example, it illustrates why naming conventions and coding standards are so important and why failing in this area will leave you and others pulling their hair out in frustration.

2.2 #1 Nondescriptive object names

Although the example of nondescriptive database names in the introduction to this chapter was rather extreme, I have seen instances of people using SQL01, SQL02, etc. as their standard naming convention—for instance names—and it really does cause a headache. Nondescriptive naming is more prevalent, however, at the code level, and that is where we focus in this chapter.

> **TIP** We will talk more about the specific problems caused by poor instance naming in chapter 8.

To discuss this, let's head back to our MagicChoc example that we introduced in chapter 1. In this chapter, we will be discussing the `SalesDB` database, which is the backend for the website. Figure 2.2 illustrates the component diagram of this database, which shows the database objects (tables, procedures, and views) within this database.

You will notice that the object names in this database really have not been well thought out. You should always strive to have code that is self-documenting. Contrary to popular belief, this does not necessarily mean littering the code with comments. Comments can certainly be helpful to explain complex logic, but far more important is that the code is written and structured in such a way that anybody who reads the code, providing that they are fluent in the language, can establish what the code is trying to achieve. Meaningful object names are a big part of this listing.

Imagine that you have been asked to fix a bug in the procedure that updates the stock inventory system after an order has been placed. You are not familiar with the process, so your first port of call might be to run a query that returns a list of stored procedures within the database. The following listing demonstrates three ways that you might wish to perform this activity. All three queries will return the same results.

Listing 2.1 Returning a list of stored procedures

```
SELECT
    name
FROM sys.procedures ;                          <-- Pulls the list from the sys
                                                   .procedures catalog view
SELECT
    name
FROM sys.objects                               Pulls the list from the sys.objects catalog
WHERE type_desc = 'SQL_STORED_PROCEDURE' ;     view, filtering by the type description

SELECT
    name
FROM sys.objects                               Pulls the list from the sys.objects
WHERE type = 'P' ;                             catalog view, filtering by the type
```

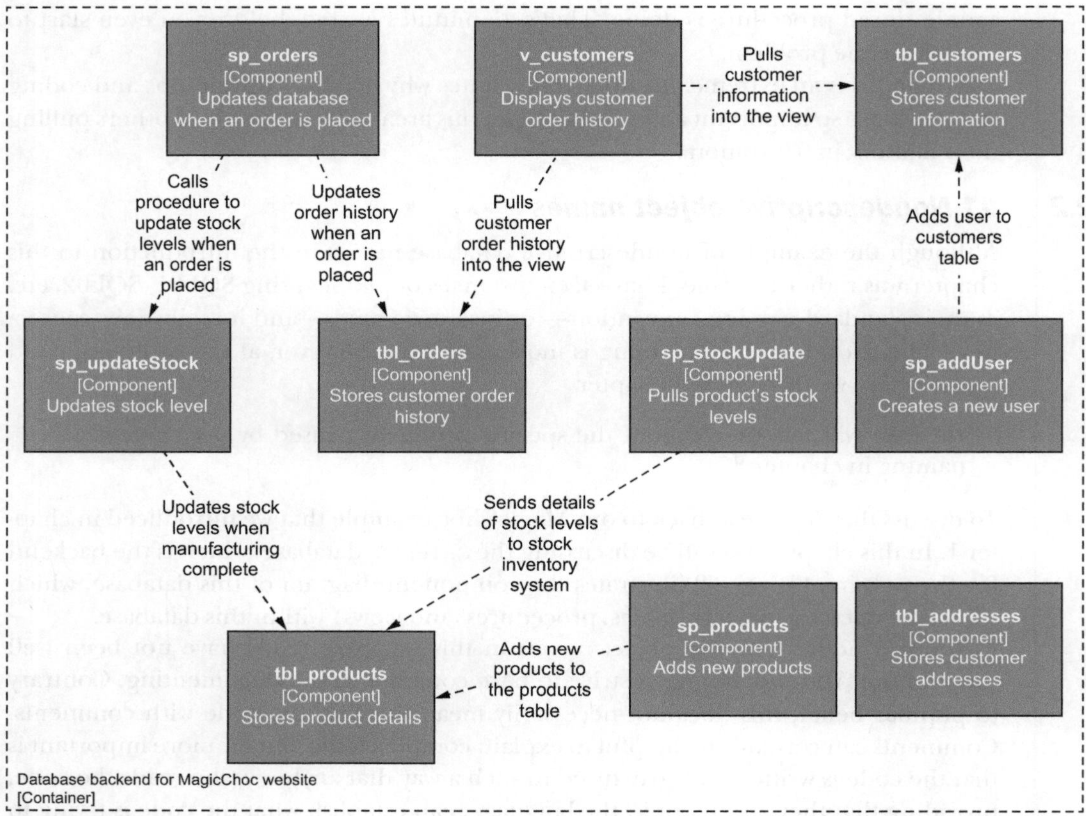

Figure 2.2 `SalesDB` component diagram

Of course, you may also choose to use SQL Server Management Studio (SSMS) to view the procedures through the GUI. However you decide to list the objects, you will find that there are procedures called `updateStock` and `stockUpdate`. Which is the procedure you need to debug? Who knows? Before you can start your assignment, you will need to either review the definitions of both stored procedures or find out where the procedure is being called to establish the name of the relevant procedure.

In our case, establishing where the stored procedure is called is going to be a little tricky because it is actually called by another stored procedure—the `sp_orders` stored procedure. Again, this procedure has a generic, fairly meaningless name, which does not articulate the purpose of the procedure. So you will have to track back to the application that triggered the process to discover the first procedure in the chain.

Now let's imagine that you have worked out that the `orders` procedure is the first stored procedure in the chain. You can find the definition of this stored procedure through SSMS, or by running the query in the following listing.

Listing 2.2 Getting the stored procedure definition

```
SELECT s.definition
FROM sys.objects o
INNER JOIN sys.sql_modules s
    ON o.object_id = s.object_id
WHERE o.name = 'sp_orders' ;
```

Joins sys.sql_modules, which stores the procedure definition to sys.objects, which stores the object name. The join is made on the object_id column, which is present in both catalog views.

> **TIP** Personally, I prefer to script a stored procedure definition from Object Explorer in SSMS, as opposed to pulling the definition from the `sys.sql_modules` catalog view. This is because pulling from `sys.sql_modules` will not preserve the formatting.

The definition of the `sp_orders` stored procedure can be found in listing 2.3. The `@AddressID` parameter is meaningless. Is it the billing address or the delivery address? The `@Address` parameter is both meaningless and confusing. The parameter's name implies an actual address, where it is meant to store an address ID. Also, which address is it referring to? Yet another meaningless parameter name is `@date`. Is this the order date? The delivery date? It could even imply a timestamp of when the record was inserted into the table! Within the body of the procedure, we also have confusing variable names. The `@stock` variable is meant to hold the quantity ordered and `@product` is holding the product ID. These names simply are not clear, and you need to wade through the code to understand their purpose.

Listing 2.3 `sp_orders` procedure definition

```
CREATE PROCEDURE sp_orders
    @CustomerID INT,
    @LineItems XML,
    @AddressID INT,
    @Address INT,
    @date DATETIME
AS
BEGIN
    DECLARE @Stock INT = 0 ;
    DECLARE @Product INT = 0 ;

    INSERT INTO tbl_orders (
        CustomerID,
        LineItems,
        BillingAddressID,
        DeliveryAddressID,
        Date
    )
    VALUES (
        @CustomerID,
        @LineItems,
        @AddressID,
        @Address,
        @date
```

```
    ) ;

    SET @Stock = @LineItems.value('(/Product/@qty)[1]', 'int') ;
    SET @Product = @LineItems.value('(/Product/@ProductID)[1]', 'int') ;

    EXEC sp_stockUpdate @product, @stock ;
END
```

TIP If you are not familiar with how to use XML in SQL Server, then you are not alone. In fact, failure to use XML appropriately is another common mistake, which we will explore in chapter 3.

By reading the definition of this stored procedure, we can already see that the meaningless names of parameters and variables are storing up trouble for us. If we need to enhance or debug functionality relating to addresses or time, then we are going to have to spend time figuring out what the data means.

For now, though, we need to fix the problem with the stock inventory update, and this stored procedure definition has allowed us to determine that the `sp_stockUpdate` procedure is likely to contain the code that we need to debug. Let's take a look at the procedure in listing 2.4.

We can see that `sp_stockUpdate` is a simple stored procedure, which updates the stock level in `SalesDB` and then uses a linked server to update the stock level in the inventory system. We can also see that the cause of the bug is inconsistent names, leading the developer to get confused and pass the product ID into the calculation that updates the quantity remaining in stock while trying to filter the product ID on the quantity of goods being ordered, instead of the actual product ID.

Listing 2.4 `sp_stockUpdate` procedure definition

```
CREATE PROCEDURE sp_stockUpdate
    @ProductStockLevel INT,
    @StockID INT
AS
BEGIN
    UPDATE tbl_products
    SET StockQty = StockQty - @productStockLevel
    WHERE ProductID = @StockID ;

    UPDATE [DCSVR01\Inventory].InventoryDB.dbo.productStock
    SET StockQty = StockQty - @productStockLevel
    WHERE ProductID = @StockID ;
END
```

Parameter names are inconsistent with both the sp_orders procedure and the table's column names.

Real-world example

This example is quite simple and is for illustrative purposes, but you can imagine that when you are dealing with complex code, these challenges will quickly become a nightmare. The example in this section is loosely based on a real-world example that I came across. A developer had written a very complex process with five layers of stored procedures and multiple entry points from external applications. Across all of the procedures, there were around 2,000 lines of code. After he moved on, a bug was discovered, and upon trying to resolve the problem, we found that the developer had used variable names, parameter names, and column names interchangeably. The bug itself was simple and should have been resolved within a couple of hours, but because of the tangled web of naming, it took three days of effort to resolve the problem. It then took another two weeks to update all the names to be consistent and perform regression testing.

TIP A positive example of good naming in listing 2.4 comes in the form of the table primary key columns. You will notice that the `tbl_products` table has a `ProductID`, the `tbl_orders` table has an `OrderID`, and the `tbl_addresses` table has an `AddressID`. A common mistake is to use `ID` as a stand-alone column name for the primary key columns in all tables, meaning that the primary key column in every table has the same name. I'm sure you can imagine how confusing this could easily become in the context of a complex stored procedure.

As you have seen, not giving due consideration to naming can introduce bugs, cost valuable time when trying to fix problems, and make it harder to enhance functionality. Therefore, spending a little time to keep names consistent and meaningful is a practice that we should all follow.

This might sound easy, and for small database projects, it usually is. But when you have a large project that is built over a long period of time by multiple developers, it can actually become quite tricky. It can become even more tricky if your project is delivered with *Agile* methodology. Unlike a traditional waterfall project, Agile projects use methodologies such as Sprint or Kanban, which break the backlog of work up into small chunks that can deliver incremental functionality at a faster pace.

The Agile approach can work very well and brings many advantages over waterfall projects. When it is delivered badly, however, there can be an assumption that design, architecture, and planning are not required. In database projects, architecture is always critical, as you must consider important design elements, such as the schema of your tables. Failure to do this will likely result in a tangled mess of tables that are not normalized and probably data duplication and performance problems, as well as increased complexity. If you are going to spend time up front looking at table design, then it is a simple and comparatively quick task to also look at other design elements, such as object naming.

A well-managed database project using Agile methodology will either have a number of design sprints at the start of the project or periodic sprints where a section (usually a schema) of the database is designed.

So what should the developer who wrote our MagicChoc stored procedures have done differently? Consider the new definition of the `sp_orders` procedure in listing 2.5. First, the address parameters are now both obviously IDs. More importantly, it is clear which parameter is for the billing address and which is for the delivery address. The @date parameter is now clearly an order date. Not only have we changed the parameter, however, but we have also updated the column name in the table, which removes the ambiguity at this level. The @product variable has been updated to @ProductID, and not only have we updated the @stock variable to be @OrderQty, but we have also updated the XML definition to match, making the data clearer, right through the stack. Finally, we have updated the execution of the sp_updateProductStockLevel procedure to pass the variable in the correct order. This final change will fix the bug.

Listing 2.5 sp_orders procedure new definition

```
ALTER PROCEDURE sp_orders
    @CustomerID INT,
    @LineItems XML,
    @BillingAddressID INT,
    @DeliveryAddressID INT,
    @OrderDate DATETIME
AS
BEGIN
    DECLARE @OrderQty INT = 0 ;
    DECLARE @ProductID INT = 0 ;

    INSERT INTO tbl_orders (CustomerID, LineItems, BillingAddressID,
DeliveryAddressID, OrderDate)
    VALUES (@CustomerID, @LineItems, @BillingAddressID, @DeliveryAddressID,
@OrderDate) ;

    SET @OrderQty = @LineItems.value('(/Product/@OrderQty)[1]', 'int') ;
    SET @ProductID = @LineItems.value('(/Product/@ProductID)[1]', 'int') ;

    EXEC sp_updateProductStockLevel @OrderQty, @ProductID ;
END
```

> **TIP** In the voice of my favorite 1980s private investigator: "I know what you're thinking, and you're right. Surely, we should have changed the procedure name as well?" However, I have kept it as is for now, as we will be discussing this name further in mistake #2.

Please also consider the new definition of the sp_stockUpdate procedure in listing 2.6. You will notice that the name of the stored procedure has been changed to sp_updateProductStockLevel, which is a much more meaningful name for the procedure. With this name, we would have had no problem finding it at the start of this example.

Listing 2.6 sp_updateProductStockLevel procedure definition

```
CREATE PROCEDURE sp_updateProductStockLevel
    @OrderQty INT,
    @ProductID INT
AS
BEGIN
```

The parameter names now match the variables being passed into them.

```
    UPDATE tbl_products
    SET StockQty = StockQty - @OrderQty
    WHERE ProductID = @ProductID ;

    UPDATE [DCSVR01\Inventory].InventoryDB.dbo.productStock
    SET StockQty = StockQty - @OrderQty
    WHERE ProductID = @ProductID ;
END
```

After reviewing the preceding two new stored procedure definitions, you will see how meaningful and consistent naming dramatically helps in making the code self-documenting. While we could add code comments in the two procedures, they would add very little benefit. Anybody who can read T-SQL can now read these definitions, and it will be very clear what the procedures are doing and what data is being passed. This doesn't mean that comments do not have their place, but this is usually to explain conceptual business logic in very long stored procedures or to specify external inputs/ outputs, such as an API contract. If your code is self-documenting, comments should not be required to explain low-level code definitions.

2.3 #2 Using object prefixes

Some developers love to use object prefixes. Object prefixes are where `tbl_` is added to the start of all table names, `sp_` is added to the start of stored procedure names, `fn_` is added to the start of function names, and `v_` is added to the start of a view.

Imagine you have a database that contains 250 tables. You are looking for the column definition of a table, so you quickly scan down the list of tables in Object Explorer. However, all of the tables have a `tbl_` prefix. This automatically increases the parse time while you scan.

That is because your brain is wired to follow common patterns. For example, you know the alphabet pretty well, right? Great! Try saying it backwards—from Z to A. It's surprisingly difficult. That's because your brain is not wired for that pattern. Even if you do train your brain to follow that pattern, it doesn't mean that everybody else will find it easy.

It's the same with scanning prefixed objects. Even if you have trained your brain to be able to easily scan a string from the fifth character onward, your fellow developers, business intelligence developers, and administrators may not have, so you will be inadvertently hindering their productivity.

If there was a good reason for doing this—and there are in some languages, such as ARM in Azure—then I would consider the tradeoff. In SQL Server, however, there is no good reason to do it. The reason that is usually citied is, "Because I need a way to easily identify which objects are of which type."

So let's use MagicChoc to explore that reason through a couple of different lenses. Specifically, in the `SalesDB`, there is a table called `tbl_Orders` and a stored procedure called `sp_orders`. Additionally, there is a table called `tbl_customers` and a view called `v_customers`. The first lens is pure identification of object type. Let's use the customer objects to think about this. There are two ways that you may wish to explore those objects: either through SSMS or through code. Figure 2.3 shows the two objects in Object Explorer.

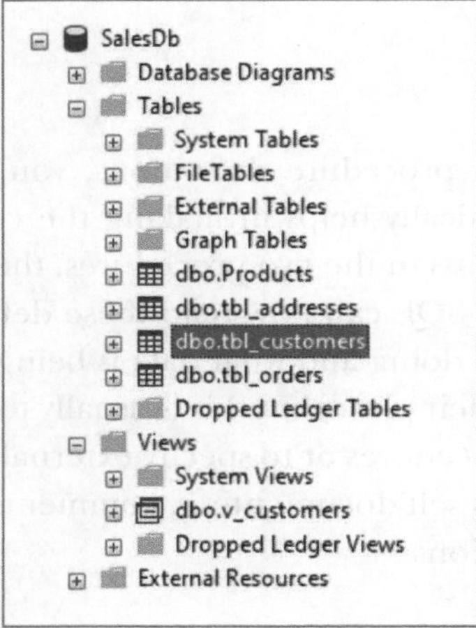

Figure 2.3 Viewing objects through Object Explorer

As you can see, it is quite easy to determine which is the table and which is the view. The table is displayed under the Tables node, and the view is displayed under the Views node.

What about if you wanted to iterate your objects through code? The query in listing 2.7 demonstrates how to pull back the details of both objects via T-SQL. You will notice that the objects are easily distinguishable by virtue of the `type_desc` column in `sys.objects`.

Listing 2.7 Returning the customers objects

```
SELECT
      name
    , type_desc
FROM sys.objects
WHERE name LIKE '%customers%' ;
```

The results of this query are

```
Name             type_desc
tbl_customers    USER_TABLE
v_customers            VIEW
```

Once again in the voice of that legendary 1980s detective, "I know what you're thinking, and you're right. If we dropped the prefix, the `customers` table and view would have an identical name, and that is not allowed." And that brings me nicely to the second lens.

You will remember that in mistake #1, we discussed having meaningful object names that made your code self-documenting. Let's think about this from the perspective of the customers objects. There is a table and a view with exactly the same name. Unless they are performing exactly the same function, that can't be right, unless the view is just returning all the data from a single underlying table. And if the view is just returning the same data as the table, then why does the view exist?

> **Reasons for views that map exactly to a table**
>
> There are two reasons why some people may have views that just return all columns from a single table. The first is a way of locking the tables to avoid people inadvertently changing the table schema. If you create a view `WITH SCHEMABINDING`, then it is not possible to alter the definition of the table without first dropping (or removing) `SCHEMABINDING` from the view. I do not recommend this approach. It is far better and more understandable to simply limit people's access to make schema modifications using an appropriate security strategy. There is a design principle called *the principle of least surprise*. I subscribe to this theory.
>
> The second reason that you may see a view returning all columns from a single table is because of a stringent policy that all applications must access data via an abstraction layer. I am certainly in favor of the principle behind this, which is to keep the complexity at the SQL Server level and allow application developers to simply pull data from views and stored procedures. When it is taken to this extreme, however, it adds extra objects to no benefit. You just have more objects to maintain.

In the `SalesDB`, the `tbl_customers` table holds details about customers. Therefore, it has a meaningful name. The `v_customers` view, however, is returning both customer data and order data. Therefore, its name is not appropriate. A more appropriate name might be `customerOrders`.

The `tbl_addresses` table does not have any corresponding views, procedures, or functions, so we can simply go ahead and remove the prefix there. The `tbl_products` table does have a corresponding stored procedure, but that procedure currently has an `sp_` prefix, so we can go ahead and rename this table as well. However, we should rename the stored procedure to `sp_addOrder` to make it meaningful.

> **TIP** You guessed it, in the words of Magnum PI: "I know what you're thinking, and you're right. Shouldn't we drop the `sp_` prefix from the stored procedures as well?" Yes, we should, but we are going to discuss this further in mistake #3; for now, we will leave them as they are.

The script in the following listing will drop the prefix from the tables and view.

Listing 2.8 Dropping the prefix

```
EXEC sp_rename 'tbl_addresses', 'addresses' ;

EXEC sp_rename 'tbl_orders', 'orders' ;

EXEC sp_rename 'tbl_customers', 'customers' ;
```

sp_rename automatically updates Foreign Key constraints.

```
DROP VIEW dbo.v_customers ;
GO

CREATE VIEW dbo.customerOrders
AS
SELECT
        c.FirstName
      , c.LastName
      , c.email
      , o.LineItems.value('(/Product/@ProductName)[1]', 'int') AS ProductName
      , o.LineItems.value('(/Product/@OrderQty)[1]', 'int') AS OrderQty
      , o.OrderDate
FROM dbo.customers c
INNER JOIN dbo.orders o
    ON c.CustomerID = o.CustomerID ;
GO

DROP PROCEDURE dbo.sp_orders ;
GO

CREATE PROCEDURE dbo.sp_addOrder
      @CustomerID INT,
      @LineItems XML,
      @BillingAddressID INT,
      @DeliveryAddressID INT,
      @OrderDate DATETIME
AS
BEGIN
      DECLARE @OrderQty INT = 0 ;
      DECLARE @ProductID INT = 0 ;

      INSERT INTO orders (
            CustomerID,
            LineItems,
            BillingAddressID,
            DeliveryAddressID,
            OrderDate
      )
      VALUES (
            @CustomerID,
            @LineItems,
            @BillingAddressID,
            @DeliveryAddressID,
            @OrderDate
      ) ;

      SET @OrderQty = @LineItems.value('(/Product/@OrderQty)[1]', 'int') ;
      SET @ProductID = @LineItems.value('(/Product/@ProductID)[1]', 'int') ;

      EXEC sp_updateProductStockLevel @OrderQty, @ProductID ;
END
GO

DROP PROCEDURE dbo.sp_updateProductStockLevel ;
GO

CREATE PROCEDURE dbo.sp_updateProductStockLevel
```

Drops the view and creates it with the new name. This allows us to also change the definition to use the new table names.

While sp_rename can be used with stored procedures, we also need to change the definitions to use the new table names.

While sp_rename can be used with stored procedures, we also need to change the definitions to use the new table names.

```
    @OrderQty INT,
    @ProductID INT
AS
BEGIN
    UPDATE products
    SET StockQty = StockQty - @OrderQty
    WHERE ProductID = @ProductID ;

    UPDATE [DCSVR01\Inventory].InventoryDB.dbo.productStock
    SET StockQty = StockQty - @OrderQty
    WHERE ProductID = @ProductID ;
END
```

2.4 #3 The dreaded sp_ prefix

In mistake #2 we spent time discussing why prefixes are not a good idea, so why do we have a mistake dedicated to the `sp_` prefix? The best way to explain why the `sp_` prefix deserves a special shout-out is with an example. Therefore, I would like you to consider the definition of the `sp_AddUser` stored procedure in the `SalesDB`, which can be found in the next listing. This procedure simply adds a new user to the application when they register for an account online via the MagicChoc website.

Listing 2.9 `sp_AddUser` procedure definition

```
CREATE PROCEDURE sp_addUser
    @UserDetails XML
AS
BEGIN

    OPEN SYMMETRIC KEY MagicChocKey
        DECRYPTION BY CERTIFICATE MagicChocCertificate ;

    INSERT INTO dbo.customers (
          FirstName
        , LastName
        , email
        , UserPassword
    )
    VALUES (
          @UserDetails.value('(/User/FirstName)[1]','nvarchar(128)')
        , @UserDetails.value('(/User/LastName)[1]','nvarchar(128)')
        , @UserDetails.value('(/User/email)[1]','nvarchar(512)')
        , ENCRYPTBYKEY(KEY_GUID('MagicChocKey'), @UserDetails.value('(/User/
 UserPassword)[1]','nvarchar(128)'))
    ) ;

    CLOSE SYMMETRIC KEY MagicChocKey ;
END
```

The details of the new user are passed from the application as an XML fragment.

The xQuery value() method is used to pull the values out of the XML fragment and insert them into the customers table.

The password is encrypted before being inserted into the table.

The application seems to be throwing a strange error. To diagnose the problem, we can simulate the application calling the stored procedure with the script in the following listing.

Listing 2.10 Calling the `sp_AddUser` stored procedure

```
DECLARE @UserDetails XML ;                    <-- Declares a variable of type XML

SET @UserDetails = N'<User>
    <FirstName>Peter</FirstName>
    <LastName>Carter</LastName>
    <email>peter@carter.com</email>
    <UserPassword>myPaSSw0rd</UserPassword>
</User>' ;
```

Passes an element-centric XML fragment into the @UserDetails variable

```
EXEC sp_adduser @UserDetails ;
```

Passes the XML fragment into the sp_AddUser stored procedure

Using this script to execute the stored procedure causes the following error to be thrown:

```
Msg 257, Level 16, State 3, Procedure sp_adduser, Line 0 [Batch Start Line 94]
Implicit conversion from data type xml to nvarchar is not allowed. Use the
CONVERT function to run this query.
```

Well, that's odd! The error shows as being on line 0 of the stored procedure, which implies an error passing the `@UserDetails` variable. But there is no NVARCHAR-to-XML conversion happening. The variable is of the XML data type and the procedure's parameter is defined as the XML data type. So what is going on?

Let's try an experiment. Let's run the procedure with no parameters, using the statement `EXEC sp_adduser`. The error output is

```
Msg 201, Level 16, State 4, Procedure sp_adduser, Line 0 [Batch Start Line
104]
Procedure or function 'sp_adduser' expects parameter '@loginame', which was
not supplied.
```

Now we have a different error, but that's even more strange. It is complaining that we are not passing the `@loginname` parameter. But our stored procedure doesn't have a `@loginname` parameter. It's almost like we are executing the wrong stored procedure.

We need to get to the bottom of this one. To do so, let's run the query in listing 2.11, which returns results from the `sys.all_objects` catalog view. This object provides a union of user objects and system objects.

Listing 2.11 Pulling details from `sys.all_objects`

```
SELECT
      name
    , SCHEMA_NAME(schema_id) AS SchemaName
    , type_desc
    , is_ms_shipped
FROM sys.all_objects
WHERE name = 'sp_adduser' ;
```

The SCHEMA_NAME() function is a system function, which converts schema IDs into schema names.

The results of this query are

name	SchemaName	type_desc	is_ms_shipped
sp_adduser	dbo	SQL_STORED_PROCEDURE	0
sp_adduser	sys	SQL_STORED_PROCEDURE	1

The results show that there are two procedures with the same name. The first result is our stored procedure. We can tell this because it is in the dbo schema and the is_ms_shipped flag is false. The second result is a system-stored procedure with the same name. We can tell it is a system-stored procedure because it is in the sys schema and the is_ms_shipped flag is true.

TIP The is_ms_shipped flag highlights objects that are created internally, by SQL Server.

System-stored procedures are stored in a "hidden" read-only database called resource, which stores all system objects. These objects appear to be in all databases, however. This means that they can be accessed easily from all databases. All system-stored procedures have an sp_ prefix, and this prefix should be reserved exclusively for system-stored procedures.

When you execute a stored procedure with an sp_ prefix, SQL Server will first look for that procedure in the master database. Only if it does not find a procedure there will it attempt to find the procedure in the local database where the procedure was executed.

This can be demonstrated using the script in listing 2.12. This script creates a procedure called sp_listing_2_12 in the master database and then executes it from the SalesDB database, using a one-part name.

Listing 2.12 Accessing a procedure in master from a user database

```
USE master
GO

CREATE PROCEDURE sp_listing_2_12
AS
BEGIN
    SELECT 'Hello! I am in the master database!' ;
END
GO

USE SalesDb
GO

EXEC sp_listing_2_12 ;
```

- Changes the context to master, before creating the procedure (annotates `USE master` / `GO`)
- Changes the context to SalesDB, before executing the procedure (annotates `USE SalesDb` / `GO`)

Now that we understand why using the sp_ prefix is a bad idea, let's clean up our procedure names. We can achieve this with the script in listing 2.13. Because we do not need to update any procedure definitions, we can use the sp_rename procedure to perform this task.

Listing 2.13 Cleaning up procedure names

```
EXEC sp_rename 'sp_addOrder', 'addOrder' ;

EXEC sp_rename 'sp_addUser', 'addUser' ;

EXEC sp_rename 'sp_updateProductStockLevel', 'updateProductStockLevel' ;

EXEC sp_rename 'sp_products', 'addProduct' ;

EXEC sp_rename 'sp_updateStock', 'updateStockLevelAfterManufacture' ;
```

As well as removing the prefix, we have also made the object names more meaningful.

Now that we have resolved all of the mistakes in our object names, it is worth taking a look at what this has done to our component diagram. The updated diagram is shown in figure 2.4.

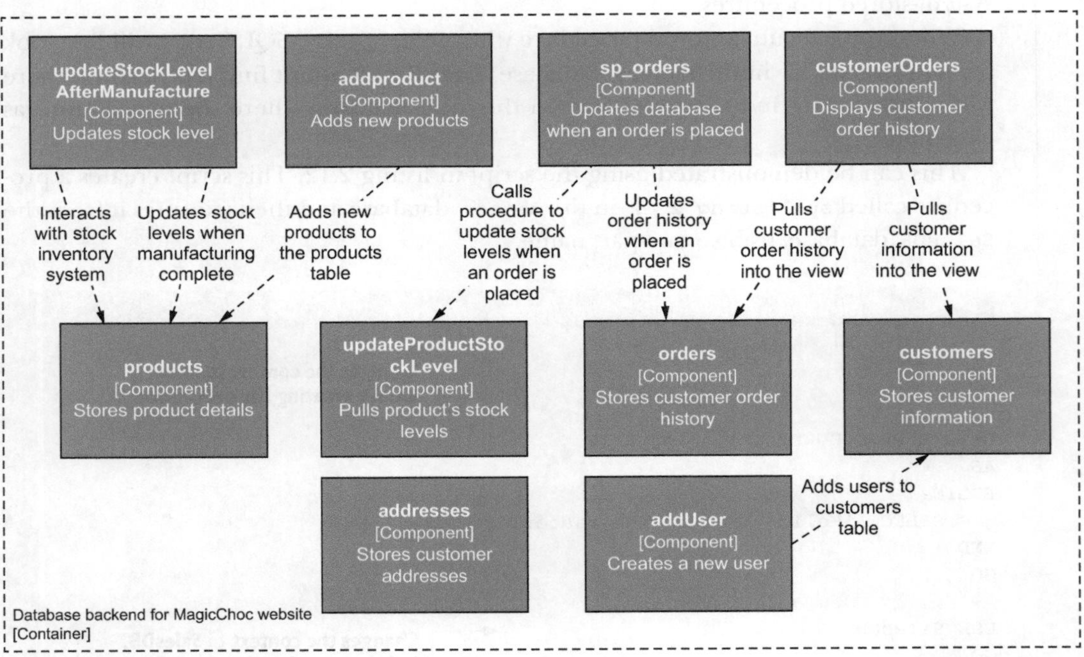

Figure 2.4 Updated component diagram

2.5 #4 Not making time for coding standards

Imagine you are on a team of 10 developers working on a large data-tier application. You are all experienced developers, and you have a tight deadline to hit. It's tempting to wade straight into writing code. After all, you have all been around the block a few times. You all know to indent your code with four spaces, right? Hold on! Is it four spaces or a tab?

The quickest way to start an argument between two developers is to talk about coding standards. Everybody has their own standards to which they adhere, and everybody thinks that their standards are the best. If we have a single standard, then not everybody will agree with it, but even if it's imperfect, the consistency means that it is better than having no standard at all.

Depending on the size and complexity of a given project, the coding standards will likely vary in their level of comprehensiveness. They will, however, cover both stylistic choices and technical considerations.

Unlike technical standards, a simple fact about stylistic standards is that it doesn't really matter what the standards are, provided that you have them and they are implemented consistently across the project.

Coding standards are where architecture comes into play. In mistake #1, we talked about the need for architecture in SQL Server projects to ensure that database schemas are optimally designed and performant. We also mentioned that this architecture should consider naming conventions. Another facet of architecture is ensuring that there is a set of coding standards to which people can adhere.

Stylistic choices may include elements such as

- Indent code with four spaces or tab?
- Should all statements be terminated with a semicolon?
- When listing column names, should the comma separator be at the end of the line or the beginning of the next line?
- Should `ON` clauses be specified on the same line as the `JOIN` clause?
- Should SQL Server keywords be all uppercase?
- Camel case versus Pascal?

Technical standards will likely include the following:

- Do not use cursors.
- Use `UNION ALL` rather than `UNION`, where possible.
- Do not use `*` in the `SELECT` list.
- Do not use `NOLOCK`.
- Avoid using `DISTINCT`.

NOTE These lists are designed to give you an idea of the considerations that go into coding standards. They are not in any way meant to be comprehensive.

So what happens if you do not have coding standards? The simple answer is that developers just do their own thing. To think about the consequences of this, we should consider stylistic choices and technical considerations separately.

For stylistic choices, the problem comes with code maintenance. In the following script (which we saw earlier in this chapter but is repeated here for convenience), we saw an extreme example of what can happen when no stylistic coding standards are in place:

```
ALTER PROCEDURE [dbo].[proc01]
AS
BEGIN
;with t3 as (select col1, col2, col3 from tbl03) select t1.col1, t2.col2,
t1.col2, t1.col3, t3.col1, t3.col2 from dbo.tbl01 t1 inner join tbl02 t2 on
t1.col1 = t2.col1 and t1.col3 < 55 inner join t3 on t3.col1 = t1.col1 union
select col1, col2, col3, NULL, NULL, '0' from dbo.tbl04 ;
END
```

While any code is unlikely to be written quite this badly in the real world, remember our conversation in mistake #2 about how our brains get used to certain patterns when parsing lists of objects. The same applies when our brains try to parse code.

Consider the queries in listing 2.14. Imagine that you have just parsed 50 queries in the style of query 1. You then reach a query that is written in the style of query 2. Depending on the complexity of the query, this is going to slow you down—maybe for a few seconds, maybe for a few minutes. The two queries return the same results. They are just written using different standards.

Listing 2.14 Changing code style

```
SELECT
      c.FirstName
    , c.LastName
    , o.LineItems
FROM dbo.customers c
LEFT JOIN dbo.orders o
    ON c.CustomerID = o.CustomerID
WHERE c.CustomerID >= 2 AND c.CustomerID <= 3
    AND c.CustomerID <> 2 ;
```

Query 1

```
SELECT
    cust.FirstName,
    cust.LastName,
    ord.LineItems
FROM dbo.customers cust
LEFT JOIN (
    SELECT CustomerID,
    LineItems
    FROM dbo.Orders
) ord ON cust.CustomerID = ord.CustomerID
WHERE cust.CustomerID BETWEEN 2 AND 3 AND cust.CustomerID != 2 ;
```

Query 2

Ultimately, not using a consistent coding style will slow down the resolution of bugs and the development of new enhancements as your data-tier application moves through its lifecycle.

When we think about the technical coding standards, these are much more prescriptive. If developers do not follow the technical standards, then your application will likely experience degraded performance or even return unexpected results. All of the technical standards listed previously are common mistakes in SQL Server and will be discussed in chapter 5.

2.6 #5 Using ordinal column position

SQL Server supports the use of ordinal column numbers in the `ORDER BY` clause. This means that, instead of ordering by a column name, you can order by its ordinal position within the `SELECT` clause. For example, consider the query in the following listing.

Listing 2.15 Ordering by ordinal column position

```
SELECT *
FROM SYS.databases
ORDER BY 54 ;
```

Orders by the 54th column in the SELECT list

So what column have we ordered the query by? The answer is the `log_reuse_wait_desc` column, but the only way of determining that would be to either count the columns in the result set until you get to the 54th column or run the query in listing 2.16, which pulls the column name from the metadata held in catalog views.

Listing 2.16 Pulling the column name from metadata

```
SELECT
    c.name
FROM SYS.all_columns c
INNER JOIN SYS.all_objects o
    ON o.object_id = c.object_id
WHERE o.name = 'databases'
    AND c.column_id = 54 ;
```

> **TIP** If the object being queried was a user object instead of a system object, then the query would also work if we joined `sys.objects` to `sys.columns`.

Another good reason to avoid the use of ordinal column positions is that they are not stable when the underlying tables are modified. If the second column was deleted from a table, for example, then we would need to update all queries that referred to an ordinal column of 3..*n*, as the ordinal positions would have changed.

Summary

- Always use object names that are meaningful, with a view to making your code self-documenting.
- Always consider database architecture, which is the design of your database, even within agile projects.
- Avoid using prefixes for database objects, as they can actually make objects harder to locate.
- Be especially careful to avoid using the `sp_` prefix for stored procedures as this indicates that they are a system stored procedure, instead of a user-defined procedure.

- Always make time to ensure that your data-tier application has coding standards. These should form part of your architectural efforts and should consider both stylistic choices as well as technical standards.
- Avoid ordering by ordinal column numbers—unless you enjoy troubleshooting!

3 Data types

This chapter covers

- Why data types are important
- The consequences of using the wrong standard data type
- Reasons for using advanced data types
- The benefits of working with XML and JSON data

In this chapter, we will explore data types and why it is important to choose the correct data types for our table's columns. We will start by exploring some simple data types that are commonly used but that many people use incorrectly. We will see the effect that this can have on cost and performance.

We will then explore some of SQL Server's advanced data types, which are significantly underused. We will investigate the use cases that make them so useful and look at the effects of avoiding them. It is worth noting, however, that while this chapter explores `HIERARCHYID`, XML, and JSON, other specialized data types exist, such as `GEOGRAPHY` and `GEOMETRY` for geospatial data. I strongly encourage you to explore all of SQL Server's advanced data types.

MagicChoc has decided that it needs a new application, which will support human resources. The script in listing 3.1 creates the `HumanResources` database and then creates the first table: `dbo.employees`. You will notice that this table has been created using the data type `NVARCHAR(MAX)` for every column. This doesn't look right, does it? But why? All of the data that we want to store can be inserted into this expansive data type. So does it really matter? We will explore this example throughout the chapter.

Listing 3.1 Creating an employees table

```
CREATE DATABASE HumanResources ;
GO

USE HumanResources ;
GO

CREATE TABLE dbo.Employees (
    EmployeeID              NVARCHAR(MAX)     NOT NULL,
    FirstName               NVARCHAR(MAX)     NOT NULL,
    LastName                NVARCHAR(MAX)     NOT NULL,
    DateOfBirth             NVARCHAR(MAX)     NOT NULL,
    EmployeeStartDate       NVARCHAR(MAX)     NOT NULL,
    ManagerID               NVARCHAR(MAX)     NULL,
    Salary                  NVARCHAR(MAX)     NOT NULL,
    Department              NVARCHAR(MAX)     NOT NULL,
    DepartmentCode          NVARCHAR(MAX)     NOT NULL,
    Role                    NVARCHAR(MAX)     NOT NULL,
    WeeklyContractedHours   NVARCHAR(MAX)     NOT NULL,
    StaffOrContract         NVARCHAR(MAX)     NOT NULL,
    ContractEndDate         NVARCHAR(MAX)     NULL
) ;
```

Designed to store 0 for staff or 1 for contractor (annotation on `StaffOrContract`)

Why is selecting the correct data type so important? Most people who have worked with SQL Server for a while understand the importance of constraints. These constraints come in many forms, such as foreign keys, check constraints, and `NULL` constraints.

Constraints are vital for ensuring data quality within a database. For example, a foreign key will ensure that a value exists in a different table before it is inserted or updated. A `NOT NULL` constraint enforces that a value in the column is mandatory and that the column cannot contain `NULL` values. A check constraint ensures that values in a column meet certain criteria, for example, ensuring that an employee's start date is not earlier than their 16th birthday.

What a lot of people fail to consider, however, is that a data type is also a constraint— a constraint that applies to every single column in every single table within every single database. It is the foundation of data quality and functionality. Additionally, it can play a part in ensuring our code is self-documenting. Self-documenting code is discussed in more detail in chapter 2.

Using the example of our `Employees` table, there are several immediate problems. First, we cannot create a primary key constraint, as primary keys are not supported on `NVARCHAR(MAX)` columns. Second, calculations of the date columns will be cumbersome and require conversion. Dates could also be inserted in conflicting formats, for example, `13/01/2023` and `01/13/2023`. Third, we can insert any data we like into any column. We could insert a date into the `Salary` column, text into the columns expecting numeric values, or dates into the textual descriptors such as `FirstName`, `LastName`, and `Department`. Finally, as we can store up to 2 GB of data in every column of every row, this table could, in theory, get very large very quickly.

We should fix these problems straight away, and the script in listing 3.2 can address them by dropping and recreating the table. It will change the numeric columns to `INT`, the date columns to `DATE`, and reduce the textual descriptor columns to an appropriate length. The table will also add a primary key to the `EmployeeID` column.

Listing 3.2 Updating the employee table column types

```
DROP TABLE dbo.Employees ;
GO

CREATE TABLE dbo.Employees (
    EmployeeID              INT           NOT NULL  PRIMARY KEY,
    FirstName               NVARCHAR(32)  NOT NULL,
    LastName                NVARCHAR(32)  NOT NULL,
    DateOfBirth             DATE          NOT NULL,
    EmployeeStartDate       DATE          NOT NULL,
    ManagerID               INT           NULL,
    Salary                  MONEY         NOT NULL,
    Department              NVARCHAR(64)  NOT NULL,
    DepartmentCode          NVARCHAR(4)   NOT NULL,
    Role                    NVARCHAR(64)  NOT NULL,
    WeeklyContractedHours   INT           NOT NULL,
    StaffOrContract         INT           NOT NULL,
    ContractEndDate         DATE          NULL
) ;
```

> **NOTE** While the newly selected data types are far more useful than blanket `NVARCHAR(MAX)`, they are also still far from perfect. We will explore this problem in the following sections of this chapter.

3.1 #6 Always storing whole numbers in INT

Imagine that we have a large data warehouse. One of the fact tables has 1 billion rows, and it joins to five dimensions, which all have 30,000 rows. Performance is poor and memory is always maxed out because of the volume of data in the buffer cache. When queries are running, a lot of data is being spooled to `TempDB`. We have optimized the queries. We have also reviewed our indexing strategy and ensured that both indexes and statistics are well maintained. It looks like the only thing to do is to throw more hardware at the problem, but we suspect, based on our trend over the last two years, that if we add more RAM, we are only pushing the problem further down the line. What should we do? A starting point would be to consider reviewing our numeric data types, especially those used in primary/foreign key relationships.

INT is the most used but also the most misused data type in SQL Server. We actually have four data types that are designed to store whole numbers specifically. These data types are detailed in table 3.1.

Table 3.1 Integer data type family

Data type	Range	Size (Bytes)
TINYINT	0 to 255	1
SMALLINT	-32,768 to 32,767	2
INT	-2,147,483,648 to 2,147,483,647	4
BIGINT	-9,223,372,036,854,775,808 to 9,223,372,036,854,775,807	8

We can also examine this in code by running the query in listing 3.3. This query uses the CAST() function to convert the value 1 into each of the integer data types. This converted value is then passed into the DATALENGTH() function, which calculates the size of the input value, in bytes.

Listing 3.3 Examining the size of data types

```
SELECT
      DATALENGTH(CAST(1 AS TINYINT)) AS TinyIntSize
    , DATALENGTH(CAST(1 AS SMALLINT)) AS SmallIntSize
    , DATALENGTH(CAST(1 AS INT)) AS IntSize
    , DATALENGTH(CAST(1 AS BIGINT)) AS BigIntSize ;
```

The results of this query are

```
TinyIntSize     SmallIntSize     IntSize     BigIntSize
1               2                4           8
```

Imagine that our five dimension tables use INT for their primary key column. There are 30,000 rows in each of the dimension tables, and there are more than 32,000 possible positive values in the SMALLINT data type. That means if we were not expecting the dimensions to grow dramatically, then we could save 2 bytes in each row.

> **TIP** There are actually more than 64,000 possible values in the SMALLINT range, but to use more than 32,000 of them, we would need to start our numbering sequence at –32,000. This may not play nicely with the principle of least surprise.

At this point, you may be thinking, "Why are we bothered about saving 2 bytes?" The answer to that requires some simple math. There are 30,000 rows in each of the five dimension tables. By moving to a SMALLINT, we would only be saving 58 KB per table. But our fact table has 1 billion rows. That means we would be saving 1.86 GB per key. Multiply that by the five dimension tables and that means for each query against the fact table that touches all rows and all five keys, we would be saving 9.3 GB. Scale that out against the eight fact tables in the data warehouse. We should also factor in the size of indexes, which are built on those foreign key columns. Now consider parallel sessions running different queries. Suddenly, our choice of data type is having a direct and tangible effect on memory consumption.

How does all of this relate to our `Employees` table? Let's document our table in the form of an *Entity Relationship Diagram (ERD)*. An ERD is a diagram that lays out data entities (tables). It shows the relationships between these entities (primary/foreign key constraint), and it details the attributes (columns) of an entity. Optionally, it can also detail the data type of each column.

When building C4 diagrams for data-tier applications, an ERD is often used as the code diagram, which documents the table structure. The ERD in figure 3.1 currently shows just our `employees` entity, but we will build on this in chapter 4. The diagram records the currently defined data types but has been annotated to call out the values that we expect in each column.

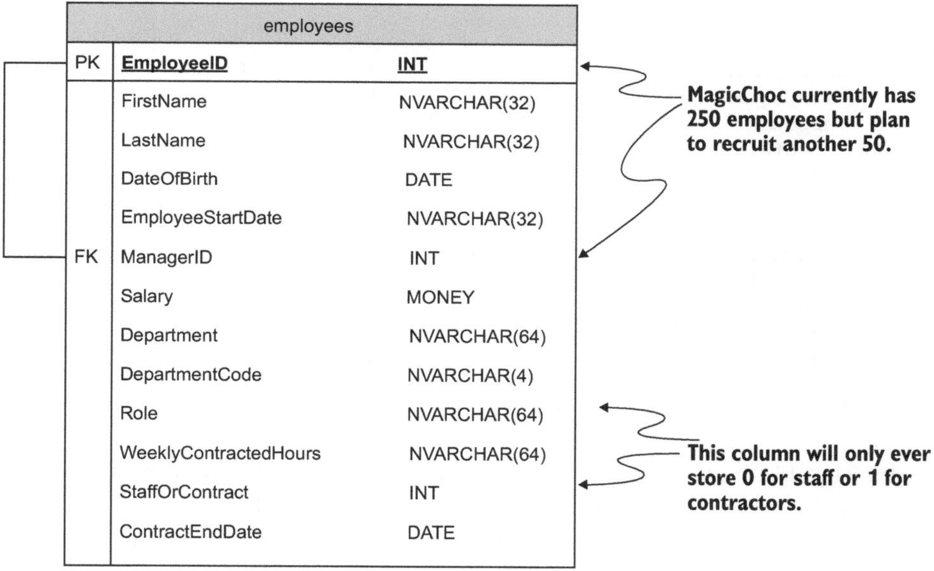

Figure 3.1 `Employees` **ERD**

The `EmployeeID` and `ManagerID` columns will require up to 300 unique values. Therefore, the `TINYINT` data type will be too restrictive. We could, however, use the `SMALLINT` data type. This will save us 2 bytes per row over the `INT` data type that we currently have.

The `StaffOrContract` column is an interesting case. It will store integer values but only in the range of 0 to 1. This brings into play an additional data type that we have not yet discussed: `BIT`. The `BIT` data type is technically an integer data type, but it can only store the values `0`, `1`, and `NULL`. It is designed to store Boolean values, such as flags, and has useful extra features.

If a user inserts `TRUE` or `FALSE` into a `BIT` column, SQL Server will automatically convert them to `1` and `0`, respectively. Additionally, if a user inserts any numeric value other than 0 or 1, then SQL Server will automatically convert the value to 1. For example, if we ran the query `SELECT CAST(86.2 AS BIT)`, then it would return the value `1`.

Additionally, if a table has multiple `BIT` columns, then SQL Server optimizes its storage. The first eight `BIT` columns only use 1 byte of space. The subsequent eight columns use an additional byte and so on. The `StaffOrContract` column is an ideal use case for the `BIT` data type and will save us 3 bytes per row.

As we have no data in the `employees` table as yet, let's drop and recreate it using our preferred integer data types. We can do this with the script in the following listing.

Listing 3.4 Changing integer column types

```
DROP TABLE dbo.Employees
GO

CREATE TABLE dbo.Employees (
    EmployeeID              SMALLINT      NOT NULL  PRIMARY KEY,
    FirstName               NVARCHAR(32)  NOT NULL,
    LastName                NVARCHAR(32)  NOT NULL,
    DateOfBirth             DATE          NOT NULL,
    EmployeeStartDate       DATE          NOT NULL,
    ManagerID               SMALLINT      NULL,
    Salary                  MONEY         NOT NULL,
    Department              NVARCHAR(64)  NOT NULL,
    DepartmentCode          NVARCHAR(4)   NOT NULL,
    Role                    NVARCHAR(64)  NOT NULL,
    WeeklyContractedHours   INT           NOT NULL,
    StaffOrContract         BIT           NOT NULL,
    ContractEndDate         DATE          NULL
) ;
```

We should always be mindful of the amount of storage space required by our data types. This is especially true if the table is very large or if the column will be used in an index. `SMALLINT` and `TINYINT` should be used instead of `INT` where we do not expect values to overflow these sizes, to reduce wasted space.

3.2 #7 Always using variable-length strings

Imagine that we have a table that stores US addresses. We are correctly trying to make sure that our data is as space efficient as possible. Therefore, we use variable-length strings for all of the columns, which include each line of the address and the zip code. We know that Mooselookmeguntic in Maine and Kleinfeltersville in Pennsylvania have the longest city names in the United States, each with 17 characters, so we set the `CityName` column to be a `VARCHAR(17)`. We know that the longest state name in the US is Rhode Island and Providence Plantations, so we set the state column to be a `VARCHAR(48)`. We know that the zip code will be exactly 10 characters, but because we know it will have the same length every time, should we use a `VARCHAR(10)` or a `CHAR(10)`? Does it even matter? Either way, the data is 10 characters long, so will take up 10 bytes of space, right? And if that is correct, why do we even have fixed-length strings at all? The fact is that this assumption is not correct. To understand why, we need to understand a little about how SQL Server stores data.

> **NOTE** Fixed-length strings `CHAR` and `NCHAR` pad out the string with white space, if it has not been filled with data. For example, if we have a `CHAR(8)` and insert the value `Hello!` then it will use 8 bytes of storage because the two spare characters will be filled with white space.

SQL Server stores data in a series of 8 KB pages, with each series of eight pages making up a 64 KB extent, which is usually the smallest amount of data that is read. Each data page has a 96-byte page header, which stores information that applies to the whole page, such as its unique ID and the object ID of the table (or index) that it belongs to.

The data that form rows are then stored in slots on the page. These slots don't just store the data, however. They also have to store a small amount of *metadata*, to allow the data to be useful. This metadata includes information about the type of record stored in that slot. For example, is it a data record or an index record? Does it include ghost data (data that has been logically deleted but not yet physically removed)?

Other metadata includes the length of fixed-length data (this does not just include fixed-length character data but also data such as integers), a NULL value bitmap that tracks if variable-length columns contain NULL values, and a version tag, which is used by operations such as online index rebuilds or transactions with optimistic transaction isolation levels. We will discuss isolation levels in chapter 10.

The piece of metadata that we are really concerned about here, however, is the *column offset array*. This is used to track where each variable-length column begins within the row. Because variable-length data can be of any length, this offset table is the only way for SQL Server to separate where one piece of data ends and the next one begins.

Each variable-length column requires a 2-byte offset in this table, meaning that every variable-length column uses 2 bytes more space than it would if it was a fixed-length column. This applies even if the column stores a `NULL` value. Therefore, if we used a `CHAR(10)` for our zip code, it would take up 10 bytes of space, but if we used a `VARCHAR(10)`, it would take up 12 bytes of space, despite the actual data length being 10 bytes.

CHAR and VARCHAR vs. NCHAR and NVARCHAR

`NCHAR` and `NVARCHAR` are able to store full UNICODE data, whereas `CHAR` and `VARCHAR` are only able to store an 8-bit codepage. From SQL Server 2019, it has been possible to use UTF-8 enabled collations, and `CHAR`/`VARCHAR` data types can store the full range of UTF-8 characters. For full UTF-16 support, however, the `NCHAR` and `NVARCHAR` data types are still required.

(continued)

CHAR and VARCHAR data types use 1 byte per character. NCHAR and NVARCHAR use 2 bytes per character. The extra space is required for the full 16-bit UTF-16 codepage. Therefore, not only do the UTF-16 data types use more space, but they limit the number of characters that can be stored on a page. SQL Server imposes a maximum length for fixed-length UTF-16 data of 4,000 characters, as opposed to the maximum length of fixed-length 8-bit codepage data, which is 8,000 characters.

It is possible to store variable-length data up to 2 GB by using the VARCHAR(MAX) and NVARCHAR(MAX) data types, but any fields that do not fit on the data page are stored in a different type of allocation unit and are referred to as row-overflow data.

The size limitation also applies across multiple columns. No matter how the columns are dispersed, the maximum length of data on a page is 8,060 bytes. Therefore, if we have a table that consists of a CHAR(5000) column and a VARCHAR(5000) column, and data is inserted into the variable-length column that has a length of 2,000 characters (4,000 bytes), then the variable-length data would dynamically be moved to a different page and stored in the row-overflow allocation unit.

Some people make an argument that because storage and memory are comparatively cheaper than they used to be, we should just use NCHAR and NVARCHAR data types to avoid any potential problems with codepage incompatibilities between columns. My view of this, which has been strengthened by the addition of UTF-8 collations, is the same as for any other data type. We should use the most restrictive data type that will not overflow.

In other words, if we know, because of the nature of our data, that we will never face any codepage incompatibility problems, then we should use the 8-bit codepage data types. This will ultimately give us the best performance and resource efficiency at the best pricepoint. If, however, this cannot be guaranteed—for example, if we need to pull in data from the internet or other untrusted sources or, indeed, if we know that we may need to mix data from multiple collations—then we should use the UTF-16 data types instead.

In the context of our Employees table, most of our columns absolutely need to be variable length. Our DepartmentCode column, however, will always contain a two-character value, such as HR for Human Resources, SA for Sales, and MA for Manufacturing. Therefore, we should change the definition of the DepartmentCode column to be a NCHAR(2). This will save 2 bytes of information per row. We are using Unicode because, in section 3.4, we will be pulling in data from an external business partner.

The statement in the following listing makes the desired update to the Employees table by using the ALTER TABLE..ALTER COLUMN command.

Listing 3.5 Updating the DepartmentCode column to a fixed-length string

```
ALTER TABLE dbo.Employees
    ALTER COLUMN DepartmentCode NCHAR(2) ;
```

Using variable-length strings is the right thing to do if the values in our column are likely to be of differing lengths. This avoids the shorter values being padded out with white space and saves space. If we expect the values of a column to always be the same length, however, then we should use a fixed-length string. Failure to do so will add an additional 2 bytes per row, which will be used for a column offset array, defining the beginning of each variable-length value.

3.3 #8 Writing your own hierarchy code

If we look at our `Employees` table, we have probably realized that the `EmployeeID` and `ManagerID` columns are designed to model an employee hierarchy. Therefore, consider the org chart in figure 3.2, which models the organizational structure of the senior management team at MagicChoc.

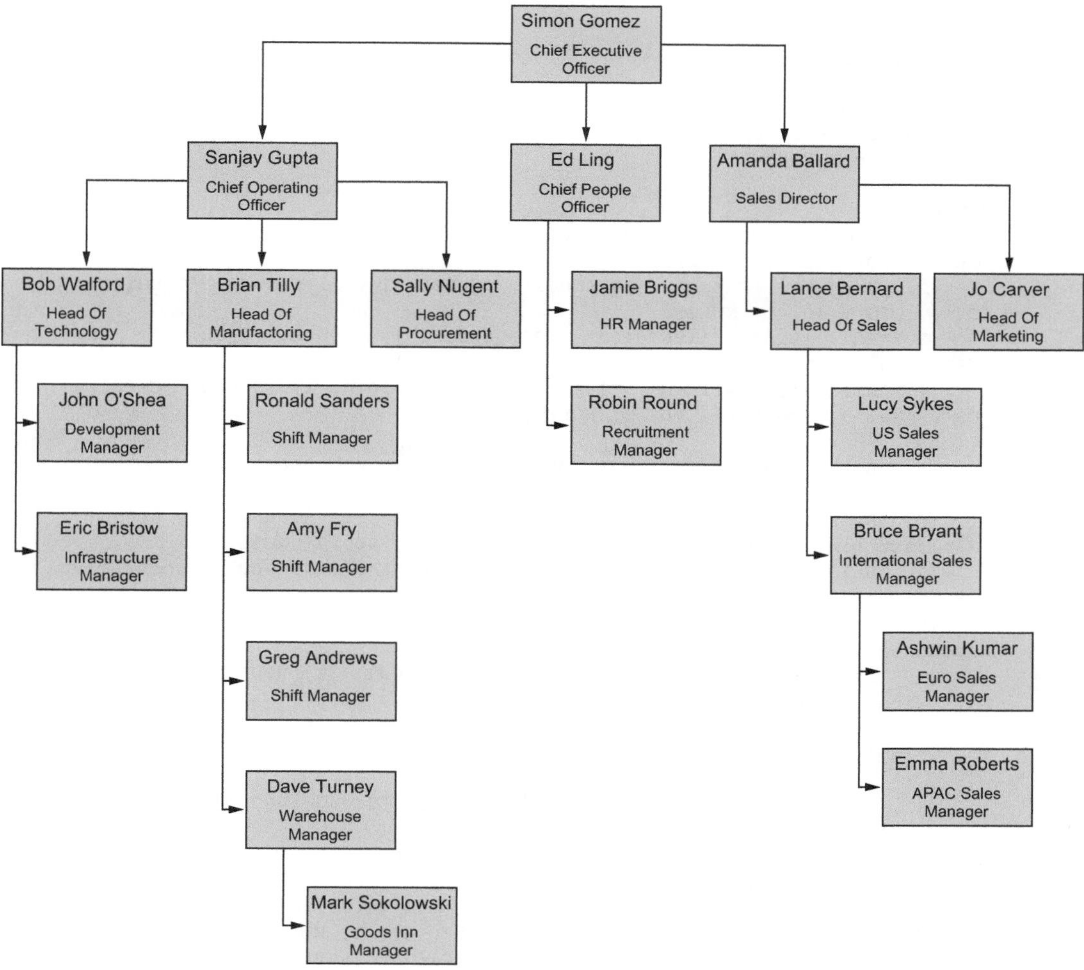

Figure 3.2 MagicChoc management org chart

To demonstrate how to model this hierarchy using a traditional approach, which a surprising number of developers still use, I invite you to run the script in listing 3.6, which will insert employee records into the `Employees` table. Notice how the `ManagerID` column contains the `EmployeeID` of the person they report to.

Listing 3.6 Inserting employee records into the `Employees` table

```
INSERT INTO dbo.Employees (
    EmployeeID
  , FirstName
  , LastName
  , DateOfBirth
  , EmployeeStartDate
  , ManagerID
  , Salary
  , Department
  , DepartmentCode
  , Role
  , WeeklyContractedHours
  , StaffOrContract
  , ContractEndDate
)
VALUES
    (1, 'Simon', 'Gomez', '19691001', '20180101', NULL, 980000, 'C-Suite',
'CS', 'CEO', 40, 1, NULL),
    (2, 'Sanjay', 'Gupta', '19761001', '20180101', 1, 640000, 'C-Suite',
'CS', 'COO', 40, 1, NULL),
    (3, 'Ed', 'Ling', '19690403', '20200801', 1, 320000, 'C-Suite', 'CS',
'CPO', 40, 1, NULL),
    (4, 'Amanda', 'Ballard', '19830401', '20200301', 1, 350000, 'C-Suite',
'CS', 'Sales Director', 40, 1, NULL),

    (5, 'Bob', 'Walford', '19780908', '20191201', 2, 96000, 'Technology',
'TE', 'Head Of Technology', 40, 1, NULL),
    (6, 'Brian', 'Tilly', '19710102', '20181001', 2, 89000,
'Manufacturing', 'MA', 'Head Of Manufacturing', 40, 1, NULL),
    (7, 'Sally', 'Nugent', '19790302', '20220601', 2, 80000, 'Procurement',
'PR', 'Head Of Procurement', 40, 1, NULL),
    (8, 'Jamie', 'Briggs', '19900102', '20190601', 3, 65000, 'Human
Resources', 'HR', 'HR Manager', 40, 1, NULL),
    (9, 'Lance', 'Bernard', '19910707', '20210601', 4, 98000, 'Sales &
Marketing', 'SA', 'Head Of Sales', 40, 1, NULL),
    (10, 'Jo', 'Carver', '19900810', '20191201', 4, 70000, 'Sales &
Marketing', 'SA', 'Head Of Marketing', 40, 1, NULL),

    (11, 'John', 'O''Shea', '19700609', '20180601', 5, 70000, 'Technology',
'TE', 'Development Manager', 40, 1, NULL),
    (12, 'Eric', 'Bristow', '20000109', '20221001', 5, 72000, 'Technology',
'TE', 'Infrastructure Manager', 40, 1, NULL),
    (13, 'Ronald', 'Sanders', '19601209', '20190101', 6, 45000,
     'Manufacturing', 'MA', 'Shift Manager', 45, 1, NULL),
    (14, 'Amy', 'Fry', '19921101', '20190101', 6, 45000, 'Manufacturing',
'MA', 'Shift Manager', 45, 1, NULL),
    (15, 'Greg', 'Andrews', '19871212', '20190101', 6, 45000,
```

```
'Manufacturing', 'MA', 'Shift Manager', 45, 1, NULL),
    (16, 'Dave', 'Turney', '19760609', '20190101', 6, 52000,
'Manufacturing', 'MA', 'Warehouse Manager', 48, 1, NULL),
    (17, 'Mark', 'Sokolowski', '19960209', '20190901', 16, 42000,
'Manufacturing', 'MA', 'Goods Inn Manager', 40, 1, NULL),

    (18, 'Robin', 'Round', '19940409', '20190601', 3, 60000, 'Human
Resources', 'HR', 'Recruitment Manager', 40, 1, NULL),
    (19, 'Lucy', 'Sykes', '19890201', '20200201', 9, 65000, 'Sales', 'SA',
'US Sales Manager', 40, 1, NULL),
    (20, 'Bruce', 'Bryant', '19860304', '20200301', 9, 70000, 'Sales',
'SA', 'International Sales Manager', 40, 1, NULL),
    (21, 'Ashwin', 'Kumar', '20010212', '20210601', 20, 55000, 'Sales',
'SA', 'Euro Sales Manager', 40, 1, NULL),
    (22, 'Emma', 'Roberts', '20000208', '20210601', 20, 55000, 'Sales',
'SA', 'APAC Sales Manager', 40, 1, NULL) ;
```

Now imagine that we have been asked to write a report that lists all of Sanjay Gupta's direct reports. This can be achieved using the following simple query:

```
SELECT
    FirstName
  , LastName
FROM dbo.Employees
WHERE ManagerID = 2 ;
```

But what if we are asked to write a query that returns all of Sanjay Gupta's direct and indirect reports? This suddenly becomes more complex. There are several ways of creating this report, including dreaded cursors (which we will discuss in chapter 5), but the best practice method would be for developers to use a recursive *common table expression (CTE)*. A CTE is a temporary result set, which can be referenced multiple times within a query. It can also reference itself, which allows for *recursion*.

> **NOTE** Recursion means that an error in the query could cause an infinite loop. To avoid this, there is an instance-wide setting that controls the maximum level of recursion. By default, this is set to 100. If we want to override this for a specific query, we can use the `MAXRECURSION` query hint.

Recursion is the key to implementing hierarchies in this scenario. For example, the query in listing 3.7 uses a CTE to return all employees who report both directly and indirectly to Sanjay Gupta, who has an `EmployeeID` of `2`. Within the definition of the CTE, the first query returns the employee record for Sanjay himself. A `UNION ALL` clause then appends the results of the second query. This second query is recursive, because it joins the results from the `Employees` table to the results of the first query within the CTE. Because the join is on `EmployeeID` in the first results set to the `ManagerID` in the second result set, the second result set contains the details of subordinate employees. The final `SELECT` statement sits outside of the CTE. It returns all records from the CTE but then joins back to the underlying `Employees` table to populate the managers' first and last names.

TIP You will notice that the semicolon that terminates the `SET` statement is at the start of the line that begins the `WITH` CTE clause. This is a stylistic choice. A CTE must always be the start of a statement. Therefore, it is a common practice to always start the statement with a semicolon. That will stop a compilation error even if we have forgotten to terminate the previous statement. Alternatively, you can enforce a standard whereby all statements are always terminated with a semicolon.

Listing 3.7 Using a CTE to return all direct and indirect employees

```
DECLARE @ManagerID INT ;

SET @ManagerID = 2

;WITH EmployeeCTE AS (
    SELECT
          EmployeeId
        , FirstName
        , LastName
        , ManagerId
    FROM dbo.Employees
    WHERE EmployeeId = @ManagerID
    UNION ALL
    SELECT
          Emp.EmployeeId
        , Emp.FirstName
        , Emp.LastName
        , Emp.ManagerId
    FROM dbo.Employees AS Emp
    INNER JOIN EmployeeCTE AS CTE
        ON CTE.EmployeeId=Emp.ManagerId
)
SELECT
      Emp.EmployeeID
    , Emp.FirstName
    , Emp.LastName
    , Emp.ManagerID
    , Mgr.FirstName AS ManagerFirstName
    , Mgr.LastName AS ManagerLastName
FROM EmployeeCTE Emp
INNER JOIN dbo.Employees Mgr
    ON Emp.ManagerID = Mgr.EmployeeID ;
```

Another typical query that we may be asked to write involves working out who manages an employee's manager. This is common when constructing escalation paths. The query in listing 3.8 demonstrates how we could establish who manages Emma Robert's manager. In this query, we add a constant of `0` in the first query within the CTE, with a column name `Level` to the result set, and specify that Emma Roberts is at level 0. The recursive query then increments the level number for each layer of the hierarchy. The final query, outside of the CTE, then filters by level 2 to return the entity two levels above Emma.

Listing 3.8 Using a CTE to return the entity two levels above in a hierarchy

```
DECLARE @EmployeeID INT ;

SET @EmployeeID = 22

; WITH EmployeeCTE AS
(
   SELECT
       employeeid
     , firstname
     , lastname
     , managerid
     , Role
     , 0 as Level
   FROM dbo.Employees
   WHERE EmployeeID = @EmployeeID
   UNION ALL
   SELECT
       emp.EmployeeID
     , emp.FirstName
     , emp.LastName
     , emp.ManagerID
     , emp.Role
     , Level + 1
   FROM dbo.employees emp
   INNER JOIN EmployeeCTE cte
      ON emp.EmployeeID = cte.ManagerID
)

SELECT
    firstname
  , lastname
  , Role
FROM EmployeeCTE
WHERE Level = 2 ;
```

The challenge with this traditional approach to implementing a hierarchy is that it requires the developer to write a lot of code. The examples in this section are simple and are for illustrative purposes, but in real-world scenarios, recursive CTEs can become complex and hard to manage. Every time a slightly different request comes from the business, developers need to write the code that will traverse the hierarchy in the appropriate way. For example, we may be asked to return a list of all managers at the third level of the org structure.

What many developers do not realize is that Microsoft has already done most of the hard work for us by implementing the `HIERARCHYID` data type. This is an advanced data type written in .NET that allows us to call methods against it, which will traverse the hierarchy for us without the need to write complex CTEs.

To see how this works, let's add a new column to the `Employees` table, called `ManagerHierarchyID`, which will be of type `HIERARCHYID`. We can achieve this with the script in the following listing.

Listing 3.9 Adding the ManagerHierarchyID column

```
ALTER TABLE dbo.Employees ADD
    ManagerHierarchyID HIERARCHYID NULL ;
```

To take advantage of SQL Server's hierarchy features, we will first need to model the hierarchy. To explain how this modeling works, consider the following section of our org chart. Simon Gomez is at the top of the hierarchy, which we will call the root.

The hierarchy is modeled using a slashed format. Therefore, the root of the hierarchy is represented as `/`. Sanjay Gupta and Ed Ling are at the second level of the hierarchy, and each needs to be uniquely identified. Therefore, Sanjay will be represented as `/1/` and Ed will be represented as `/2/`.

Jamie Briggs and Robin Round both report to Ed Ling. Therefore, they are both at the third level of the hierarchy, but they also need to be uniquely identified. Therefore, they would be represented as `/1/2/1/` and `/1/2/2/`, respectively. The levels continue to build from there. They are then stored in the table as bit strings and displayed, unformatted, as hexadecimal values. For example, the hierarchy ID for Simon Gomez at the root level is stored as `0x`, whereas Sanjay Gupta at the second level is stored as `0x58` and Ed Ling, also at the second level, is stored as `0x68`. Jamie Briggs and Robin Round are stored as `0x6AC0` and `0x6B40`, respectively.

But fear not: there is no need to model the hierarchy manually. Instead, we will take a two-step approach, which takes the hard work out of the modeling process. The first step is to create a temporary table that consists of three columns: `EmployeeID`, `ManagerID`, and a row number, which we will generate by using the `ROW_NUMBER()` function and partitioning the numbers by `ManagerID`. This function will give us the incremental numbers that we need at each level of a hierarchy branch.

The second step is to define a CTE, built on our temporary table, which will define the root of the hierarchy by using the `GetRoot()` global method against the `HIERARCHYID` type for Simon Gomez, who sits at the top of the hierarchy and therefore has a `NULL` `ManagerID`.

The recursive query will build the subsequent levels of the hierarchy by concatenating the next subsequent hierarchy level with the incremental value that we generated using `ROW_NUMBER()`. We can then use an `UPDATE` statement to pull the modeled hierarchy IDs from the CTE and update the `Employees` table, based on joining the `EmployeeID`. This is demonstrated in the following listing.

Listing 3.10 Generating HierarchyIDs for the Employees table

```
SELECT
     EmployeeID
   , ManagerID
   , ROW_NUMBER()
         OVER (PARTITION BY ManagerID ORDER BY ManagerID) AS Incremental
INTO #Hierachy
FROM dbo.Employees
```

```
;WITH HierarchyPathCTE AS (
    SELECT
         hierarchyid::GetRoot() AS ManagerHierarchyID
       , EmployeeID
    FROM #Hierachy AS C
    WHERE ManagerID IS NULL
    UNION ALL
    SELECT
        CAST(hpc.ManagerHierarchyID.ToString() +
            CAST(h.Incremental AS VARCHAR(30)) +
            '/' AS HIERARCHYID)
       ,h.EmployeeID
FROM #Hierachy AS h
JOIN HierarchyPathCTE AS hpc
   ON h.ManagerID = hpc.EmployeeID
)

UPDATE e
    SET ManagerHierarchyID = hp.ManagerHierarchyID
FROM dbo.Employees e
INNER JOIN HierarchyPathCTE hp
    ON e.EmployeeID = hp.EmployeeID ;
```

Case sensitivity

An important note when working with the HIERARCHYID data type is that methods are case sensitive. For example, the following query will return an error:

```
SELECT ManagerHierarchyID.tostring() FROM dbo.Employees ;
```

whereas the following query would execute successfully:

```
SELECT ManagerHierarchyID.ToString() FROM dbo.Employees ;
```

From this point on, working with hierarchies becomes incredibly simple. Think back to the query we wrote to generate a list of all people who report directly and indirectly to Sanjay Gupta. We can replace this whole recursive query with the simple query in the following listing, which uses the `IsDescendantOf()` method to filter the query by identifying anyone who sits within Sanja Gupta's branch of the hierarchy.

Listing 3.11 Returning all of Sanjay Gupta's direct and indirect reports

```
DECLARE @Manager HIERARCHYID ;

SELECT @Manager = ManagerHierarchyID
FROM dbo.Employees
WHERE EmployeeID = 2 ;

SELECT
      EmployeeID
    , FirstName
    , LastName
```

```
    , ManagerHierarchyID.ToString()
FROM dbo.Employees
WHERE ManagerHierarchyID.IsDescendantOf(@Manager) = 1 ;
```

In a similar vein, think back to the recursive query that we wrote to discover who manages Emma Robert's manager. This can be replaced with the simple script in the following listing, which uses the `GetAncestor()` method to traverse the hierarchy.

Listing 3.12 Discovering who manages Emma Robert's manager

```
DECLARE @EmployeeID INT ;

SET @EmployeeID = 22 ;

SELECT
    FirstName
    , LastName
    , Role
    , ManagerhierarchyID.ToString() AS ManagerHierarchyID
FROM dbo.Employees
WHERE ManagerHierarchyID = (
    SELECT ManagerHierarchyID.GetAncestor(2)
    FROM dbo.Employees
    WHERE EmployeeID = @EmployeeID
) ;
```

You may remember that I also mentioned that we could be asked to traverse the hierarchy in a number of ways and suggested that we may encounter the need to find hierarchy siblings. To explore how simple this is, imagine that MagicChoc is performing a salary benchmarking exercise. Specifically, Amy Fry has requested a pay increase, and the HR team want to know if her salary is on a par with other people at her level of the organization.

In this scenario, we can use the `GetLevel()` method to determine the level of the hierarchy that she is on and then return details of all other employees at the same level. This technique is demonstrated in the following listing.

Listing 3.13 Returning all employees who are organizational siblings of Amy Fry

```
DECLARE @EmployeeID INT ;

SET @EmployeeID = 14 ;

SELECT
    FirstName
  , LastName
  , Salary
FROM dbo.Employees
WHERE ManagerHierarchyID.GetLevel() = (
    SELECT
        ManagerHierarchyID.GetLevel()
    FROM dbo.Employees
    WHERE EmployeeID = @EmployeeID
) ;
```

3.4 #9 Not storing XML data as native XML

When XML data is passed to a database, developers often feel compelled to store that data in relational data structures. This is sometimes out of a sense of best practice—the suggestion that this is a database, so surely it's better to store the data in a relational format? Other times the choice is made through a fear of XML and the potential need to write complex XQuery statements to get at the data. Frankly, there are many occasions where storing data in a relational format is a good idea, but this is far from true in some scenarios.

Let's think back to our `Employees` table. So far, we have only added employee records for the management team, who are all permanent staff. The warehouse, however, often employs temporary staff through a job agency called Total Warehouse Jobs. MagicChoc does a lot of business with this agency, and the companies have therefore decided to integrate their systems.

When a temp leaves MagicChoc, their employee record is deleted from the system. However, Total Warehouse Jobs keeps a record of their past contracts. If a person signs a new contract with MagicChoc, then there is a requirement for Total Warehouse Jobs to provide a list of their previous contracts, with the roles they performed. This helps MagicChoc assign them appropriate work, in which they have experience.

The nature of XML means that it is extensible and human readable, supports schema validation, and can be universally processed. This makes it a popular choice for system integration. In our scenario, it has been agreed that, once a contract is signed, Total Warehouse Jobs will send details of the employee's previous contracts in an XML document. This information needs to be stored in the `HumanResources` database.

The warehouse application uses this data on a daily basis to calculate which people will be assigned which tasks, based on the daily manufacturing priorities. An ETL process needs to send the data to the warehousing application in XML format.

3.4.1 Shredding XML

The way in which I have seen some developers approach this scenario is to shred the XML data that is received into a relational table and then reconstruct an XML document to send it on to the recipient.

> **TIP** Shredding XML is the process of removing (or shredding) the markup from the data and organizing the data into relational values.

If we were to take this approach in our MagicChoc example, the first thing we would need to do is create a schema that will hold the historic contract data. The nature of the data means that we will need three tables to avoid duplicating data. This is a key concept of normalization, which we will discuss in chapter 4. An example of what this table might look like can be found in the following listing.

Listing 3.14 Creating table structures for historic contract data

```
CREATE TABLE dbo.ContractHistory (
    ContractHistoryID     SMALLINT     NOT NULL     PRIMARY KEY     IDENTITY,
```

```
  EmployeeID              SMALLINT     NOT NULL
      REFERENCES dbo.Employees(EmployeeID),
  ContractStartDate       DATE         NOT NULL,
  ContractEndDate         DATE         NOT NULL
) ;

CREATE TABLE dbo.Skills (
  SkillsID    SMALLINT    NOT NULL    PRIMARY KEY    IDENTITY,
  Skill       VARCHAR(30) NOT NULL
) ;

CREATE TABLE dbo.ContractSkills (
  ContractSkillsID     INT          NOT NULL    PRIMARY KEY    IDENTITY,
  ContractHistoryID    SMALLINT     NOT NULL
      REFERENCES dbo.ContractHistory(ContractHistoryID),
  SkillID              SMALLINT     NOT NULL
      REFERENCES dbo.Skills(SkillsID)
) ;
```

Because the `Skills` table we just created is a reference table, before we move on, let's add some sample data using the script in the following listing.

Listing 3.15 Adding data to the `Skills` table

```
INSERT INTO dbo.Skills (Skill)
VALUES
   ('Picker'),
   ('Packer'),
   ('Stock Take'),
   ('Forklift Driver'),
   ('Machine 1 operator'),
   ('Machine 2 operator'),
   ('Machine 3 operator'),
   ('Machine 4 operator') ;
```

The historic contract data consists of an element-centric XML document, with a root element called `<EmployeeContracts>`.

Element-centric vs. attribute-centric mappings

In an element-centric XML document, an element contains child elements, which hold the element's properties. This is opposed to an attribute-centric XML document, where an element's properties are stored in attributes of the element. For example, in the fragment

```
<Employee ID="23"></Employee>
```

`ID` is an attribute of the `<Employee>` element and has a value of `23`. For simple documents, elements versus attributes is largely a stylistic choice. If you have complex nodes, however, that will repeat or must be in a certain sequence, then elements must be used, as this cannot be achieved with attributes.

Under the root element, there is a complex element called `<Employee>`, which contains the child elements that will be stored in our `Employees` table. It also contains a nested complex element called `<Contracts>`, which contains a repeating element called `<Contract>`, containing the details of each contract that the employee has had. A further complex element is nested under `<Contract>`, called `<Skills>`, containing in turn a repeating element called `<Skill>`. An example of the data that we receive from Total Warehouse Jobs is as follows:

```
<EmployeeContracts>
    <Employee>
        <EmployeeID>23</EmployeeID>
        <FirstName>Robert</FirstName>
        <LastName>Blake</LastName>
        <DateOfBirth>19781212</DateOfBirth>
        <Contracts>
            <Contract>
                <StartDate>20200101</StartDate>
                <EndDate>20203006</EndDate>
                <Skills>
                    <Skill>Forklift driver</Skill>
                    <Skill>Picker</Skill>
                    <Skill>Packer</Skill>
                </Skills>
            </Contract>
            <Contract>
                <StartDate>20210101</StartDate>
                <EndDate>20211212</EndDate>
                <Skills>
                    <Skill>Picker</Skill>
                    <Skill>Stock Take</Skill>
                </Skills>
            </Contract>
        </Contracts>
    </Employee>
</EmployeeContracts>
```

So to use the approach of storing this dataset in a traditional relational structure, our first job will be to shred the data we receive. To do this, we could either use the `OPENXML()` function, which will return a rowset from an XML document, or use a combination of the `nodes()` and `value()` XQuery methods. In this example, we will use `OPENXML()` because it is the method I see people use most often.

The first complexity with the `OPENXML()` function is that it does not have a built-in XML parser. Instead, we must parse the XML document using an MSXML parser before passing it to the function. We can perform this document preparation by using the `sp_xml_preparedocument` stored procedure. This procedure will parse the document, and the output object will contain a handle to the in-memory tree representation of the nodes within the document, which can then be passed to the function.

NOTE When using `sp_xml_preparedocument`, it is important to use the `sp_xml_removedocument` procedure after the `OPENXML()` function. This will release the memory that is being consumed.

We also need to pass the `OPENXML()` function, an XPath pattern that identifies the rows to be processed. We will point this XPath expression to the lowest level of our hierarchy, and then, in our mappings, we will use the `../` operator to traverse the higher levels.

> **TIP** XPath is defined by W3C and is a language used to navigate through nodes in an XML document. An XPath expression is used to select specific nodes in an XML document.

The final parameter is optional and indicates how to populate the spillover column. The possible values are detailed in table 3.2.

Table 3.2 Spillover column population options

Value	Description
0	Attribute-centric mapping
1	Applies attribute-centric mapping followed by element-centric mapping
2	Applies element-centric mapping followed by attribute-centric mapping
8	Does not copy data to the overflow property

A `WITH` clause is used with `OPENXML()` to specify the data type and mappings on nodes within the document. If the `WITH` clause is omitted, then SQL Server returns an *XML edge table*, which details the fine-grain document structure, including information such as namespace URI, namespace prefix, and pointers to next and previous sibling elements.

The script in listing 3.16 demonstrates what the process of shredding the data and inserting it into the tables might look like. The first thing we do is to declare variables to store the raw XML document and the handle to the in-memory parse tree of the prepared document. Next come two table variables. The first will store the results of the `OPENXML()` function, while the second simply holds some internal employee data that we are simulating pulling from the HR application and that is required to populate the `Employees` table. Next, we parse the XML data before calling the `OPENXML()` function and insert the results into the table variable. After that, we run queries to duplicate the data and insert it into the tables. These `INSERT` statements are wrapped in a transaction (which will be discussed in chapter 10), which means if one of the inserts fails, all of the inserts will be rolled back. This prevents us from ending up with inconsistent data between the tables that we would have to manually unpick in the event of a failure. Before the transaction begins, `XACT_ABORT` is turned on. This will stop the transaction from continuing, even if a statement has only failed for a minor error, such as a failed foreign key constraint.

> **TIP** Yes! You are absolutely right! We should add error handling to this code, especially as the XML data is coming from an external source. We will discuss error handling in chapter 7.

Listing 3.16 Shredding the data with OPENXML()

```
DECLARE @RawContractDetails XML ;              <-- Declares a variable to store the raw XML
DECLARE @ParsedContractDetails INT ;           <-- Declares a variable to store the pointer to the in-memory parse tree
DECLARE @ShreddedData TABLE (
      EmployeeID           INT
    , FirstName            NVARCHAR(32)
    , LastName             NVARCHAR(32)
    , DateOfBirth          DATE
    , ContractStartDate    DATE
    , ContractEndDate      DATE
    , Skill                NVARCHAR(30)
) ;
DECLARE @InternalEmployeeData TABLE (
      EmployeeStartDate        DATE
    , ManagerID                SMALLINT
    , Salary                   MONEY
    , Department               NVARCHAR(64)
    , DepartmentCode           NCHAR(2)
    , Role                     NVARCHAR(64)
    , WeeklyContractedHours    INT
    , StaffOrContract          BIT
    , ContractEndDate          DATE
    , ManagerHierarchyID       HIERARCHYID
) ;

INSERT INTO @InternalEmployeeData
VALUES (
    '20230101',
    14,
    39000,
    'Manufacturing',
    'MA',
    'Warehouse Operative',
    40,
    0,
    '20231231',
    '/1/2/2/1/'
) ;

SET @RawContractDetails = N'<EmployeeContracts>
    <Employee>
        <EmployeeID>23</EmployeeID>
        <FirstName>Robert</FirstName>
        <LastName>Blake</LastName>
        <DateOfBirth>19781212</DateOfBirth>
        <Contracts>
            <Contract>
                <StartDate>20200101</StartDate>
                <EndDate>20200603</EndDate>
                <Skills>
                    <Skill>Forklift driver</Skill>
                    <Skill>Picker</Skill>
                    <Skill>Packer</Skill>
                </Skills>
            </Contract>
```

```
            <Contract>
                <StartDate>20210101</StartDate>
                <EndDate>20211231</EndDate>
                <Skills>
                    <Skill>Picker</Skill>
                    <Skill>Stock Take</Skill>
                </Skills>
            </Contract>
        </Contracts>
    </Employee>
</EmployeeContracts>' ;

EXEC sp_xml_preparedocument @ParsedContractDetails OUTPUT,
@RawContractDetails ;

INSERT INTO @ShreddedData
SELECT *
FROM OPENXML(@ParsedContractDetails,
'/EmployeeContracts/Employee/Contracts/Contract/Skills/Skill', 2)
WITH (
    EmployeeID          SMALLINT        '../../../../EmployeeID',
    FirstName           NVARCHAR(32)    '../../../../FirstName',
    LastName            NVARCHAR(32)    '../../../../LastName',
    DateOfBirth         DATE            '../../../../DateOfBirth',
    ContractStartDate   DATE            '../../StartDate',
    ContractEndDate     DATE            '../../EndDate',
    Skill               NVARCHAR(30)    'text()'
) ;

SET XACT_ABORT ON ;

BEGIN TRANSACTION
    INSERT INTO dbo.Employees
    SELECT
          s.EmployeeID
        , s.FirstName
        , s.LastName
        , s.DateOfBirth
        , i.EmployeeStartDate
        , i.ManagerID
        , i.Salary
        , i.Department
        , i.DepartmentCode
        , i.Role
        , i.WeeklyContractedHours
        , i.StaffOrContract
        , i.ContractEndDate
        , i.ManagerHierarchyID
    FROM @ShreddedData s
    INNER JOIN @InternalEmployeeData i
        ON 1=1
    GROUP BY
          s.EmployeeID
        , s.FirstName
        , s.LastName
        , s.DateOfBirth
```

Parses the XML document (annotation for EXEC sp_xml_preparedocument)

Shreds the XML data and inserts the relational values into a table variable (annotation for INSERT INTO @ShreddedData …)

Turns on XACT_ABORT, so that if any statements in the transaction fail, the whole transaction will roll back. (annotation for SET XACT_ABORT ON)

Begins a transaction to perform the table updates, so that if one statement fails, the transaction will roll back (annotation for BEGIN TRANSACTION)

```
        , i.EmployeeStartDate
        , i.ManagerID
        , i.Salary
        , i.Department
        , i.DepartmentCode
        , i.Role
        , i.WeeklyContractedHours
        , i.StaffOrContract
        , i.ContractEndDate
        , i.ManagerHierarchyID ;

    INSERT INTO dbo.ContractHistory(
        EmployeeID,
        ContractStartDate,
        ContractEndDate
    )
    SELECT
          EmployeeID
        , ContractStartDate
        , ContractEndDate
    FROM @ShreddedData
    GROUP BY
          EmployeeID
        , ContractStartDate
        , ContractEndDate ;

    INSERT INTO dbo.ContractSkills(ContractHistoryID, SkillID)
    SELECT
          ch.ContractHistoryID
        , s.SkillsID
    FROM @ShreddedData sd
    INNER JOIN dbo.Skills s
        ON TRIM(s.Skill) = TRIM(sd.Skill)
    INNER JOIN dbo.ContractHistory ch
        ON sd.EmployeeID = ch.EmployeeID
            AND sd.ContractStartDate = ch.ContractStartDate
            AND sd.ContractEndDate = ch.ContractEndDate ;

COMMIT

EXEC sp_xml_removedocument @ParsedContractDetails ;
```

Removes the parse tree from memory

Okay, so that was hard work, right? It was hard work for SQL Server too! In my lab environment, which is a t2.large EC2 instance running nothing but this script, it took 31ms to execute the script. That's 31ms to process five rows of data into three tables. So far, all we have done is shred the data. In the next section, we will look at the process required to reconstruct the XML document so that it can be sent to the client. Perhaps you are starting to see why I am not recommending this approach for our particular use case.

3.4.2 Reconstructing XML

Now that we have shredded the XML data into tables, we need to write the process that the ETL will use to send the data to the warehouse application. This means reconstructing the XML document from the data stored in the tables. We can achieve this by using a `SELECT` statement that specifies a `FOR XML` clause. `FOR XML` has four possible modes, and these are detailed in table 3.3.

Table 3.3 `FOR XML` modes

Mode	Description
`RAW`	The most basic mode for constructing XML. It generates a flat XML document with one element per row.
`AUTO`	Generates XML documents with nested elements. The nesting is controlled by the join conditions within the query. The automatic formatting means that we have minimal control over the formatting of the XML.
`PATH`	Allows advanced control over the format of the XML document by mapping columns in the query to XML nodes in a given location of the hierarchy.
`EXPLICIT`	Offers similar control over formatting as `PATH` mode but is overly complex. There is generally no need to use this mode.

To create the correct shape for our XML document, we will need to use `FOR XML PATH`, with subqueries, which also use the `FOR XML PATH` clause. The subqueries are required so that we can deal with the repeating elements at the child level of the document.

The query in listing 3.17 demonstrates how we can achieve this by using two layers of subqueries. The innermost query returns the skills associated with a given contract. These results are converted to XML using `FOR XML PATH`. This clause uses the `TYPE` keyword to define that the results will be well-formed XML and uses `ROOT` to specify the name of the root node within the document. The outer subquery uses the same process to pull the details from the repeating `Contracts` element. Finally, the outer query returns the employee details, which will sit at the top of the hierarchy.

Listing 3.17 Reconstructing the XML document

```
SELECT
      e.EmployeeID 'EmployeeID'
    , e.FirstName 'FirstName'
    , e.LastName 'LastName'
    , e.DateOfBirth 'DateOfBirth'
    , (
        SELECT
              ch.ContractStartDate 'StartDate'
            , ch.ContractEndDate 'EndDate'
            , (
                SELECT
                    s.Skill 'Skill'
              FROM dbo.Skills s
              INNER JOIN dbo.ContractSkills cs
                  ON s.SkillsID = cs.SkillID
                    WHERE cs.ContractHistoryID = ch.ContractHistoryID
                    FOR XML PATH(''), TYPE, ROOT('Skills')
    )
        FROM dbo.ContractHistory ch
```

```
        WHERE EmployeeID = e.EmployeeID
        FOR XML PATH('Contract'), TYPE, ROOT('Contracts')
    )
FROM dbo.Employees e
WHERE EmployeeID = 23
FOR XML PATH('Employee'), ROOT('EmployeeContracts') ;
```

In my lab environment, this query took 52 ms to complete. Now think about a production environment where these processes are being run constantly by multiple people. Think too about where such processes need to run against large, complex XML documents. You can see why it can start to become quite costly.

3.4.3 Avoiding the overhead by storing data as XML

Converting the XML into relational data and back again took a fair amount of fiddling and also took a combined total of 83 ms. We could have saved development time and compile/execution time if we had stored the data in XML format. So let's explore the development and processing impact if we were to store the data in its native format.

Because all of the details of skills and contracts for an employee are stored in a single XML document, there is no need to have the `EmployeeContracts` and `EmployeeSkills` tables. Instead, we can simply insert the XML document into the `Employees` table. Before we get started, let's update the `Employees` table and add a column called `PreviousContracts`, which will store the data. The following listing contains a command that we can run to achieve this.

Listing 3.18 Adding a `PreviousContracts` column to the `Employees` table

```
ALTER TABLE dbo.Employees
    ADD PreviousContracts XML NULL ;
```

In our specific scenario, we will not be able to avoid using a small amount of XQuery. This is because the data will be keyed on the `EmployeeID`, and this is supplied by Total Warehouse Jobs inside the XML document. Therefore, we will need to extract this value along with the employee's name and date of birth.

A script that we can use to add the new user to the `Employees` table is demonstrated in listing 3.19. As in our previous example, we are simulating our HR system to provide some of the values that will populate our `Employees` table with a table variable called `@InternalEmployeeData`. We then use the XQuery `value()` method to extract the `EmployeeID`, `FirstName`, `LastName`, and `DateOfBirth` nodes from the XML document. The `value()` method is passed an XPath to the node we want to extract, followed by the SQL Server data type that the node will be mapped to. `value()` requires a singleton value; therefore the desired node index is mandatory, even if the node does not repeat. Note that the `EmployeeID` in the XML document has been incremented to avoid the insert failing because of a violation of the primary key constraint.

> **TIP** We are extracting the value of an element, but if we were extracting an attribute, then we would need to prefix the attribute name with an `@` symbol.

Listing 3.19 Adding an employee to the `Employees` table

```
DECLARE @RawContractDetails XML ;
DECLARE @InternalEmployeeData TABLE (
      EmployeeStartDate             DATE
    , ManagerID                     SMALLINT
    , Salary                        MONEY
    , Department                    NVARCHAR(64)
    , DepartmentCode                NCHAR(2)
    , Role                          NVARCHAR(64)
    , WeeklyContractedHours         INT
    , StaffOrContract               BIT
    , ContractEndDate               DATE
    , ManagerHierarchyID            HIERARCHYID
) ;

INSERT INTO @InternalEmployeeData
VALUES (
    '20230101',
   14,
   39000,
   'Manufacturing',
   'MA',
   'Warehouse Operative',
   40,
   0,
   '20231231',
   '/1/2/2/1/'
) ;


SET @RawContractDetails = N'<EmployeeContracts>          <-- Defines the XML document
   <Employee>
         <EmployeeID>25</EmployeeID>
         <FirstName>Robert</FirstName>
         <LastName>Blake</LastName>
         <DateOfBirth>19781212</DateOfBirth>
         <Contracts>
               <Contract>
                     <StartDate>20200101</StartDate>
                     <EndDate>20200603</EndDate>
                     <Skills>
                           <Skill>Forklift driver</Skill>
                           <Skill>Picker</Skill>
                           <Skill>Packer</Skill>
                     </Skills>
               </Contract>
               <Contract>
                     <StartDate>20210101</StartDate>
                     <EndDate>20211231</EndDate>
                     <Skills>
                           <Skill>Picker</Skill>
                           <Skill>Stock Take</Skill>
                     </Skills>
               </Contract>
         </Contracts>
```

```
    </Employee>
</EmployeeContracts>' ;

INSERT INTO dbo.Employees
SELECT
     @RawContractDetails.value('(/EmployeeContracts/Employee/EmployeeID)[1]',
     'SMALLINT') AS EmployeeID
   ,@RawContractDetails.value('(/EmployeeContracts/Employee/FirstName)[1]',
     'NVARCHAR(32)') AS FirstName
    ,@RawContractDetails.value('(/EmployeeContracts/Employee/LastName)[1]',
     'NVARCHAR(32)') AS LastName
   ,@RawContractDetails.value('(/EmployeeContracts/Employee/DateOfBirth)[1]',
     'DATE') AS DateOfBirth
    , EmployeeStartDate
    , ManagerID
    , Salary
    , Department
    , DepartmentCode
    , Role
    , WeeklyContractedHours
    , StaffOrContract
    , ContractEndDate
    , ManagerHierarchyID
    , @RawContractDetails AS PreviousContracts
FROM @InternalEmployeeData ;
```

The SELECT list consists of calls to the value() method to extract nodes from the XML document.

This script took 33 ms to execute in my lab environment. We can now retrieve the XML document for the warehouse application with the simple `SELECT` statement in the following listing.

Listing 3.20 Retrieving the XML document for the warehouse application

```
SELECT
    PreviousContracts
FROM dbo.Employees
WHERE EmployeeID = 25 ;
```

This `SELECT` statement took less than 1 ms to execute in my lab environment. If we round it up to 1 ms, that means the insertion and the return of the XML data took a combined total of 34 ms. This means that, overall, the end-to-end processing was more than twice as fast when we avoided shredding.

Does this mean that we should never shred XML data? No, absolutely not! There are many good reasons for shredding the data. The general rule that I use is that T-SQL is much more efficient than XQuery. Therefore, if our scenario requires us to frequently query the data, then it is a good idea to shred it. Conversely, if we frequently write the data but rarely query it, then storing the data in native XML format is the best approach. The mistake that we should avoid is always shredding the data (or, equally, always storing the data as XML). Instead, make your design decision based on your application's requirements.

3.5 #10 Ignoring JSON

Just as SQL developers have a tendency to avoid XML data, they also have a tendency to avoid JSON data. Just as we saw when talking about XML, this can lead to suboptimal table design and suboptimal performance. Let's imagine that we have been asked to expand our data schema for the `employees` entity so that it allows us to store their home addresses.

A typical model for modeling addresses in SQL Server would be to have an `Addresses` table with an `AddressID` as a primary key, which then has a column of the same name in the `Employees` table and also potentially other tables where an address is relevant, such as `Offices` or `Sites` in the case of an HR database. The column in the `Employees` table would have a foreign key constraint, so that only applicable values from the `Addresses` table can be stored.

This model is okay, but it will become a wide, sparse table because not all addresses have the same number of lines, and we need to be able to cater to any eventuality. This is made worse in the case of MagicChoc, which is an international company. Think of zip codes. They are known as post codes in the UK, *yóu dì qū hào* in Thailand, and block numbers in Bahrain, to name but a few. Because they have different formats in different countries, we would either store these in a very permissive data type or we could use separate, sparsely populated columns for each. It is also worth noting that many countries, such as Bahamas, Dominica, Fiji, and many African nations, do not have any equivalent to a zip code, further increasing the sparse nature of the table.

Depending on our application requirements, what may be a better data design is to store the data in JSON format. Like XML, JSON has a semistructured format that allows for irrelevant data to be omitted. It is becoming increasingly popular as it is a very lightweight format with significantly less tagging than XML.

Because of the efficiency of T-SQL for querying data, when I'm modeling data, I work to the same rule with JSON as I do with XML. Namely, if the data will be written often and queried infrequently, then JSON is a good choice. If the data is queried far more than it is written, however, then I prefer to store the data relationally.

Other use cases for JSON include modeling data domains that would otherwise need to be split across relational data and NoSQL. This is because, with SQL Server, both types of data can be stored in the same schema, supporting communication with REST APIs or other system integrations that send and receive data in JSON format. It is now also feasible to store and analyze log data in SQL Server, where the logs are JSON based.

So let's see how we could avoid the mistake of ignoring JSON by modeling our employee address data in JSON format. If our addresses could relate to multiple entities, such as offices or sites, then we may still want to build an `Addresses` table so that the JSON-formatted addresses can be used by multiple entities. We are, however, convinced that `Employees` is the only entity that will need to interact with address data, so we will add an additional column to our `Employees` table to store the address data. The following listing shows a command that will create that column.

ingListing 3.21 Adding an `Address` column to the `Employees` table

```
ALTER TABLE dbo.Employees
    ADD Address NVARCHAR(MAX) ;
```

> **NOTE** But wait a minute! We are going to model data in JSON, so why have we just created a column of type `NVARCHAR(MAX)`? The answer to this is, at the time of writing, a JSON data type is in preview in Azure SQL Database, but for SQL Server in IaaS or on-prem, JSON doesn't have its own data type. It is stored as `VARCHAR` or `NVARCHAR` and is then indexed as text. This makes JSON fully compatible with any SQL Server functionality that supports text.

First, let's look at the format of the JSON document we will use to store addresses. The JSON format uses simple `name:value` pairs, encapsulated in `""`. Nesting is designated with {}. The use of `[]` designates an array. Our address document has a root of `EmployeeAddress` and contains nodes for `EmployeeID` and `Address`. The `Address` node has further nodes, nested underneath, which store each line of the address. Additional lines can be added or the existing nodes replaced, depending on the requirements of each address, meaning that we remove the problem of sparse data. An example document is as follows:

```
{
    "EmployeeAddress":[
        {
            "EmployeeID":1,
            "Address":{
                "Line1":"5331 Rexford Court",
                "City":"Montgomery",
                "State":"AL",
                "ZipCode":"36116"
            }
        }
    ]
}
```

We can generate this document using a `SELECT` statement with a `FOR JSON` clause. There are two `FOR JSON` processing options: `AUTO` and `PATH`. `AUTO` can be used to automatically format the document based on the order of columns and the table `JOIN` sequence order. `PATH` mode gives granular control over the formatting.

> **TIP** `FOR JSON AUTO` can only be used against a table, so in theory it cannot be used in the way we plan, but it is easy to work around this limitation by adding a `FROM` clause to an arbitrary table. I tend to use `sys.tables` for this purpose, but any table will suffice. If we use this technique, we will need to add a `TOP 1` to our `SELECT` clause to avoid returning a node for each record in the table.

The query in listing 3.22 will generate our sample JSON document. Note that we are using PATH mode, so each column has an alias that specifies the name of the node and its position within the JSON hierarchy.

Listing 3.22 Generating a JSON document

```
SELECT
      1 AS 'EmployeeID'
    , '5331 Rexford Court' AS 'Address.Line1'
    , 'Montgomery'         AS 'Address.City'
    , 'AL'                 AS 'Address.State'
    , '36116'              AS 'Address.ZipCode'
FOR JSON PATH, ROOT ('EmployeeAddress') ;
```

The script in listing 3.23 demonstrates how we could update the Employees table to add an employee address if we were given the address data in JSON format. The WHERE clause of the UPDATE statement uses the JSON_VALUE() function to retrieve the EmployeeID from inside the document. The first parameter that this function accepts is the JSON document in which to search. The second parameter specifies the path to the node. A JSON path always begins with $., which represents the whole document. The root node, EmployeeAddress, is an array (denoted by the square brackets), meaning that we need to pass an array index to specify which record we wish to return a value for. If we do not pass this index, then we will return a NULL result, even if there is only a single record, as there is in our scenario.

Listing 3.23 Updating the Employees table with address data

```
DECLARE @EmployeeAddress NVARCHAR(MAX) ;

SET @EmployeeAddress = (
    SELECT
          1 AS 'EmployeeID'
        , '5331 Rexford Court' AS 'Address.Line1'
        , 'Montgomery'         AS 'Address.City'
        , 'AL'                 AS 'Address.State'
        , '36116'              AS 'Address.ZipCode'
    FOR JSON PATH, ROOT ('EmployeeAddress')
) ;

UPDATE dbo.Employees
SET Address = @EmployeeAddress
WHERE EmployeeID =
    JSON_VALUE(@EmployeeAddress, '$.EmployeeAddress[0].EmployeeID') ;
```

If we ever need to shred this JSON document into a relational format, then we can use the OPENJSON() function. The format and functionality of OPENJSON() will look familiar to those of you who have read about OPENXML() earlier in this chapter. The advantage of the OPENJSON() function, however, is that there is no need to prepare the document before use. This saves on resource utilization.

In listing 3.24, we use the `OPENJSON()` function to shred our employee address document. The first parameter passed to the function is the JSON document itself. The second parameter specifies the path to the highest level of the hierarchy that we wish to interrogate. Remember that `$` represents the whole document, and just like when we used `JSON_VALUE()`, the path we pass needs to take account of the array by specifying an array index. The `WITH` clause specifies the columns that we want to return from the document, along with the SQL data types that they will map to and the path to the relevant node, where the node is not at the same level as the path expression.

Listing 3.24 Shredding the JSON data into relational values

```
DECLARE @EmployeeAddress NVARCHAR(MAX) ;

SET @EmployeeAddress = (
    SELECT
          1 AS 'EmployeeID'
        , '5331 Rexford Court' AS 'Address.Line1'
        , 'Montgomery'         AS 'Address.City'
        , 'AL'                 AS 'Address.State'
        , '36116'              AS 'Address.ZipCode'
    FOR JSON PATH, ROOT ('EmployeeAddress')
) ;

SELECT *
FROM OPENJSON(@EmployeeAddress, '$.EmployeeAddress[0]')
WITH (
    EmployeeID SMALLINT,
    Line1 NVARCHAR(64) '$.Address.Line1',
    City NVARCHAR(64) '$.Address.City',
    [State] NCHAR(2) '$.Address.State',
    ZipCode NVARCHAR(10) '$.Address.ZipCode'
) ;
```

We can see that JSON can play an important role in SQL Server if used appropriately. We can use SQL Server's JSON support to denormalize data and simplify complex data models, integrate with NoSQL, or avoid processing data that is sent to and from APIs.

Summary

- Always use the most restrictive data type that will allow you to store all potentially required values. This is especially true for integer values that are used in key constraints or values that are indexed.
- Always use fixed-length strings to reduce storage overhead when the length of strings is consistent within a column. Always use variable-length strings when the length will not be consistent.
- Avoid writing your own code and creating self-referenced tables when you are modeling and creating hierarchies. Instead, use the `HIERARCHYID` data type, as the type includes multiple methods, which take the heavy lifting out of the development.

- When we are faced with XML data, we shouldn't feel we need to always shred that data into a relational model. Always consider the application requirements and model the data schema accordingly. This may or may not include storing data as native XML.
- Don't shy away from JSON data. There are use cases where using JSON data is a good choice to simplify our data models.

4 Database design

This chapter covers

- Design mistakes in SQL Server and why it is important to avoid them
- The mistake of failing to normalize your database
- Mistakes made when designing and creating keys

In this chapter, we will discuss common mistakes that are made when designing databases. These mistakes can cause multiple challenges, leading to issues such as poorly performing code.

Design mistakes are introduced at the earliest stage of the development lifecycle before any code has been written. To illustrate this, let's focus on MagicChoc. The company feels that its processes are too fragmented, so it has commissioned a new application, which will combine its non-internet sales and procurement functions into a single interface with a single backend. For this purpose, the MagicChoc management team has stated that they want to store the following data items:

- Sales Order Date
- Sales Order Number
- Sales Person Name
- Sales Person Email
- Sales Area Name
- Sales Area Manager
- Customer Company Name
- Customer Contact Name
- Customer Contact Email
- Customer Invoice Address
- Customer Delivery Addresses
- Sales Order Delivery Due Date
- Sales Order Delivery Actual Date
- Sales Order Item
- Sales Order Quantities
- Currier Used for Delivery
- Product Name
- Product Stock Level
- Product Next Manufacture Date
- Product Next Manufacture Quantity
- Back Order Manufacturing ID
- Product Type Name
- Product Type Description
- Product Category Name
- Product Category Description
- Product Subcategory Name
- Product Subcategory Description
- Supplier Name
- Supplier Contact Name
- Supplier Contact Email
- Supplier Address
- Purchase Order Date
- Purchase Order Number
- Purchase Order Items
- Purchase Order Quantities

In this chapter, we will design the table structure that we need to store this data. Along the way, we will explore how to avoid common design mistakes. Specifically, we will look at the issues that can arise if we fail to normalize our database. We will then look at the performance problems that can be associated with a poor choice of primary key. Finally, we will explore the consequences of not creating foreign key constraints.

4.1 #11 Failing to normalize

Many times, I have asked developers, "Is the database normalized?" The answer invariably is "Yes!" Unfortunately, on many occasions, the developers were relatively inexperienced in database design and misunderstood my question to mean "Have you designed an Online Transaction Processing (OLTP) database as opposed to a data warehouse?" In reality, instead of normalizing their database, they have just used their own judgment to decide on the database schema.

To design our database schema, we will create an Entity Relationship Diagram (ERD), which is a diagram that describes the *entities*, which are objects within a data model, and *attributes*, which are used to describe the data object. An ERD also describes how objects relate to each other within the model.

TIP An ERD is often the code-level diagram within a C4 model when C4 is being used to document the design of a database. Therefore, in this section, we will implicitly build a C4 code diagram.

In the following sections, we will first explore the wrong way to design a database schema, which is to use the judgment approach. In this approach, we will use nothing but our experience to organize the data. Because everybody's experience is not only at different levels but also simply different, there are multiple issues that can arise when we use this unstructured approach. We will examine some of the more common issues that can occur, such as nonatomic values and data duplication.

Finally, we will explore how to avoid our mistakes by using normalization to design our schema. We will explore this structured approach to database modeling, which was first developed by Edgar Codd in the 1970s and has really stood the test of time. It is a set of methodical steps that is used to remove redundancy from our data. When using this approach, we will follow a strict set of rules, which are aimed at avoiding data duplication and making the schema as efficient as possible. We will also touch on how we can test our normalization by using an Entity Relationship Diagram and look at the concept of data generalization.

4.1.1 Designing a schema using judgment

Let's use our judgment to design the schema of the new sales and procurement database that MagicChoc has requested. It wants to model 35 data items, so let's make things a bit easier and break them down into sections. Let's start with the Sales Order data—specifically, the following data items:

- Sales Order Date
- Sales Order Number
- Sales Person Name
- Sales Person Email
- Sales Area Name
- Sales Area Manager
- Sales Order Delivery Due Date
- Sales Order Delivery Actual Date
- Sales Order Item
- Sales Order Quantities
- Currier Used for Delivery

The Sales Order Number attribute will be unique, so this looks like a good contender as a key for our entity. The troublesome aspect is the relationship between Sales Order Item and Sales Order Quantities. We notice that there is an obvious *one-to-many relationship*. This is a relationship between entities where a single record in one entity can be associated with multiple entities in another. In this instance, there could be more than one product ordered on any given order, so we decide to split the items ordered into a different entity. We also think that, as we have a requirement to store general product details, it would make sense to leave out the product details and just key to the Products entity, which we will design shortly.

> **Keys**
>
> Relational databases join tables together using the concept of keys. There are two basic types of keys—a primary key and a foreign key. A primary key is used to uniquely identify a row in a table. A foreign key is used to point to a primary key value or a unique constraint from a secondary table.

(continued)

For example, imagine a table of employees. You need to record the office where each employee works. You could add an `Office` column to the `Employees` table, but that would mean duplicating the same handful of office names (and possibly addresses, phone numbers, etc.) over and over again. So if you move the office details out into an `Offices` table, you can use a primary key, let's say `OfficeID`, to uniquely identify each office. Then, you can use a foreign key in the `Employees` table (often, but not always, with the same name as the primary key). This foreign key will refer to the values in the primary key column of the `Offices` table to ensure that only values are entered into the foreign key, which exists in the primary key. This enforces what is known as *referential integrity*.

If a key has a business meaning, such as `SocialSecurityNumber`, then it is known as a *natural key*. If a key does not have business meaning, such as an arbitrary, incrementing number, like `EmployeeID`, then it is called an *artificial key*.

A natural key may consist of multiple columns. If a key consists of multiple columns, it is called a *composite key*. It's best to minimize the use of composite keys when possible.

Similarly, as we assume customers may place multiple orders, and we know we need to store customer details as part of the requirements, we decide we should create a key in the `Orders` table that will join the `Customers` table when we create it. Finally, we notice that there is not a good candidate for a primary key, so we will create an artificial key. This leaves us with the beginning of an ERD, which can be seen in figure 4.1.

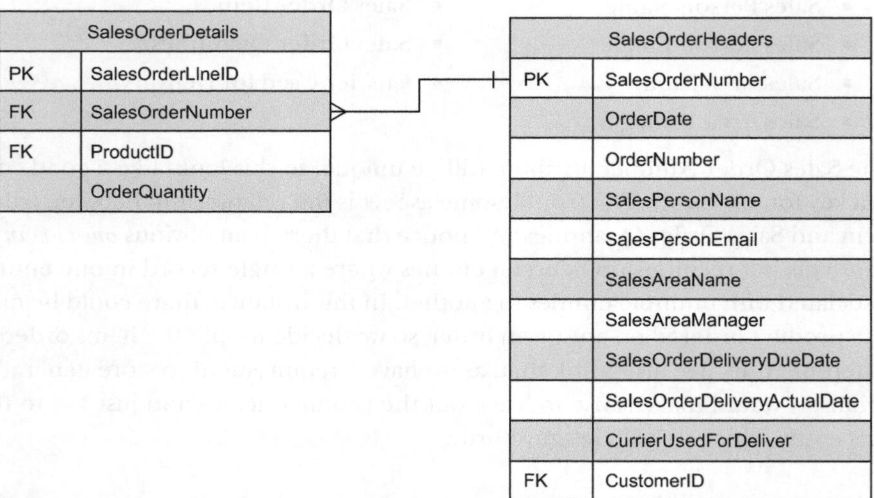

Figure 4.1 ERD for Sales Orders

Next, we will look at the requirements around Product data, where we need to store the following data:

- Product Name
- Product Stock Level
- Product Next Manufacture Date
- Product Next Manufacture Quantity
- Backorder Manufacturing ID
- Product Type Name
- Product Type Description
- Product Category Name
- Product Category Description
- Product Subcategory Name
- Product Subcategory Description

We decide to have a table for Products, and as there is no obvious natural key, we will create an artificial key, which will link to the ProductID attribute in the Sales Order Details entity. We also notice that there could be a one-to-many relationship between products and product categories, so we decide to create a separate Product Categories entity, which we will join to the Products entity with another artificial key. If we combine these entities with the Sales Orders entities, we will have the ERD shown in figure 4.2.

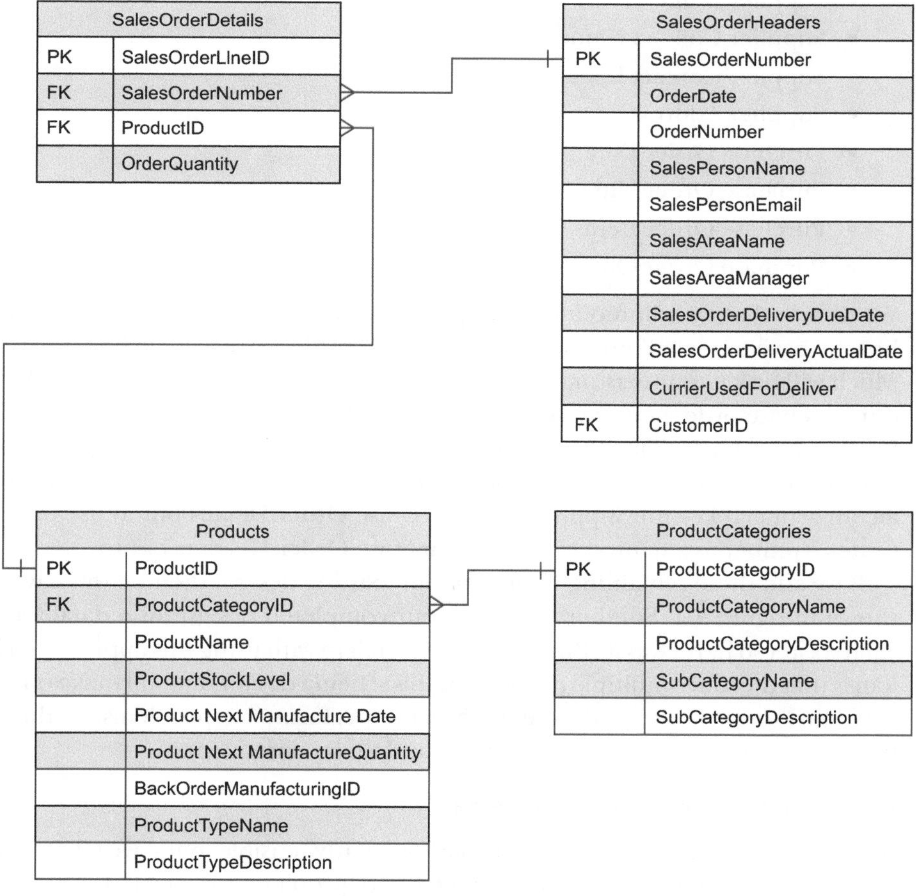

Figure 4.2 ERD with Products added

Next, we will build the Customers entity, which we know will have the following attributes:

- Customer Company Name
- Customer Contact Name
- Customer Contact Email
- Customer Invoice Address
- Customer Delivery Addresses

To avoid a wide, sparse table, we decide to move addresses into a different entity. We also realize that we can have a single Addresses entity that keys to both Customer Invoice Address and Customer Delivery Address. This avoids duplicating data if the invoice address is the same as the delivery address. We achieve this by adding flags for each address type. We will create artificial keys for both entities. Appending these entities to our existing design gives us the ERD shown in figure 4.3.

Finally, let's add the entities for Suppliers and Purchase Orders. The data attributes that we need to model for these entities are

- Supplier Name
- Supplier Contact Name
- Supplier Contact Email
- Supplier Address
- Purchase Order Date
- Purchase Order Number
- Purchase Order Items
- Purchase Order Quantities

We decide that we will model our Suppliers and Purchase Orders in a way similar to how we have modeled our Customers and Sales Orders. We will have a Suppliers entity, which will link to our existing Addresses entity to store supplier addresses. We will split our purchase orders into two entities: one for Purchase Order Headers and the other for Purchase Order Details. Again, this is to allow us to order multiple items in the same order without having to duplicate the order data for each item. We decide to create an artificial key for Suppliers and Purchase Order Details but to use the Purchase Order Number as a natural key in the Purchase Order Headers entity.

If we add these remaining entities to our existing design, then we will have the ERD shown in figure 4.4. So, there, we have our completed design for a database schema. That wasn't so hard, was it? But what is the problem with using this approach? The problem is that there are multiple mistakes in this schema design that will make our database very hard to work with and potentially cause performance problems. In the next section, we will discuss some of the mistakes and their consequences.

4.1.2 Problems with our database schema

At first glance, our database schema may look fairly sensible, but if we take a closer look at some of our design choices, we will see where problems will occur. Let's start by looking at customer and supplier names, which is one of the easiest issues to spot.

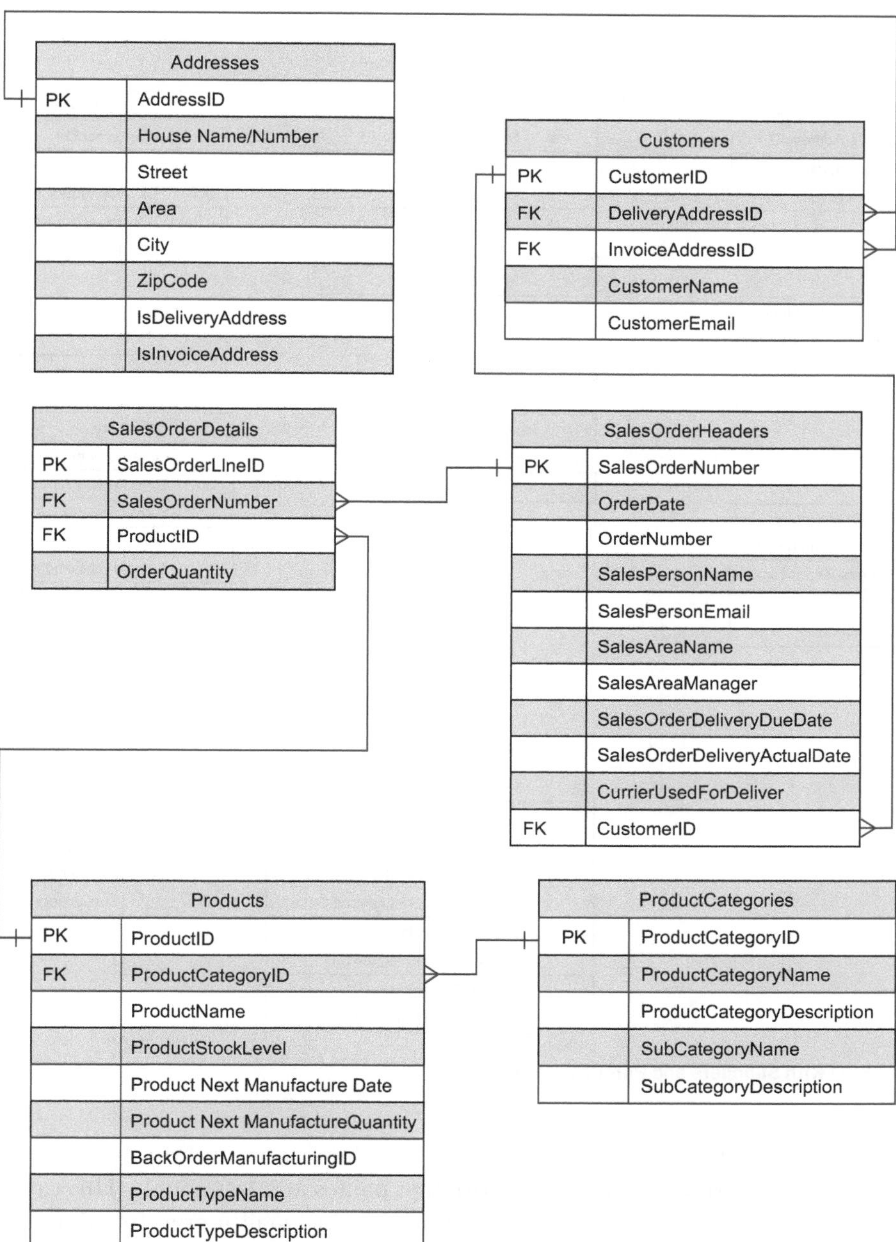

Figure 4.3 ERD with Customers added

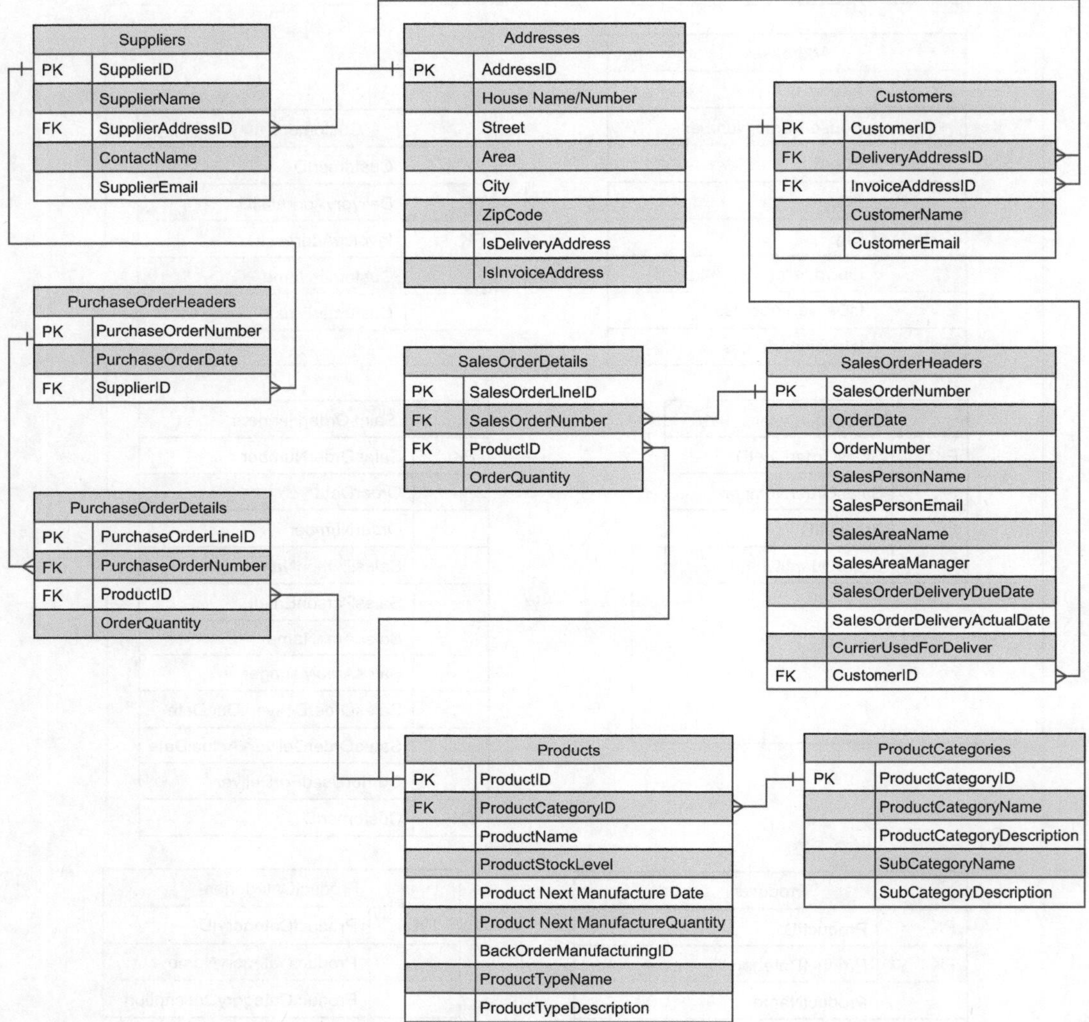

Figure 4.4 ERD with Suppliers and Purchase Orders

Both the `SupplierName` attribute of the Suppliers entity and the `CustomerName` attribute of the Customers entity will store first names and last names. This can cause various issues. Imagine that our sales application has mail merge functionality, and we wish to start letters to customers with "Dear Robert," where Robert is the first name of a customer. To retrieve this first name, we would need to run a query such as

```
SELECT SUBSTRING(CustomerName, 0, CHARINDEX(' ', CustomerName, 1))
FROM Customers ;
```

This not only makes our code more complex to read and write but is also less efficient than simply selecting a `FirstName` column from a table. Therefore, we should always make sure our values are atomic. An *atomic value* is the one that cannot be broken down further and still retain its meaning. For example, the name Peter A. Carter could be broken down into three atomic values—first name, middle initial, and last name. The argument that it could be broken down into 12 characters doesn't hold because these values would have no contextual meaning.

> **TIP** The exception to this rule is when, after normalizing a schema, you intentionally make the decision to denormalize your data. For example, you may decide to store your address data as JSON, as discussed in chapter 3. Other reasons to avoid normalization include where we are working with analytical data or creating staging tables.

Another problem lies in our `ProductCategories` entity. This entity consists of both product categories and subcategories. But there are likely to be multiple subcategories within a category. This means that we will have to duplicate the `ProductCategoryName` and `ProductCategoryDescription` for each product subcategory. Duplicating the data wastes space, which will make the table bigger and hence slower to read, as well as taking up more memory and making index operations less efficient. The larger problem, however, is with inserts and updates. These will become much less efficient as we will need to update product category details on multiple rows. We could have avoided this by breaking the data down into more entities and joining them with a primary/foreign key relationship.

We have decided to store `SalesAreaName` in the `SalesOrderHeader` entity. This means that the name will be duplicated multiple times, as it can apply to multiple rows. It also means that our Sales Area Manager has to be repeated for every record. Again, if sales area details had been broken into a different entity and joined back with a primary/foreign key relationship, then this could have been avoided.

We have a similar issue with the `SupplierContactName`. Not only is the value not atomic, but depending on the business rules, we could also end up duplicating the data. What if two of our suppliers were owned by the same person? Also, what if we have future requirements to store additional contact information, such as a contact-specific phone number? This will just compound the issue, as well as make our suppliers entity very wide.

This leaves us with many questions. How could we have avoided these design problems? Are there any more issues with our design? How can we even test it to find out, without building the entire schema and populating it with data?

The answer to all these questions is to use the process of normalization to design our data schema. We will discuss how to use this process in the following section.

> **NOTE** An additional issue we would not be able to spot without an understanding of the business data and business rules is that the sales order numbers will be in the format ABC1234D-E12. This will give us a very wide primary key. This topic will be discussed in a later section of this chapter.

4.1.3 Designing a database schema using normalization

As mentioned earlier in the chapter, normalization is a formal data modeling process that was first created by Edgar Codd in the 1970s and has really stood the test of time. There are 10 normal forms, or steps, in the process, which have been added to the methodology over time. The most recent addition of Essential Tuple Normal Form was added as recently as 2012. Specifically, the normal forms are

- First Normal Form (1NF)
- Second Normal Form (2NF)
- Third Normal Form (3NF)
- Elementary Key Normal Form (EKNF)
- Boyce-Codd Normal Form (BCNF or 3.5NF)
- Fourth Normal Form (4NF)
- Essential Tuple Normal Form (ETNF)
- Fifth Normal Form (5NF)
- Domain-key Normal Form (DKNF)
- Sixth Normal Form (6NF)

In the vast majority of cases, there is no need to go past 3NF. It is also important to note that other problems can arise if we overnormalize a schema. Therefore, this chapter will focus on modeling our data schema into 3NF.

To model data into 1NF, we will be ensuring that all attributes are atomic and uniquely named and that their order is irrelevant. We will also ensure that repeating groups of attributes are moved into a different entity and that the order of rows is not important.

When we model data into 2NF, we will ensure that all attributes are dependent on all attributes that constitute a composite primary key. If they don't, we will move them into a new entity. Finally, when we model the data into 3NF, we will ensure that attributes are not dependent on attributes that are not currently part of the primary key. If they are, then again, this is a sign that they should be moved to a new entity.

Normalization tips

While some data normalization tools are available, I honestly find that the best tool for the process is a simple spreadsheet. Personally, for smaller datasets, such as the one we are discussing here, I use a column per normal form, with row gaps between entities. This allows me to compare my models side by side and think through the logic that I am using.

Another important tip for normalization is to understand your data. This means working with the business analyst, or the application owner, to understand the business meaning and business rules behind each attribute. Failure to do this will inevitably result in false assumptions, which affect your model.

Ensuring you have this understanding will help you, or your business analyst, create another important document called a *data dictionary*. Again, this is often created within a spreadsheet and details information such as

- Attribute name
- Attribute description/meaning
- Business rules, such as expected values, uniqueness, etc.
- Example data
- Data type
- Upstream dependencies
- Data lineage

Data lineage is important in complex data-tier applications. It tracks the path that a data item has taken to reach the table that it currently resides in. For example, if we had a database used for internet marketing, you may be storing a cookie ID. The lineage here could be something like

1. Tracking ID (in Impressions CSV delivered from cookie provider) >
2. TrackingID (in `Cookies` table in staging schema) >
3. CookieID (In `Cookies` table marketing schema)

Finally, don't be afraid to make mistakes. Build your model, test it, and, if you have made a mistake, then simply fix it, rinse, and repeat.

Before we begin, we will arrange our attributes into three broad data types: Sales, Purchasing, and Products, which relate to both Sales and Purchasing. This gives us our starting data in an unnormalized form, as shown in the following:

```
Sales
Sales Order Date
Sales Order Number
Sales Person Name
Sales Person Email
Sales Area Name
Sales Area Manager
Customer Company Name
Customer Contact Name
Customer Contact Email
Customer Invoice Address
Customer Delivery Addresses
Sales Order Delivery Due Date
Sales Order Delivery Actual Date
Sales Order Item
Sales Order Quantities
Currier Used for Delivery

Purchasing
Supplier Name
Supplier Contact Name
Supplier Contact Email
Supplier Address
Purchase Order Date
Purchase Order Number
Purchase Order Items
Purchase Order Quantities
```

```
Products
Product Name
Product Stock Level
Product Next Manufacture Date
Product Next Manufacture Quantity
Back Order Manufacturing ID
Product Type Name
Product Type Description
Product Category Name
Product Category Description
Product Subcategory Name
Product Subcategory Description
```

FIRST NORMAL FORM

For a relation to be in 1NF, it must meet the following rules:

- All attributes are atomic.
- Every attribute has a unique name.
- The order of attributes is irrelevant.
- Repeating groups are removed.
- All rows must be unique (there must be a key).

NOTE In normalization, a relation is the equivalent of an entity in an ERD or a table in a database.

In our example, every attribute already has a unique name, and the order of attributes is irrelevant, so we are off to a good start. We do, however, need to break down some of our attributes to be atomic. We also need to check our data for repeating groups, which are groups of columns that repeat. We also need to find a *candidate key*, which is a set of columns that form a *minimal super key*. A super key is a key that uniquely identifies every row, and it is minimal if the removal of any column in that key would result in an inability to uniquely identify every row.

First, let's identify keys that will be used to uniquely identify rows in each relation. The Sales data can be uniquely identified by the Sales Order Number. Therefore, there is no need to use a *composite key*, which is a key consisting of multiple attributes. If a key consists of a single attribute, then it is known as a *prime attribute*.

The Purchasing data can be uniquely identified by the Purchase Order Number. Therefore, it is a super key in its own right, and we can again use this as a single attribute candidate key.

The Products data cannot be identified by the Product Name alone, as some parts ordered from suppliers have the same name as the products that are sold to customers. Therefore, we need to use both the Product Name and the Product Type Name to uniquely identify any given record, and these two attributes will therefore form our candidate key.

This process has already helped us to spot the first issue with our data model. Both our Sales data and our Purchasing data hold product names (Sales Order Items and

Purchase Order Items, respectively). The issue is that we have found that we require both Product Name and Product Type Name to uniquely identify a Product. Therefore, let's add Product Type Name to each of those entities. We should also add relationships to each relation that joins to the Products relation. While we are there, let's change the names of the Sales Order Items attribute and the Purchase Order Items attribute to be Product Name, to make the relationship clear.

Next, we should look for nonatomic values. The nonatomic values in our unnormalized data, which we need to break down, are

- *Sales Person Name*—We will break this down to Sales Person First Name and Sales Person Last Name.
- *Sales Area Manager*—We will break this down to Sales Area Manager First Name and Sales Area Manager Last Name.
- *Customer Contact Name*—We will break this down to Customer Contact First Name and Customer Contact Last Name.
- *Customer Invoice Address*—We will break this down into the following attributes:
  - Invoice Address Street
  - Invoice Address Area
  - Invoice Address City
  - Invoice Address Zip Code
  - Invoice Address Country
- *Customer Delivery Address*—We will break this down into the following attributes:
  - Delivery Address Street
  - Delivery Address Area
  - Delivery Address City
  - Delivery Address Zip Code
  - Delivery Address Country
- *Product Name and Product Type Name (in the Sales relation)*—This is a tricky one. This attribute will store multiple products that have been ordered on a single order, but we can't really break this down into multiple attributes, as there is not a defined number of items that can be placed on a single order. Therefore, we will separate this out into a different relation and carry down the Sales Order Number, which we have selected as the key, so that the new relation can join back to the original relation. We will also bring with it the Sales Order Quantities (which we will shorten to Quantity), which would otherwise suffer from the same issue.
- *Supplier Contact Name*—We will break this down into Supplier Contact First Name and Supplier Contact Last Name.
- *Supplier Address*—We will break this down into the following attributes:
  - Supplier Address Street

  - Supplier Address Area
  - Supplier Address City
  - Supplier Address Zip Code
  - Supplier Address Country
- *Product Name and Product Type Name (in the Purchasing relation)*—As with the Sales relation, we will need to move these attributes out to a new relation and carry across the Purchase Order Number so that we can join the entities. Again, we will bring the Purchase Order Quantities attribute and shorten it to Quantity.

Finally, we need to look for repeating groups. You may have already noticed from the bulleted list that the attributes that make up the Invoice Address are an exact repeat of the attributes that make up the Delivery Address within the Sales relation. Therefore, we should move both of these addresses out into a new relation, which we will call Addresses. We will add an additional attribute to the new relation, for which the candidate key will be Street and Zip Code. We will then bring these back into the Sales relation twice, once for invoice address and again for delivery address.

TIP While it's not explicitly called for within the rules of normalization, at this point it would make sense to add Supplier Address to the Addresses relation as well. We will then have a single relation that stores all addresses in our database. This minimizes duplication and, in the specific case of address, means that a single address validation leaves it ready to be consumed by any entity.

Data generalization

By adding all three address types to a single relation, we have performed a data modeling technique called generalization, where we pull together attributes from a set of relations or entities and create a new entity that is more generic.

A more advanced type of *generalization* would be to create supertypes and subtypes. With this technique, we may, for example, decide to generalize salespeople, customer contacts, supplier contacts, and sales area managers. All their common attributes, such as First Name, Last Name, and Email, would be moved into a People entity.

Some of the person types may have unique attributes, however. For example, a salesperson may also have attributes for Sales Target and Employee Number. In this case, we could create an additional entity for Sales Persons that would contain the unique attributes and join back to the People entity.

In this instance, People becomes a supertype. Sales Persons is a subtype of the People entity. There is a good example of this modeling within the AdventureWorks database, which is a SQL Server sample database. In this database, the `Employees` table is a subtype of the Person supertype.

The AdventureWorks database can be downloaded from https://mng.bz/oOod.

The following structure illustrates how our data is modeled into 1NF, using the previous discussion points:

```
    Sales
    Sales Order Date
PK  Sales Order Number
    Sales Person First Name
    Sales Person Last Name
    Sales Person Email
    Sales Area Name
    Sales Area Manager First Name
    Sales Area Manager Last Name
    Customer Company Name
    Customer Contact First Name
    Customer Contact Last Name
    Customer Contact Email
FK  Invoice Address Street
FK  Invoice Address Zip Code
FK  Delivery Address Street
FK  Delivery Address Zip Code
    Sales Order Delivery Due Date
    Sales Order Delivery Actual Date
    Currier Used for Delivery

      Sales Order Details
PK FK Product Name
PK FK Product Type Name
      Quantity
PK FK Sales Order Number

    Address
PK  Street
    Area
    City
PK  Zip Code

    Purchasing
    Supplier Name
    Supplier Contact First Name
    Supplier Contact Last Name
    Supplier Contact Email
FK  Supplier Address Street
FK  Supplier Address Zip Code
    Purchase Order Date
PK  Purchase Order Number

      Purchase Order Details
PK FK Product Name
PK FK Product Type Name
      Quantity
PK FK Purchase Order Number

    Products
PK  Product Name
```

```
    Product Stock Level
    Product Next Manufacture Date
    Product Next Manufacture Quantity
    Back Order Manufacturing ID
PK  Product Type Name
    Product Type Description
    Product Category Name
    Product Category Description
    Product Subcategory Name
    Product Subcategory Description
```

So that's great. Our relations are starting to look a bit more like a database schema. But having a database modeled to 1NF is usually considered a bad design. So let's move on and start looking at how we can bring our database into 2NF.

SECOND NORMAL FORM

For relations to be in 2NF, they must comply with the following rules:

- The relations must be in 1NF.
- All attributes must be functionally dependent on the whole of the key.

Okay, so we know that our relations are already in 1NF, but how do we ensure functional dependency on the whole of the key? Well, first it is worth noting that this rule only applies to relations that have a composite key. By definition, if a natural key consists of a prime attribute, then all other attributes must be dependent upon it.

In our example, we only have a single attribute that is not dependent on all attributes within a composite key. This is the Product Type Description attribute within the Product relation. This attribute is solely dependent on the Product Type Name attribute. Therefore, let's pull the Product Type Name and Product Type Description attributes out into a separate relation, where Product Type Name becomes the prime attribute. We will also push the Product Type Name back up to the Product relation as a foreign key.

Therefore, the following represents our data when modeled in 2NF:

```
    Sales
    Sales Order Date
PK  Sales Order Number
    Sales Person First Name
    Sales Person Last Name
    Sales Person Email
    Sales Area Name
    Sales Area Manager First Name
    Sales Area Manager Last Name
    Customer Company Name
    Customer Contact First Name
    Customer Contact Last Name
    Customer Contact Email
FK  Invoice Address Street
FK  Invoice Address Zip Code
FK  Delivery Address Street
FK  Delivery Address Zip Code
    Sales Order Delivery Due Date
```

```
    Sales Order Delivery Actual Date
    Currier Used for Delivery

      Sales Order Details
PK FK Product Name
PK FK Product Type Name
      Quantity
PK FK Sales Order Number

    Address
PK  Street
    Area
    City
PK  Zip Code

    Purchasing
    Supplier Name
    Supplier Contact First Name
    Supplier Contact Last Name
    Supplier Contact Email
FK  Supplier Address Street
FK  Supplier Address Zip Code
    Purchase Order Date
PK  Purchase Order Number

      Purchase Order Details
PK FK Product Name
PK FK Product Type Name
      Quantity
PK FK Purchase Order Number

      Products
PK    Product Name
      Product Stock Level
      Product Next Manufacture Date
      Product Next Manufacture Quantity
      Back Order Manufacturing ID
PK FK Product Type Name
      Product Category Name
      Product Category Description
      Product Subcategory Name
      Product Subcategory Description

    Product Types
PK  Product Type Name
    Product Type Description
```

Third Normal Form

Lastly, we need to transform our relations into 3NF. The rules of 3NF state

- Relations must be in 2NF.
- All attributes must be nontransitively dependent on the key.

Our relations are already in 2NF, which is great. But we need to ensure *nontransitive dependence,* which means that attributes are not dependent on any nonprime attributes within the relation.

If we look through our data, we will see that we have quite a few examples of attributes that depend more on nonprime attributes than they do the candidate key. The first example is in the Sales relation: the Sales Person First Name and the Sales Person Last Name. It is reasonable to expect that the Sales Person Email will be unique, which means that it could be used to identify each unique combination of these attributes. Therefore, we will move all three of these attributes into a new Sales Person relation, where Sales Person Email is the prime attribute, and bring the Sales Person Email attribute back up into the Sales relation as a foreign key.

The Sales relation also has Sales Area Manager First Name and Sales Area Manager Last Name. Both of these attributes can be uniquely identified by the Sales Area Name attribute. Therefore, we will bring them down into a Sales Areas relation and retain Sales Area Name as a foreign key.

The Customer Contact First Name, Customer Contact Last Name, Customer Email, along with the delivery address keys and the invoice address keys can all be uniquely identified by the Customer Company Name attribute. Therefore, we will move these out into a Customers relation and join it back on the Customer Company Name key. This is an interesting example, however, as once we have created this new relation, you may notice that we can also now identify the Customer Contact First Name and Customer Contact Last Name by using the Customer Email. Therefore, we should move these attributes out to yet another relation, called Customer Contact, which will join back to the Customer relation using the Customer Contact Email as a key.

In a similar fashion, when we look at the Purchasing relation, we will see that the Supplier Contact First Name, Supplier Contact Last Name, and the Supplier Address keys can all be uniquely identified using the Supplier Name and therefore should move into a Suppliers relation. But the Supplier Contact First Name, Supplier Contact Last Name, and Supplier Contact Email should then move down to a Supplier Contact relation, keyed on the Supplier Contact Email.

> **TIP** Supplier Contacts, Customer Contacts, and Sales Person would be good candidates for generalization. If we wanted to generalize this data, we could create a single Contacts entity, which would hold all contact types. To make filtering easier, we could create a Contact Type attribute in the entity. This entity would then join to the Suppliers, Customers, and Sales entities.

In the Products relation, the Product Category Name, Product Category Description, and Product Subcategory description can all be uniquely identified by the Product Subcategory name, so we will move these attributes down into a Product Subcategories relation. Furthermore, we should then move the Product Category Description down into a Product Categories relation, which is keyed on the Product Category Name attribute.

Finally, the `ProductNextManufactureDate` and `ProductNextManufactureQuantity` attributes can be identified by the `BackOrderManufacturingID` attribute, so we will move these attributes down to a new Back Orders relation.

We should now find that our data is in 3NF, as shown in the following:

```
     Sales
     Sales Order Date
PK   Sales Order Number
FK   Sales Person Email
FK   Sales Area Name
FK   Customer Company Name
     Sales Order Delivery Due Date
     Sales Order Delivery Actual Date
     Currier Used for Delivery

     Sales Person
     Sales Person First Name
     Sales Person Last Name
PK   Sales Person Email

     Sales Areas
PK   Sales Area Name
     Sales Area Manager First Name
     Sales Area Manager Last Name

     Customer
PK   Customer Company Name
FK   Customer Contact Email
FK   Invoice Address Street
FK   Invoice Address Zip Code
FK   Delivery Address Street
FK   Delivery Address Zip Code

     Customer Contact
     Customer Contact First Name
     Customer Contact Last Name
PK   Customer Contact Email

       Sales Order Details
PK FK Product Name
PK FK Product Type Name
       Quantity
PK FK Sales Order Number

     Address
PK   Street
     Area
     City
PK   Zip Code

     Purchasing
FK   Supplier Name
     Purchase Order Date
```

```
PK  Purchase Order Number

    Suppliers
PK  Supplier Name
FK  Supplier Contact Email
FK  Supplier Address Street
FK  Supplier Address Zip Code

    Supplier Contact
    Supplier Contact First Name
    Supplier Contact Last Name
PK  Supplier Contact Email

      Purchase Order Details
PK FK Product Name
PK FK Product Type Name
      Quantity
PK FK Purchase Order Number

      Products
PK    Product Name
      Product Stock Level
FK    Back Order Manufacturing ID
PK FK Product Type Name
FK    Product Subcategory Name

    Product Types
PK  Product Type Name
    Product Type Description

    Product SubCategories
FK  Product Category Name
PK  Product Subcategory Name
    Product Subcategory Description

    Product Categories
PK  Product Category Name
    Product Category Description

    BackOrders
    ProductNextManufactureDate
    ProductNextManufactureQuantity
PK    BackOrderManufacturingID
```

We should now take the time to tidy up a few things. First is our relation names. After the modeling, Sales is no longer a meaningful name for the data it represents. Let's change this to Sales Order Header. Also, Purchasing no longer adequately represents its attributes, so we should change it to Purchase Order Header.

Wide primary keys are bad. I won't go into too much detail here, as we will be discussing this in the next mistake, but currently all of our keys are *natural keys*, which are keys that have business meaning. Where we have composite keys, we should replace these with *artificial keys*, which are keys that store an arbitrary value with no business meaning—usually an incrementing number. We should also replace keys that are text-based with artificial keys. Again, this makes the keys narrower.

With this in mind, we will make the following changes:

- Sales Person will have a new key called Sales Person ID.
- Sales Areas will have a new key called Sales Area ID.
- Customers will have a new key called Customer ID.
- Customer Contacts will have a new key called Customer Contact ID.
- Sales Order Details will have a new key called Sales Order Details ID.
- Addresses will have a new key called Address ID.
- Suppliers will have a new key called Supplier ID.
- Supplier Contacts will have a new key called Supplier Contact ID.
- Purchase Order Details will have a new key called Purchase Order Details ID.
- Products will have a new key called Product ID.
- Product Types will have a new key called Product Type ID.
- Product Subcategories will have a new key called Product Subcategory ID.
- Product Categories will have a new key called Product Category ID.

Finally, we should remove all spaces from our relation and attribute names. This is to make them database friendly when we create our database tables and columns. If we had any special characters or reserved words, which are words that are used by SQL Server, such as "SELECT" or "table," in our relation and attribute names, we should consider changing these as well. If we did not take this step, then we would have to use delimited identifiers when we referenced the objects in SQL Server. This means encapsulating the name in square brackets. For example, `SELECT MyColumn FROM MyTable` would become `SELECT [MyColumn] FROM [MyTable]` Delimited identifiers are considered poor practice because they clutter our code and because, if we need to use them, we have not followed the standard rules and conventions for naming identifiers.

We have now finished our design, but how can we test it? There is no hard and fast answer to this, but we will get a good idea if we create an ERD. When examining the ERD, we should notice that all entities that need to be joined are joined with a 1:many join type. If we find any many:many or 1:1 joins, then there is likely a mistake in the model. So let's see how our model looks if we build an ERD. This ERD can be seen in figure 4.5.

Our final task is to write a script that will create our database objects. The script in listing 4.1 will generate these objects, some of which we will use in later mistakes.

> **NOTE** There is an intentional mistake in the script. The `PurchaseOrderDetails` table has a `PurchaseOrderNumber` column, but a foreign key has not been created, to join it back to the `PurchaseOrderHeaders` table. We will explore the consequences of this in a later section of this chapter.

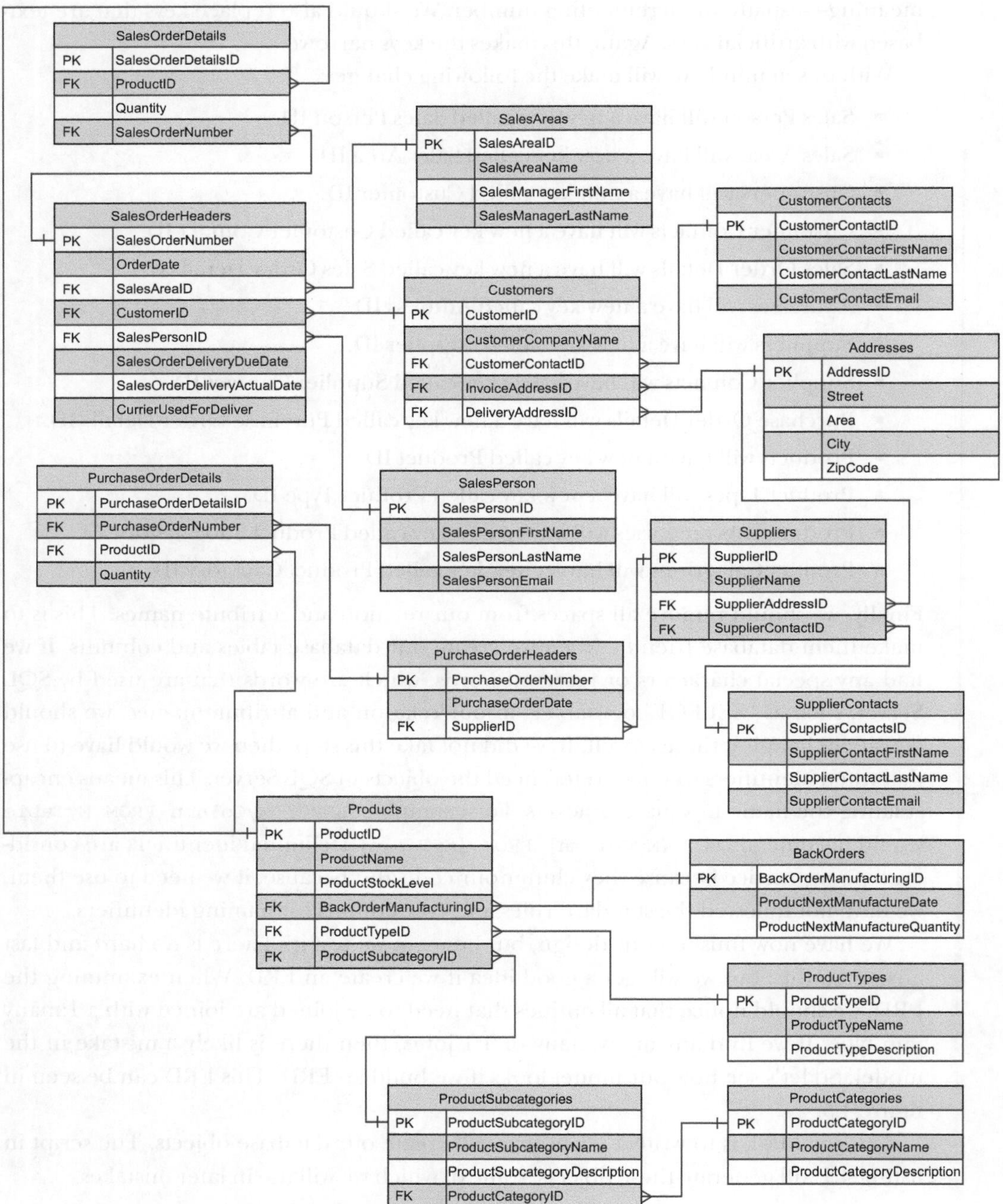

Figure 4.5 ERD from normalized design

Listing 4.1 Creating the database objects

```
CREATE DATABASE MagicChoc ;
GO

USE MagicChoc ;
GO

CREATE TABLE dbo.BackOrders (
    BackOrderManufacturingID            INT     NOT NULL
        IDENTITY    PRIMARY KEY,
    ProductNextManufactureDate          DATE    NOT NULL,
    ProductNextManufactureQuantity      INT     NOT NULL
) ;

CREATE TABLE dbo.ProductCategories (
    ProductCategoryID               SMALLINT          NOT NULL
        IDENTITY    PRIMARY KEY,
    ProductCategoryName             NVARCHAR(64)      NOT NULL,
    ProductCategoryDescription      NVARCHAR(256)     NULL
) ;

CREATE TABLE dbo.ProductSubcategories (
    ProductSubcategoryID                SMALLINT          NOT NULL
        IDENTITY    PRIMARY KEY,
    ProductCategoryID                   SMALLINT          NOT NULL
        REFERENCES dbo.ProductCategories(ProductCategoryID),
    ProductSubcategoryName              NVARCHAR(64)      NOT NULL,
    ProductSubcategoryDescription       NVARCHAR(256)     NULL
) ;

CREATE TABLE dbo.ProductTypes (
    ProductTypeID               SMALLINT        NOT NULL
        IDENTITY    PRIMARY KEY,
    ProductTypeName             NVARCHAR(64)    NOT NULL,
    ProductTypeDescription      NVARCHAR(256)   NOT NULL
) ;

CREATE TABLE dbo.Products (
    ProductID                       INT                 NOT NULL
        IDENTITY    PRIMARY KEY,
    ProductName                     NVARCHAR(64)        NOT NULL,
    ProductStockLevel               INT                 NOT NULL,
    BackOrderManufacturingID        INT                 NULL
        REFERENCES dbo.BackOrders(BackOrderManufacturingID),
    ProductTypeID                   SMALLINT            NOT NULL
        REFERENCES dbo.ProductTypes(ProductTypeID),
    ProductSubcategoryID            SMALLINT            NOT NULL
        REFERENCES dbo.ProductSubcategories(ProductSubcategoryID)
) ;

CREATE TABLE dbo.Addresses (
    AddressID     INT                 NOT NULL
        IDENTITY    PRIMARY KEY,
    Street        NVARCHAR(128)       NOT NULL,
    Area          NVARCHAR(64)        NULL,
```

```
    City          NVARCHAR(64)      NOT NULL,
    ZipCode       NVARCHAR(10)      NOT NULL
) ;

CREATE TABLE dbo.SupplierContacts (
    SupplierContactID          INT                NOT NULL
        IDENTITY    PRIMARY KEY,
    SupplierContactFirstName   NVARCHAR(32)       NOT NULL,
    SupplierContactLastName    NVARCHAR(32)       NOT NULL,
    SupplierContactEmail       NVARCHAR(256)      NOT NULL
) ;

CREATE TABLE dbo.Suppliers (
    SupplierID          INT               NOT NULL
        IDENTITY    PRIMARY KEY,
    SupplierName        NVARCHAR(32)      NOT NULL,
    SupplierContactID   INT               NOT NULL
        REFERENCES dbo.SupplierContacts(SupplierContactID),
    SupplierAddressID   INT               NOT NULL
        REFERENCES dbo.Addresses(AddressID)
) ;

CREATE TABLE dbo.PurchaseOrderHeaders (
    PurchaseOrderNumber   INT     NOT NULL    PRIMARY KEY,
    SupplierID            INT     NOT NULL
        REFERENCES dbo.Suppliers(SupplierID),
    PurchaseOrderDate     DATE    NOT NULL
) ;

CREATE TABLE dbo.PurchaseOrderDetails (
    PurchaseOrderDetailsID    INT    NOT NULL
        IDENTITY    PRIMARY KEY,
    ProductID                 INT    NOT NULL
        REFERENCES dbo.Products(ProductID),
    Quantity                  INT    NOT NULL,
    PurchaseOrderNumber       INT    NOT NULL
) ;

CREATE TABLE dbo.CustomerContacts (
    CustomerContactID          INT                NOT NULL
        IDENTITY    PRIMARY KEY,
    CustomerContactFirstName   NVARCHAR(32)       NOT NULL,
    CustomerContactLastName    NVARCHAR(32)       NOT NULL,
    CustomerContactEmail       NVARCHAR(256)      NOT NULL
) ;

CREATE TABLE dbo.Customers (
    CustomerID            INT               NOT NULL
        IDENTITY    PRIMARY KEY,
    CustomerCompanyName   NVARCHAR(32)      NOT NULL,
    CustomerContactID     INT               NOT NULL
        REFERENCES dbo.CustomerContacts(CustomerContactID),
    InvoiceAddressID      INT               NOT NULL
        REFERENCES dbo.Addresses(AddressID),
    DeliveryAddressID     INT               NOT NULL
        REFERENCES dbo.Addresses(AddressID)
```

This column is missing a foreign key constraint, which should join it back to the PurchaseOrderHeader table.

```
) ;

CREATE TABLE dbo.SalesAreas (
    SalesAreaID                    SMALLINT        NOT NULL
        IDENTITY    PRIMARY KEY,
    SalesAreaName                  NVARCHAR(32)    NOT NULL,
    SalesAreaManagerFirstName      NVARCHAR(32)    NOT NULL,
    SalesAreaManagerLastName       NVARCHAR(32)    NOT NULL
) ;

CREATE TABLE dbo.SalesPersons (
    SalesPersonID           SMALLINT        NOT NULL
        IDENTITY    PRIMARY KEY,
    SalesPersonFirstName    NVARCHAR(32)    NOT NULL,
    SalesPersonLastName     NVARCHAR(32)    NOT NULL,
    SalesPersonEmail        NVARCHAR(256)   NOT NULL
) ;

CREATE TABLE dbo.SalesOrderHeaders (
    SalesOrderNumber                NCHAR(12)       NOT NULL    PRIMARY KEY,
    SalesOrderDate                  DATE            NOT NULL,
    SalesPersonID                   SMALLINT        NOT NULL
        REFERENCES dbo.SalesPersons(SalesPersonID),
    SalesAreaID                     SMALLINT        NOT NULL
        REFERENCES dbo.SalesAreas(SalesAreaID),
    CustomerID                      INT             NOT NULL
        REFERENCES dbo.Customers(CustomerID),
    SalesOrderDeliveryDueDate       DATE            NOT NULL,
    SalesOrderDeliveryActualDate    DATE            NULL,
    CurrierUsedforDelivery          NVARCHAR(32)    NOT NULL
) ;

CREATE TABLE dbo.SalesOrderDetails (
    SalesOrderDetailsID    INT          NOT NULL    IDENTITY    PRIMARY KEY,
    ProductID              INT          NOT NULL
        REFERENCES dbo.Products(ProductID),
    Quantity               INT          NOT NULL,
    SalesOrderNumber       NCHAR(12)    NOT NULL
        REFERENCES dbo.SalesOrderHeaders(SalesOrderNumber)
) ;
GO
```

Modeling data using normalization can seem complex at first, but after a few attempts, it starts to come naturally. It certainly has many benefits over the judgment modeling approach and is far less prone to errors. It allows us to apply a methodology that has well and truly stood the test of time.

4.2 #12 Using a wide primary key

As mentioned in the previous section, we have selected `SalesOrderNumber` as the primary key of the `SalesOrderHeaders` table, but the format of the order numbers is ABC1234D-E12. This means that our column is of data type `NCHAR(12)`. This means that for each row, the column uses 24 bytes of space, as opposed to the 4 bytes of space that an `INT` would take. Even a `BIGINT` would only consume 8 bytes of space.

We spoke about the benefits of using the smallest possible data types in chapter 3, but this data has letters in it. Depending on the business rules, we may be able to use a `CHAR(12)`, but even that will consume 12 bytes of storage per row—so what can we do? And what is the significance of it being a primary key column?

To answer these questions, let's think about our indexing strategy for the `SalesOrderHeaders` table. The primary key column, by default, will have a *clustered index.* A clustered index organizes data into a *B-tree.* This is a structure consisting of multiple layers of index pages, which provide pointers to index pages on lower levels of the structure. There is always one root level, consisting of a single page, known as the *Index Allocation Map (IAM).* There are then zero or more intermediate levels, depending on the size of the table. The bottom (leaf) level of a clustered index is the actual data pages of the table.

TIP There is a full discussion around indexes in chapter 11.

Because the data within the index is ordered, records can be found very quickly by using an operation called a *clustered index seek.* This operation traverses the levels of an index to locate a record. This is opposed to a *clustered index scan*, which is an operation where every page of the leaf level of the index has to be searched until the required record is found. These operations, along with an example of the B-tree structure, are illustrated in figure 4.6. You will notice that whenever a single row is searched, the maximum number of pages read by a seek operation is equal to the number of levels of the B-tree. The maximum number of pages read by an index scan, however, is equal to the

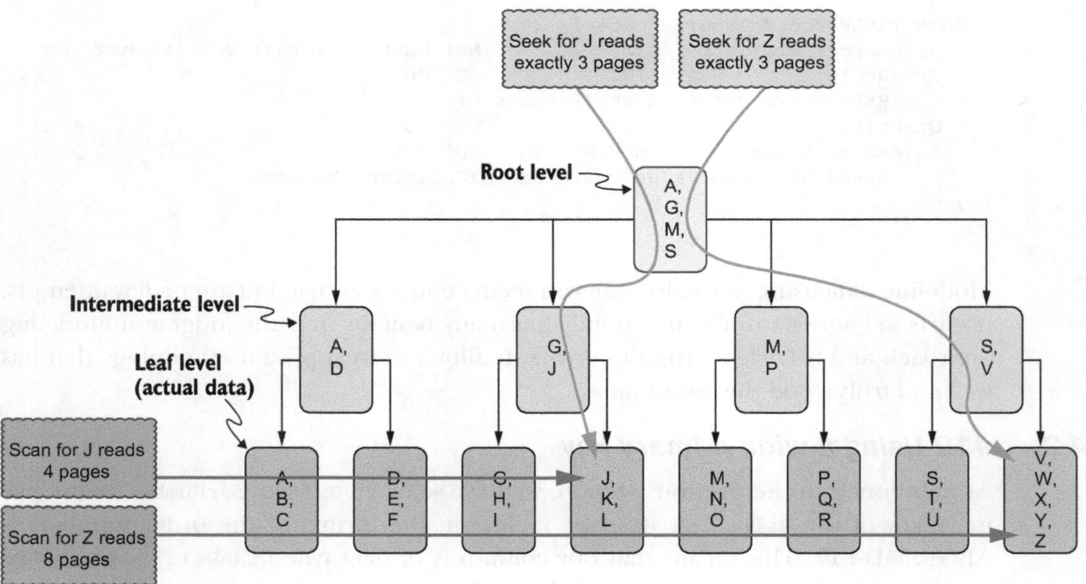

Figure 4.6 Clustered index seeks and scans against a B-tree

number of data pages that comprise the leaf level of the index and therefore the table. If multiple rows can be returned by the operation, then a seek is used to find the start point for reading the leaf level.

> **TIP** Because a clustered index orders the data pages of the table itself, there can only ever be a single clustered index on a table. A table that does not have a clustered index is called a *heap*. In a heap, records are stored in no particular order. Heaps are often used for purposes such as staging tables, which have large inserts of ephemeral data, where order is irrelevant, as this can optimize performance.

The business has told us that they often search sales orders by filtering the order date. Therefore, we want to optimize these queries by creating a nonclustered index on the `SalesOrderDate` column. A nonclustered index creates a B-tree structure that is very similar to a clustered index. The difference is that instead of the leaf level of the index containing actual data, it contains pointers to the data within the clustered index or heap. Because the leaf level is just pointers, this means that the actual data is not being ordered. Thus we can have multiple nonclustered indexes on a single table. The pointers to the clustered index consist of the clustered index key. This means that a wide clustered key is replicated to all nonclustered indexes.

> **NOTE** If a nonclustered index has `INCLUDE` columns, then the actual data values of these columns will be stored in the index along with the pointer to the index or heap.

Additionally, the business has told us that sales order queries will usually include sales area information and customer information. This data is stored in different tables, so we will also want to create nonclustered indexes on the `SalesAreaID` and `CustomerID` columns, which are the foreign keys for these tables. By creating nonclustered indexes on the foreign keys, the keys are ordered in the same way as their primary key counterparts in the tables that we join to. This can allow for more efficient join operations.

To see the consequences of having a wide primary key, let's first add some data to the relevant tables. The script in listing 4.2 adds a small amount of data to the relevant tables. It then creates the nonclustered indexes on the `SalesOrderHeaders` table. There is no need to create the clustered index, as this was created automatically when we created the primary key on the table.

Listing 4.2 Adding data and creating nonclustered indexes

```
INSERT INTO dbo.SalesPersons (
    SalesPersonFirstName,
    SalesPersonLastName,
    SalesPersonEmail
)
VALUES
    ('Robin', 'Wells', 'robin.wells@magicchoc.com'),
    ('Jack', 'Jones', 'jack.jones@magicchoc.com'),
    ('Jane', 'Smith', 'jane.smith@magicchoc.com') ;
```

```
INSERT INTO dbo.SalesAreas (
    SalesAreaName,
    SalesAreaManagerFirstName,
    SalesAreaManagerLastName
)
VALUES
    ('US', 'Lucy', 'Sykes'),
    ('Euro', 'Ashwin', 'Kumar'),
    ('APAC', 'Emma', 'Roberts') ;

INSERT INTO dbo.Addresses (Street, Area, City, ZipCode)
VALUES
    ('744 Saxon Rd', NULL, 'Crawfordsville', '47933'),
    ('267 Old York Ave.', NULL, 'Reno', '89523'),
    ('923 Taylor Ave.', NULL, 'Charlotte', '28205'),
    ('942 Cactus Street', NULL, 'Albany', '12203'),
    ('32 Selby Drive', NULL, 'Pittsfield', '01201'),
    ('65 New Street', 'Landford', 'Salisbury', 'SP5 2QP') ;

INSERT INTO dbo.CustomerContacts (
    CustomerContactFirstName,
    CustomerContactLastName,
    CustomerContactEmail
)
VALUES
    ('Ralphie', 'Buchanan', 'Ralphie.Buchanan@Pitt.com'),
    ('Bettie', 'Peters', 'bpeters@cookingschmooking.co.uk'),
    ('Zackery', 'McEachern', 'Zackery.McEachern@wilsonindustries.com') ;


INSERT INTO dbo.Customers (
    CustomerCompanyName,
    CustomerContactID,
    InvoiceAddressID,
    DeliveryAddressID
)
VALUES
    ('Pitt and Co', 1, 1, 2),
    ('Cooking Schmooking', 2, 3, 4),
    ('Wilson Industries', 3, 6, 6) ;


INSERT INTO dbo.SalesOrderHeaders (
    SalesOrderNumber,
    SalesOrderDate,
    SalesPersonID,
    SalesAreaID,
    CustomerID,
    SalesOrderDeliveryDueDate,
    SalesOrderDeliveryActualDate,
    CurrierUsedforDelivery
)
VALUES
    ('COO1634D-U06', '20230501', 1, 1, 1, '20230503', '20230503', 'LHD'),
    ('WIL1635D-E16', '20230616', 2, 2, 3, '20230630', NULL, 'GoodSpeed
International'),
```

```
    (,PIT1636D-U04', ,20230616', 3, 1, 1, ,20230706', NULL, ,LHD') ;
GO

CREATE NONCLUSTERED INDEX NI_SalesOrderHeaders_OrderDate
    ON SalesOrderHeaders(SalesOrderDate) ;
CREATE NONCLUSTERED INDEX NI_SalesOrderHeaders_SalesAreaID
    ON SalesOrderHeaders(SalesAreaID) ;
CREATE NONCLUSTERED INDEX NI_SalesOrderHeaders_CustomerID
    ON SalesOrderHeaders(CustomerID) ;
```

Next, to demonstrate the issue, we need to see what is stored on the index pages of one of the indexes that we have just created. Let's use the `NI_SalesOrderHeaders_OrderDate` index here, but we could pick whichever index we like.

There are three steps that are required to view inside the index pages. The first step is to determine the index ID of our index. This is not the object ID, which is unique across the instance. Instead, this is the index identifier within the table. We can list the details for a given index by interrogating `sys.indexes` and filtering by the name of the index, as shown in the following listing.

Listing 4.3 Determining the index ID

```
SELECT
    name
  , index_id
  , type_desc
FROM sys.indexes
WHERE name = 'NI_SalesOrderHeaders_OrderDate' ;
```

The index ID that I have is 2, but you may find the ID is different if you created the indexes in a different order. Now that we have the index ID, the next step is to use the `DBCC IND` command to list out all of the pages that make up the index.

The command lists out the IAM chain of the index, from the root level through to the leaf level. There is one row returned for every page within the index that includes page numbers, index level, and page pointers for traversing the index, as well as other useful information.

The command accepts three parameters, namely, database name (or database ID), table name, and index ID. The following listing demonstrates how to use this command.

Listing 4.4 Using `DBCC IND` to discover index page numbers

```
DBCC IND ('MagicChoc', 'SalesOrderHeaders', 2) ;
```

> **WARNING** My results are shown next, but please note that you will almost certainly find that your page numbers differ. Please make sure you use your own page numbers in the following examples.

The results are shown in figure 4.7. You will notice that there are only two pages. The first page is the root page of the index. There will always be exactly one root page, regardless of index size. There are no intermediate levels of the index because it is too small. The leaf level of the index consists of exactly one page, because there are only three records in the table, so everything sits comfortably inside a single page.

Results | Messages

	PageFID	PagePID	IAMFID	IAMPID	ObjectID	IndexID	PartitionNumber	PartitionID	iam_chain_type	PageType	IndexLevel	NextPageFID	NextPagePID	PrevPageFID	PrevPagePID
1	1	579	NULL	NULL	1669580986	2	1	72057594046906368	In-row data	10	NULL	0	0	0	0
2	1	600	1	579	1669580986	2	1	72057594046906368	In-row data	2	0	0	0	0	0

Figure 4.7 Results of `DBCC IND`

The final step is to use another DBCC command, called `DBCC PAGE`. This command can be used to display the contents of a data or index page. The command accepts four parameters, namely, the database name, the file ID, the page ID (taken from `DBCC IND`), and a parameter that specifies the formatting option. It is important to note, however, that before running `DBCC PAGE`, we must ensure that trace flag 3604 is turned on. Trace flags are used to toggle features on and off, and we will discuss some of these in chapter 10. This particular flag sends DBCC output to the console. The following listing demonstrates how to use this command.

Listing 4.5 Using `DBCC PAGE` to view the page contents

```
DBCC TRACEON(3604) ;
DBCC PAGE('MagicChoc', 1, 600, 3) ;
```

My results from running this command are displayed in figure 4.8. As expected, you will see the index key value in the `SalesOrderDate` (key) column. But look at the column next to it: the `SalesOrderNumber` (key) column. The value of the primary key is stored in every row. This provides the pointer back to the data in the clustered index.

Results | Messages

	FileId	PageId	Row	Level	SalesOrderDate (key)	SalesOrderNumber (key)	KeyHashValue	Row Size
1	1	600	0	0	2023-05-01	COO1634D-U06	(f1ae9621c514)	31
2	1	600	1	0	2023-06-16	PIT1636D-U04	(efc14f137f43)	31
3	1	600	2	0	2023-06-16	WIL1635D-E16	(411ea115e4a3)	31

Figure 4.8 Results of `DBCC PAGE`

Therefore, the primary key is not only taking up 12 bytes per row in the table but also up to 12 bytes for every row in every single nonclustered index on the table. What is worse is that our nonclustered indexes are not unique. If a nonclustered index is unique, then the clustered key value is only stored on the leaf level of the index. For nonunique, nonclustered indexes, however, the clustered key value is stored on every row at all levels of the index.

This wide key is not only using additional disk space and memory, but it is also going to damage the performance of the indexes. Remember that a page can only store 8,000 bytes of data. Therefore, the wider the key, the more index pages are required. In turn, SQL Server then must read more pages to retrieve the required data.

In this scenario, where we either find ourselves with a wide column as our primary key or we find that our primary key is a composite of multiple columns, my advice is to create an artificial primary key and automatically populate it with `IDENTITY`. If we need to enforce uniqueness on our natural key, we can still achieve this without bloating our clustered and nonclustered indexes by building a unique nonclustered index on the column.

Globally unique identifiers as primary keys

One of the examples of wide primary keys I have seen is the use of globally unique identifiers (GUIDs).

GUIDs can be generated by using the `NEWID()` function and provide a mechanism for generating values that are unique across the whole server. We sometimes must use GUIDs as primary keys, however. For example, there are some COTS (commercial off the shelf) products that specifically mandate it.

There are two considerations with using GUIDs as a primary key. The first is the size. GUIDs are 16 bytes wide, so we need to ask ourselves: do we really need a value that is globally unique, or do we just need it to be unique within the context of the table? If it needs to be unique across a database, then there may be other methods, such as the `SEQUENCE` feature, that can achieve this in a more appropriate way.

The other consideration is the random nature of a GUID. A clustered index, by definition, orders the data within the table by the values in the clustered index, which is usually based on the primary key. If these values are random, then SQL Server will have to keep reordering the data pages. This means that the index can suffer from a problem known as *page splits*.

When a page split occurs, data will be moved between pages to ensure that the data remains ordered. This will lead to increased IO and reduced performance for `UPDATE` and `INSERT` operations. Additionally, it will lead to index fragmentation, which we will discuss in chapter 11. Fragmentation will reduce the performance of `SELECT` operations until such time as the index is rebuilt.

This issue can be offset by using a low fill factor on the clustered index and rebuilding indexes at a low rate of fragmentation, but generally I recommend creating a nonclustered primary key and then generating the clustered index on a column of integer data type. We can then create the primary key on the column containing the GUIDs.

4.3 #13 Not using foreign keys

Missing foreign key constraints is a mistake that I have seen some less experienced developers make, usually citing the reason that if they need to quickly insert data into a table, then having the constraints make it too time consuming. I have most often seen this view taken, in situations like ours, when the key is a natural key and therefore has business meaning and is controlled by a frontend application.

The challenge with this train of thought is that a frontend application simply cannot guarantee data integrity in the same way that SQL Server constraints can. To discuss this topic in more detail, let's use the example of our `PurchaseOrderHeaders` and `PurchaseOrderDetails` tables.

You may remember that there is a mistake in our database creation script in listing 4.1, resulting in the `PurchaseOrderNumber` column existing in the `PurchaseOrderDetails` table, but as a foreign key was not created, there is no join back to the `PurchaseOrder-Headers` table.

Before we go any further, let's run the script in the following listing to insert data into the relevant tables.

Listing 4.6 Inserting data into product and purchasing tables

```
INSERT INTO dbo.ProductCategories (
    ProductCategoryName,
    ProductCategoryDescription
)
VALUES
    ('Raw Ingridience', NULL),
    ('Machine Parts', 'Parts used by manufacturing for machine maintenance'),
    ('Misc', 'Office supplies and other miscelaneous stock items'),
    ('Services', 'Non-stock purchases, such as transport'),
    ('Confectionary Products', NULL),
    ('Non-confectionary Products', NULL) ;

INSERT INTO dbo.ProductSubcategories (
    ProductCategoryID,
    ProductSubcategoryName,
    ProductSubcategoryDescription
)
VALUES
    (1, 'Chilled Ingredience', 'Ingredience that must be kept between 1C
and 5C'),
    (1, 'Frozen Ingredience', 'Ingredience must be kept below -18C'),
    (1, 'Ambient Ingredience', 'Ingredience that should be kept in cool,
dry storage'),
    (2, 'Line 1 Components', 'Components required for manufacturing line 1'),
    (2, 'Line 2 Components', 'Components required for manufacturing line 1'),
    (2, 'Line 3 Components', 'Components required for manufacturing line 1'),
    (2, 'Line 4 Components', 'Components required for manufacturing line 1'),
    (3, 'Office Supplies', 'Stationary, etc'),
    (3, 'Misc', NULL),
    (4, 'Curriers', NULL),
    (4, 'Building Maintenance', NULL),
    (5, 'Boxes of chocolates', NULL),
    (5, 'Sweets', NULL),
    (5, 'Chocolate Bars', NULL),
    (6, 'Packaging', 'Product Packaging'),
    (6, 'Merchandise', 'Non-core items which are procured and sold, such as
    mugs and branded gifts') ;

INSERT INTO dbo.ProductTypes (ProductTypeName, ProductTypeDescription)
VALUES
    ('Purchased Product', 'Products which are purchased'),
    ('Sold products', 'Products which are sold'),
    ('Traded Products', 'Products which are both bought and sold') ;
```

```
INSERT INTO dbo.SupplierContacts (
    SupplierContactFirstName,
    SupplierContactLastName,
    SupplierContactEmail
)
VALUES
    ('John', 'Smith', 'john.smith@smithfields.com'),
    ('John', 'Doe', 'john.doe@unknownengineering.com'),
    ('Michael', 'Knight', 'mknight@knightridercurriers.com') ;

INSERT INTO dbo.Addresses (
    Street,
    City,
    ZipCode
)
VALUES
    ('8648 Columbia Street', 'Beachwood', '44122'),
    ('83 Addison Dr.', 'Westerville', '43081'),
    ('508 Mill Pond Street', 'Clinton Township', '48035') ;

INSERT INTO dbo.Suppliers (
    SupplierName,
    SupplierContactID,
    SupplierAddressID
)
VALUES
    ('Smithfeilds', 1, 7),
    ('Unknown Engineering', 2, 8),
    ('Knight Rider Curriers', 3, 9) ;

INSERT INTO dbo.Products (
    ProductName,
    ProductStockLevel,
    ProductTypeID,
    ProductSubcategoryID
)
VALUES
    ('Large head sprocket', 3, 1, 4),
    ('Long weight', 6, 1, 4),
    ('Staples', 8900, 1, 8),
    ('Magic Mug', 38, 3, 16),
    ('Massive Magic Box', 18, 2, 12),
    ('Delivery', -1, 3, 10) ;
```

We will now simulate our frontend application inserting purchase orders into the table using the script in listing 4.7. The application is turning on XACT_ABORT and wrapping both INSERT statements inside a transaction. That's good. It means if one statement fails, the other will also fail, helping to keep the data consistent.

Listing 4.7 Adding a purchase order

```
SET XACT_ABORT ON ;

BEGIN TRANSACTION
```

```
    SELECT @@TRANCOUNT ;

    INSERT INTO dbo.PurchaseOrderHeaders  (
        PurchaseOrderNumber,
        SupplierID,
        PurchaseOrderDate
    )
        VALUES
            (6826, 2, '20230601'),
            (6827, 2, '20230617') ;

    INSERT INTO dbo.PurchaseOrderDetails (
        ProductID,
        Quantity,
        PurchaseOrderNumber
    )
    VALUES
        (4, 3, 6826),
        (5, 4, 6827),
        (4, 1, 6827) ;
COMMIT
```

But let's think about the driver for leaving out a foreign key: the fact that we may want the ability to quickly and easily update a table. Consider the following scenario. We have a call from the head of procurement, who says, "There has been a problem with a purchase order. I need you to fix it in the backend, as the application isn't letting me deal with it. I need you to move the ordered items from purchase order 6827 onto purchase order 6828—pronto!"

We are under pressure, so we, perfectly rationally, do exactly what the head of procurement asked us to do, by running the statement in the following listing.

Listing 4.8 Amending a purchase order

```
UPDATE dbo.PurchaseOrderDetails
SET PurchaseOrderNumber = 6828
WHERE PurchaseOrderNumber = 6827 ;
```

This would not have been possible if a foreign key constraint was used.

Unfortunately, what the head of procurement really wanted us to do was "Create a new purchase order, with a purchase order number of 6828, transfer the ordered items across, and then delete purchase order 6827."

So now we are in a situation where our data is in an inconsistent state. If we were to run a query, such as the query in listing 4.9, which returns details of purchase orders from across the two tables, then neither purchase order 6827 nor purchase order 6828 would be returned.

If we had created a foreign key constraint, then this would not have been possible because referential integrity would have been enforced, and we would not have been able to update the `PurchaseOrderNumber` to a value that did not exist in the `PurchaseOrderHeaders` table.

Listing 4.9 Returning purchase order information

```
SELECT
      poh.PurchaseOrderNumber
    , poh.PurchaseOrderDate
    , pod.ProductID
    , pod.Quantity
FROM dbo.PurchaseOrderHeaders poh
INNER JOIN dbo.PurchaseOrderDetails pod
    ON poh.PurchaseOrderNumber = pod.PurchaseOrderNumber ;
```

To avoid this pitfall, ensure that you always use foreign key constraints. We can fix the mistake in the MagicChoc database by running the script in listing 4.10. Before creating the constraint, we fix the data values; otherwise, the constraint creation would fail.

Listing 4.10 Adding a foreign key constraint

```
UPDATE dbo.PurchaseOrderDetails
SET PurchaseOrderNumber = 6827
WHERE PurchaseOrderNumber = 6828 ;

ALTER TABLE dbo.PurchaseOrderDetails ADD CONSTRAINT
    FK_PurchaseOrderDetails_PurchaseOrderHeaders
        FOREIGN KEY (PurchaseOrderNumber)
            REFERENCES dbo.PurchaseOrderHeaders(PurchaseOrderNumber) ;
```

When tables have relationships with each other, it is always good practice to create primary and foreign key relationships between them. Even if logic is built into the application to avoid inconsistent data, this logic will not be able to deal with mistakes that happen outside the application.

Summary

- Always normalize your data, rather than trying to design your schema using judgment, to avoid mistakes.
- Where appropriate, consider using data generalization to create supertypes and subtypes, as this can enhance your database design.
- Use an ERD to help validate, as well as to document your design. This diagram will visualize the entities with their attributes, as well as their primary and foreign keys, with the relationships between them.
- Avoid using wide columns or multiple columns as a primary key, as the primary key will often become the clustered index and thus will be replicated in your nonclustered indexes and can lead to performance degradation.
- Always use a foreign key constraint, where tables are related to each other, to avoid data consistency issues.

5 T-SQL development

This chapter covers

- Mistakes that can cause unexpected results
- Mistakes that can lead to performance problems
- Avoiding looping with cursors in T-SQL
- Deleting large numbers of rows

SQL is an ANSI and ISO standard language that allows database developers to interrogate and manipulate data within a relational database. T-SQL is SQL Server's dialect of the SQL language and is used to interact with SQL Server instances and the databases hosted within.

In chapter 4, we designed and created the tables for a new MagicChoc database. In this chapter, we will explore some of the common mistakes that can be made in T-SQL by developers who are less experienced with the language. For examples of T-SQL development, we will look to MagicChoc, which wants us to develop the logic that will be used by its frontend applications. We will use this as an opportunity to start exploring some of the common mistakes that can be made in T-SQL by developers who are less experienced with the language.

Getting to grips with SQL can be a challenge for developers who are more familiar with writing application code, using languages such as C# or Visual Basic, because of the large conceptual difference between how the languages work. For example, looping in .NET languages is perfectly acceptable, but in the set-based world of SQL, it can cause serious performance problems.

Most development mistakes in T-SQL cause performance issues, and that will be the main focus of this chapter. The first two sections, however, will focus on mistakes leading to unexpected results. Finally, we will look at a common mistake that is made when deleting large numbers of rows.

5.1 #14 Dealing incorrectly with NULL values

MagicChoc has asked us to look at the data and confirm how many product subcategories do not have a description. Therefore, we run the query in the following listing.

Listing 5.1 Incorrectly counting `NULL` values

```
SELECT COUNT(*)
FROM dbo.ProductSubcategories
WHERE ProductSubcategoryDescription = NULL ;
```

`0` is returned as the result. Fantastic. Every product subcategory has a description, right? We know there are 16 subcategories in total, so let's just double-check our result by flipping the query to count the number of rows where the description isn't `NULL`, using the query in the following listing.

Listing 5.2 Incorrectly counting non-`NULL` values

```
SELECT COUNT(*)
FROM dbo.ProductSubcategories
WHERE ProductSubcategoryDescription <> NULL ;
```

Wait a minute! This query is returning `0` as the result as well. What is going on here? What developers new to SQL sometimes don't realize is that a `NULL` is an unknown value. Therefore, in comparison, a `NULL` is not equal to another `NULL`.

To understand this, think about the following analogy. How many stars are there in our galaxy? Personally, I do not know the answer to this. How many grains of sand are there in the world? Again, I personally have no idea. Does that mean that the number of stars in the galaxy is equal to the number of grains of sand in the world? No, of course, it doesn't. It might be; it might not be. I have no idea. Therefore, just as I cannot say that two values that I don't know are the same or different, SQL Server cannot tell us if two values it does not know are the same or different.

To deal with this problem, we just need to tweak our syntax when dealing with `NULL` values to use `IS` or `IS NOT` instead of `=` and `<>`. For example, the script in the following listing successfully returns a count of product subcategories that do not have a description, followed by a count of product subcategories that do have a description.

Listing 5.3 Successfully returning a count of NULL and non-NULL values

```
SELECT COUNT(*)
FROM dbo.ProductSubcategories
WHERE ProductSubcategoryDescription IS NULL ;

SELECT COUNT(*)
FROM dbo.ProductSubcategories
WHERE ProductSubcategoryDescription IS NOT NULL ;
```

Another aspect of dealing with `NULL` values that can confuse people who are new to SQL is the use of `IS NULL` versus the `ISNULL()` function. As we have just seen, `IS NULL` is used in a `WHERE` clause to filter a result set so that it returns only rows where the column contains `NULL` values.

The `ISNULL()` function, on the other hand, is used in a `SELECT` list, `JOIN` clause, or the `SET` clause of an `UPDATE` statement to replace a `NULL` value with a value that is not `NULL`. For example, the query in the following listing will return a complete list of product subcategories, but descriptions that are `NULL` will be replaced with the value `No description available`.

Listing 5.4 Using the ISNULL() function to replace a NULL value

```
SELECT
      ProductSubcategoryName
    , ISNULL(ProductSubcategoryDescription, 'No description available')
FROM dbo.ProductSubcategories ;
```

Always take care when dealing with `NULL` values. Remember that a `NULL` value is not equal to another `NULL` value. Also remember that the `IS NULL` syntax is used to filter a query to return `NULL` values, while the `ISNULL()` function is used to replace a `NULL` value with a non-`NULL` value.

5.2 #15 Using NOLOCK as a performance tweak

MagicChoc's sales application has a drop-down box filled with addresses related to a customer, which allows the salesperson to select the delivery address they want an order to be shipped to. When the delivery address screen loads, however, the drop-down list is slow to populate, and we have been asked to improve the performance of the query.

We have heard that locking and blocking can cause performance issues in SQL Server, and someone has mentioned that there is a query hint, called `NOLOCK`, which can improve performance. We therefore amend the query that populates the delivery address drop-down, so that it reads as per the following listing.

Listing 5.5 Adding the NOLOCK query hint

```
DECLARE @CustomerID INT ;
SET @CustomerID = 2 ;
```

```
SELECT
      Street
    , Area
    , City
    , ZipCode
FROM dbo.Addresses a WITH(NOLOCK)
INNER JOIN dbo.Customers c
    ON a.AddressID = c.DeliveryAddressID
WHERE CustomerID = @CustomerID ;
```

Everything is fine for a while, but one day, an order is delivered to an incorrect address, and we are asked to investigate how this could have happened.

Imagine the following scenario. A salesperson is processing an order for Cooking Schmooking. At the same time, an administrator is speaking to another member of the Cooking Schmooking team about updating various details, including a change of address. The administrator realizes that they have input the incorrect address and cancels the customer update before it completes. The administrator then continues on to input the correct address. Let's examine the exact sequence of events in figure 5.1.

SQL Server uses locking to make sure that a transaction cannot read data that is currently being modified by a different transaction. By using the `NOLOCK` query hint, we have prevented our `SELECT` statement from taking out any locks. The result is that the salesperson reads the address from the table while the transaction performing the update is in flight. The transaction that was performing the update is then rolled back. This results in the salesperson reading a delivery address that was never actually committed and, therefore, never really existed in the database.

There are many ways to optimize SQL Server performance, and tuning locking through the use of transaction isolation levels, which affect how locks are maintained, is one option. We will be discussing this in chapter 10. I would always recommend, however, avoiding the use of `NOLOCK` against a query, as it is an opaque optimization that usually adds more risk than reward.

5.3 #16 Using SELECT * as standard

Let's now take a look at mistakes that can lead to performance issues. Let's start by considering a scenario where we are developing a procedure that returns information regarding sales areas. We can't remember the columns in the table, or what the data looks like; therefore, we run the following ad hoc query:

```
SELECT *
FROM SalesAreas
```

A colleague then asks us, "Do we store best-before dates for products?" We are not sure, so we run the following ad hoc query, so that we can answer our colleague:

```
SELECT *
FROM Products
```

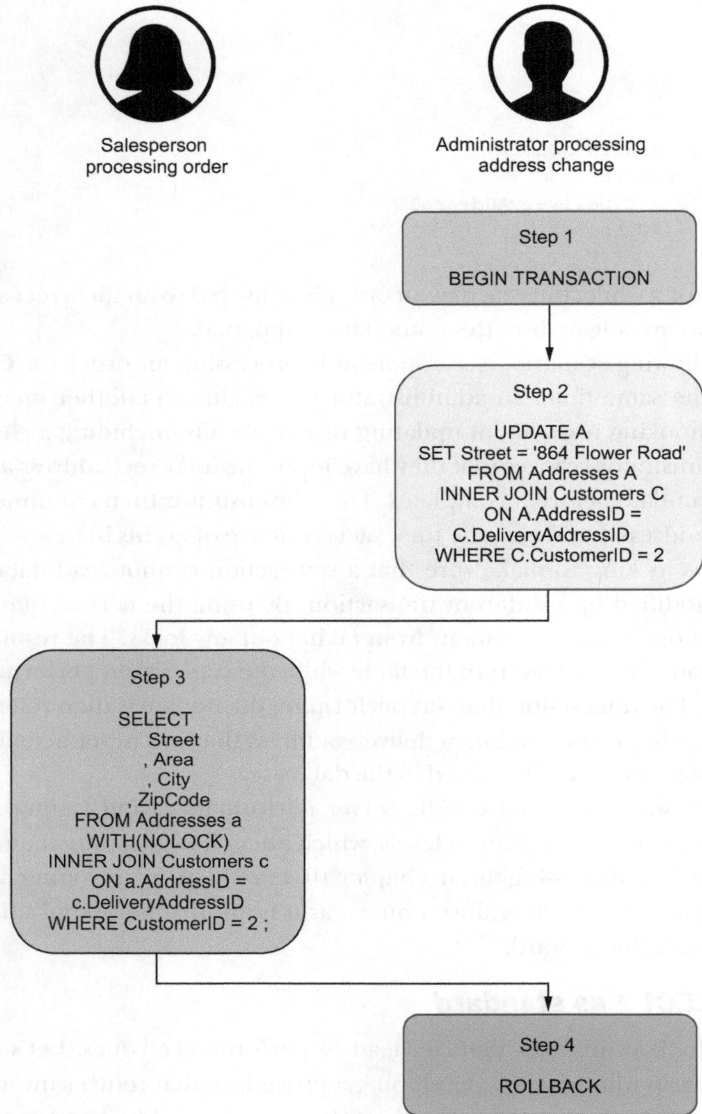

Figure 5.1 Sequence of events

Both of these examples are a perfectly valid usage of `SELECT *`. The mistake that I want to discuss is when developers use `SELECT *` in code that they plan to release and maintain.

Let's imagine that our application is going to perform some analysis on how long orders take to be delivered and how many of them are late. To meet this requirement, we need to return the following columns to the frontend application:

- SalesOrderDate
- SalesOrderDeliveryDueDate
- SalesOrderDeliveryActualDate

Instead of selecting these three specific columns, however, we decide to use SELECT *. There are three reasons why this practice is a mistake: performance, code maintenance, and code readability. Let's first discuss performance.

There are two aspects of performance that we should consider when we think of SELECT *. The first is sending data to the application tier. In this case, our application needs us to send it three columns, totaling 9 bytes. If we were to send all columns to the application, then the size per row would be up to 61 bytes per row. That is an extra 51 bytes per row. Imagine that there are 2.5 million sales orders in the table. That's an extra 121MB of data that we are sending across the network for no reason.

Now imagine that we used the same technique for a table that had several NVARCHAR (MAX) columns, which can store up to 2 GB each. What if multiple users were running the same query at the same time? You can see how this can easily become an issue.

The second aspect of performance we should consider relates to indexes. To explain this problem, let's imagine that the exact requirement is to return the three columns, filtered by SalesOrderDate. To satisfy this query in the most efficient way, we could create what is known as a *covering index*—that is, an index that includes all columns that we want to return.

For example, listing 5.6 creates an index built on the SalesOrderDate column but then includes the SalesOrderDeliveryDueDate and SalesOrderDeliveryActualDate. When you use the INCLUDE syntax, SQL Server generates the index on the main column(s) but then includes the values of the included columns at the leaf level. This is especially useful for covering queries, where you need to filter or join on a given column but then also wish to return a small set of other columns in the results. This is because it minimizes the size of the index while avoiding a lookup operation to the clustered index to retrieve the other columns.

Listing 5.6 Creating a covering index

```
CREATE NONCLUSTERED INDEX [OrderDate-Including-DueDate-ActualDate]
    ON dbo.SalesOrderHeaders (SalesOrderDate)
INCLUDE(SalesOrderDeliveryDueDate,SalesOrderDeliveryActualDate) ;
```

Unfortunately, if you use SELECT *, then indexes like this will almost certainly not be used, as they do not include all the columns that you are returning. It would, of course, be possible to include every column in the table, but this would make a very wide, inefficient index. Then, if we were to add another column to the table, the index would stop working unless we remembered to update the index definition as well.

That brings us nicely to the second problem with the SELECT * approach, which is code maintenance. Imagine an application that acts as a middleware layer. It pulls order dates from the SalesOrderHeaders table using a query such as

```
SELECT *
FROM dbo.SalesOrderHeaders
WHERE SalesOrderDate = '20230616' ;
```

The data is then passed into a stored procedure on another instance, which performs the analytics. Because we are passing all columns from the table, the table type on the analytics instance is created as follows:

```
CREATE TYPE SalesOrdersForAnalysis AS TABLE
(
   SalesOrderNumber               NCHAR(12)          NOT NULL,
   SalesOrderDate                 DATE               NOT NULL,
   SalesPersonID                  INT                NOT NULL,
   SalesAreaID                    INT                NOT NULL,
   CustomerID                     INT                NOT NULL,
   SalesOrderDeliveryDueDate      DATE               NOT NULL,
   SalesOrderDeliveryActualDate   DATE               NULL,
   CurrierUsedforDelivery         NVARCHAR(32)       NOT NULL
) ;
```

The stored procedure is then declared in the following way:

```
CREATE PROCEDURE dbo.AsyncAnalysis
   @DatesForAnalysis SalesOrdersForAnalysis READONLY
AS
BEGIN
   SELECT *
   FROM @DatesForAnalysis ;

   --Analysis logic here...
END
```

In this scenario, if we add a column to the `SalesOrderHeaders` table, we will need to then perform the following steps:

1 Drop the `AsyncAnalysis` stored procedure, because it depends on the `Sales-OrdersForAnalysis` type.
2 Drop the `SalesOrderForAnalysis` type.
3 Recreate the `SalesOrderForAnalysis` type.
4 Recreate the `AsyncAnalysis` stored procedure.

In short, the code update would have been far simpler if we had just used the columns that we needed, as opposed to all columns in the table. There have been multiple times in my career where I have come across problems like this, and it exponentially increases the time it takes to perform a simple change.

The final reason why we should avoid the `SELECT *` approach relates to code readability. In chapter 2, we discussed the benefits of having self-documenting code. Using `SELECT *` breaks the self-documenting code model and makes your code more opaque and harder for you and other developers to maintain in the future, as what you are trying to achieve is less obvious.

I recommend always avoiding `SELECT *` in code that you need to release and maintain. It can have a negative impact on performance due to increasing network load and forcing the use of less efficient index operations to retrieve the data. It makes your code harder to maintain in cases where there are downstream dependencies. It also makes your code harder to read and breaks the self-documentation model.

5.4 #17 Unnecessarily ordering data

We have been asked to perform some reporting against our customer contacts, and we have decided that the data might be more useful if we order it by email addresses. Before we examine this, however, let's generate some data for the `CustomerContacts` table, using the script in the following listing, which will generate 3.2 million rows of data.

Listing 5.7 Generating data for the `CustomerContacts` table

```
DECLARE @FirstName TABLE (FirstName NVARCHAR(32)) ;

DECLARE @LastName TABLE (LastName NVARCHAR(32)) ;

DECLARE @domain TABLE (Domain NVARCHAR(250)) ;

DECLARE @topleveldomain TABLE (TLD NVARCHAR(6)) ;

DECLARE @email TABLE (Email NVARCHAR(256)) ;

INSERT INTO @FirstName
VALUES
    ('Rachel'),
    ('Seth'),
    ('Tony'),
    ('Angel'),
    ('Isabell'),
    ('Robert'),
    ('Adelaide'),
    ('Jessie'),
    ('Paxton'),
    ('London'),
    ('Jadyn'),
    ('Corey'),
    ('Maximo'),
    ('Johan'),
    ('Mariah'),
    ('Raven'),
    ('Hamza'),
    ('Cristofer'),
    ('Molly'),
    ('Malcolm') ;

INSERT INTO @LastName
VALUES
```

```
        ('Hill'),
        ('Acosta'),
        ('Oconnell'),
        ('Jefferson'),
        ('Cross'),
        ('Patel'),
        ('House'),
        ('Price'),
        ('Morales'),
        ('Reeves'),
        ('Rice'),
        ('Drake'),
        ('Briggs'),
        ('Henry'),
        ('Aguilar'),
        ('Holloway'),
        ('Burnett'),
        ('Aguilar'),
        ('Simon'),
        ('Barry') ;

INSERT INTO @domain
SELECT
    CONCAT(FirstName, LastName)
FROM @FirstName
CROSS JOIN @LastName ;

 INSERT INTO @topleveldomain
 VALUES
        ('.net'),
        ('.com'),
        ('.co.uk'),
        ('.eu'),
        ('.ru'),
        ('.edu'),
        ('.gov'),
        ('.ninja'),
        ('.io'),
        ('.co'),
        ('.ai'),
        ('.ca'),
        ('.me'),
        ('.de'),
        ('.fr'),
        ('.ac'),
        ('.am'),
        ('.ax'),
        ('.ba'),
        ('.ch') ;

INSERT INTO @email
SELECT
    CONCAT(Domain, TLD)
FROM @domain
CROSS JOIN @topleveldomain ;
```

```
INSERT INTO dbo.CustomerContacts(
    CustomerContactFirstName,
    CustomerContactLastName,
    CustomerContactEmail
)
SELECT
      FirstName
    , LastName
    , Email
FROM @FirstName
CROSS JOIN @LastName
CROSS JOIN @email ;
```

Now that we have some data, let's meet our brief and write a query that returns the `CustomerContactFirstName`, `CustomerContactLastName`, and `CustomerContactEmail` columns from the `CustomerContacts` table. Before running this query, the script in the following listing runs the command `SET STATISTICS TIME ON`, which will return execution time statistics in the messages window of SSMS.

Listing 5.8 Returning required data from the `CustomerContacts` table

```
SET STATISTICS TIME ON ;

SELECT
      CustomerContactFirstName
    , CustomerContactLastName
    , CustomerContactEmail
FROM dbo.CustomerContacts ;
```

On my test rig, that query took 20,679 ms to run. So now let's try that again, but this time we will order the data by `CustomerContactEmailAddress`, as shown in the following listing.

Listing 5.9 Returning data from `CustomerContacts` ordered by email

```
SET STATISTICS TIME ON ;

SELECT
      CustomerContactFirstName
    , CustomerContactLastName
    , CustomerContactEmail
FROM dbo.CustomerContacts
ORDER BY CustomerContactEmail ;
```

> **TIP** If you are following along with measuring performance, it is important to note that your mileage may vary depending on the performance of your hardware, as well as other processes that may be running. I also advise against capturing execution plans at the same time as testing performance, as this will affect the result of the time collection.

On the same test rig, this query took 27,415 ms to execute. That is 25% slower than the unordered version of the query. The reason for this is that relational databases are built on the branch of mathematics known as *set theory*, where we consider a *set*, which is a distinct group of objects, and a *bag (or multiset)*, which is a collection of objects that may contain duplicates. In both mathematical concepts, the order of the results is unimportant. Therefore, ordering data is not a set-based operation. Instead, it is a presentational operation only. Therefore, you should order data only if you really need to.

We can see this represented in the relative cost of the sort operation if we look at the execution plan, which is the steps, or operators, that the query optimizer has decided to take to satisfy the query. You can access execution plans in multiple ways, including via Query Store, which we will discuss in chapter 10, or metadata, which we will also discuss in chapter 10, or simply by pressing the "Include Actual Execution Plan" button on the toolbar in SQL Server Management Studio prior to executing the query.

The execution plan generated for the query in listing 5.9 is illustrated in figure 5.2. You will notice that the sort operation is 91% of the estimated cost of the query.

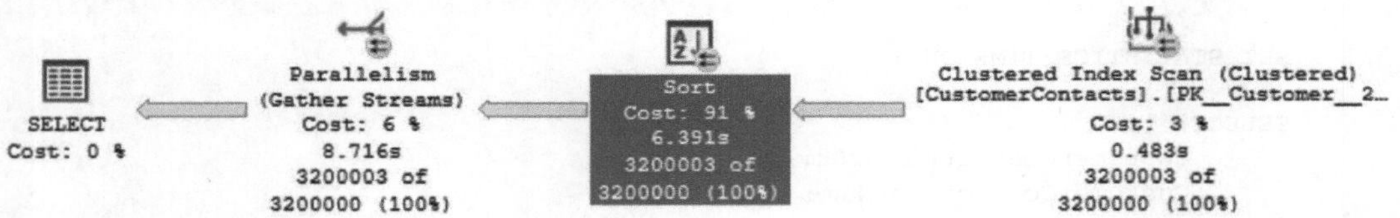

Figure 5.2 Execution plan sort operation cost

> **Execution plan of sort operation cost**
>
> In the context of an execution plan, there are a couple of things to bear in mind. First, cost is estimated when the query is compiled, and SQL Server does not update the costs post-execution. Therefore, even when displaying the actual execution plan (as opposed to the estimated execution plan—which can be viewed prior to query execution)—you will see estimated costs. These costs can be incorrect due to factors such as inaccurate statistics.
>
> Second, cost is not a direct measurement of performance. It is a weighted value, calculated based on a proprietary algorithm that estimates a relative cost for processor and IO and then sums these values to derive a total cost for the operator, known as a *subtree cost*.

If a situation arises where you simply must order your data for presentational reasons, then using indexes can help. For this query, the ideal index to cover the query would be built on `CustomerContactEmail` as the index key and include the `CustomerContactFirstName` and `CustomerContactLastName` columns at leaf level. This index, which can be created using the command in listing 5.10, is ordered by the `CustomerContactEmail` column, so no sort operation is required. Because the other required columns are included at the leaf level, there is not even any need to perform a lookup operation to the clustered index.

Listing 5.10 Creating a covering index to improve performance

```
CREATE NONCLUSTERED INDEX
    [NI-CustomerContactEmail-Include-FirstName-LastName]
        ON dbo.CustomerContacts(CustomerContactEmail)
        INCLUDE(CustomerContactFirstName, CustomerContactLastName) ;
```

Now that we have a covering index, let's run the query in listing 5.9 again and see what that does to the execution plan, which is illustrated in figure 5.3, and also the execution time. You can see that, this time, the optimizer has chosen to perform a nonclustered index scan, and on my test rig, the query took 20,904 ms to execute, which is roughly the same as the original, unordered query.

Figure 5.3 Execution plan using a nonclustered index scan

While creating the index has worked well for this specific query, we need to remember that nothing is ever free. Although the index has resolved the performance of the query that has ordered the data by email address, the existence of the index will decrease the performance of `INSERT`, `UPDATE`, and `DELETE` operations made against the table, as SQL Server will need to also update the nonclustered index.

Therefore, it is always better to avoid ordering data unless absolutely necessary, as performance will decrease. If you do have to order data, for presentation reasons, consider your index strategy, but bear in mind that this will have an impact on the performance of write operations to the table.

5.5 #18 Using DISTINCT without good reason

We have been asked to return a list of unique suppliers. I have seen less experienced developers use the `DISTINCT` keyword, just to make sure that the results are unique. To examine this, we could achieve the same results using either of the queries in listing 5.11. Because (unless we have a serious data quality issue) the same supplier will not be listed twice in our table, the use of the `DISTINCT` keyword is redundant.

Listing 5.11 Return suppliers with and without using DISTINCT

```
SELECT SupplierName
FROM dbo.Suppliers ;

SELECT DISTINCT SupplierName
FROM dbo.Suppliers ;
```

Even though we don't need the `DISTINCT` keyword, does it make any difference if we use it? To answer that, let's examine the execution plan in figure 5.4. If both queries had the same cost, then they would each have a query cost, relative to batch, of 50%. In this case, however, you can see that the query with the `DISTINCT` keyword has a relative cost of 82%, meaning it was far less efficient. You can see this reflected in the Distinct Sort operator.

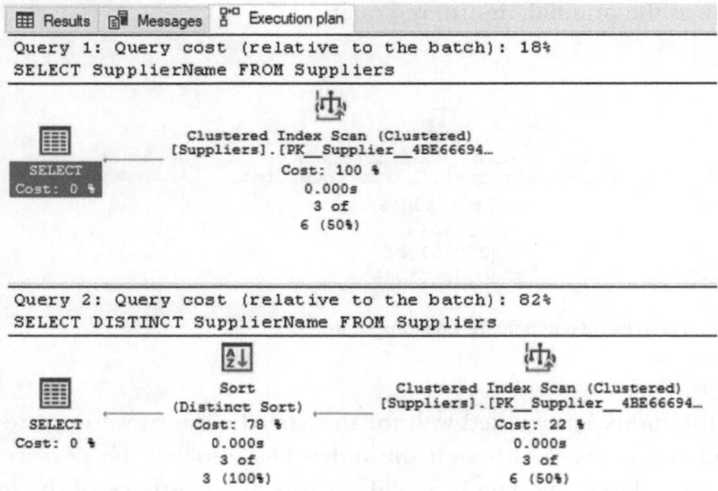

Figure 5.4 Execution plans with and without DISTINCT

There may be some occasions where we simply must uniquify our results. For example, imagine that we have been asked to return a unique list of the suppliers from which MagicChoc purchased large head sprockets in June 2023. We could return the list of suppliers using the query in the following listing.

Listing 5.12 Returning a list of suppliers of large head sprockets

```
SELECT DISTINCT s.SupplierName
FROM dbo.Suppliers s
INNER JOIN dbo.PurchaseOrderHeaders poh
    ON poh.SupplierID = s.SupplierID
```

```
INNER JOIN dbo.PurchaseOrderDetails pod
    ON pod.PurchaseOrderNumber = poh.PurchaseOrderNumber
WHERE MONTH(poh.PurchaseOrderDate) = 6
    AND YEAR(poh.PurchaseOrderDate) = 2023
AND pod.ProductID = 4 ;
```

The trouble is that, because we have purchased the item twice from Unknown Engineering within this time period, this query returns two results for the Supplier. We could, of course, use the `DISTINCT` keyword, but we know that it will degrade performance. Are there any other options?

The three queries in listing 5.13 are all functionally equivalent. The first query uses the `DISTINCT` keyword to uniquify the results, the second uses the `GROUP BY` clause, and the third uses the `ROW_NUMBER()` windowing function.

Listing 5.13 Using the `DISTINCT` key word

```
SELECT DISTINCT s.SupplierName
FROM dbo.Suppliers s
INNER JOIN dbo.PurchaseOrderHeaders poh
    ON poh.SupplierID = s.SupplierID
INNER JOIN dbo.PurchaseOrderDetails pod
    ON pod.PurchaseOrderNumber = poh.PurchaseOrderNumber
WHERE MONTH(poh.PurchaseOrderDate) = 6
    AND YEAR(poh.PurchaseOrderDate) = 2023
AND pod.ProductID = 4 ;

SELECT s.SupplierName
FROM dbo.Suppliers s
INNER JOIN dbo.PurchaseOrderHeaders poh
    ON poh.SupplierID = s.SupplierID
INNER JOIN dbo.PurchaseOrderDetails pod
    ON pod.PurchaseOrderNumber = poh.PurchaseOrderNumber
WHERE MONTH(poh.PurchaseOrderDate) = 6
    AND YEAR(poh.PurchaseOrderDate) = 2023
AND pod.ProductID = 4
GROUP BY s.SupplierName ;

SELECT SupplierName FROM (
    SELECT s.SupplierName, ROW_NUMBER() OVER(ORDER BY s.SupplierName) AS rn
    FROM dbo.Suppliers s
    INNER JOIN dbo.PurchaseOrderHeaders poh
        ON poh.SupplierID = s.SupplierID
    INNER JOIN dbo.PurchaseOrderDetails pod
        ON pod.PurchaseOrderNumber = poh.PurchaseOrderNumber
    WHERE MONTH(poh.PurchaseOrderDate) = 6
        AND YEAR(poh.PurchaseOrderDate) = 2023
    AND pod.ProductID = 4
) a WHERE rn = 1 ;
```

In our specific case, because the number of rows in question is tiny and because my test rig is not under load, there was no performance difference between the three, and the versions with `DISTINCT` and `GROUP BY` both generated the same execution plan.

In a production environment, however, with complex queries and large amounts of data, you may find that you have three entirely different plans and that some are significantly more efficient than others. Therefore, if you find that you have a performance issue using the `DISTINCT` keyword, it is worth trying the other two approaches to see if you can improve performance.

> **TIP** I could make the `ROW_NUMBER()` query outperform the `DISTINCT` and `GROUP BY` queries in the preceding example simply by loading more data into the table. This example demonstrates, however, the importance of performance testing based on realistic data. We will explore this further in chapter 7.

We should never use `DISTINCT` for its own sake. If there is a genuine requirement to uniquify the results of a query, however, and if you experience performance issues when using `DISTINCT`, then you can explore other approaches to improve performance. If `DISTINCT` is really required and there are no performance issues observed, then I would recommend sticking with this approach, as it is the least opaque of the three options. It is immediately apparent what you are doing, and that helps make the code self-documenting.

> **TIP** A genuine need to use `DISTINCT` may be because of an underlying issue with the database schema. Please see chapter 4 for more details.

5.6 #19 Using UNION unnecessarily

Just like unnecessarily ordering data and unnecessarily removing duplicates, developers who are new to SQL Server also make a similar mistake with the `UNION` clause. A union is a way of horizontally joining two sets of results, and there are two different ways to produce this union. Specifically, you can use a `UNION` clause or a `UNION ALL` clause.

The difference between `UNION` and `UNION ALL` is that `UNION ALL` will return all results from both queries. `UNION`, however, will remove duplicate results. For example, imagine that we have been asked to compile a list of MagicChoc's contacts from both the `CustomerContacts` table and the `SupplierContacts` table. The first query in listing 5.14 uses `UNION` to create a distinct list of contacts. The second query uses `UNION ALL` to create a list that may include duplicates.

> **TIP** There are additional horizontal join operators called `INTERSECT` and `EXCEPT`. `INTERSECT` will return the results from query 1, which also appear in the results from query 2. `EXCEPT` will return the results from query 1 that are not present in query 2.

Listing 5.14 Creating contacts lists with and without duplicates

```
SELECT SupplierContactFirstName, SupplierContactLastName
FROM dbo.SupplierContacts
UNION
SELECT CustomerContactFirstName, CustomerContactLastName
```

```
FROM dbo.CustomerContacts ;

SELECT SupplierContactFirstName, SupplierContactLastName
FROM dbo.SupplierContacts
UNION ALL
SELECT CustomerContactFirstName, CustomerContactLastName
FROM dbo.CustomerContacts ;
```

We can see from the execution plans in figure 5.5 that the cost of deduplicating the list was significantly higher, so it would be worth checking the requirement. Do we really need to deduplicate the list? If we don't, then we should not deduplicate just for the sake of it.

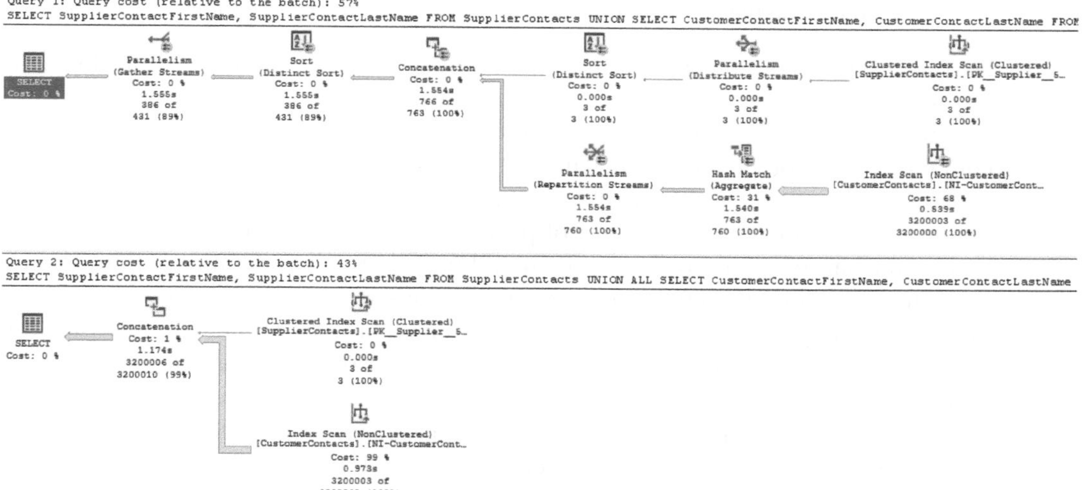

Figure 5.5 Execution plans for horizontal joins

There will be times where we need to use `UNION`, but we should only use it when there is a genuine requirement to do so. If duplicates are unimportant, or cannot occur because of business logic, then use `UNION ALL` instead.

5.7 #20 Using cursors

The head of procurement at MagicChoc would like us to produce a report that shows how many products we have in stock grouped by each product category. Rather than in a vertical format, however, we must produce the reports in a horizontal format, where the column names are the product categories, with a single row detailing the quantity of products in stock relating to each category.

The mistake that a lot of developers make at this point is to use a cursor. A cursor is a mechanism within T-SQL for looping over a set of rows, processing them one row at a time. Cursors can be used for many purposes, including pivoting data and generating and executing dynamic T-SQL scripts such as running a command against every table. They can also be used to find a value within any column of a table or to rank data.

The problem is that cursors are a dreadfully inefficient way to process relational data. Each iteration of a cursor has the same overhead as running the command in a standalone manner. For example, if you have a cursor that iterates through 1 million rows, it would have the same overhead as running 1 million statements against the table. Furthermore, the language enhancements to T-SQL over the past 25 years have nullified any requirement to use cursors. I cannot think of a single situation where a cursor is required to achieve the desired outcome, and you will most likely (at least hopefully) have a coding standard in place that disallows you from using cursors anyway.

> **TIP** Even DBAs who formerly used cursors to iterate over a number of objects within a database have no reason to do so. We will discuss this more in chapter 9.

So, moving back to our scenario, if we went ahead and used a cursor to produce our pivoted report, we could use a script like the one in listing 5.15. The script first creates a temporary table with the final structure of our report. We then insert a holding row containing zero for each column. This will give us the base that we can update. When declaring our variable, we also declare a cursor to include the full result set that we will iterate. In our scenario, that is a list of product categories and quantities in a vertical tabular format. We then open our cursor and use a `FETCH` statement to pull in the first row. The `WHILE` loop then tells our cursor the actions we want to perform—in our case, updating the appropriate column in the temporary table based on the values inside the cursor. At the end of the `WHILE` loop, we pull the next row into the cursor. The `WHILE` loop exits when `@@FETCH_STATUS = 0`. This system variable lets us know when there are no rows left to fetch. Finally, we simply run a select statement from the temporary table before cleaning up the temporary objects so they don't clutter the memory.

Listing 5.15 Using a cursor to pivot data

```
CREATE TABLE #Categories (
    [Raw Ingredients]                       INT,
    [Machine Parts]                         INT,
    [Misc]                                  INT,
    [Confectionary Products]                INT,
    [Non-confectionary Products]            INT
  ) ;

INSERT INTO #Categories
VALUES (0,0,0,0,0) ;

DECLARE @Category as varchar(32) ;
DECLARE @Stock as varchar(32) ;

DECLARE product_cursor CURSOR FOR
SELECT
      pc.ProductCategoryName
```

```
    , SUM(ISNULL(p.ProductStockLevel,0)) Stock
FROM dbo.ProductCategories pc
INNER JOIN dbo.ProductSubcategories ps
    ON pc.ProductCategoryID = ps.ProductCategoryID
LEFT JOIN dbo.Products p
    ON ps.ProductSubcategoryID = p.ProductSubcategoryID
GROUP BY ProductCategoryName ;

OPEN product_cursor  ;

FETCH NEXT FROM product_cursor INTO @Category, @Stock  ;

WHILE @@FETCH_STATUS = 0
BEGIN
    IF @Category = 'Raw Ingredients'
        UPDATE #Categories
        SET [Raw Ingredients] =
            [Raw Ingredients] + @Stock
    ELSE IF @Category = 'Machine Parts'
        UPDATE #Categories
        SET [Machine Parts] =
            [Machine Parts] + @Stock
    ELSE IF @Category = 'Misc'
        UPDATE #Categories
        SET [Misc] = [Misc] + @Stock
    ELSE IF @Category = 'Confectionary Products'
        UPDATE #Categories
        SET [Confectionary Products] =
            [Confectionary Products] + @Stock
    ELSE IF @Category = 'Non-confectionary Products'
        UPDATE #Categories
        SET [Non-confectionary Products] =
            [Non-confectionary Products] + @Stock ;

    FETCH NEXT FROM product_cursor INTO @Category, @Stock  ;
END

SELECT
      [Raw Ingredients]
    , [Machine Parts], [Misc]
    , [Confectionary Products]
    , [Non-confectionary Products]
FROM #Categories ;

CLOSE product_cursor ;

DEALLOCATE product_cursor ;

DROP TABLE #Categories ;
```

Instead of using a costly cursor, we could have used the `PIVOT` operator. This operator will do the hard work for us and do it as a set-based operation, which will be far more efficient than a cursor.

Real-world example

About 10 years ago, I was working with one of the world's largest advertising companies, which worked with very large datasets that were harvested from search engines and cookie service providers. They asked me to look at a performance problem they had on an ETL job that pivoted a large dataset.

Their original implementation used a cursor. I rewrote the process to use a `PIVOT` statement instead of a cursor. Doing so reduced the execution time from over 3 hours to 48 seconds!

The single query in listing 5.16 achieves the same result as the cursor. The outer query specifies the columns that we want to return from the query. Here we can use `*`, or we can specify a column list. If we use a column list, then there is no obligation to select all the pivoted columns. The subquery pulls a flat list of categories and stock levels. Finally, the `PIVOT` operator defines the final result set by specifying the aggregation that we want to use against the stock column and the values within the `ProductCategoryName` column that we want as our pivoted columns.

Listing 5.16 Pivoting data using the `PIVOT` operator

```
SELECT
      [Raw Ingredients]
    , [Machine Parts]
    , [Misc]
    , [Confectionary Products]
    , [Non-confectionary Products]
FROM (
    SELECT
          pc.ProductCategoryName
        , ISNULL(p.ProductStockLevel,0) Stock
    FROM dbo.ProductCategories pc
    INNER JOIN dbo.ProductSubcategories ps
        ON pc.ProductCategoryID = ps.ProductCategoryID
    LEFT JOIN dbo.Products p
        ON ps.ProductSubcategoryID = p.ProductSubcategoryID
) AS WorkingTable
PIVOT
(
    SUM(Stock)
    FOR ProductCategoryName IN (
        [Raw Ingredients],
        [Machine Parts],
        [Misc],
        [Confectionary Products],
        [Non-confectionary Products]
    )
) AS PivotTable ;
```

To demonstrate the difference in query cost, we can copy the `PIVOT` query into the same query window as our cursor operation. If we then look at the execution plan for this statement, we can see that it is only 9% of the cost of the whole batch, meaning that the combined total cost of the statements we had to execute for the cursor-based approach was estimated as more than 10× less efficient than using the PIVOT operator. The relevant section of the execution plan is shown in figure 5.6.

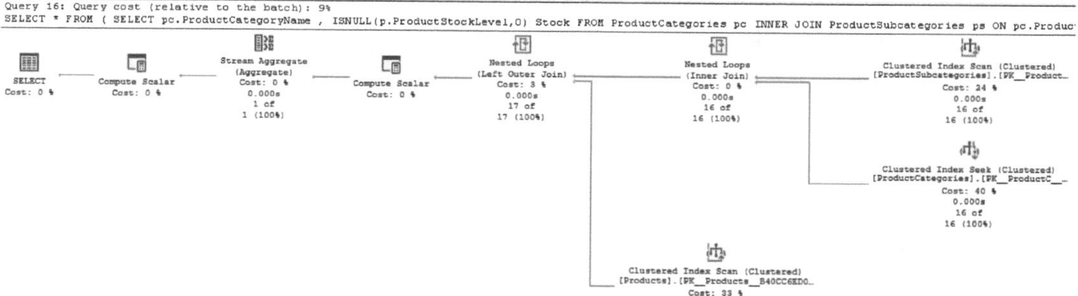

Figure 5.6 Relative cost of a query using PIVOT against an equivalent cursor

5.8 #21 Deleting many rows in a single transaction

It is not uncommon for SQL developers to be asked to remove old data from tables. This is often followed by a database shrink operation, which will reclaim space. We will be discussing database shrink operations again in chapters 9 and 11.

The most efficient way to remove a large amount of data from a table is to use a command called TRUNCATE TABLE. This command removes data from a table while leaving the table structure intact by deallocating data pages. The trouble here is that there is no WHERE clause with a truncate operation. It's all or nothing, or in other words, you have to remove every single row.

Even if you do wish to remove every single row from a table, there are other limitations with table truncation. For example, you cannot perform the operation if a column in the table is referenced by a foreign key constraint or *edge constraints*, which enforce semantics and ensure the integrity of *edge tables*, which represent relationships within a graph database. Additionally, truncation cannot be used if the table is a base table within an index view, participates in either transactional or merge replication, or is a *system-versioned temporal table*, which is a table used to track the full data change history of another table to allow for point-in-time analysis.

These limitations often leave developers having to use DELETE statements to remove large quantities of rows from tables. The mistake I have seen here, many times, is that developers will try to delete all rows from a table in a single transaction. For example, consider a table that has many millions (or even billions) of rows.

The script in listing 5.17 creates a table and populates it with a very large number of rows. The number of rows it creates will vary depending on the tables and columns within your database, but on my test rig, it will generate just under 3.5 billion rows.

WARNING This script will take a long time to run.

Listing 5.17 Creating a very large table

```
CREATE TABLE dbo.VeryLargeTable (
    ID          BIGINT                  IDENTITY    PRIMARY KEY,
    TextCol     NVARCHAR(4000)
) ;

DECLARE @LoopCounter INT = 0 ;

WHILE @LoopCounter < 2000
BEGIN
    INSERT INTO dbo.VeryLargeTable (TextCol)
    SELECT 'Yet another row in a very, very, very large table. In fact,
this table is going to take a very long time to create, and you will not be
able to delete all rows in one go!'
    FROM sys.columns c1
    CROSS APPLY sys.columns c2 ;

    SET @LoopCounter = @LoopCounter + 1 ;
END
```

Let's try to delete all rows from this table in a single transaction using the query in listing 5.18. Remember that if we do not start an explicit transaction, then each statement will run inside an autocommit transaction. In other words, the lowest granularity of a transaction is a single statement.

Listing 5.18 Deleting rows in a single transaction

```
DELETE FROM dbo.VeryLargeTable ;
```

This statement will result in a very large transaction. While a transaction is open, the transaction log cannot truncate itself to free up space. This is true even in the `SIMPLE` recovery model (we will discuss recovery models in chapter 12). The transaction will become so large, in fact, that we will run out of space in the transaction log, and the query will roll back, causing a 9002 error to be thrown, as illustrated in figure 5.7.

```
Messages
  Msg 9002, Level 17, State 4, Line 19
  The transaction log for database 'MagicChoc' is full due to 'ACTIVE_TRANSACTION' and the holdup lsn is (1271:88633:22).

  Completion time: 2023-06-19T20:53:40.9360874+00:00
```

Figure 5.7 9002 error thrown when the transaction log becomes full

Instead, we need to break the `DELETE` operation down into multiple statements and hence multiple transactions. Assuming the database is in the `SIMPLE` recovery model, this will prevent the transaction log from becoming full, as it will be able to truncate itself between statement executions. This is one of the very few scenarios where I would consider using a WHILE loop in a production environment, and that is only because this is an ad hoc script. I would always avoid putting a WHILE loop into code that I intend to deploy, for the same reasons I avoid the use of cursors. In listing 5.19, we have set the script to delete rows in batches of 250,000. You can tweak this number to optimize performance depending on the characteristics of your environment.

> **WARNING** This script will take a long time to run.

Listing 5.19 Deleting rows in batches

```
DECLARE @RowCounter BIGINT ;

SET @RowCounter = 1 ;

WHILE @RowCounter > 0
BEGIN
    DELETE TOP(250000)
    FROM dbo.VeryLargeTable ;

    SET @RowCounter = (SELECT COUNT(*) FROM dbo.VeryLargeTable) ;
    PRINT @RowCounter ;
END
```

Operations that modify data, such as DELETE operations, can cause the transaction log to become full when they are run against large tables. To avoid this issue, break the operation into multiple statements and iterate over them.

Summary

- Remember that a NULL is an unknown value and is therefore not equal to another NULL value.
- Avoid using the NOLOCK query hint as a performance optimization as it can lead to unexpected results, which return data that never existed in the database.
- Avoid SELECT * in anything other than ad hoc queries, as it can cause issues with performance and code maintenance, and it's an antipattern for self-documenting code.
- Ordering data is a presentation feature rather than a set-based feature. Only order data if it is absolutely necessary.
- Do not uniquify results unless you really need to. If DISTINCT causes performance issues, consider other techniques such as GROUP BY or ROW_NUMBER().
- UNION is more expensive than UNION ALL because it removes duplicates. Therefore, if duplicates are either unimportant or not possible, use UNION ALL instead of UNION.
- Cursors should be avoided. They are very expensive, and in modern versions of SQL Server, there are no operations that can't be performed via other methods.
- Deleting many rows from a table in a single transaction can cause the transaction log to become full. Avoid this by splitting the deletion into multiple batches.

6 SSIS development

This chapter covers

- An introduction to SSIS and SSIS development mistakes
- Losing bad data
- Not optimizing data loads
- Using SSIS as a T-SQL orchestration tool
- Always extracting all the data from a source table

SQL Server Integration Services, commonly known as SSIS, is a tool that ships with SQL Server Enterprise and Standard editions, although there are feature limitations in the Standard edition. It is an *extract, transform, and load* (*ETL*) tool that allows developers to build data movement and transformation pipelines within a drag-and-drop GUI.

NOTE Examples in this chapter will use SQL Server Data Tools, which can be downloaded from https://mng.bz/RNB0. The Integration Services extension also needs to be installed and is available in Extensions | Manage Extensions and then by searching for SQL Server Integration Services Projects 2022 from the marketplace.

An SSIS package always consists of a single *control flow*, which orchestrates the tasks that the package will run. Within the control flow, we can create zero or more *data flows*, which are used to import, export, and transform data within memory buffers.

Tasks on the control flow are joined by precedence constraints. This allows us to design our packages to run tasks serially, instead of all tasks running in parallel. Tasks following a precedence constraint are always run after the task(s) preceding the constraint.

Constraints

SSIS has three types of constraint: success, failure, and completion. These allow us to control the flow of our package and create custom error-handling logic. Tasks connected to constraints have the following behavior:

- A task connected to a success constraint will be executed following the successful completion of the preceding task. If the preceding task fails, it will not be executed.
- A task connected to a failure constraint will be executed following the failure of the preceding task. If the preceding task succeeds, it will not be executed.
- A task connected to a completion constraint will run following the execution of the preceding task. It will be executed regardless of the success or failure of the preceding task.

In the SSIS control flow, a success constraint is shown in green, a failure constraint in red, and a completion constraint in blue.

Precedence constraints within the control flow should not be confused with data paths within the data flow. In the data flow, a blue data path indicates that rows that successfully pass through the preceding component are passed to the subsequent component. A red data path indicates that rows that fail the preceding component will be passed to the subsequent component. There is no completion data path.

When we create a project from the Integration Services Project template, we will see an empty control flow in front of us, with the SSIS Toolbox in the left-hand pane. This toolbox is where we can drag out tasks onto the control flow or our components onto a data flow. The toolbox is context sensitive, so if we are in a data flow, we will see data flow components instead of control flow tasks.

Each data flow is actually a task on our control flow, so we can create a data flow by dragging a data flow task onto the control flow. We can then view the data flow by either double-clicking the task or switching to the Data Flow tab at the top of our design surface.

Connection managers are used to create connections to data sources, such as databases and flat files. Out-of-the-box connection managers include OLE DB connections, ADO.NET connections, Files, Flat Files, and Analysis Services. For performance, when connecting to SQL Server instances within data flows, OLE DB is often the optimal choice. ADO.NET connection managers are often used for connecting to SQL Server for Execute T-SQL Statement tasks on the control flow.

OLE DB configuration

Some years ago, OLE DB was deprecated by Microsoft. It was then undeprecated in 2018 and a new OLE DB driver was released. SQL Native Client 11 is still deprecated, however, and does not ship with SQL Server 2022. Therefore, to use SQL Server OLE DB with applications that connect to SQL Server, including SSIS, you will need to download and install the Microsoft OLE DB Driver 19 for SQL Server, which can be found at https://mng.bz/AagK.

The Microsoft Visual C++ Redistributable is a prerequisite for this driver, however, so this will need to be installed first. This redistributable can be found at https://mng.bz/ZVXO.

Once these packages are installed, the correct OLE DB driver will appear in the Provider drop-down. By default, however, the connection manager will set the Use Encryption For Data property to `Mandatory`. Unless you have certificates configured for your SQL Server instance, you will need to change this to `Optional`. The property can be found by using the Data Links button in the connection manager dialog box and navigating to the All tab.

Developers can make various mistakes when developing SSIS packages. In this chapter, we will explore a mistake that can result in data loss. We will explore the results of not optimizing data loads. We will also look at the effects of using SSIS purely as an orchestration tool and not taking advantage of data pipelines. Finally, we will look at the mistake of not filtering our data extraction.

To explore some of the mistakes that are commonly made when using SSIS, we will continue with the MagicChoc example and use the following scenario. The marketing department is going to start advertising online and wants to track the impressions (views of online advertising banners) that are seen by potential customers. The impressions data will be received in a CSV file, where it will be picked up by an SSIS package, which will be scheduled to run once per day. The package will put the data into a table in the `staging` schema of the `Marketing` database. It will then transform the data into a table in the `marketing` schema. Finally, it will roll the data up and insert it into an aggregated table in the `reporting` schema, before truncating the staging table.

If you wish to follow along with the examples in this chapter, see the sample CSV file in the code repository for this book. It is called `impressions.csv`. You will also need to create the `Marketing` database using the script in the following listing.

Listing 6.1 Creating the `Marketing` database

```
CREATE DATABASE Marketing ;
GO

USE Marketing ;
GO

CREATE SCHEMA staging ;
GO
```

```
CREATE SCHEMA marketing ;
GO

CREATE SCHEMA reporting ;
GO

CREATE TABLE staging.ImpressionsStage (
    ImpressionUID          VARCHAR(MAX)     NULL,
    ReferralURL            VARCHAR(MAX)     NULL,
    CookieID               VARCHAR(MAX)     NULL,
    CampaignID             VARCHAR(MAX)     NULL,
    RenderingID            VARCHAR(MAX)     NULL,
    CountryCode            VARCHAR(MAX)     NULL,
    StateID                VARCHAR(MAX)     NULL,
    BrowserVersion         VARCHAR(MAX)     NULL,
    OperatingSystemID      VARCHAR(MAX)     NULL,
    CostPerMille           VARCHAR(MAX)     NULL,
    EventTime              VARCHAR(MAX)     NULL,
    BidPrice               VARCHAR(MAX)     NULL
) ;

CREATE TABLE marketing.Impressions (
    ImpressionID        BIGINT              NOT NULL     PRIMARY KEY  IDENTITY,
    ImpressionUID       UNIQUEIDENTIFIER    NOT NULL,
    ReferralURL         VARCHAR(512)        NOT NULL,
    CookieID            UNIQUEIDENTIFIER    NOT NULL,
    CampaignID          BIGINT              NOT NULL,
    RenderingID         BIGINT              NOT NULL,
    CountryCode         TINYINT             NULL,
    StateID             TINYINT             NULL,
    BrowserVersion      BIGINT              NOT NULL,
    OperatingSystemID   BIGINT              NOT NULL,
    BidPrice            MONEY               NOT NULL,
    CostPerMille        MONEY               NOT NULL,
    EventTime           DATETIME            NOT NULL
) ;

CREATE TABLE reporting.ImpressionAggregates (
    ImpressionAggregateID     BIGINT     NOT NULL     PRIMARY KEY  IDENTITY,
    CampaignID                BIGINT     NOT NULL,
    CountryCode               TINYINT    NOT NULL,
    EventDate                 DATE       NOT NULL,
    AvgBidPrice               MONEY      NOT NULL,
    AvgCostPerMille           MONEY      NOT NULL
) ;
```

In Visual Studio, we will create a new project called `ImpressionsLoad`, which will use the Integration Services project type (which needs to be installed). The solution should have the same name, and the project can be created in the same directory as the solution.

Online marketing terminology

For some context, see the following definitions of some terms used within this data domain:

(continued)

- Cost per mille (CPM) is the actual cost charged for 1,000 views, following an automated auction of the banner space.
- The bid price is the maximum cost per 1,000 views that the advertiser is willing to pay in the automated auction.
- The referral URL is the website on which the view occurred.
- The cookie ID is the unique ID of the tracking cookie. Therefore, it is synonymous with a user.

It may also be interesting to note that "views" is synonymous with "impressions," also known in the industry as "eyeballs."

6.1 #22 Throwing away bad data

One of the most common mistakes that I see SSIS developers make is throwing away rows that they can't load. Often, misconceptions around how SSIS works means that developers do not even know they are doing this. To explore this, let's create a simple SSIS package with a data flow that will load the impression data from our `impressions.csv` file (which I have placed in the root of `c:\`) into our `staging.impressions` table.

Let's begin by dragging a data flow task onto the control flow and renaming it Load Impressions Staging. We should also create two connection managers: one for the CSV file and the other for the SQL Server instance.

To create the connection manager for the CSV file, we should choose a flat file connection. On the General Page of the dialog box, we can configure the basic details of the connection, such as the name of the file, file encoding, and type of file (delimited, fixed width, or ragged right). In the Columns page of the dialog box (figure 6.1), we should ensure that the column delimiter is configured as a comma. Other possible delimiters include tab, semicolon, and vertical bar, among others. The Advanced page allows us to specify the properties of individual columns, such as data type. The Preview page displays the first 100 rows within the file.

In the Advanced page of the dialog box, we should set our data types. SSIS can suggest data types for us, based on the first 100 rows, but unless we are sure that the first 100 rows adequately cover the possibilities within our data, we should select the data types ourselves. Because we are loading into a staging table with expansive data types, however, we will just leave the data types as 50-character-length strings for now.

Our second connection manager will be an OLE DB connection manager, which points to the SQL Server instance that hosts the marketing database. In this connection manager, we will first choose the OLE DB provider that we want to use from the drop-down. In our case, we will select the Native OLE DB\Microsoft OLE DB Driver 19 for SQL Server. We will then specify the name of the SQL Server instance and the name of the database (initial catalog) that we will be connecting to. Additionally, we can select how we want to authenticate to the instance. If we use Windows integrated security, then the package will authenticate as the identity that runs the package. If we choose

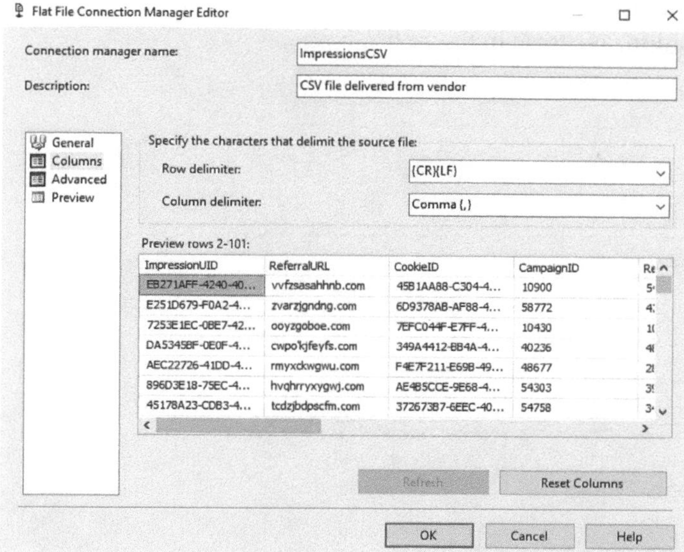

Figure 6.1 Flat file connection manager—Columns page

a SQL Server username and password, then the package will authenticate using second-tier authentication, also known as SQL authentication.

Back in the data flow, we can now create a flat file source, which will use our flat file connection manager, and an OLE DB destination, which will use our OLE DB connection manager.

The Columns page of the data flow source allows us to map *external columns*, which are columns coming from the data source, to *output columns*, which are the columns that are passed from our component to the next component in the data flow. We can remove external columns by deselecting them in the top window, and we can change the names of the output columns. For our use case specifically, we will map the `ImpressionUID` external column to an output column called `ImpressionID`.

On the Error Output page of the flat file source, we can define the behavior of the component if there is a failure of any given row that passes through it. We can differentiate between and specify different behaviors of the component based on general errors or data truncations. For now, we will leave the default values in place, which means that if a row fails to be passed through the source into the data flow, it will cause the component to fail.

To complete the simple data flow, we will also need an OLE DB destination. In the destination, we can choose if we want to load data into a named object or an object that will be pulled from a variable. For each of these options, we can also choose if we want to see the fast load options. These options will allow us to optimize the performance of the load; we will talk more about this in the next section of the chapter. In our case, we will use the table or view fast load data access mode and select the `staging.ImpressionStage` as the destination, as shown in figure 6.2.

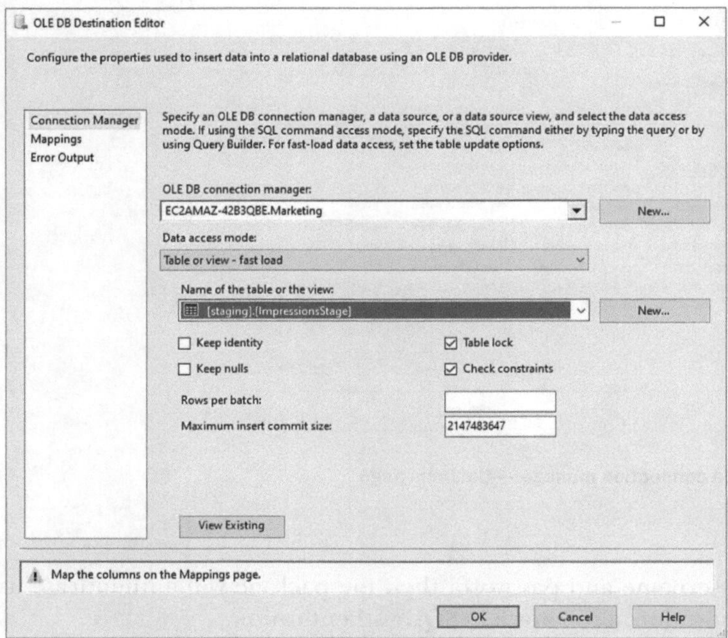

Figure 6.2 OLE DB destination editor—Connection Manager page

> **NOTE** Leaving the default settings for the fast load options is a mistake. We should always spend time configuring these options. This forms part of the mistake of not optimizing the load, and we will discuss this in the next section.

On the Mappings page of the OLE DB destination, any input columns (columns coming from the previous component) will automatically be mapped to the destination columns (in the destination table) if their names are the same. The `ImpressionID` column is not mapped, however, because the name is different. Therefore, we must select it from the drop-down list. We could also modify the automappings if we needed to.

The Error Output page of the destination defines the behavior of the component should a row fail to be inserted. Just like the error output on the source, however, we will leave it with the default Fail Component. The columns in our destination table are so expansive that there is little chance of a recoverable row failing.

Now let's execute the package in debug mode by clicking the Start button in the toolbar and see what happens. The results are shown in figure 6.3. You will notice that we have successfully loaded 954,912 rows into the staging table, but then there was an error at the Impressions CSV source. This is indicated by the red cross.

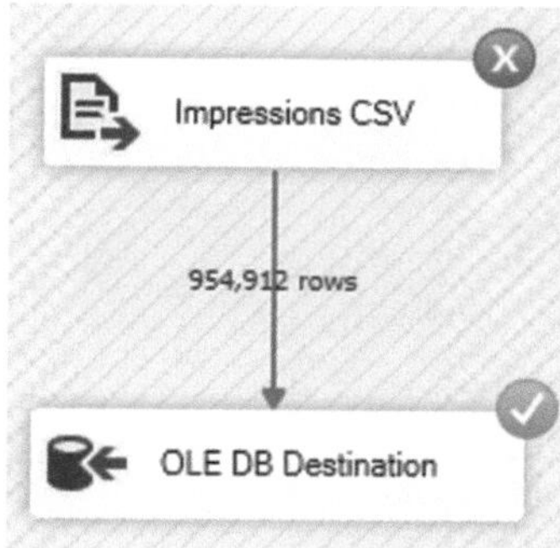

Figure 6.3 Failed data flow

If we move over to the Progress tab, we can see that there was a data truncation error on row 999,969, as shown in figure 6.4.

[SSIS.Pipeline] Information: Execute phase is beginning.
[Impressions CSV [2]] Error: Data conversion failed. The data conversion for column "ImpressionUID" returned stat
[Impressions CSV [2]] Error: The "Impressions CSV.Outputs[Flat File Source Output].Columns[ImpressionID]" failed
[Impressions CSV [2]] Error: An error occurred while processing file "C:\impressions.csv" on data row 999969.
[SSIS.Pipeline] Error: SSIS Error Code DTS_E_PRIMEOUTPUTFAILED. The PrimeOutput method on Impressions
[SSIS.Pipeline] Information: Post Execute phase is beginning.

Figure 6.4 Error in the Progress tab

How annoying! There are only 1 million rows in the file! We don't want to lose the whole file because of one bad row, do we? So let's go back into the Error Output page of the flat file source editor and change the behavior of the component so that if any errors are encountered, we will ignore the row(s) with the error and continue loading the data. This is shown in figure 6.5.

> **TIP** Click the Stop Debugging button before modifying the package.

> **TIP** Before running the package again, truncate the staging data to avoid double-loading the data. We can do this with a `TRUNCATE TABLE Staging.ImpressionsStage` command.

Now if we run the package again, we will see that the data flow was successful. This will be denoted by each component having a green tick. So that's great, right? Well, not really. In fact, it's a mistake. It may have solved the short-term problem, but what if the next file has five bad rows? Or 50? What if it has 5,000 bad rows? The cookie ID is a significant column, which we need, so we should not be throwing away this bad data. But we also don't want our package to fail every time. So what should we do?

The answer is to redirect bad rows to a different destination so that they can be examined by the application support team to decide if they can safely be thrown away or if we

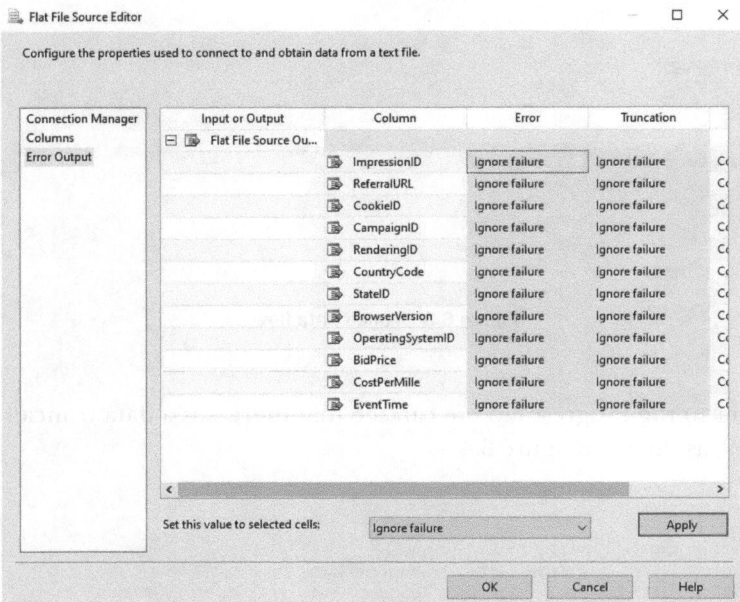

Figure 6.5 Flat file source editor—Error Output page set to ignore failure

can fix the data. It might even be the case that the application owner needs to reach out to the vendor and request a new data extract. Data coming from untrusted sources is often dirty, and we should account for this in our code.

To fix the problem, let's first create a new table, which will hold any rows that fail the task. We can achieve this using the script in the following listing.

Listing 6.2 Creating an error table

```
CREATE TABLE staging.ImpressionLoadFailures (
    FlatFileSourceErrorOutputColumn    VARCHAR(MAX)    NOT NULL,
    ErrorCode                          VARCHAR(MAX)    NOT NULL,
    ErrorColumn                        VARCHAR(MAX)    NOT NULL
) ;
```

Next, we will create a new OLE DB destination and name it Failed Rows. Pull the red connector from the data source onto the new data flow destination. With our current configuration, this will immediately cause the Configure Error output dialog box to be displayed. This dialog box is identical to the Error Output page of the data source editor. We should configure this page to redirect rows with errors and truncations.

Let's now configure the new destination. On the Connection Manager page, we will point to our new `ImpressionLoadFailures` table as the destination table. On the Mappings page, we will need to manually map the Flat File Source Error Output Column, as our table does not have spaces in the column name, so automapping will not work. Our data flow will now look like figure 6.6.

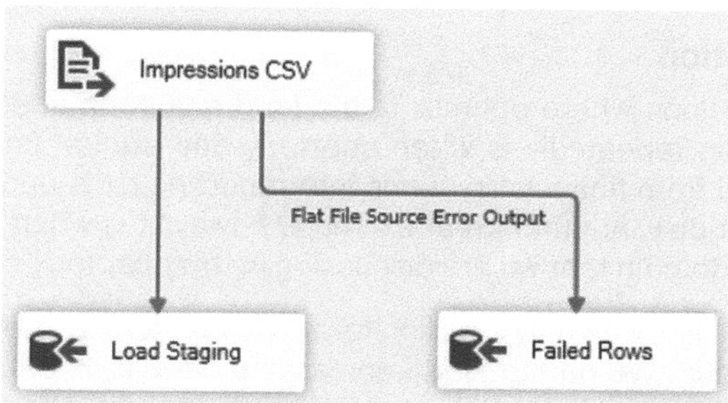

Figure 6.6 Data flow with error output

If we now run the package again, the failed row will be inserted into our `Impression-LoadFailures` table. We can examine that row:

```
91C27789-2805-41EB-8E06-A4F5AD147817;jouktjkatujr.com,
7D522130-5A00-4C4B-83D5-EA0A7E1777CF,
54879,4433265,220,NULL,128,142,3.3635,1.2668,02/07/2023 07:56
```

We know that we are expecting the file to be comma separated, but we can see after the first Globally Unique Identifier (GUID) that there is a semicolon instead of a comma. This will cause the row to fail because of a truncation error on the Cookie ID column. This is because we have used the suggested data type of a 50-character string, and the length of the column (until we hit the first comma) is 53 characters.

> **TIP** In some scenarios, we would also want to add a failure constraint to the data source destination. In our scenario, however, we have configured the staging table, so that all columns are `VARCHAR(MAX)`, and that is as expansive as we can be. Therefore, there is no need for a failure source, as we could not make its columns any more expansive.

We should always avoid throwing away bad data. The ignore-row behavior may be convenient, but if the data is important enough to load, it should be important enough to keep, even if a later review of the data reveals that we can't repair it. If a particular column is not needed, then we should avoid loading it. It increases our chances of the package failing, and it makes the rows larger than they need be, which could also carry a performance penalty. This is discussed later in the chapter.

6.2 #23 Not optimizing data loads

In the previous section, while building our data flow, you may have noticed an additional mistake that we made—namely, not optimizing our data load. Without this optimization, our package will never perform optimally.

To optimize the load, we should configure properties on the data flow, which control the size of the data buffers that the data will be loaded into when they are read out of the CSV file. There are then fast load options on the OLE DB destination that can be used to optimize the bulk load into SQL Server.

Real-world package optimization

There have been numerous occasions where optimizing the load has been absolutely essential. An example I have seen repeatedly is when quarterly and annual financial transaction data has been loaded from financial systems into reporting tools and must be completed in a certain time window. Another great example, however, is when I have been working with the same data domain that we are discussing in this chapter.

In this chapter, we have a single flat file, with only 1 million rows in it. I remember, however, working for a large advertising group. We had to load impressions data, click data, and event data on a nightly basis, and then perform a complex click-path analysis. There were multiple files from multiple cookie providers. There were hundreds of millions of impressions, tens of millions of clicks, and millions of events that had to be processed every night.

Because of the size of our sample file, we will be looking to save seconds. In the real-world scenario, however, optimizing the data loads saved many minutes. This was crucial, as the files were often not delivered until after midnight and they had to be ready for the business by the start of the working day. The ETL processes took many hours to complete, and without the load optimizations, they would have overrun their windows, causing a business impact on a daily basis.

The properties on the data flow that control its size are `DefaultBufferMaxRows`, which controls the maximum number of rows within the buffer, and `DefaultBufferSize`, which controls the maximum size of the data buffer. The default maximum number of rows is 10,000, and the default maximum size is 1MB. The buffer size will be controlled by the limit that is reached first.

This can be confusing, so I recommend setting the `AutoAdjustBufferSize` property to `True`. This will result in not having to worry about the `BufferSize` property, as it will automatically be configured to match our chosen maximum number of rows within the buffer.

The fast load options within the OLE DB destination allow us to specify if an identity specification should be disabled on a column, if `NULL` values should be kept, if check constraints should be disabled, and if a table lock should be used. It also allows us to specify the maximum number of rows per batch and the maximum commit size of the insert.

Because we are loading data into a staging table, which is a flat heap that has no keys, constraints, or `NULL` constraints, we can ignore these settings for our scenario. If we did have these constraints, however, then there would be a performance penalty for having them enabled. We will ensure that the table lock option is checked, however, as this will avoid contention and reduce the overhead of lock escalation.

The maximum batch size and commit size are important values to configure. By default, data will be loaded into the table in a single transaction. This is likely to cause performance issues, due to excessive use of `TempDB` and filling up the transaction log. We suspect that reading data from the flat file will be slower than inserting data into the staging table, so we will keep the maximum batch and commit size in line with the number of rows in our data flow source.

Unfortunately, there is no magic number for the number of rows that should be in each buffer or in each batch. The optimum values will be very specific to your unique environment, resource profile, workload profile, and data profile. The way to find the optimum value is to test the data flow with multiple size options.

> **TIP** When doing this, I usually start with a small value and increase the size in increments. This usually results in incremental performance improvements, which start to tail off. When execution times start to increase, I know that I have hit the optimum size.

Table 6.1 contains the results of various tests I performed on the data flow. The first column details the maximum number of rows in the buffer, which is aligned with the maximum number of rows per batch. The second column shows the execution time, in seconds, for the package. These execution times can be pulled from the Progress tab before stopping execution or from the Execution Results tab after execution stops.

Table 6.1 Buffer size performance tests

Buffer/batch size	Execution time (seconds)
1,000	49.032
5,000	36.828
10,000	35.813
20,000	34.875
50,000	34.328
75,000	35.125

> **TIP** If you want to run the tests on your own environment, remember to truncate the staging table each time to keep it a fair test. Also remember that your mileage will vary, depending on the specifications of your computer and other processes that may be running.

In my environment, it is clear to see that 50,000 rows is the optimal size of the buffer. We should also check out the hypothesis that the flat file source will be the limiting factor, however. Therefore, let's run some more tests. This time, we will keep the `MaximumRowsPerBuffer` at 50,000 for each test but tweak the batch size. The results of these tests can be found in table 6.2. Once again, remember that the results will be specific to your unique environment, so your mileage may vary.

Table 6.2 Batch size performance tests

Batch size	Execution time (seconds)
25,000	35.125
75,000	34.962

As expected, the results show that reading the flat file was the limiting factor and we cannot gain a performance improvement by removing the alignment of the batch size from the buffer size.

We should always optimize our load performance. Suboptimal performance can cause packages to overshoot their ETL windows. This could have an effect on the business or on maintenance processes such as backups.

6.3 #24 Using SSIS as a T-SQL orchestration tool

A common mistake I see made by developers who are new to SSIS is to avoid using data flows and to simply perform loads between tables or transformations using Execute T-SQL tasks on the control flow.

This approach results in developers not harnessing the power of SSIS. It means that we are just running standard T-SQL. The ETL will not become loosely coupled from our data sources, ETL developers who come after us will not have a graphical representation of the logic, and we will not be able to take advantage of SSIS error handling and logging. A bad row will result in a whole query failing, rather than being able to redirect an individual bad row. Additionally, we will lose the ability to explore where our data is within a pipeline, making it harder to debug performance issues.

> **SSIS performance**
>
> It is worth noting that if the source and destination tables are both in the same server, then using native T-SQL will likely be more performant than transforming data using data flow pipelines, because it performs better at operations like joining and merging data. Therefore, for some large loads, where a single database server is involved, native T-SQL might be the correct approach, especially if we have a narrow ETL window. We should use the right tool for the job.
>
> Arguably, however, in this scenario, there may be little benefit in the overhead of running SSIS at all, and we may be better off running a SQL Server Agent job and using job steps to orchestrate the workflow. When loading and transforming data between servers, SSIS can normally outperform a linked server.
>
> It is also worth weighing up performance versus functionality. If we do not have any constraints around the length of the ETL window, we may consider that the error handling, logging, and debugging tools of SSIS are more important considerations than speed.

To explore the effects of using SSIS as a pure orchestration tool, let's expand our package to transform data from our staging table into our core marketing table and then on into the reporting table. Finally, our package should truncate the staging table. The following section will discuss how these tasks may be created using the control flow as an orchestration tool for Execute T-SQL Statement tasks.

6.3.1 Creating an Execute T-SQL Statement orchestration

Our first step in enhancing the package will be to create a new ADO connection manager. This connection manager will be used by our Execute T-SQL Statement tasks to connect to our SQL Server instance.

Once we have a connection manager, we can now create our tasks that will execute our SQL statements. We should configure the first new Execute T-SQL Statement task to execute the query in listing 6.3. This query performs an `INSERT` statement, converting data where SQL Server is not able to perform an implicit conversion. The `SET DATEFORMAT` statement at the start is required, so that SQL Server recognizes the dates in the `EventTime` column. Without this, the task would fail with data type overflow errors.

Listing 6.3 Loading data into the `Impressions` table

```
SET DATEFORMAT DMY
INSERT INTO marketing.Impressions (
    ImpressionUID,
    ReferralURL,
    CookieID,
    CampaignID,
    RenderingID,
    CountryCode,
    StateID,
    BrowserVersion,
    OperatingSystemID,
    BidPrice,
    CostPerMille,
    EventTime
)
SELECT
      ImpressionUID
    , ReferralURL
    , CookieID
    , CampaignID
    , RenderingID
    , CASE
        WHEN CountryCode = 'NULL' THEN NULL
        ELSE CountryCode
      END CountryCode
    , CASE
        WHEN StateID = 'NULL' THEN NULL
        ELSE StateID
      END StateID
    , BrowserVersion
    , OperatingSystemID
    , CAST(BidPrice AS MONEY)
    , CAST(CostPerMille AS MONEY)
    , EventTime
FROM staging.ImpressionsStage ;
```

The next Execute T-SQL Statement task we will create is called Merge Aggregates, which is used to populate the `reporting.ImpressionAggregates` table. For this task, we should use the query in listing 6.4. This query uses a `MERGE` statement to roll the data up by `CampaignID`, `CountryCode`, and `EventDate` before loading the aggregated table. If a row already exists for the campaign, country, and date, then the average bid price and average CPM will be updated. Otherwise, a row will be inserted.

Listing 6.4 Loading the `Aggregates` table

```
MERGE INTO reporting.ImpressionAggregates AS Target
USING (
    SELECT
          CampaignID
        , CountryCode
        , AVG(BidPrice) AS AvgBidPrice
        , AVG(CostPerMille) AS AvgCostPerMille
        , CAST(EventTime as DATE) AS EventDate
    FROM marketing.Impressions
    GROUP BY
          CampaignID
        , CountryCode
        , CAST(EventTime as DATE)
) AS source
ON (
    Source.CampaignID = Target.CampaignID
        AND Source.CountryCode = Target.CountryCode
        AND Source.EventDate = Target.EventDate
)
WHEN MATCHED THEN
    UPDATE SET
          AvgBidPrice = Source.AvgBidPrice
        , AvgCostPerMille = Source.AvgCostPerMille
WHEN NOT MATCHED THEN
    INSERT (
           CampaignID,
           CountryCode,
           EventDate,
           AvgBidPrice,
           AvgCostPerMille
           )
    VALUES (
           Source.CampaignID,
           Source.CountryCode,
           Source.EventDate,
           Source.AvgBidPrice,
           Source.AvgCostPerMille
           ) ;
```

Our final task will truncate the staging table at the end of the load using the statement in listing 6.5. Truncating a table is a perfectly acceptable usage of an Execute T-SQL Statement task. This task cannot be performed as part of the data flow. We will keep this task, even when we optimize the package to replace the previous Execute T-SQL Statement tasks with data flows.

Listing 6.5 Truncating the `Staging` table

```
TRUNCATE TABLE staging.ImpressionsStage ;
```

All our tasks should be joined together by success constraints. This will force the tasks to run sequentially. It also means that if a task fails, the subsequent tasks will not run. Figure 6.7 illustrates how our control flow will look at this point.

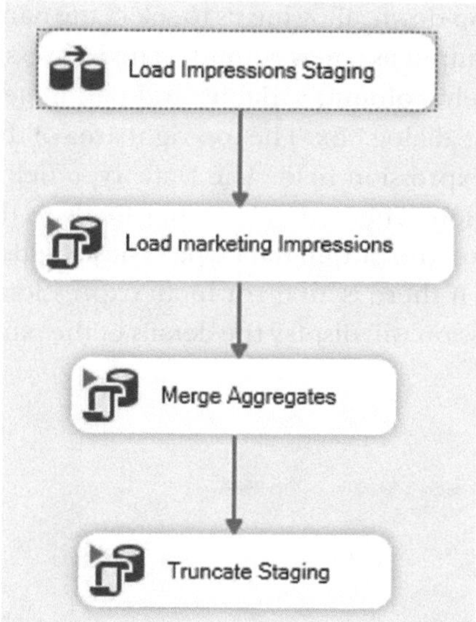

Figure 6.7 Package used to orchestrate T-SQL tasks

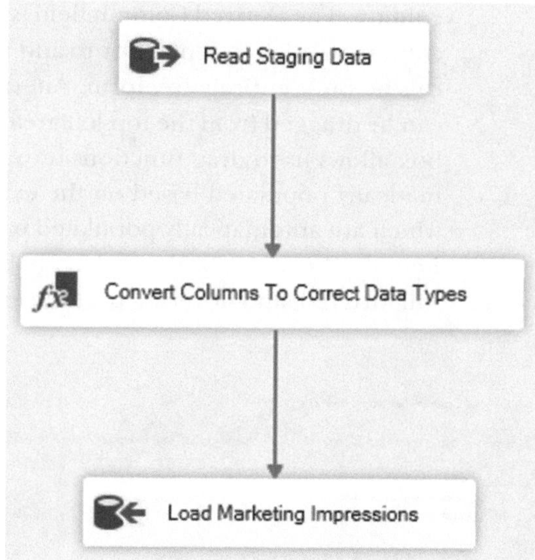

Figure 6.8 Load Marketing Impressions data flow

The package is now complete, but it is less than ideal for loading data, as in this case, the data comes from an untrusted source and is likely to be dirty. Let's imagine that we have loaded a dirty row into our staging data. Because of the expansive columns in our staging table, we have managed to get the data this far, but when we try to load the `marketing.Impressions` table, the row fails because of a failure to convert between data types. In this scenario, the whole task will fail. It will also be tricky to track down the reason for the failure, as SQL Server will not report the specific row that failed.

So how could we create a better package? The answer is to use data flow tasks. To do this, let's delete the Load Marketing Impressions and Merge Aggregate tasks. The following section will discuss how to replace them with data flows.

6.3.2 Converting Execute T-SQL Statement tasks to data flows

The Load Marketing Impressions data flow will look similar to the flow illustrated in figure 6.8. You will see that there is a source, which is reading the data from the staging table. There is then a derived column transformation, which converts the columns to the correct data types, before a data flow destination inserts the rows into the `marketing.Impressions` table.

The source and destination are straightforward components. It is the derived column transformation where the magic happens. In figure 6.9, you will notice that we have used *SSIS expressions,* which are a combination of columns, functions, operators, and literals, to create new output columns that contain the converted values. The Derived Column Name field is free text and allows us to specify a name for the output column. The Derived Column field is a drop-down, allowing us to select the name of the column we wish to replace or to add the output as a new column. The Expression field can be built entirely freeform. Alternatively, column, variable, and parameter names can be dragged from the top-left area of the dialog box. The top-right area of the dialog box allows us to drag functions into the expression field. The Data Type field is automatically populated based on the expression. There are also other fields to the right, which are automatically populated based on the output data type. These fields include Length, Precision, Scale, and Code Page. If there is an error in an expression, then it will turn red, and hovering over the expression will display the details of the parse error.

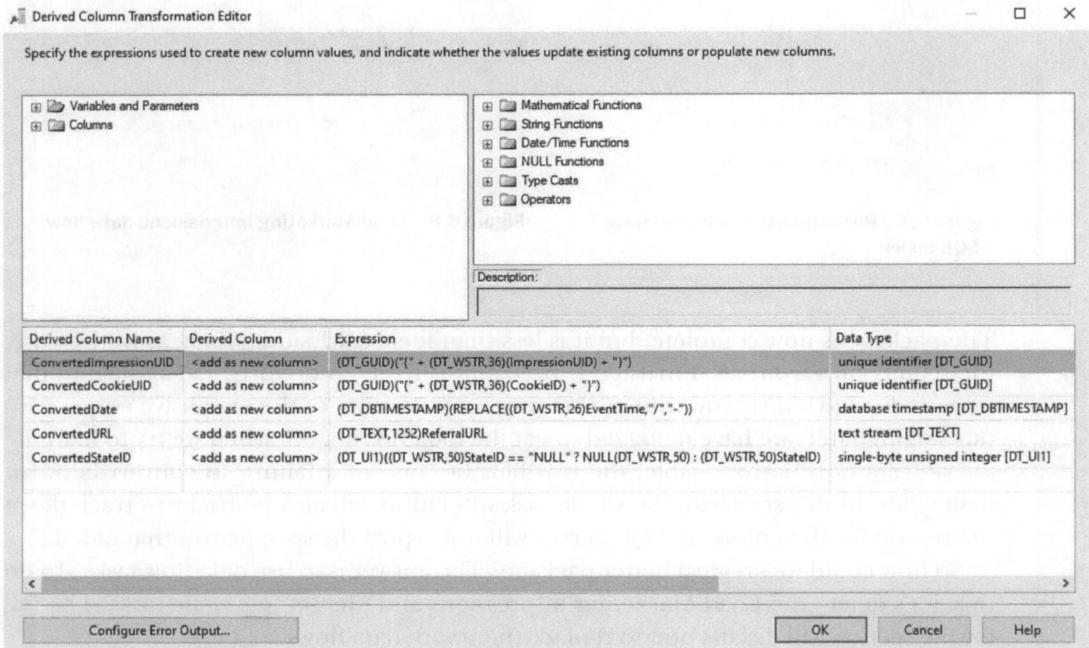

Figure 6.9 Derived column transformation

The first two expressions are converting GUID values. For SSIS to recognize the values as GUIDs, they must be enclosed in curly braces. Therefore, we explicitly cast the input column to a 36-character Unicode string and add the curly braces before and after. We then convert the entire value to the `DT_GUID` data type.

The expression to convert the `EventTime` column first explicitly converts the input to a 26-character string, replacing the `/` characters with `-` characters. This is because SSIS can't recognize the data format used in the staging table. Finally, we cast the results to the `DB_TIMESTAMP` data type.

The expression to convert the URL simply performs an explicit cast to a string with the 1252 code page. This code page is synonymous with the Windows 1252 code page.

The expression to convert the `StateID` column is arguably the most interesting of the expressions. We are using this expression not just to change the data type but also to replace the string value of `"NULL"` with a `NULL` value. To those of you with a .NET background, the syntax may be somewhat familiar, but to understand this expression, let's break it down into parts. The first part is to the right of the `:` and passes `StateID` as an input column, after explicitly casting it as a 50-character string. On the left side of the `:` we are checking if the value within `StateID` (which, again, has to be explicitly cast) is equal to `"NULL"`. If it is, then we replace this value with a `NULL` value. There is another cast here, because in SSIS there is a different `NULL` value type for every data type. For example, a `NULL(DT_WSTR,50)` is a different type to a `NULL(DT_I4)`. Finally, outside of the brackets, on the far left, we convert the final value to a `DT_UI1`, which is a single-byte unsigned integer.

The expressions used in this transformation are detailed in the following listing.

Listing 6.6 SSIS expressions

```
(DT_GUID)("{" + (DT_WSTR,36)(ImpressionUID) + "}")       ConvertedImpressionUID
(DT_GUID)("{" + (DT_WSTR,36)(CookieID) + "}")             ConvertedCookieUID
(DT_DBTIMESTAMP)(REPLACE((DT_WSTR,26)EventTime,"/","-"))  ConvertedDate
(DT_TEXT,1252)ReferralURL                                 ConvertedURL
(DT_UI1)((DT_WSTR,50)StateID == "NULL" ? NULL(DT_WSTR,50) :
(DT_WSTR,50)StateID)                                      ConvertedStateID
```

The biggest advantage of this data flow over the corresponding Execute T-SQL Statement task is the ability to handle errors. As discussed earlier in this chapter, we could enhance this data flow to include error paths so that failed rows can be redirected to a data errors table. This would allow an application support team to deal with bad rows that cannot be converted into the more restrictive data types as part of business-as-usual operations. With the Execute T-SQL Statement task, the entire insert would fail and need to be debugged, and the data fixed, before any data from the load is available to the business.

The Merge Aggregates data flow will look similar to figure 6.10. This flow starts with a data flow source, which reads the impressions from the `marketing.Impressions` table. There is then a derived column transformation, which rolls up the date and time data to rounded dates. The aggregate transformation then calculates the average bid price and CPM. Finally, there is an upsert destination, which inserts rows into the `reporting.ImpressionAggregates` table if the key combination does not already exist or updates the aggregated values if the key combination does already exist.

Transformational data flows such as this are often far more complex than this example. For complex transformations, a data flow can have many advantages over an

Execute T-SQL Statement task. Not only can failed rows be redirected individually, but we also have a graphical view of our logic. This can help make the business logic clear to other developers. We also have the ability to watch our flow execute in real time and understand where errors occur or where performance is slow. This can assist the development process.

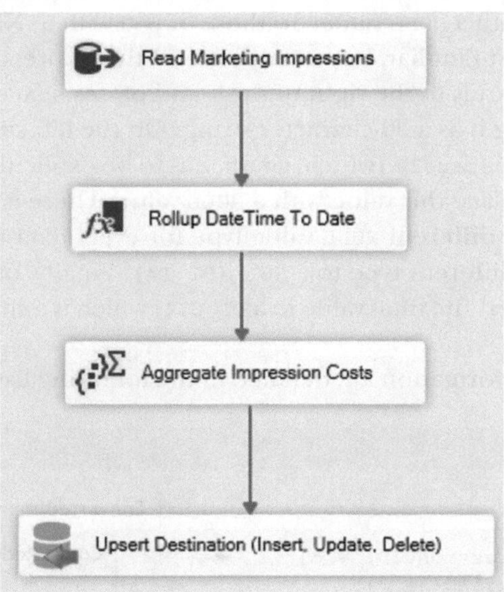

Figure 6.10 Merge Aggregates data flow

The Read Marketing Impressions source is a simple read from the base table. The Rollup DateTime To Date transformation is a derived column transformation, which generates a new output column using the SSIS expression `(DT_DBTIMESTAMP)(DT_DBDATE)EventTime`. This expression first converts the value to `DT_DBDATE`, which removes the time component. For ease of data type matching, it then immediately converts the value back to `DT_DBTIMESTAMP`, which adds a time component back in, but as the time information is now missing, it will be set to `00:00:00.000`.

The Aggregate Impression Costs transformation uses the aggregate transformation to calculate the average values of `BidPrice` and `CostPerMille`, grouped by the `CampaignID`, `CountryCode`, and `EventTime` columns. Figure 6.11 shows the Aggregations page of the Aggregate Transformation Editor. You will notice that in the top half of the dialog box we have selected the appropriate input columns for the transformation, and in the lower half, we have specified the appropriate aggregation that we want to apply. For the measures, we have selected Average, and we have selected Group By for the key columns. This will generate different average cost data for each unique combination of `CampaignID`, `CountryCode`, and `EventTime`.

TIP Other aggregate functions available are Count, Count Distinct, Sum, Minimum, and Maximum.

Blocking transformations

It is worth noting that SSIS transformations can either be blocking or non-blocking. *Non-blocking* transformations, such as the derived column transformation, will output rows within batches as soon as those batches have been processed. Other transformations, however, do not pass any outputs until all rows have been processed. These are known as *blocking* transformations, as downstream components cannot begin until the blocking transformation has completely finished its processing. The aggregate transformation is a blocking transformation. This is because it cannot confirm aggregate values until all rows are received. Otherwise, it could be processing and passing out incorrect aggregations, as the aggregate values would likely change if more rows with the same group by keys were received.

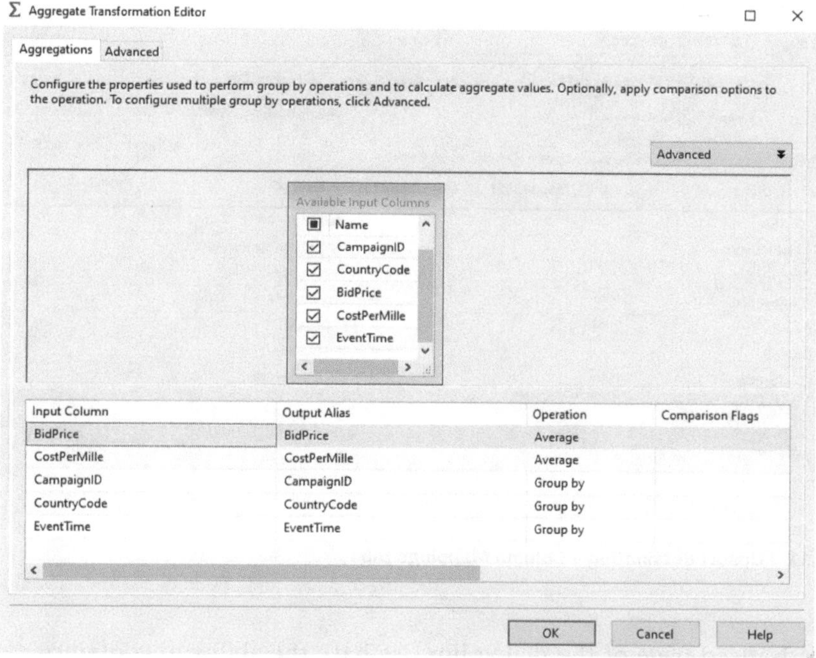

Figure 6.11 Aggregate Transformation Editor

The upsert destination is not an out-of-the-box SSIS component. While there are various methods to achieving the result with native SSIS components, they are deemed a poor practice, as they often exhibit very poor performance. There are various upsert destinations available, including offerings from COZYROC and SentryOne, but for this chapter, we will use the destination from ZappySys, which is part of their SSIS PowerPack offering. It can be purchased from https://mng.bz/2gVd.

In the Settings page of the Upsert Destination dialog box, we will choose the operation that we want to perform. In our scenario, that is an upsert, but the component also supports sync (upsert + delete), bulk update, and bulk delete. We will then select the data source we want to use and the table that will be our destination. We can also tweak our batch size for performance.

In the Column Mappings tab of the Upsert Destination dialog box, shown in figure 6.12, we will map all of our source columns and check the Key option against `CampaignID`, `CountryCode`, and `EventTime`. The key columns designate the business keys that will be used to match the rows when deciding if a row should be inserted or if an update should be made.

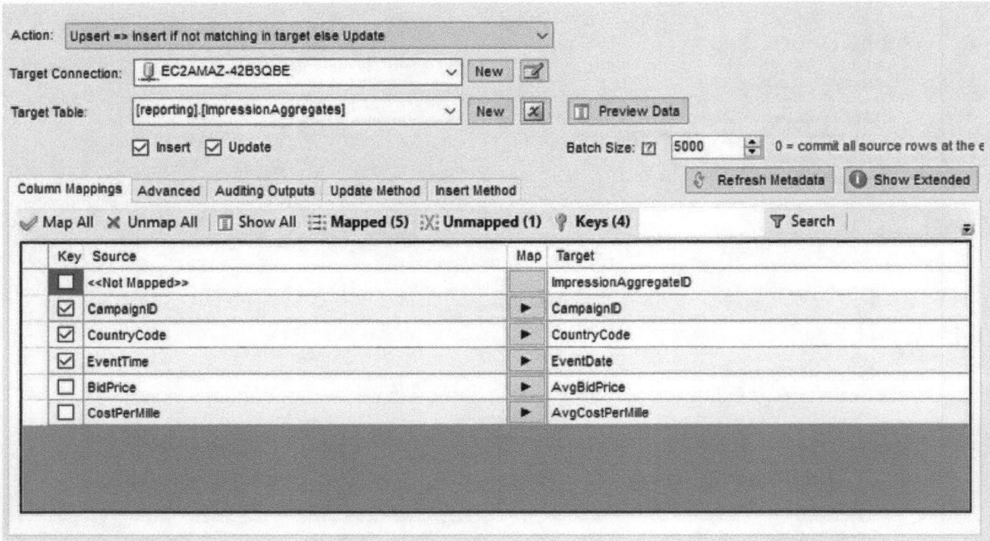

Figure 6.12 Upsert destination—Column Mappings tab

In the Advanced page of the dialog box, we have the ability to configure commands that will be executed before and after the insert. This can be useful for creating and removing indexes that will support the load. It can also be used for specifying hints, such as imposing a table lock.

When performing ETL operations between servers, using data flows is invariably a good idea as opposed to using SSIS as an orchestration tool for executing T-SQL scripts. When performing ETL operations between tables on the same server, SSIS can perform slower than a T-SQL script; however, it may still be a better option if we need the out-of-the-box logging, error handling, and debugging features, as well as the ability to fail individual rows.

6.4 #25 Extracting all data when we only need a subset

When building a data flow, it can be tempting to always configure our data flow source to read all data from the source table. Extracting a whole table is the default option. Choose our table in the drop-down box and away we go.

In some scenarios, we really will need to extract and process all data from a table, and if this is the case, then there is nothing wrong with using this option. If we only need a subset of the data from a table, however, then doing this can have a drastic impact on performance. Let's take our Merge Aggregates data flow, for example. In the previous section, we configured the data flow source to simply pull all data from the `marketing.Impressions` table, as shown in figure 6.13.

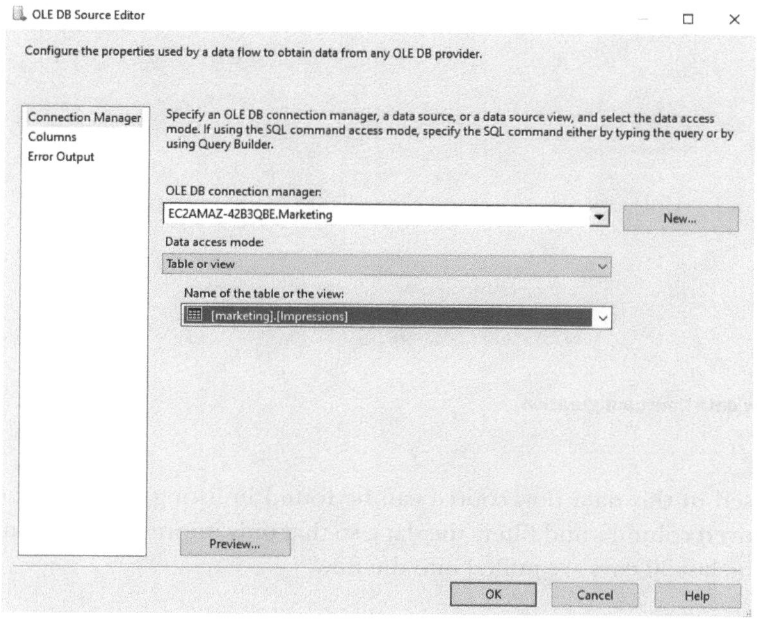

Figure 6.13 Original data source configuration

If I execute the data flow task on my test rig, it takes 16.403 seconds to complete.

If we examine the data flow, however, we will notice that the only columns we need in the flow are `CampaignID`, `CountryCode`, `EventTime`, `BidPrice`, and `CostPerMille`. If we removed the other columns, which are unnecessary, then the buffers would be smaller and more performant.

Let's also imagine that there is a business rule, which means that backdated impression data is only supplied for the last 30 days. Therefore, we know that any data older than 30 days won't change, so the aggregates do not need to be reprocessed. We could reduce the number of data buffers that the data flow needs to process by filtering the data at source.

To achieve this, let's reconfigure our data flow source to load data using a command rather than extracting all data from the table. The reconfigured data flow is shown in figure 6.14.

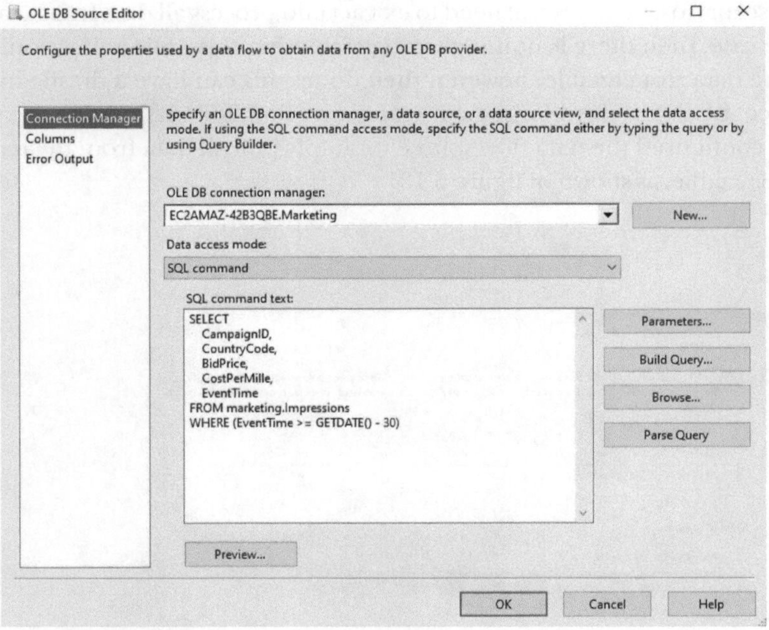

Figure 6.14 New data flow configuration

The query used in this data flow source can be found in listing 6.7. The query pulls only the required columns and filters the data, so that only impressions with an `EventTime` inside the last 30 days are pulled into the flow.

Listing 6.7 Loading impression data

```
SELECT
    CampaignID,
    CountryCode,
    BidPrice,
    CostPerMille,
    EventTime
FROM marketing.Impressions
WHERE (EventTime >= GETDATE() - 30) ;
```

When I executed the data flow on my test rig with the new configuration, it completed in 2.937 seconds. If we have a tight ETL window, performance enhancements like this, implemented throughout our packages, could make a huge difference.

> **TIP** Because the filter is based on date, if you are following along with this example in the future, it is likely that you will not return any rows. You can resolve this by either updating the event times in your base table or altering the `WHERE` clause in the data flow source query.

If we do not need all of the data from our source, then we should filter it at source to reduce the size and number of data buffers required within our flow.

Summary

- When loading data from an external source, we should always try to keep as much data as possible. Consider using staging tables with expansive column types, and use the Redirect Rows feature to pull bad rows into an error-handling table.
- Tweaking data flow settings, such as the `MaximumRowsPerBuffer`, can have a significant impact on performance. This can be important, especially when we have a tight ETL window.
- When loading data into SQL Server, use OLE DB sources and destinations where possible for performance. Always tweak OLE DB destination fast load options to optimize performance for your environment.
- There is no magic bullet configuration. Test various configurations to see which performs best in a particular environment.
- Avoid using SSIS as an orchestration tool for Execute T-SQL tasks. Doing this loses many of the benefits of using SSIS, such as out-of-the-box logging and error handling.
- Avoid extracting all the data from a table unless you really need to. We can get good performance improvements in our package by limiting the number of columns and rows returned to match what is required by our data flow. If you don't need all the data in the table, use a data flow source with a SQL command and filter the data at source.

7 Error handling, testing, source control, and deployment

This chapter covers

- Handling T-SQL errors
- Troubleshooting code
- Performance testing
- Modern development practices

When one thinks of the role of a database developer, it is easy to focus exclusively on writing efficient T-SQL code. In reality, however, the modern database developer has to consider many other things. Error handling is the first of these areas. If a procedure throws an error in production, we will want that error to be handled gracefully to mitigate risks such as inconsistent data. Error handling can even make a piece of code retry to avoid an application support team having to step in. We will invariably also want to be notified if an error does occur so that it can be investigated.

We also need to be able to debug code errors efficiently. Code ends up with bugs. That is a fact of life. When there are bugs in our code, we need to be able to debug them in an efficient manner. There is no point in writing a piece of code in a day if it then takes a week to debug it. Therefore, understanding debugging methodology is essential when working with complex code.

A common mistake I see being made by SQL developers is a lack of testing. We will explore unit testing as part of a wider look at the (lack of) adoption of modern development practices by SQL developers. We will explore the benefits of keeping our code in source control, writing unit tests, and using an automated build-and-deploy pipeline. In chapter 4 we created a database called `MagicChoc`, and in chapter 6 we created a database called `Marketing`. We will be using both databases in this chapter.

Modern development practices require code to be kept in source control and for DevOps processes to be used for deploying code. These practices have been the norm for many years now, but SQL developers seem to be late adopters. I have seen many SQL Server teams who still store their "source code" in database backups and manually run complex, lovingly handcrafted scripts to deploy their data-tier applications. We will explore both of these mistakes in this chapter.

Development tools

So far in this book, except for when we explored SQL Server Integration Services (SSIS), I have been using SQL Server Management Studio (SSMS) to create the examples, and my assumption is that you have probably been using SSMS to follow along. It is very familiar to SQL Server professionals, and it's very easy to use.

There are several other tools that we can use to develop T-SQL, however, such as Visual Studio Code, SQL Server Data Tools (SSDT), and Azure Data Studio. For some advanced development techniques, we need to use some of these additional development tools. For mistakes #28 to #32 in this chapter, we will use the SQL Server Database Project template in Visual Studio. This can be downloaded from the Visual Studio marketplace, or we can install SSDT.

7.1 #26 Writing code that doesn't handle errors

If our code fails in production, the last thing we want is for an unhandled error to occur. If our code fails, we want it to fail gracefully and provide useful diagnostic information to the application support team, who will need to try and resolve the issue. To explore the issue, let's first examine a stored procedure that has no error handling and take a look at some of the consequences.

The stored procedure in listing 7.1 can be created inside the `MagicChoc` database. It is a simple stored procedure that accepts the parameters required to create a new sales order. It generates the required prefix for the `SalesOrderNumber` based on the customer and then inserts a record into the `SalesOrderHeaders` and `SalesOrderDetails` tables.

Listing 7.1 Creating the `dbo.InsertSalesOrder` stored procedure

```
CREATE PROCEDURE dbo.InsertSalesOrder
    @SalesOrderNumber NVARCHAR(12),
    @SalesOrderDate DATE,
    @SalesPersonID INT,
    @SalesAreaID INT,
```

```
    @CustomerID INT,
    @SalesOrderDeliveryDueDate DATE,
    @SalesOrderDeliveryActualDate DATE,
    @CurrierUsedForDelivery NVARCHAR(32),
    @ProductID INT,
    @Quantity INT
AS
BEGIN
    BEGIN TRANSACTION

        DECLARE @CustomerPrefix NVARCHAR(12) ;
        SET @CustomerPrefix = (
            SELECT SUBSTRING(CustomerCompanyName,1,3)
            FROM dbo.Customers
            WHERE CustomerID = @CustomerID
        ) ;

        INSERT INTO dbo.SalesOrderHeaders
        VALUES (
            @CustomerPrefix + @SalesOrderNumber
            , @SalesOrderDate
            , @SalesPersonID
            , @SalesAreaID
            , @CustomerID
            , @SalesOrderDeliveryDueDate
            , @SalesOrderDeliveryActualDate
            , @CurrierUsedForDelivery
        ) ;

        INSERT INTO dbo.SalesOrderDetails (
            ProductID
            , Quantity
            , SalesOrderNumber
        )
        VALUES (
            @ProductID
            , @Quantity
            , @CustomerPrefix + @SalesOrderNumber
        ) ;

    COMMIT
END
```

Let's take a look at this in practice by using our stored procedure to try to create some sales orders. The script in the following listing will execute our stored procedure, and the sales order will be successfully inserted into both the `SalesOrderHeaders` and `SalesOrderDetails` tables.

Listing 7.2 Successfully inserting a sales order

```
EXEC dbo.InsertSalesOrder
      '1635D-U06'
    , '2023-08-19'
    , 1
```

```
    , 1
    , 2
    , '2023-09-01'
    , NULL
    , 'Get Me There!'
    , 5
    , 1 ;
```

So far, so good! The procedure ran successfully, and a sales order was added. Let's execute the stored procedure again using the script in listing 7.3. This time, before executing the stored procedure, we are going to change the name of the `SalesOrderDetails` table to be `SalesOrderLines`. Naturally, this will cause a failure inside the transaction.

Listing 7.3 Attempting to insert into a table that does not exist

```
EXEC sp_rename 'dbo.SalesOrderDetails', 'SalesOrderLines' ;
GO

EXEC dbo.InsertSalesOrder
      '1637D-U06'
    , '2023-08-19'
    , 1
    , 1
    , 2
    , '2023-09-01'
    , NULL
    , 'Get Me There!'
    , 5
    , 1 ;
```

Two errors have been thrown, as shown:

```
Msg 208, Level 16, State 1, Procedure dbo.InsertSalesOrder, Line 35 [Batch
Start Line 2]
Invalid object name 'dbo.SalesOrderDetails'.
Msg 266, Level 16, State 2, Procedure dbo.InsertSalesOrder, Line 35 [Batch
Start Line 2]

Transaction count after EXECUTE indicates a mismatching number of BEGIN and
COMMIT statements. Previous count = 0, current count = 1.
```

As we would expect, the first error is caused by the incorrect table name. The second error is more interesting, however. It states that the number of open transactions is higher at the end of the execution of the stored procedure than it was at the start. We can test this by running `SELECT @@TRANCOUNT`. Assuming we have no other open transactions, this value will show as `1`, whereas it should ideally be `0`. This is because the transaction did not automatically roll back. We need to manually run the `ROLLBACK` command to clear up this transaction, and if you are following along, you should do that now. You should then run the following code to correct the name of the table:

```
EXEC sp_rename 'dbo.SalesOrderLines', 'SalesOrderDetails' ;
GO
```

The code inside the stored procedure is wrapped inside a *transaction*, which is a collection of one or more T-SQL statements that update data and are committed or undone as a single logical unit. At the most basic level, a transaction must have four key properties, which are known as ACID. *ACID* is an acronym that stands for atomic, consistent, isolated, and durable.

When we say that a transaction is atomic, it means that all statements are either committed or undone ("rolled back") as a single unit. They either all succeed or they all fail. When we say that they are consistent, we mean that the data in the tables will be left in a consistent state at the end of the transaction. For a transaction to be isolated, it cannot interact with other transactions that are happening concurrently. For a transaction to be durable, the updated data cannot be lost after a transaction has been committed, even if SQL Server were to crash.

SQL Server uses many mechanisms to ensure that transactions have ACID properties, including locking, which enforces isolation by stopping other transactions from updating other rows at the same time, and logging by means of a transaction log, which is flushed to disk before the commit of a transaction is completed to ensure durability.

It is very important to note, however, that SQL Server is a large, complex product, and there are many nuances. For example, transaction isolation can be varied by using different transaction isolation levels, and we will examine these in chapter 10.

Another nuance is durability. A feature called *delayed durability* can improve performance by reducing IO contention on busy systems but at the expense of durability. In other words, an ill-timed system crash could result in committed data being lost.

Regarding error handling, a very important nuance is around atomicity and consistency. While a transaction should ensure that all data is either committed or rolled back as a single unit, the setting of `XACT_ABORT` will define how strictly this rule is adhered to. If `XACT_ABORT` is set to `OFF`, which is the default value, then some errors, such as data truncation, will not prevent the transaction from committing other statements.

Let's look at another example. The script in listing 7.4 executes our stored procedure again. This time, the object names are correct, but we are trying to insert a `ProductID` that does not exist. This will cause a primary key violation.

Listing 7.4 Inserting an incorrect product ID into a sales order

```
EXEC dbo.InsertSalesOrder
      '1655D-U06'
    , '2023-08-19'
    , 1
    , 1
    , 2
    , '2023-09-01'
    , NULL
    , 'Get Me There!'
    , 86
    , 1 ;
```

The output of this execution is

```
(1 row affected)
Msg 547, Level 16, State 0, Procedure dbo.InsertSalesOrder, Line 35 [Batch
Start Line 0]
The INSERT statement conflicted with the FOREIGN KEY constraint
"FK__SalesOrde__Produ__619B8048". The conflict occurred in database
"MagicChoc", table "dbo.Products", column 'ProductID'.
```

In this output, we can see that the insert into the `SalesOrderHeaders` table succeeded, but the insert into the `SalesOrderDetails` table failed. If we were to run `SELECT @@TRANCOUNT` at this point, we would return a value of `0`. This means that the transaction has been committed. Specifically, it has committed the insert from the first statement, despite the second insert failing.

This is because if `XACT_ABORT` is turned off, which is the default behavior, then some runtime errors, such as deadlocks or incorrect object names, will cause a transaction to abort, but other errors, such as key violations, will allow the transaction to continue and only fail the statement.

This has left our data in an incomplete state. The sales order exists in the `SalesOrderHeaders` table, but it has no line items associated with it. What's more, the error was not of high enough severity to be written to the error log, which will make it more opaque to debug.

The first takeaway from these examples is that it is good practice to turn on `XACT_ABORT`. This can be done within the stored procedure, or batch, by using `SET XACT_ABORT ON`. However, I would recommend turning it on globally for connections to the instance using the script in the following listing.

Listing 7.5 Turning `XACT_ABORT` on globally for instance connections

```
EXEC sp_configure
     'user options'
   , '16384' ;
GO

RECONFIGURE WITH OVERRIDE ;
GO
```

The second, larger takeaway is that it really is a good idea to properly handle errors within our code. SQL Server provides comprehensive error-handling functionality, but not taking advantage of it is a mistake I see far too often.

Therefore, let's explore how we could have written our stored procedure to better encompass error handling. To do this, the first feature to be aware of is a construct called `TRY..CATCH`, which may be familiar to those of you with a .NET background.

> **TIP** For .NET developers, please be aware that SQL Server does not support a `FINALLY` block, which is a third aspect of the construct in .NET languages that allows for code to be run regardless of the success or failure of the `TRY` block.

Within a TRY..CATCH block, SQL Server will attempt to execute the code within the TRY block. If the code completes successfully, then SQL Server will exit the construct. If an error occurs, however, SQL Server will jump out of the TRY block at the line that caused the error and move into the CATCH block. The code within the CATCH block will then be executed.

This means that we can attempt to execute code, but if it fails, we can put error-handling logic inside the CATCH block. This logic could include rolling back a transaction and raising meaningful errors.

There are two ways to throw meaningful errors in SQL Server. The first involves calling the RAISERROR() function. The second is a simpler error-handling feature called THROW. While the two pieces of functionality both exist to raise errors, there are differences, which we will explore.

> **TIP** Did you spot the mistake in RAISERROR()? If not, look again. There is a spelling mistake. But the mistake is not in this book; it is in SQL Server. It is probably the most famous and definitely the most ironic spelling mistake in the industry!

Within the context of a CATCH block, we have access to system functions that expose information about the error that has occurred. Specifically, the functions available, each having an intuitive name, are

- ERROR_NUMBER()—Returns the error number of the error that caused the CATCH block to execute
- ERROR_SEVERITY()—Returns the severity level of the error
- ERROR_STATE()—Returns the state number of the error, which can help identify the cause of the error
- ERROR_MESSAGE()—Returns the complete text of the error message
- ERROR_PROCEDURE()—Returns the name of the stored procedure or trigger where the error occurred
- ERROR_LINE()—Returns the line number within the procedure or trigger where the error occurred

These functions can be used to enhance the error-handling logic. For example, we could branch the code within the CATCH block based on the error number. We could also push this data to an error-logging table.

Let's see how we could enhance our stored procedure to use a TRY..CATCH block. After we begin our transaction, we will begin a TRY block, which contains our business logic. The last statement within the TRY block will COMMIT our transaction.

The TRY block is immediately followed by a CATCH block, which contains our error-handling logic. In here, we ROLLBACK the transaction and then throw an error using the THROW command.

There are two ways that we can use the THROW command. We can use the keyword THROW on its own, which will cause the original error to be thrown. Alternatively, we can specify a custom error number, error message, and state to be thrown by adding these to the THROW statement. What the THROW statement cannot do is throw an error message that is stored in the sys.messages table, and we cannot provide an error severity. The severity of an error raised by the THROW command is always level 16, which means that it is not logged.

Error severity levels

In SQL Server, there are 25 error severity levels. Severity levels 0 through 10 are not really errors. Instead, they are informational messages. Errors of severity level 10 are informational messages that are converted to severity level 0 for reasons of compatibility.

Errors with severity levels of 11 through 16 are regarded as errors that can be fixed by the user, such as incorrect object names, syntax errors, permission-denied errors, and deadlocks.

Error severity levels 17 through 19 are errors that can usually only be fixed by an administrator, such as running out of resources, exceeding limits enforced by the Database Engine, and issues within the Database Engine that have caused the statement to fail without the connection to the instance being closed.

Errors with a severity level of 20 through 24 are fatal errors, such as encountering database or media corruption. Errors with a severity level of 19 through 24 are written to the error log.

When thinking about error handling, there are a few things about severity levels that we should bear in mind. First, only errors with a severity of 11 through 19 will cause code execution to move to the CATCH block. If an error with severity 0 through 10 is thrown, then execution will continue because the error was just informational. If the severity is 20 or over, on the other hand, then there is no point moving to the CATCH block because the error was fatal and, in many cases, the connection will even be terminated.

The next thing to bear in mind is that, as mentioned earlier, errors raised by THROW have a fixed severity of 16, meaning that they will never be written to the error log, which, in many cases, will make the errors opaque to anyone trying to troubleshoot.

THROW can only raise either the original system error or an ad hoc error, meaning an error that is not stored in sys.messages. Therefore, the error number we throw must be 50,000 or higher.

Finally, we need to bear in mind that although each severity level has a defined meaning (for example, severity level 22 means that a table or index has been damaged by a hardware or software issue), these levels only apply to system errors. It is perfectly possible to create a custom error message and "hijack" an error severity for our own purposes, which may not correspond to the intended severity level. This, of course, would not be good practice, however, as it is likely to cause confusion for colleagues.

The script in listing 7.6 shows the updated stored procedure definition, which has been encapsulated in a TRY..CATCH block. If the code in the TRY block fails, then execution will jump to the CATCH block, where the transaction will be rolled back, and then the error thrown using the THROW statement.

Listing 7.6 Adding a `TRY..CATCH` block to `InsertOrders`

```
ALTER PROCEDURE dbo.InsertSalesOrder
    @SalesOrderNumber NVARCHAR(12),
    @SalesOrderDate DATE,
    @SalesPersonID INT,
    @SalesAreaID INT,
    @CustomerID INT,
    @SalesOrderDeliveryDueDate DATE,
    @SalesOrderDeliveryActualDate DATE,
    @CurrierUsedForDelivery NVARCHAR(32),
    @ProductID INT,
    @Quantity INT
AS
BEGIN
    BEGIN TRANSACTION
    BEGIN TRY
        DECLARE @CustomerPrefix NVARCHAR(12) ;
        SET @CustomerPrefix = (
            SELECT SUBSTRING(CustomerCompanyName,1,3)
            FROM dbo.Customers
            WHERE CustomerID = @CustomerID
        ) ;

            INSERT INTO dbo.SalesOrderHeaders
            VALUES (
                @CustomerPrefix + @SalesOrderNumber
              , @SalesOrderDate
              , @SalesPersonID
              , @SalesAreaID
              , @CustomerID
              , @SalesOrderDeliveryDueDate
              , @SalesOrderDeliveryActualDate
              , @CurrierUsedForDelivery
            ) ;

        INSERT INTO dbo.SalesOrderDetails (
              ProductID
            , Quantity
            , SalesOrderNumber
        )
        VALUES (
            @ProductID
          , @Quantity
          , @CustomerPrefix + @SalesOrderNumber
        ) ;

    COMMIT
    END TRY
    BEGIN CATCH
        ROLLBACK ;
        THROW ;
    END CATCH
END
```

So far, this does not give us a huge benefit, however. If we executed the command in listing 7.4 again, we would receive the following error:

```
Msg 2627, Level 14, State 1, Procedure dbo.InsertSalesOrder, Line 23 [Batch
Start Line 0]
Violation of PRIMARY KEY constraint 'PK__SalesOrd__CF6C70EEA96DBC48'.
Cannot insert duplicate key in object 'dbo.SalesOrderHeaders'. The
duplicate key value is (Coo1655D-U06).
```

Therefore, let's enhance our `InsertSalesOrder` procedure even further. The script in listing 7.7 will update the procedure again. This time, we will branch the code within the `CATCH` block using `IF` statements, combined with the system functions that expose error information, so that the `CATCH` bock behaves differently, depending on the error thrown. If the error is a primary key violation, a custom error message will be thrown. If the error is a deadlock, then the `GOTO` command will be used to attempt to execute the code in the `TRY` block again. If any other error is raised, then the original error will be thrown.

Listing 7.7 Updating `InsertSalesOrder` procedure to branch `CATCH` block

```
ALTER PROCEDURE dbo.InsertSalesOrder
    @SalesOrderNumber NVARCHAR(12),
    @SalesOrderDate DATE,
    @SalesPersonID INT,
    @SalesAreaID INT,
    @CustomerID INT,
    @SalesOrderDeliveryDueDate DATE,
    @SalesOrderDeliveryActualDate DATE,
    @CurrierUsedForDelivery NVARCHAR(32),
    @ProductID INT,
    @Quantity INT
AS
BEGIN
    BEGIN TRANSACTION
    RETRY:
    BEGIN TRY
        DECLARE @CustomerPrefix NVARCHAR(12) ;
        SET @CustomerPrefix = (
            SELECT SUBSTRING(CustomerCompanyName,1,3)
            FROM dbo.Customers
            WHERE CustomerID = @CustomerID
        ) ;

       INSERT INTO dbo.SalesOrderHeaders
        VALUES (
              @CustomerPrefix + @SalesOrderNumber
            , @SalesOrderDate
            , @SalesPersonID
            , @SalesAreaID
            , @CustomerID
            , @SalesOrderDeliveryDueDate
            , @SalesOrderDeliveryActualDate
            , @CurrierUsedForDelivery
```

```
        ) ;

        INSERT INTO dbo.SalesOrderDetails (
              ProductID
            , Quantity
            , SalesOrderNumber
        )
        VALUES (
              @ProductID
            , @Quantity
            , @CustomerPrefix + @SalesOrderNumber
        ) ;
    COMMIT
    END TRY
    BEGIN CATCH
        IF ERROR_NUMBER() = 2627                          Error is a primary
        BEGIN                                             key violation.
          ROLLBACK ;
              THROW 50001,
                'A duplicate sales order has been entered.', 1 ;
        END
        IF ERROR_NUMBER() = 1205                          Error is a deadlock.
        BEGIN
            ROLLBACK ;
             GOTO RETRY ;
        END
        IF ERROR_NUMBER() <> 2627                         Any other error
            AND ERROR_NUMBER() <> 1205
        BEGIN
        ROLLBACK ;
            THROW ;
        END
    END CATCH
END
```

If we were to execute the command in listing 7.4 again, we would now receive the following error:

```
Msg 50001, Level 16, State 1, Procedure dbo.InsertSalesOrder, Line 52
[Batch Start Line 0]
A duplicate sales order has been entered.
```

To make the best use of SQL Server's error-handling functionality, we may want to mix and match `THROW` with `RAISERROR()`. For example, in our scenario, if a generic error occurs, we may want to continue to use `THROW` so that the original error message bubbles up. We may choose to use `RAISERROR()` for primary key violations, however, so that we can send the error to the error log.

If we want to take this approach, we will first need to create a custom error message, which can be raised by `RAISERROR()`. To do this, we will use the `sp_addmessage` system stored procedure, as demonstrated in the following listing.

Listing 7.8 Creating a custom error message

```
EXEC sp_addmessage
      @msgnum = 50001
    , @severity = 16
    , @msgtext = 'A duplicate sales order has been entered.' ;
```

The `InsertSalesOrder` procedure can then be updated to call `RAISERROR()`, as shown in listing 7.9. The `WITH LOG` syntax will cause the error to be written to the SQL Server error log, despite the severity only being 16.

Listing 7.9 Updating `InsertSalesOrder` procedure to use `RAISERROR()`

```
ALTER PROCEDURE dbo.InsertSalesOrder
    @SalesOrderNumber NVARCHAR(12),
    @SalesOrderDate DATE,
    @SalesPersonID INT,
    @SalesAreaID INT,
    @CustomerID INT,
    @SalesOrderDeliveryDueDate DATE,
    @SalesOrderDeliveryActualDate DATE,
    @CurrierUsedForDelivery NVARCHAR(32),
    @ProductID INT,
    @Quantity INT
AS
BEGIN
    BEGIN TRANSACTION
    RETRY:
    BEGIN TRY
        DECLARE @CustomerPrefix NVARCHAR(12) ;
        SET @CustomerPrefix = (
            SELECT SUBSTRING(CustomerCompanyName,1,3)
            FROM dbo.Customers
            WHERE CustomerID = @CustomerID
        ) ;

       INSERT INTO dbo.SalesOrderHeaders
        VALUES (
              @CustomerPrefix + @SalesOrderNumber
            , @SalesOrderDate
            , @SalesPersonID
            , @SalesAreaID
            , @CustomerID
            , @SalesOrderDeliveryDueDate
            , @SalesOrderDeliveryActualDate
            , @CurrierUsedForDelivery
        ) ;

        INSERT INTO dbo.SalesOrderDetails (
              ProductID
            , Quantity
            , SalesOrderNumber
        )
```

```
        VALUES (
              @ProductID
            , @Quantity
            , @CustomerPrefix + @SalesOrderNumber
        ) ;

    COMMIT
    END TRY
    BEGIN CATCH
        IF ERROR_NUMBER() = 2627
        BEGIN
            ROLLBACK ;
            RAISERROR(50001, 16, 1) WITH LOG ;
        END
        IF ERROR_NUMBER() = 1205
        BEGIN
         ROLLBACK ;
            GOTO RETRY ;
        END
        IF ERROR_NUMBER() <> 2627
            AND ERROR_NUMBER() <> 1205
        BEGIN
             ROLLBACK ;
             THROW ;
        END
    END CATCH
END
```

If we were to then execute the command in listing 7.4 again, not only would our custom error be returned to the client, but it will also be written to the SQL Server error log, as shown in figure 7.1.

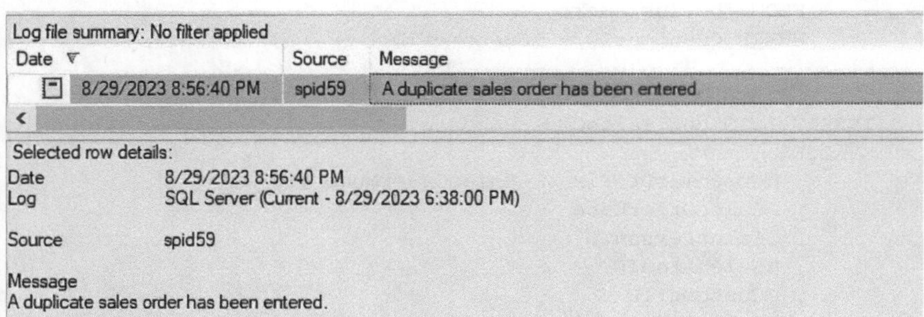

Figure 7.1 Custom error in SQL Server error log

The alternative to using `RAISERROR() WITH LOG` is to use a custom error table. For example, the script in listing 7.10 first creates an error log table. It then updates the stored procedure again, reverting it back to using `THROW`. This time, however, it updates the `CATCH` block to log the error to our newly created table.

Listing 7.10 Adding a custom logging table to `InsertSalesOrder`

```
CREATE TABLE dbo.ErrorLog (
    ID              INT     PRIMARY KEY IDENTITY,
    ErrorMessage    NVARCHAR(MAX),
    ErrorNumber     INT,
    ErrorSeverity   INT
) ;
GO

ALTER PROCEDURE dbo.InsertSalesOrder
    @SalesOrderNumber NVARCHAR(12),
    @SalesOrderDate DATE,
    @SalesPersonID INT,
    @SalesAreaID INT,
    @CustomerID INT,
    @SalesOrderDeliveryDueDate DATE,
    @SalesOrderDeliveryActualDate DATE,
    @CurrierUsedForDelivery NVARCHAR(32),
    @ProductID INT,
    @Quantity INT
AS
BEGIN
    BEGIN TRANSACTION
    RETRY:
    BEGIN TRY
        DECLARE @CustomerPrefix NVARCHAR(12) ;
        SET @CustomerPrefix = (
            SELECT SUBSTRING(CustomerCompanyName,1,3)
            FROM dbo.Customers
            WHERE CustomerID = @CustomerID
        ) ;

        INSERT INTO dbo.SalesOrderHeaders
        VALUES (
              @CustomerPrefix + @SalesOrderNumber
            , @SalesOrderDate
            , @SalesPersonID
            , @SalesAreaID
            , @CustomerID
            , @SalesOrderDeliveryDueDate
            , @SalesOrderDeliveryActualDate
            , @CurrierUsedForDelivery
        ) ;

        INSERT INTO dbo.SalesOrderDetails (
              ProductID
            , Quantity
            , SalesOrderNumber
        )
        VALUES (
              @ProductID
            , @Quantity
            , @CustomerPrefix + @SalesOrderNumber
        ) ;
```

```
    COMMIT
    END TRY
    BEGIN CATCH
        IF ERROR_NUMBER() = 2627
        BEGIN
            ROLLBACK ;
            INSERT INTO dbo.ErrorLog (
                ErrorMessage,
                ErrorNumber,
                ErrorSeverity
            )
            SELECT
                  ERROR_MESSAGE()
                , ERROR_NUMBER()
                , ERROR_SEVERITY() ;
            THROW 50001,
                'A duplicate sales order has been entered.', 1 ;
        END
        IF ERROR_NUMBER() = 1205
        BEGIN
         ROLLBACK ;
            GOTO RETRY ;
        END
        IF ERROR_NUMBER() <> 2627
            AND ERROR_NUMBER() <> 1205
        BEGIN
            ROLLBACK ;
             THROW ;
        END
    END CATCH
END
```

Adds an INSERT statement that adds the data to our logging table

Replaces the RAISERROR() with a THROW

WARNING If we take the custom error-logging approach, then the ordering of statements is very important. The `INSERT` statement must be after the `ROLLBACK` and before the `THROW`. If the `INSERT` was before the `ROLLBACK`, then it would be part of the transaction and would therefore be rolled back along with the code in the `TRY` block. If the `INSERT` was after the `THROW` statement, it would not be executed.

We should consider adding error handling to our code that modifies data. This allows us to roll back transactions and raise meaningful error messages. We should also consider logging error messages where appropriate. In certain circumstances, such as deadlocks, we may even wish to code retry logic into our procedures.

7.2 #27 Failing to alert on errors

Once our stored procedures are in production, depending on the nature of the code, there are various ways that it may be executed. It may be executed by an ETL tool, such as SSIS; it may be executed by a SQL Server Agent job, which is an orchestrated series of actions that can be scheduled to run at a specific time; or it could be called by a client application.

If a procedure is called by a client application and if the application is well written, errors should bubble up to the user and be noticed. If the procedure is called by an automated process, however, then it may be opaque to discovery. It will require an application support person to proactively check the SQL Server Agent logs, `SSISDB` logs, or custom logging tables to discover a failure.

> **TIP** As discussed in the previous section, depending on the severity of the error and the method used to raise the error, it may not be logged within the SQL Server error log. That makes the error log an unreliable place to check for application errors.

Proactive checks are often not undertaken, and even if they are, then they are subject to human error and *opportunity cost*, which means someone is spending their time performing menial tasks rather than higher value work. All of this means that it is very easy for a failure to go without being noticed until a user reports that the data looks incorrect.

So how can we solve this issue? The answer is alerting. If we look at any layers of an IT infrastructure stack, from the network layer through to the operating system, support teams will invariably have alerting in place to notify them if an error occurs that they need to investigate or take action to correct. When it comes to data-tier applications, however, alerting is often overlooked, and this is a mistake.

Depending on the scale and priorities of our application, we may be lucky enough to have enterprise-grade observability software, such as SolarWinds or LogicMonitor. If this is the case, then we should use this software to create a custom check that will alert if a failure occurs. If we take this path, then our custom data source will usually be written to read data out of a logging table at regular intervals and raise an alert if an error has been written to the log. When custom logging and log tables within `SSISDB` are used, this will usually involve a simple `SELECT` statement. If we need to read information from the SQL Server Agent log, however, then we will need to use the `sp_help_jobsteplog` stored procedure. For example, if we had a SQL Server Agent job called `Populate_Fact_Tables`, then we could use the following command to pull the log information for that step:

```
EXEC msdb.dbo.sp_help_jobhistory
      @job_name = 'Populate_Fact_Tables'
    , @mode = 'FULL' ;
```

If we are not lucky enough to have an enterprise-grade monitoring tool that we can harness to generate alerts, then we can use SQL Server's built-in functionality. In this scenario, we will use a feature called Database Mail, along with the SQL Server Agent alerting subsystem.

> **Database Mail**
>
> It is worth noting, at this point, that Database Mail is much maligned in the community, as it is not an enterprise-grade tool. While I broadly agree with this assessment, frankly speaking, if our organization has not invested in a third-party tool that we can use to do

(continued)

the job, then we need to work with what we have, and I have been in this situation several times.

One of the main complaints about the feature is that it does not scale. The functionality resides in `msdb`, and in today's complex SQL Server environments, a failover event may result in the tool ceasing to work correctly.

This issue has been partly addressed by the introduction of contained availability groups, which contain their own copy of the `master` and `msdb` system databases. At the time of writing, however, and hopefully not at the time of reading, there was a bug in contained availability groups that prevents the Database Mail functionality from working.

It is also worth noting that, to use the functionality, we will require access to an SMTP relay server. Database Mail does not have SMTP services built in. It needs to send the mail via an existing SMTP service.

A full discussion of Database Mail is beyond the scope of this book, but further details can be found at https://mng.bz/PND9.

Let's explore how we can create an alert that will fire in response to an error message. Assuming that Database Mail is already configured, there are two artifacts that we will need to create. The first is an operator, which will be configured to use a Database Mail profile, and the second is the alert itself.

It is important to note that SQL Server Agent alerts rely on the Windows application log to know when SQL Server has fired an event. Events are forwarded to the application log when they are written to the SQL Server error log. Therefore, if an event does not create a log entry, then it will not cause an alert to fire. This means that when we use this approach we must ensure that our error messages are raised with `RAISERROR()` using the `WITH LOG` option. This means that they will be logged and the alert will fire even if the severity level is below 19.

Let's use the script in listing 7.11 to create an operator called Pete, who will be notified if an alert is fired.

TIP In a real-world scenario, we would preferably use a group email address or a distribution list.

Listing 7.11 Creating a SQL Server Agent operator

```
EXEC msdb.dbo.sp_add_operator
      @name= ,Pete'
    , @enabled=1
    , @email_address= ,pete@onehudredsqlmistakes.com' ;
```

TIP SQL Server currently supports pager notifications as well as email, provided that we have third-party pager-to-email software. This functionality is deprecated, however, and should not be used.

To create the alert, we can choose New Alert from the context of the Alerts node under SQL Server Agent in SSMS. This will cause the New Alert dialog box to be displayed. The General page of this dialog box is shown in figure 7.2. Here we have given the alert a name and specified that we want it to respond to a SQL Server event. Other options are to make the alert respond to a WMI event or a SQL Server performance condition. In the Database Name drop-down, we can leave the default of all databases or we can select a specific database that the alert must be raised in. Finally, we can choose if we want the alert to fire in response to either a specific error number or a specific severity level.

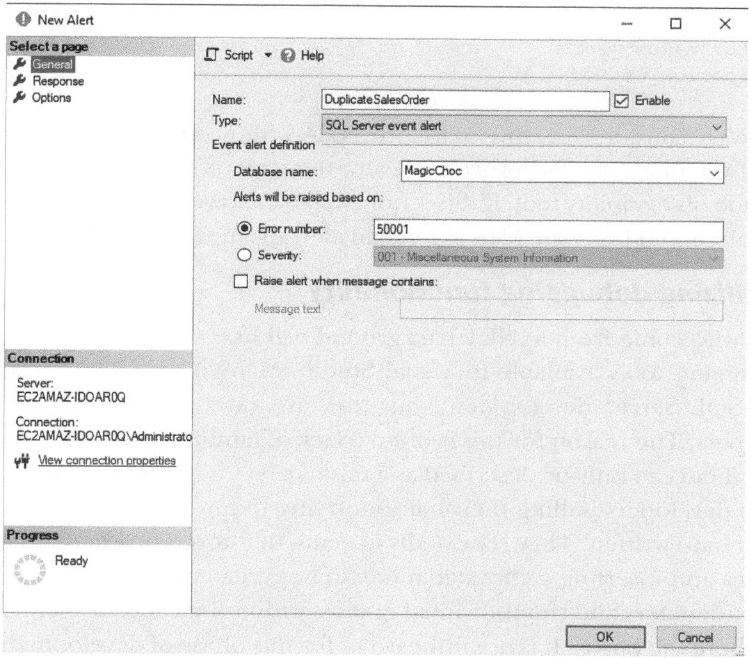

Figure 7.2 Database Mail New Alert dialog box—General page

In the Response page of the dialog box, we can choose if we want to execute a SQL Server Agent job in response to the alert, which will try to remediate the issue, or if we want to send an alert to an operator, or both. For our purpose, we will tick the Notify Operators option. This will cause the Operator list to become active, and we can select Email next to the Pete operator.

On the Options page of the dialog, we can create additional notification text that will be sent with the email. We can also specify a delay between alerts being sent. This functionality can be used to reduce noise alerts when an alert fires repeatedly in quick succession.

Alternatively, instead of using the GUI, we could have created the alert using the `sp_add_alert` and `sp_add_notifcation` stored procedures, in the `msdb` database. This is demonstrated in the following listing.

Listing 7.12 Creating an alert using T-SQL

```
EXEC msdb.dbo.sp_add_alert
      @name= 'DuplicateSalesOrder'
    , @message_id=50001
    , @enabled=1
    , @database_name= 'MagicChoc' ;

EXEC msdb.dbo.sp_add_notification
      @alert_name= 'DuplicateSalesOrder'
    , @operator_name= 'Pete'
    , @notification_method = 1 ;
```

We should always consider creating alerts for code within our data-tier applications, which are run via an automated process. Ideally, these alerts will be created within an enterprise-grade observability tool. If this is not available, however, then we can use SQL Server Agent alerts and Database Mail to send an alert via an existing SMTP server.

7.3 #28 Not utilizing debugging functionality

Those of you who come from a .NET background will likely be familiar with the vast array of debugging tools available in Visual Studio. Many of these features are also available for SQL Server development, but they are rarely used by inexperienced T-SQL developers. The reason for this is often a lack of familiarity with the feature set, but not using them can only be described as a mistake.

I have seen developers pulling their hair out trying to find a bug in a stored procedure that they have written. They repeatedly execute the stored procedure, commenting out queries and inserting `PRINT` statements. They create variables to simulate the procedure's parameters and run individual queries within the code, desperately trying to work out where the bug is. It is not unheard of for this phase of development to take as long as the creation of the procedure itself.

T-SQL developers could save a great deal of time if they used the debugging functionality of Visual Studio in combination with the SQL Server Database Project template. To follow along with examples in this section, you should create a SQL Server Database Project called `Marketing` and then import the `Marketing` database that we created in chapter 6. You can import the database using the Project | Import | Database option from the context menu of the `Marketing` project. You will need to create a connection.

Once the project is configured, let's add a new item to the project and create a stored procedure using the definition in listing 7.13. The stored procedure accepts parameters for `CampaignID` and `Budget` and uses these to create a campaign summary. Two result sets are generated. The first is a financial summary of the advertising campaign, and the second is a distinct list of `ReferralURL` and `RenderingID`.

Listing 7.13 Creating a `CalculateCampaignSummary` stored procedure

```
CREATE PROCEDURE dbo.CalculateCampaignSummary
    @CampaignID INT,
    @Budget MONEY
AS
BEGIN
    DECLARE @AvgCPM DECIMAL ;
    DECLARE @CampaignCost MONEY ;
    DECLARE @NoOfImp INT ;
    DECLARE @AvgBidPrice MONEY ;
    DECLARE @CostOfBidPerc DECIMAL ;
    DECLARE @BudgetDifference MONEY ;

    SELECT
          @NoOfImp = COUNT(*)
        , @CampaignCost = (SUM(CostPerMille) / 1000) * COUNT(*)
    FROM marketing.Impressions
    WHERE CampaignID = @CampaignID
    GROUP BY CampaignID ;

    SELECT
          @avgcpm = AvgCostPerMille
        , @avgbidprice = AvgBidPrice
    FROM reporting.ImpressionAggregates
    WHERE CampaignID = @CampaignID ;

    SET @CostOfBidPerc = (@AvgBidPrice / @AvgCPM) * 100 ;
    SET @BudgetDifference = @budget - @CampaignCost ;

    SELECT
          @CampaignID CampaignID
        , @AvgCPM AvgCPM
        , @CampaignCost CampaignCost
        , @NoOfImp ImpQty
        , @CostOfBidPerc CostToBidPercentage
        , @BudgetDifference ;

    SELECT DISTINCT
          ReferralURL
        , RenderingID
    FROM marketing.Impressions
    WHERE CampaignID = @CampaignID ;
END
```

The first debugging tool that we should discuss is the Error List window, which can be found in the View menu. This is an incredibly useful window, which analyzes our code in real time and reports on build errors and IntelliSense errors. For example, if I were to add the text `Lets add an error to our code` in between the final query and the END statement, then the Error List window would update within moments, as shown in figure 7.3.

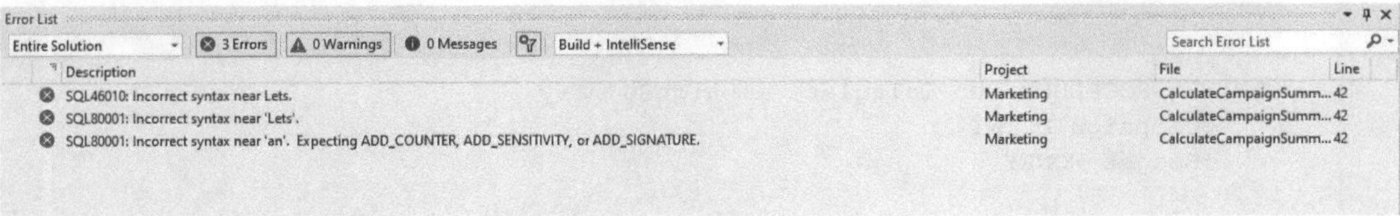

Figure 7.3 Errors in Error List window

Now let's publish our database. We can do this by selecting Publish from the context menu of the project. Select the connection (that we created earlier) to our `Marketing` database on our server from the Publish Database dialog box. This will result in our stored procedure being deployed to our SQL Server instance.

> **CAUTION** If you inserted the erroneous text along with me, you will need to remove this before publishing; otherwise, the build will fail.

Now let's execute our new stored procedure using the command in listing 7.14. Open a new query window from the context menu of the SQL Server instance in SQL Server Object Explorer and execute the procedure by using the pale-green start button on the Query window task bar.

Listing 7.14 Executing the `CalculateCampaignSummary` stored procedure

```
USE Marketing ;
GO

EXEC dbo.CalculateCampaignSummary
    22961,
    52 ;
```

At this point, we will see that the procedure throws a divide-by-zero error on line 26.

So let's execute the stored procedure again; but this time let's use the debugger. If we click the drop-down next to the pale-green start button, we will see an extra option. This is represented by a dark-green play button labeled Execute With Debugger.

When we select this option, the execution will begin, but the first statement (in our case, the `USE Marketing` statement) will be highlighted in yellow. This indicates that the execution is paused at this point. We now have several options, which are described in table 7.1.

Table 7.1 Code debugging navigation options

Option	Shortcut	Description
Continue	F5	Continue execution until the next breakpoint.*
Step Over	F10	Will step through the top layer of code but continue through lower levels, such as procedures or functions, without debugging them (unless a breakpoint is hit)*

Table 7.1 Code debugging navigation options (*continued*)

Option	Shortcut	Description
Step Into	`F11`	Will step through all layers of code. When a procedure or function is encountered, it will step into that code block and pause execution at the first statement.

* Discussed shortly

As we need to debug our stored procedure, the most appropriate choice is Step Into. So let's use F11 to step into our stored procedure. As we step through each query, we will notice the values of each variable (and parameters) being updated in the Locals window. After the first two queries have been run, the Locals window should look similar to figure 7.4.

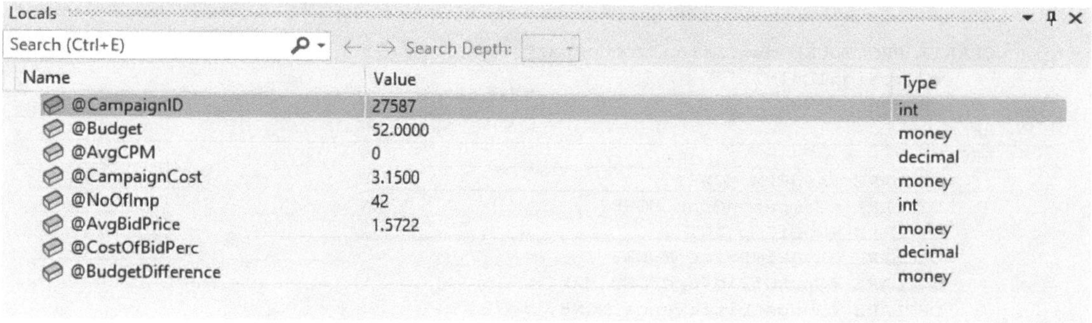

Locals

Search (Ctrl+E) Search Depth:

Name	Value	Type
@CampaignID	27587	int
@Budget	52.0000	money
@AvgCPM	0	decimal
@CampaignCost	3.1500	money
@NoOfImp	42	int
@AvgBidPrice	1.5722	money
@CostOfBidPerc		decimal
@BudgetDifference		money

Figure 7.4 Locals window

We can now see the cause of the divide-by-zero error. The value of the `@AvgCPM` variable is `0`, and the next statement will divide the `@AvgBidPrice` by this value. Let's try to get to the bottom of this. Without pausing execution, we can run queries in the Immediate window. Let's use the Immediate window to run the query in the following listing, which will ensure that we are only returning a single row, from the second query in our procedure.

Listing 7.15 Running a query in the Immediate window

```
SELECT COUNT(*) FROM reporting.ImpressionAggregates WHERE CampaignID =
@CampaignID
```

This returns the number 42. Well, that explains things! The second query in our procedure returns 42 rows, or to put it another way, we are trying to assign 42 different values to each of our variables.

Bonus mistake

For those of you who may be wondering why `@AvgCPM` and `@AvgBidPrice` behaved differently, have a look at the data types. `@AvgCPM` is a `DECIMAL`, whereas `@AvgBidPrice` is `MONEY`. Therefore, `@AvgBidPrice` is using the final value to be returned.

This was an unintentional mistake that I made when creating these examples, which is why it does not appear in the debugging example. I decided to leave it in, as the behavior is actually quite interesting and may not be what you would expect, but we should set `@AvgCPM` to be `MONEY` as well.

We had better update the second query within our stored procedure to get the average values, which is what we need. We can do this by publishing the procedure definition in the following listing.

Listing 7.16 Fixing the stored procedure

```
CREATE PROCEDURE dbo.CalculateCampaignSummary
    @CampaignID INT,
    @Budget MONEY
AS
BEGIN
    DECLARE @AvgCPM MONEY ;
    DECLARE @CampaignCost MONEY ;
    DECLARE @NoOfImp INT ;
    DECLARE @AvgBidPrice MONEY ;
    DECLARE @CostOfBidPerc DECIMAL ;
    DECLARE @BudgetDifference MONEY ;

    SELECT
          @NoOfImp = COUNT(*)
        , @CampaignCost = (SUM(CostPerMille) / 1000) * COUNT(*)
    FROM marketing.Impressions
    WHERE CampaignID = @CampaignID
    GROUP BY CampaignID ;

    SELECT
          @avgcpm = AVG(AvgCostPerMille)
        , @avgbidprice = AVG(AvgBidPrice)
    FROM reporting.ImpressionAggregates
    WHERE CampaignID = @CampaignID ;

    SET @CostOfBidPerc = (@AvgBidPrice / @AvgCPM) * 100 ;
    SET @BudgetDifference = @budget - @CampaignCost ;

    SELECT
          @CampaignID CampaignID
        , @AvgCPM AvgCPM
        , @CampaignCost CampaignCost
        , @NoOfImp ImpQty
        , @CostOfBidPerc CostToBidPercentage
        , @BudgetDifference ;
```

```
    SELECT DISTINCT
          ReferralURL
        , RenderingID
    FROM marketing.Impressions
    WHERE CampaignID = @CampaignID ;
END
```

> **NOTE** For SQL Server Database Projects, the Immediate window does have limitations. Specifically, we cannot run anything that will require the execution environment to be loaded. In general, this means that we can return scaler values, such as counts, but not result sets. It also means that some other functionality, such as system functions like `ERROR_NUMBER()` or `ERROR_MESSAGE()`, are not usable. Items such as system variables are available, however. Therefore, we could, for example, `SELECT @@trancount`.

Now that we have fixed our stored procedure, let's run it in debug mode again. But before we do, let's have a quick chat about breakpoints. A *breakpoint* is a point in the code where a developer indicates that they want execution to pause. This is an incredibly useful feature when debugging code, as it allows a developer to perform actions such as checking variable values and determining execution paths within logic.

Now that we know what a breakpoint is, let's set a breakpoint on line 26 (`SET @CostOfBidPerc = (@AvgBidPrice / @AvgCPM) * 100 ;`). We can create a simple breakpoint by simply clicking in the left margin, next to where we want the break to occur. If we now start debugging our stored procedure and use F5 instead of F11, execution will continue until the breakpoint is hit. At this point, we can check to ensure that our `@AvgCPM` and `@AvgBidPrice` variables have expected values in the Locals window before hitting F5 again to allow execution to finish.

> **WARNING** Visual Studio supports advanced breakpoints, which allow us to add conditions to breakpoints. These conditions are not supported by T-SQL, however.

Use modern debugging techniques within the SQL Server Database project template for Visual Studio to debug code. This saves time and makes the process of debugging our code a far less frustrating experience.

7.4 #29 Not making use of Schema Compare

When we are making large changes to a complex programmable object, it can be hard to keep track of what we have done. A mistake that I often see T-SQL developers make is deploying large code changes into their environment without a complete grasp of what they are going to change. This is a mistake that can lead to multiple issues in production.

Additionally, poor change and deployment processes, combined with emergency fixes, can lead to code drift between different environments. For example, if we have a development environment, a test environment, a staging environment, and a production environment, it is possible to end up with deployments out of sequence.

To avoid these issues, developers can use the *SSDT Schema Compare utility*. This is a tool that can compare databases in two different environments and highlight the differences between them. We also have the option of using a Schema Compare tool to bring the databases into synchronization.

To explore this, let's update the `CalculateCampaignSummary` stored procedure within our `Marketing` project. We are missing an alias for `@BudgetDifference` in our summary, and we also want to add a parameter that will control whether the second result set is returned. We can make the changes to the definition using the script in the next listing. Save the changes, but don't publish them yet.

Listing 7.17 Enhancing the `CalculateCampaignSummary` definition

```
CREATE PROCEDURE dbo.CalculateCampaignSummary
    @CampaignID INT,
    @Budget MONEY,
    @Detailed BIT
AS
BEGIN
    DECLARE @AvgCPM MONEY ;
    DECLARE @CampaignCost MONEY ;
    DECLARE @NoOfImp INT ;
    DECLARE @AvgBidPrice MONEY ;
    DECLARE @CostOfBidPerc DECIMAL ;
    DECLARE @BudgetDifference MONEY ;

    SELECT
          @NoOfImp = COUNT(*)
        , @CampaignCost = (SUM(CostPerMille) / 1000) * COUNT(*)
    FROM marketing.Impressions
    WHERE CampaignID = @CampaignID
    GROUP BY CampaignID ;

    SELECT
          @avgcpm = AVG(AvgCostPerMille)
        , @avgbidprice = AVG(AvgBidPrice)
    FROM reporting.ImpressionAggregates
    WHERE CampaignID = @CampaignID ;

    SET @CostOfBidPerc = (@AvgBidPrice / @AvgCPM) * 100 ;
    SET @BudgetDifference = @budget - @CampaignCost ;

    SELECT
          @CampaignID CampaignID
        , @AvgCPM AvgCPM
        , @CampaignCost CampaignCost
        , @NoOfImp ImpQty
        , @CostOfBidPerc CostToBidPercentage
        , @BudgetDifference BudgetDifference$ ;


    IF @Detailed = 1
    BEGIN
        SELECT DISTINCT
```

```
                ReferralURL
              , RenderingID
            FROM marketing.Impressions
            WHERE CampaignID = @CampaignID ;
    END
END
```

Before deploying our updated procedure, we can analyze the changes we are making. To do this, select Schema Compare from the context menu of the `Marketing` project in SQL Server Object Explorer within Visual Studio. This will cause a Compare window to appear, and we can use Select Target on the top right to select the `Marketing` database in our instance. Hitting the compare button at the top of the Compare window taskbar will now cause the comparison to be executed.

The results of this comparison are displayed in figure 7.5.

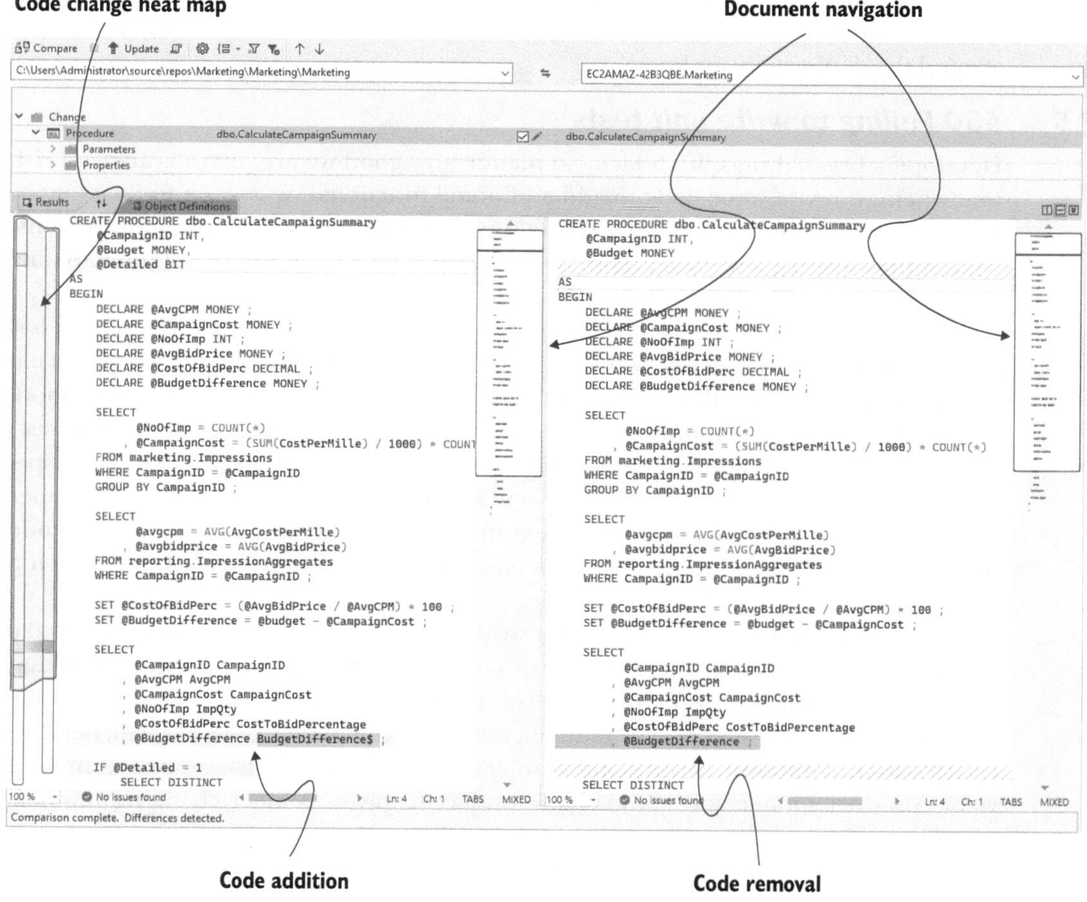

Figure 7.5 Schema Compare analysis

The pane at the top of the window shows each object that has changed, and if we select an object, the definitions of the source and target are shown in the lower pane.

You will notice that the changes are highlighted in yellow for additions and red for removals. The bar on the left of the lower pane shows where within the code the changes have happened, and we can click this bar to move to an area of interest. The box to the right of the source and target panes show which part of the code is currently visible on screen. This is also clickable, to allow us to move to different locations.

The task bar at the top of the window gives us buttons to update the target and generate an updated script. An options button allows us to set object-exclusion rules and define any differences that should be ignored. The group-objects button will toggle grouping between object type and schema, and there are also buttons that will toggle the display of unsupported actions and objects that have not changed. We can also use the up- and down-arrow buttons to move between changed objects.

When changing large, complex objects, we should use Schema Compare prior to deployment to ensure that we fully understand the changes that we are making and that we are not going to overwrite any emergency fixes that have not yet made their way back around the deployment cycle.

7.5 #30 Failing to write unit tests

Developers break things. It's a fact. No matter how good we are, there is always a risk that when we revise some code to add additional functionality, or even to fix a bug in existing functionality, we will break something else. This can happen for many reasons, from simply making a mistake to not being aware of a code module's full functionality and purpose.

In an old-fashioned SQL Server development environment, especially one that has grown organically over the years, it's likely that no developers who still work on the data-tier application will be fully aware of every requirement being met by every code module within a large application. This is even more of a truism in large, complex projects.

The solution to this problem is to write unit tests. A *unit test* is designed to test a specific piece of functionality. This gives two main benefits. First, it prevents a developer from inadvertently breaking a piece of existing functionality when they update a code module. Second, in the spirit of self-documentation, it creates a mapping between a business requirement and a code module.

In the modern development era, not writing unit tests is a mistake—but a mistake that I see all too often in the SQL Server community. It is an even bigger mistake if the data-tier application is being delivered through *Agile project methodology*. In Agile methodologies, such as Scrum or Kanban, an application is delivered in small, iterative cycles. This has multiple benefits for a project, such as the ability to deliver a minimum viable product sooner and allowing the project to pivot to meet changing business needs more easily.

With such a project methodology, however, it is more likely that we will need to revisit more code modules later on, which increases the risk of breaking previously written functionality. This makes unit testing even more important.

Real-world example

Between 2000 and the 2010s, I was lucky enough to lead the development of some of the largest data-tier applications built in London during that period. The difference in methodology over this period was dramatic. The first and last of these projects were both multiyear projects, involving multiple companies, with more than 20 developers at their peak. They both dealt with 40 to 50 TB of data, which required complex processing.

One project involved building and analyzing click paths from disparate data sources spanning two search engines and four cookie servers. The full user journey had to be calculated, from viewing online banners or search engine searches to actually buying a product on an advertiser's website.

The other had complex data, including a 30-hour clock and a hierarchy of 36 overlapping advertising regions, where the views of an advert had to be mapped to the correct region at the correct level (or sometimes levels) of the hierarchy. Both applications were written in the SQL Server stack, and both ended up with more than 1 million lines of code.

The first of these projects had a traditional development methodology. We wrote code on a development server. Code modules were scripted out and stored in Team Foundation Server (TFS). TFS had many features; one of them was a pessimistic form of source control. We promoted the code to a User Acceptance Testing (UAT) environment using a manually scripted approach. The business would then test new features before the code was manually promoted to preproduction.

Everything was fine until the final testing phase of the project. At this point, many bugs were discovered, where developers had added new functionality and broken the original functionality in the process. Nobody had spotted it, because when code was promoted, only the new functionality was tested. Even worse, because the project lasted more than two years, developers who had written some of the early code had left, and we then had to work out what the modules were supposed to be doing. The result was a nine-month delay in go-live. Not a situation I ever wanted to repeat!

In the last of these projects, with lessons learned, we took a more modern approach. We stored our code in GitHub so that we could work more effectively as a team (see the next section); we also used Jenkins and Octopus Deploy to create a CI/CD pipeline (see section 7.6.2). We created unit tests for every code module that we wrote. The CI/CD pipeline would execute the unit tests, and the build would fail if the tests were not successful. This took a little extra effort up front to write the tests, but it meant that at the end of the project, there was not a huge backlog of bugs, and the project went live on time.

Let's follow good practice and create a unit test for our `CalculateCampaignSummary` stored procedure. To start this process, we will select the Create Unit Tests option from the context menu of our stored procedure in the SQL Server Object Explorer window in Visual Studio. This will cause the Create Unit Tests dialog box to be displayed. In the top half of this window, we can select the objects. In the lower half, we can choose if we want the testing project, which will be created as an additional project within our solution, to be based on C# or Visual Basic. Quite honestly, for the purpose of writing SQL Server unit tests, it doesn't matter too much. I generally choose C#, but that is only because I am more familiar with it. If you already have a testing project created, then you will be able to select it from this drop-down list. Give the project a name and specify a name for the output class.

The Unit Test file will then be displayed in a helpful editor. If we have multiple tests, then we can switch between them in the drop-down on the top left of the window. In the drop-down to the right of this, we can select our pretest script, test script, or posttest script.

The pretest script should be used for setting up our environment for the test. This may include tasks such as populating a table before the test is executed. We will run our script against our SQL Server instance, so there is no need for us to create a pretest script.

In the posttest script, we can clean up after ourselves. For example, if we were testing a stored procedure that adds a sales order, we would use the posttest script to delete that sales order.

The test script is where we will execute our code module. Visual Studio helpfully templates the code for us, so we can simply add in the values for the parameters that we require. For our test, we will use a `CampaignID` of `27587` and a `Budget` of `10`, and we will set the `Detailed` parameter to `1`.

We then want to create four test conditions. The first three will be scaler value conditions, which we will configure to check if the following are true:

- Column 2 = 1.7876
- Column 5 = 195
- Column 6 = 6.85

The final condition will be a Row Count condition. This condition will ensure that the second result set returns 42 rows. We can delete the inconclusive condition that is automatically generated.

To delete the inconclusive condition, highlight it in the lower pane and use the red cross button to remove it. We can then add the desired conditions by selecting the required type from the drop-down list and then using the green add button. Each condition can be configured using the properties window. Figure 7.6 shows the test code windows and the test conditions.

Once we have saved the test, we can run it by navigating to the Test Explorer window and running all tests by using the double play button on the left-hand side of the task bar. Unselecting the filters by clicking the funnel button on the task bar will cause all tests to be displayed with their statuses. We can drill through the test hierarchy and click on a test to see granular information.

To see how a test looks when it has failed, go back to the test we created, change the value of one of the expected results, and run the test again.

TIP It's important to remember that, if a test fails, it is possible that there is no error in the code. There could be an error in the test!

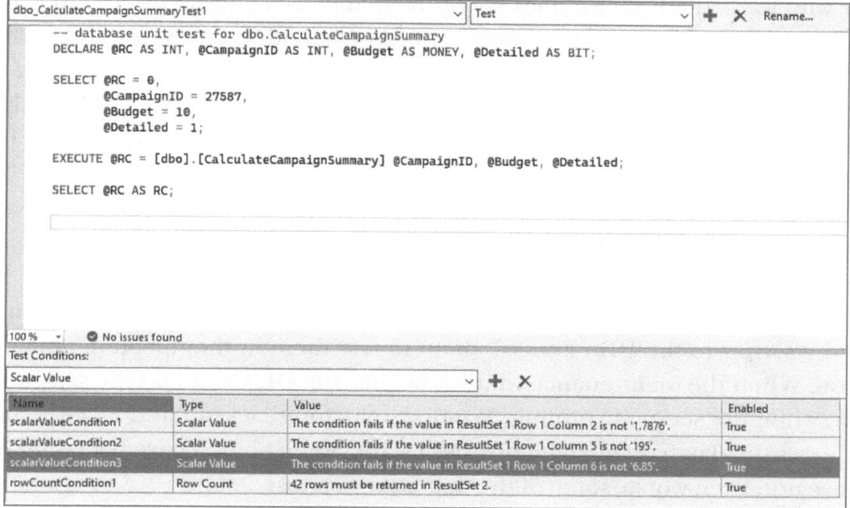

Figure 7.6 Creating a unit test

We should always consider writing unit tests for our T-SQL code modules. This is especially true for modules that branch code or update data. This practice reduces the risk of bugs caused by adding new functionality, and helps make our code self-documenting by mapping business requirements to code modules.

7.6 Modern development techniques

In the following sections, we will discuss modern development techniques that SQL Server developers should, but often do not, use to manage their code. The first of these techniques is the use of source control. The second is using a CI/CD pipeline to manage code deployments.

But why should we bother with these techniques? What is wrong with the old, familiar processes that database professionals have followed? Regarding how we store our code, in the past it was common to find that the only copy of a database schema outside of production was on a development server. Developers would update objects directly on the development server until they were released into production. In a few environments we might find that, once the objects had been created, they would be scripted out and stored as code on another platform. Sometimes this was a developer's computer, sometimes it was SharePoint, and in really advanced environments, the scripts may even have been stored in Team Foundation Server.

As for deployments, in the past it was common for developers to write very complex deployment scripts, which they would then expect production database administrators (DBAs) to execute on live systems with little or no context. Everyone involved would cross their fingers and hope that there was not an environment-specific issue halfway through the deployment.

So why were these techniques so problematic? Well, let's consider the following example. MagicChoc's development team has decided to follow a traditional mechanism for storing and deploying code. Specifically, they store their code on their development instance. They consider this to be acceptable, because they take a weekly backup of the development environment, so they can restore object definitions from backup if need be.

They also use a manual deployment process. This involves the developers writing complex scripts, which will script data out to temporary tables, drop and recreate tables and programable objects, and then script the data back in.

They are ready to deploy the new version of their database to production, so they send the scripts to the DBA and ask them to run them in the upcoming maintenance window. When the maintenance window begins, the DBA kicks off the script. Unfortunately, while the script is running, Windows patching kicks in and restarts the server. This leaves the database in an inconsistent state. Some objects have been updated; others have not. Even worse, some of the data has been lost.

The maintenance window is short, so there is a sense of panic in the air, and the DBA decides to restore the database from the backup they took just before the incident. In their haste, they restore the database over the development instance instead of the production instance. Realizing their error, they restore the database to production as well.

The developers are understanding of the DBA's mistake and ask them to restore the development database back to the development server. Unfortunately, when the DBA tries to do this, they realize that the last backup of the development server failed, so there has not been a backup in 13 days. In short, the developers have lost almost 2 weeks of work, which includes all of their effort for the release, and they will have to start again from scratch.

NOTE While this sounds like a very unlikely scenario, it is based on the experience of a friend of mine who is a SQL developer.

So how could MagicChoc have avoided these issues? Simply put, it could have used modern development practices. If it had stored its data in source control, it could have very quickly and easily retrieved its code. If it had used a CI/CD pipeline, then it could have mitigated the risk of the issue occurring in the first place. Of course, better release management could have avoided it completely, but that's another story!

In the following sections, we will explore the GitHub workflow for SQL Server and the concepts behind CI/CD for SQL Server deployments to get a feel for how MagicChoc could have done things better. I would encourage you to read further on both topics, however.

7.6.1 #31 Not keeping code in source control

In our scenario, MagicChoc was unable to recover its code because it was relying on a development server with backups. To avoid this mistake, our developers could have stored their code in source control.

With the growth of *Git*, which is an open source version control system, and since the introduction of products such as *GitHub*, which is a SaaS hosting service for managing Git repositories (repos), source control has now become a far better way of managing and storing our code.

Integrating with Git allows multiple developers to work on the same parts of a project in parallel. The source control is optimistic, which means that files are not locked, so there can still be conflicts, but these conflicts can be managed. We have access to our version history, so if we were to introduce a bug, it can easily be rolled back. It also means that we have a copy of our code stored in a known, secure, reliable location. All of these benefits of source control mean that not using it in this day and age is a clear mistake, but one I see many SQL developers still making.

To avoid this mistake, within our SQL Server Database project in Visual Studio, navigate to the Git Changes window and choose Create Git Repository. This causes the Create a Git Repository dialog box to be displayed.

As shown in figure 7.7, the top half of the screen allows us to specify the initialization settings for the repo—specifically, the local path to the repo on your computer, the license template (if any) to use, and the *gitignore template*. This is used to specify the files within the repo that should not be tracked by Git. In the bottom half of the dialog, we specify the GitHub account that we want to use. Clicking here will launch the GitHub login page. We will also specify the name, optional description, and owner of the repo.

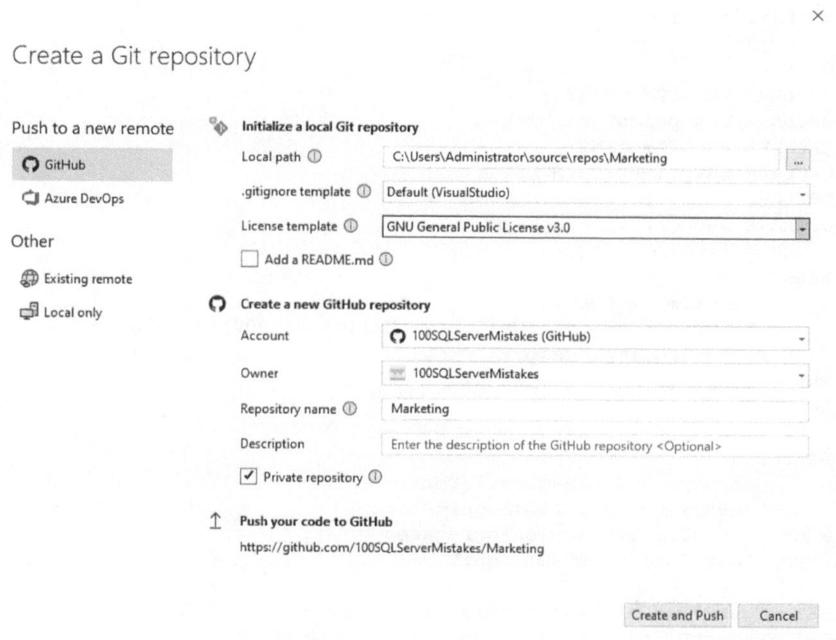

Figure 7.7 Creating and configuring a repo in GitHub

Now that our GitHub configuration is in place, our first task will be to create a branch. This will be our code branch, which we can make sure we are happy with before merging it into the trunk, which is usually called `master` or `main`. We can do this by using the branch drop-down at the top of the Git Changes window and selecting New Branch. In the Create a New Branch dialog, we can then give our branch a name (call it `CalculateCampaignSummary` if you want to follow along). We then choose the branch to base it on, which will be the trunk, in our case. Be sure to check the boxes to check out the branch and track remote changes.

NOTE At the time of writing, `master` is still the default name for a trunk in Git, but thankfully Git plans to change it to a more inclusive name soon.

Now let's see how code changes work in practice by making a small change to our `CreateCampaignSummary` stored procedure. The script in listing 7.18 adds a `BEGIN..END` around our `IF` branch.

TIP In an `IF` block, `BEGIN..END` is mandatory if there are multiple statements in the branch but optional if there is only a single statement.

Listing 7.18 Making a change to `CalculateCampaignSummary`

```
CREATE PROCEDURE dbo.CalculateCampaignSummary
    @CampaignID INT,
    @Budget MONEY,
    @Detailed BIT
AS
BEGIN
    DECLARE @AvgCPM MONEY ;
    DECLARE @CampaignCost MONEY ;
    DECLARE @NoOfImp INT ;
    DECLARE @AvgBidPrice MONEY ;
    DECLARE @CostOfBidPerc DECIMAL ;
    DECLARE @BudgetDifference MONEY ;

    SELECT
          @NoOfImp = COUNT(*)
        , @CampaignCost = (SUM(CostPerMille) / 1000) * COUNT(*)
    FROM marketing.Impressions
    WHERE CampaignID = @CampaignID
    GROUP BY CampaignID ;

    SELECT
          @avgcpm = AVG(AvgCostPerMille)
        , @avgbidprice = AVG(AvgBidPrice)
    FROM reporting.ImpressionAggregates
    WHERE CampaignID = @CampaignID ;

    SET @CostOfBidPerc = (@AvgBidPrice / @AvgCPM) * 100 ;
    SET @BudgetDifference = @budget - @CampaignCost ;

    SELECT
```

```
            @CampaignID CampaignID
          , @AvgCPM AvgCPM
          , @CampaignCost CampaignCost
          , @NoOfImp ImpQty
          , @CostOfBidPerc CostToBidPercentage
          , @BudgetDifference BudgetDifference$ ;

    IF @Detailed = 1
        BEGIN
            SELECT DISTINCT
                  ReferralURL
                , RenderingID
            FROM marketing.Impressions
            WHERE CampaignID = @CampaignID ;
        END
END
```

After we have saved the file, we should look again at the Git Changes window. The window has been refreshed to show our changed artifact. Clicking the plus sign next to the change will stage the change. The reverse arrow will roll the change back. Let's hit the plus icon to stage the change.

The changes will be moved to a Staged Changes folder, and we can now add a commit comment and commit the changes using the Commit Staged button, shown in figure 7.8.

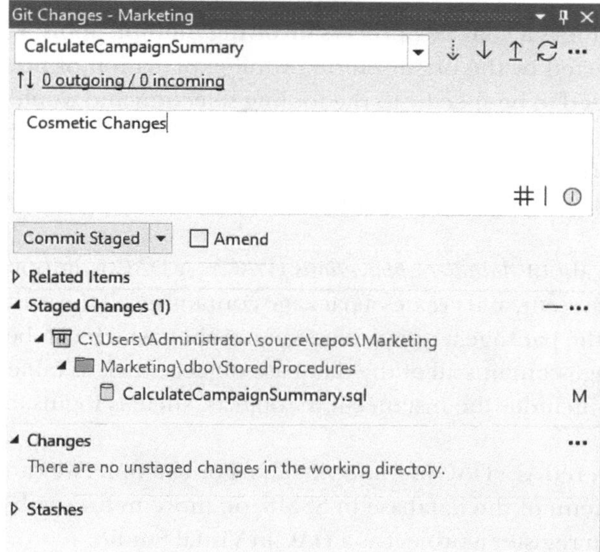

Figure 7.8
Committing changes

Pressing the up-arrow button, next to the branch drop-down, will push the changes to the remote branch. This will cause a message in a yellow banner to be displayed at the top of the Git Changes window, which contains a link to create a pull request.

If we have pushed our code to the trunk, then we can simply use the branch drop-down to switch to the trunk and then use the down-arrow button to pull the trunk down to our local repo. If we pushed to a remote branch, however, then we can follow the Create Pull Request link, which will take us to the GitHub website. Here we can create a request for a repository contributor to review our changes and merge them into the trunk.

> **TIP** Git and GitHub are worthy of a slim volume in their own right, so if you are not familiar with the products, then I would strongly suggest you dig deeper into these topics, as we have hardly been able to scratch the surface in this section. The Git and GitHub learning resources page is a good place to start; it can be found at https://mng.bz/JN90.

7.6.2 #32 Not deploying code with a CI/CD pipeline

In our scenario, the deployment issue occurred in part due to the methodology used to deploy the new release of the database into production. MagicChoc could have avoided this mistake and reduced the risks of the deployment by packaging its application and deploying it through a CI/CD pipeline.

These processes have multiple benefits, leading to a shorter time to market for incremental releases, a lower risk of bugs being deployed into production, and less complexity and time consumption for deployments. It is a process that fits well with today's Agile project methodologies.

Creating a CI/CD pipeline is a complex process involving multiple tools, which will usually be strategically selected by the organization. A full explanation of how to configure the tooling would need to be specific to the tooling selection and would warrant a volume in its own right. The chosen pipeline elements would also be specific to the requirements of your enterprise. Therefore, instead of attempting to explain a granular configuration, I will discuss the concepts and encourage you to undertake further reading.

First, however, let's talk about *data-tier applications* (DAC). A DAC is important in a continuous delivery environment, as it creates a package containing all the artifacts that make up a DAC and gives the package a unique version number, which can be used by the CD process. The package contains all of the database objects, such as tables, procedures, and users, and also includes the instance-level objects, such as logins, on which the database depends.

A database can be registered as a DAC in multiple ways. For example, we can register a DAC from the context menu of the database in SSMS, or, more in line with the concepts of this chapter, we can register a project as a DAC in Visual Studio.

To register a DAC in Visual Studio, simply publish the project. After the project has been built, the Deployment dialog box will be displayed. In this dialog box, there is a check box for Register As a Data-tier Application. If this option is checked, then an additional check box will become available, allowing us to block the deployment if the target database has drifted.

The `dacpac` file that is output from the build is a zip file containing XML files with the object definitions of the database. It is essentially just a zip file, so we can explore the contents by changing the file extension from `.dacpac` to `.zip`.

The main components in a CI/CD pipeline for SQL databases are

- Developer workstations
- Build services
- Deployment services
- Source control
- Environments

The developer workstations will be equipped with development tools, such as Visual Studio, SSDT, Git, Visual Studio Code, etc. Developers create artifacts locally and then commit them to a branch in their source control repository and raise a pull request. The pull request will often trigger the build services. These build services could be orchestrated through tooling such as GitHub actions, Azure DevOps pipelines, or Jenkins.

The build services will run the unit tests that we discussed in the previous section, ensuring that our code has not broken anything. It will then create the package of the DAC. This package will output into a `dacpac` file.

If the build succeeds and the code is merged into the trunk of source control, then the DAC can be deployed. Deployment services can consist of tools such as Octopus Deploy, Azure DevOps, or Redgate Deploy and will deploy the DAC to the lowest of the environments within our release stack. In some projects, this may be a further development environment; in others it may be an integration testing environment, and in a few, it may be UAT or staging. After code has been signed off in this environment, the deployment services can be used to deploy the DAC to the next environment until it finally reaches production.

> **NOTE** While the level of automation should, by definition, be high, different environments will have different human gates. For example, you may configure your environment so that a human reviews a pull request and then the build services are triggered by the merge into the trunk.

The diagram in figure 7.9 illustrates a typical CI/CD process for a SQL Server database.

> **TIP** The further reading that you will want to undertake likely depends on the tooling that your organization has adopted. However, Microsoft has a blog series of walk-throughs using GitHub, GitHub Actions, and Visual Studio Code that may be of interest. The first in the series can be found at https://mng.bz/M18W. You could also explore the Manning title *Grokking Continuous Delivery* by Christie Wilson, which can be found at www.manning.com/books/grokking-continuous-delivery.

We should look at implementing CI/CD pipelines for our database projects. Doing so can help make us more agile, reduce time to market, and avoid the risks of complexity.

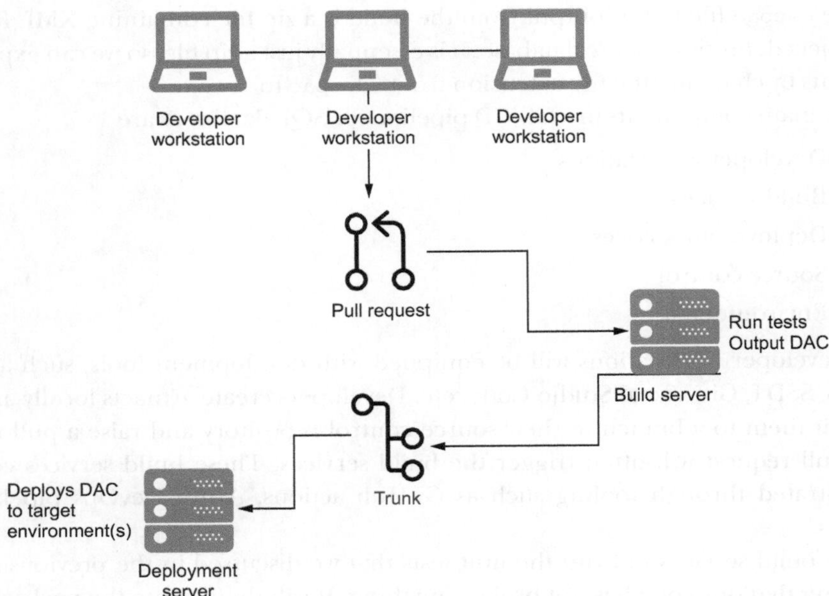

Figure 7.9 CI/CD process

Using DAC can help simplify deployments by packaging all required artifacts together and versioning them.

Summary

- ACID is a set of basic rules for transactions, which state that they must be atomic, consistent, isolated, and durable.
- `XACT_ABORT` is used to determine if an entire transaction is terminated when low severity errors cause a statement to fail.
- We should always write error handling for our code. Use `TRY..CATCH` to trap errors.
- Use `THROW` and `RAISERROR()` to raise meaningful error messages.
- Error severity levels, ranging from 0..24, denote the severity of an error, from informational message through to critical hardware or software failures.
- If an application has unattended processes, consider alerting if errors are raised so that the application support team can deal with them.
- Use an enterprise observability tool to raise alerts if possible. Otherwise, use Database Mail and the SQL Server Agent alerting subsystem.
- Make use of Visual Studio to debug code. This can save time and make troubleshooting more straightforward.

- Visual Studio Database Projects have built-in SQL schema comparison functionality. Use this functionality to ensure that code has not drifted before it's deployed.
- Use SSDT Schema Compare functionality to ensure a full understanding of the changes that will be made and the functionality that will be impacted.
- Always keep T-SQL code in a source control repository. This will provide a version history and a rollback mechanism, as well as help streamline the development of a project with multiple developers.
- Always write unit tests for programmable objects. Doing so will take a little more time up front but will save more time when resolving issues with bugs breaking existing functionality.
- Use modern deployment techniques. A CI/CD pipeline can provide many benefits, including improving time to market and reducing deployment complexity.

8 SQL Server installation

This chapter covers

- Meaningful instance names
- Using the correct OS and SQL Server edition
- Automated installation
- SQL Server's footprint
- Installation considerations in cloud

In this chapter, we will discuss the large array of options that we have for installing SQL Server. If we go back a decade, planning a SQL Server deployment was comparatively straightforward. We had to choose the most appropriate edition of SQL Server to install, and we had to think about how we would install it (GUI vs. script). We needed to consider the features required for the instance and give it an appropriate name, but that was about all.

Fast forward to the present day and the possibilities for SQL Server installation are endless. This can lead to a raft of mistakes, many of which stem from performing traditional installations without considering more optimal alternatives.

In this chapter, we will install a series of SQL Server instances for MagicChoc and explore some of the pitfalls that can await the accidental database administrator

(DBA). This will cover multiple aspects of planning and executing deployments, ranging from instance naming to selecting the appropriate operating system environment and SQL Server edition. We will also explore the challenges with manual installations, installing features that are not required, and overconsolidating instances.

8.1 #33 Using obscure instance names

In chapter 2, we discussed naming standards and the consequences that can arise from using object names that have not been well thought out. We can have similar issues with SQL Server instances if we do not think through the instance names. To explore this, let's imagine that MagicChoc has asked us to build four SQL Server instances, split across two servers, which will host databases used by the following applications:

- Choc Maker, which is used by manufacturing
- Magic Sales, a sales team application
- Temperature Smart, an application used in the manufacturing process
- HR Manager, a tool used by the human resources team

There are four applications and four instances, so we decide to create four instances across the two servers and give them names that are aligned to the application names:

- MagicServer1\ChocMaker
- MagicServer1\MagicSales
- MagicServer2\TempSmart
- MagicServer2\HRManager

At the time, this sounds perfectly sensible. A few months later, however, we realize it was a mistake. The database lead asks us to consolidate the Choc Maker and Temperature Smart applications into a single instance.

We now have three options. We can either have Choc Maker running in an instance called `TempSmart`, which will likely cause a degree of confusion in the future; we can have Temperature Smart running in an instance called `ChocMaker`, which will cause an equal amount of confusion; or we can rename the SQL Server instance as `Manufacturing`, which can generate a heap of extra work, depending on how applications are accessing the instance and the features being used.

So am I recommending naming SQL Server instances by department rather than application? No, I'm certainly not. This could come with its own set of challenges, such as having multiple instances with the same name on different servers—or worse, needing to have two instances with the same name on the same server (which isn't possible). There is also the risk of a department changing its name as part of a restructure, of course. For example, the Sales department could split into two departments, called Sales and Marketing, respectively.

How we should name instances is specific to our organization and the way the SQL Server estate is structured. For example, as well as naming an instance after an application or department, it could also be named after a business service.

It may also be a requirement to have a naming convention, which includes various aspects within the name. As an example of this, consider the instance name MAPRDENTLON01. This instance name reflects the department with a two-letter code, MA = Manufacturing. It reflects the ecosystem with a three-letter code—in this case, PRD = Production. The next three letters specify the license applied to the instance. In this example, ENT = Enterprise Edition. The next three characters in our name identify the location on the instance: LON = London. Finally, there is a two-digit incrementing identifier.

In short, my recommendation is simply to give due consideration to instance names and name them appropriately and in a way that will not cause confusion in the future. The naming standard should be consistent across the estate.

8.2 #34 Using Windows indiscriminately

Until 2017, SQL Server could only be run on Windows. This makes a lot of sense in the context of both products being developed by Microsoft. In SQL Server 2017, however, there was a dramatic shift, with Microsoft introducing support for SQL Server to run on Ubuntu, SUSE, and Red Hat flavors of Linux. It is even supported to run in Docker containers. But doesn't this seem a little odd? Surely, we would only ever want to run SQL Server on Windows, right? Well, let's explore a scenario with MagicChoc.

In chapter 4, we discussed how MagicChoc felt that its processes were too fragmented, so it commissioned a new application to combine its non-internet sales and procurement functions into a single interface with a single backend. What we didn't discuss is that this application will be written in Go and will be hosted on VMs running Ubuntu. Performance and stability are of paramount importance for the application.

The application team had originally planned to use MySQL, but MagicChoc's DBA team was not experienced in MySQL. They also wanted to use advanced SQL Server features, such as AlwaysOn, and the application team realized that they could benefit from other advanced T-SQL features, such as HIERARCHYID data type and windowing functions.

Therefore, it was decided that the DBA team would build SQL Server instances on VMs running Windows Server 2022. But for this scenario, that was a mistake. The clues as to why this was a mistake are all in the case study.

First, the DBA team did not want to support MySQL due to a lack of skills in that area, but at the same time they expected Linux-based developers to switch to a Windows environment for the Database Engine. The barrier to entry would have been lower if SQL Server were hosted on Linux.

The second reason is that the application was being built on Ubuntu. This is a license-free distribution of Linux, which implies that cost is a big factor. Many enterprise applications are built on Red Hat or SUSE distributions, as these have a license cost but also external support. If SQL Server were installed on Ubuntu rather than Windows, then the Windows Server license cost could have been avoided.

The final reason is the requirement for the application to be fast and stable. While SQL Server boasts both of these requirements on any operating system in its own right, they are somewhat enhanced in Linux due to the nature of the operating system.

Linux is a very lightweight operating system. This means that fewer things can go wrong. Even though Windows stability has drastically increased over the last decade, Linux distributions still lead the way in this regard. The lightweight nature can also offer performance advantages. In 2021, official benchmarks rated Red Hat Linux as the most performant operating system for SQL Server.

Of course, all these benefits in this scenario do not mean that Linux should be a default choice for SQL Server installation. It does mean that when architecting the platform environment for the data tier of an application that uses SQL Server, Linux should be considered. There are occasions where Linux is the optimal choice, but in many situations, Windows will still be a better option.

For example, if the application is a Windows-based application, then we would only be adding complexity by introducing a Linux server. We may also be reducing security by having to enable SQL Server authentication, instead of relying solely on Windows authentication.

> **NOTE** It is possible to enroll Linux servers in Active Directory (AD), but this is an atypical configuration.

Depending on our organization, we may be lacking Linux skills. If this is the case, then we are unlikely to want to install a complex product like SQL Server on an OS we will struggle to support.

There are also a few feature limitations in Linux. For example, SQL Server Reporting Services is not supported. Other graphical tools, such as SQL Server Management Studio (SSMS), are not supported on the Linux server, but we can install that on a Windows device and connect to the instance hosted on Linux like we could for any other instance.

A possible decision tree that can be worked through is shown in figure 8.1.

In brief, SQL Server's hosting environment should be carefully considered when planning an installation. We should consider the nature and requirements of the application tier, the technical requirements for SQL Server, operating system license costs, the support model, and the skills of the team before making a decision. Installation on Linux should always be in the back of our mind, however.

> **TIP** The installation of SQL Server on Linux is beyond the scope of this book. Microsoft has a walk-through at https://mng.bz/aVO7. Alternatively, you can find guidance on this as well as a walk-through in my book *Pro SQL Server 2022 Administration*, which can be found at https://mng.bz/gA9V.

8.3 #35 Forgetting how useful containers can be

When I first started working with SQL Server, it was always installed on a physical server, or "bare metal." Over time, VMs became increasingly popular, and although SQL Server was a little late to the party, it eventually became the norm to install SQL Server on VMs. In more recent years, containers have become ever more popular, and SQL Server has been supported on containers since SQL Server 2017.

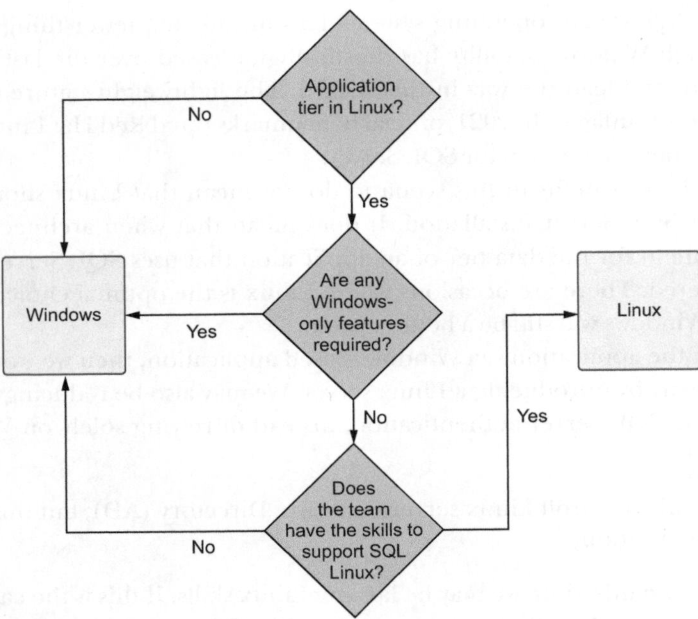

Figure 8.1 Windows vs. Linux decision tree

Unlike a VM, which virtualizes hardware, a container virtualizes the kernel of the operating system. This makes containers portable, isolated, and lightweight. Containers bring many advantages, such as their use in microservice applications, and make it very simple to deploy applications, especially in DevOps scenarios.

Despite Microsoft arriving at the container party in surprisingly good time, a constant mistake I see among DBAs is a failure to adopt them. This is often caused by a lack of understanding and a failure to see their value for SQL Server. With that in mind, let's take a look at a MagicChoc scenario.

MagicChoc has just signed a deal with a consultancy to build a new, integrated application for managing the production process. It's a large project that is forecast to take over a year to complete, and the project team will consist of 15 developers and 5 testers. Each member of the project team needs a dedicated SQL Server instance.

Some members of the project team use Windows laptops, but most of them use Macs. Therefore, they can't just install SQL Server on their laptops. One of the developers mutters something about using containers, but the DBAs shut that conversation down, because containers are stateless, so the developers would not be able to save their work. Instead, the DBA asked the Windows team to spin up 15 VMs. Unfortunately, there was not enough capacity left on the VMware cluster to do this. Instead, they spun up 1 large VM, and the DBA installed 20 instances of SQL Server.

This scenario is fairly typical of conversations that happen in the IT departments of large organizations, but unfortunately, it is riddled with misconceptions and mistakes.

The most optimal answer to this scenario would have been to use containers. Let's explore the misconceptions in a little more detail.

The DBA team was reluctant to use containers because they are stateless, and therefore, they thought that the developers would not be able to save their work. While it is absolutely true that containers are stateless, the assumption that the developers could not have saved their work is not. When using SQL Server in a container, it is imperative that data is persisted. Otherwise, when the container is removed, everything inside the container, including the databases and code, will be lost.

To persist data outside of a container, we will use a *Docker volume,* which is a Docker-managed resource that points to a file system location outside of the container. The built-in driver is `local`. Simply, this means that the SQL Server instance will be hosted inside the container, but the Docker volume exists on the host. We can create a Docker volume called `sqldata` using the command in the following listing.

Listing 8.1 Creating a Docker volume

```
sudo docker volume create sqldata
```

TIP Other driver plugins are available for Docker. For example, Flocker enables us to create Docker volumes on external storage such as Elastic Block Storage in AWS.

Once the Docker volume has been created, we can then use the `-v` switch when creating the container to map the internal file system to the external volume, as shown in listing 8.2. This will create a container called `production` and map the folder where the system databases are stored to the `sqldata` Docker volume.

NOTE This example assumes that Docker is installed and running and that you have downloaded the default SQL Server 2022 container image.

Listing 8.2 Creating a SQL Server container using a Docker volume

```
sudo docker run -e "ACCEPT_EULA=Y" \
-e "MSSQL_SA_PASSWORD=Pa$$w0rd" \
-p 1433:1433 \
--name production \
--hostname production \
-v sqldata:/var/opt/mssql \
-d mcr.microsoft.com/mssql/server:2022-latest
```

The alternative is to directly mount a host directory as a data volume inside the container. Using Docker volumes has several advantages, however. When we use a Docker volume, then we can manage it using the Docker CLI. This makes volumes easier to migrate or share between containers. Unlike mounting a host directory, Docker volumes have the additional advantage of not being dependent on the directory structure of the host.

Containers certainly have a place in the life of any modern DBA. They provide process and user isolation for applications and can dramatically reduce the deployment and management overhead of development environments for large teams. Data can be persisted by being stored outside of the container, despite the SQL Server engine running inside the container. This means that the data can survive a container being removed.

8.4 #36 Using Desktop Experience unnecessarily

Previously in this chapter, we discussed why we should consider Linux as a potential hosting platform when planning an installation of SQL Server. At the same time, however, if we decide that Windows is definitely required, then we should consider if we really need a GUI. Many times, the answer will be no, and if this is the case, then SQL Server can be installed on Windows Server Core.

To explore this, let's look at another MagicChoc requirement. In chapter 6, we created a `Marketing` database. We also built an SSIS package that would populate the `Impressions` data within this database. The business intelligence developers have no experience with Linux and are reluctant to provide application support on this platform. Therefore, the DBA team has decided that the SQL Server instance should be built on Windows Server 2022.

A VM is built, and they use the installation wizard to install a default instance of SQL Server. They made this decision because SSIS packages are developed in a GUI using Visual Studio. This was a mistake, but why?

Windows Server Core is Windows Server but without the GUI. Instead of a GUI, the server is administered using PowerShell. Removing the GUI removes much of the bloat of Windows, making it a more lightweight, secure operating system. It consumes less disk space, processor, and memory than the Desktop Experience, meaning it is more efficient, and because there are fewer components and services running, the attack surface is reduced. In other words, there are fewer features for a bad actor to attack. These characteristics make it a great operating system for running SQL Server.

But the developers will be using Visual Studio to develop the packages, and Visual Studio can't run on Server Core, so surely we need a GUI in this scenario? Well, that is not correct; this also highlights another "mini mistake." Specifically, quite a few administrators think that developers require Visual Studio to be installed on servers that run SSIS or other elements of the business intelligence stack in production environments. In fact, this should be avoided. There is no technical justification for it. Integrated development environments (IDEs) should ideally run on developers' workstations or in rare cases on a development server.

IDEs on development servers

The ideal scenario is for developers to use IDEs exclusively on their workstations and connect the IDEs to the databases hosted on the development server. I have encountered scenarios where this is not practical, however.

> One specific scenario that I encountered was when I was developing SSIS packages for a very large data warehouse. I had to develop against a full dataset, because some of the transformations required multiple months of data to produce meaningful results, and the business analysts were not able to construct a sample dataset that reflected the business rules.
>
> The data was so vast that my workstation simply didn't have enough RAM to run the packages efficiently. Additionally, I was frequently working remotely, and pulling that amount of data over the VPN with a slow internet connection was not working out well.
>
> Therefore, to develop the packages in a timely manner, I had to use Remote Desktop Protocol to connect to the development server and run the packages locally. This is very much the exception rather than the rule, however.

Allowing developers to have an IDE installed on a production server increases the attack surface of the production environment, but it also gives developers a back door into production. This back door leaves administrators with the risk of developers performing actions, or even releasing code, without the administrator's knowledge, which puts the service at risk and makes the server impossible to support. Organizations may also find that they fall foul of regulatory requirements that ensure proper separation of duties.

With this mini-mistake in mind, there is actually no requirement for an operating system in our scenario, and administrators should have built the SQL Server instance on a server running Windows Server Core.

Figure 8.2 expands on figure 8.1 to add Windows Server Core into the decision tree.

Is installing SQL Server on Windows Server Desktop Experience always a mistake? No; it is the right choice in some scenarios. The mistake is installing SQL Server on Windows Server with Desktop Experience because it's "what we have always done." Installing SQL Server on Windows Server Core should always be considered and only disregarded if there are legitimate reasons. Those legitimate reasons are a requirement for graphical features, such as when there is a requirement for SQL Server Data Quality Services (DQS) or Master Data Services.

8.5 #37 Using Enterprise Edition indiscriminately

SQL Server is expensive. To make SQL Server more accessible and reduce the cost to customers, Microsoft offers multiple editions of the product, each with different features and license constraints. For example, Express edition is free, but it has significant technical restrictions such as a maximum 10 GB database size and a maximum compute capacity of one socket or four cores. There are also many feature restrictions. Developer edition, on the other hand, is also free, but it has the full set of features supported by Enterprise edition. The only restriction is that the license does not permit use in a production environment.

MagicChoc is trying to determine the correct edition of SQL Server to use to host the data-tier portion of their Marketing application. It has decided to host it on Enterprise

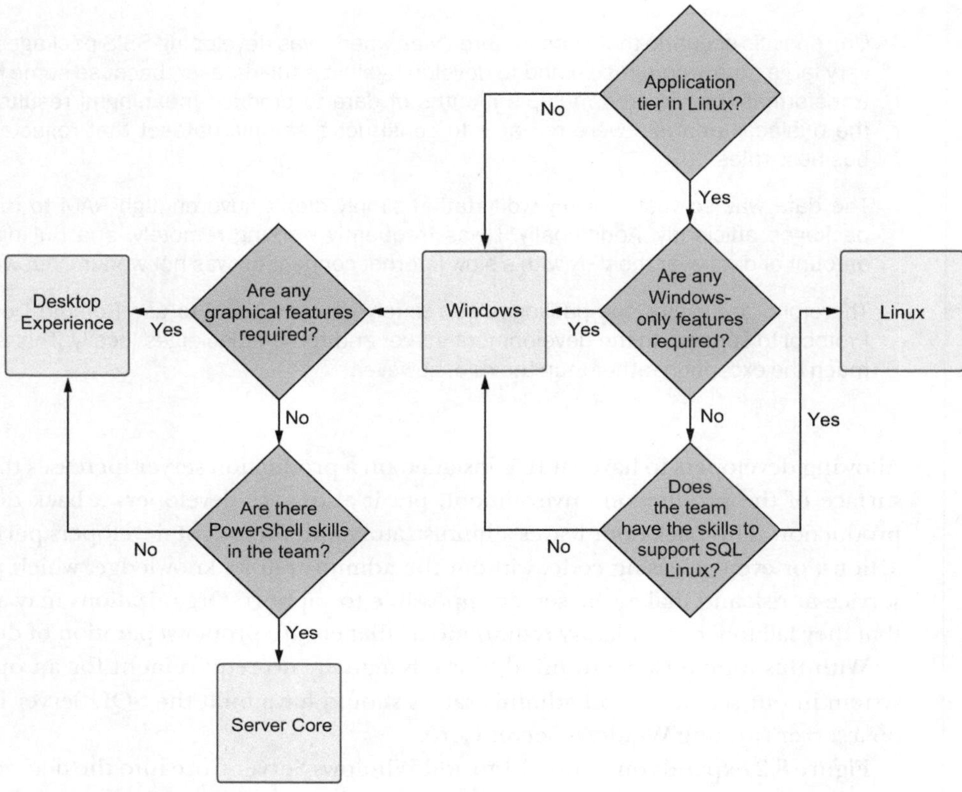

Figure 8.2 Decision tree including Server Core

edition, because it is a large 2 TB database, it needs to be hosted on an availability group with a synchronous replica, and it is running SSIS. This was a mistake. To understand why, let's break down the requirements.

First, if we consider the size of the database, Standard edition supports databases up to 524 PB, the same as Enterprise edition. The thinking may have been that, because it is a large database, it will require a large amount of processor capacity and RAM, and these are restricted on Standard edition.

This is true, but the requirements make no mention of capacity planning. It is simply an assumption. Given that Standard edition supports 128 GB of RAM and 24 cores (or 4 sockets) of processor, this assumption should be tested with capacity planning. Otherwise, there is a good chance that our organization will be spending a lot of extra money. At the time of writing, the list price for a two-core pack of Enterprise licenses is $15,123. This is compared to a two-core pack of Standard licenses with a list price of $3,945. If capacity planning shows that the data-tier application requires 16 cores, using Standard edition would reflect a cost savings of $89,424.

CAPEX vs. OPEX

If we build VMs in a public cloud environment, such as Azure or AWS, we can include the cost of the SQL Server license in the hourly cost of the EC2 instance. This has some advantages, such as being able to stop paying for the license when it is no longer needed and not paying for the license during hours when the instance is turned off. This conversion of capital expenditure (CAPEX) to operational expenditure (OPEX) is also in line with the cloud financial model, as opposed to the data center–hosting model.

On the flip side, however, if we know that our application will have longevity, then over time, we will end up paying more than we would for a perpetual license. This should be a consideration in the financial model of our business case for new applications or applications that we are looking to migrate to cloud.

Let's also think about the feature requirements. MagicChoc has stated that the application should be hosted on availability groups, and this is a common reason I hear as a requirement for Enterprise edition. But MagicChoc has requested a single, synchronous replica, and Standard edition supports a feature called *Basic Availability Groups.* This feature is a cut-down version of availability groups that offers a single replica (either synchronous or asynchronous). The replica must be inactive until the point of failover. This means that it does not support advanced functionality such as readable secondaries, backup on secondary, or integrity checks on secondary. It does, however, meet MagicChoc's requirements, so there is no reason to use Enterprise edition. We will discuss availability groups more in chapter 13.

The final reason for Enterprise edition was that SSIS is required. This is a common misconception that even some quite experienced DBAs make. In reality, SSIS is supported on Standard edition, with only a few restrictions. These restrictions include the ability to operate as a scale-out master and some advanced control flow tasks and data source transformations. For example, there are restrictions on change data capture (CDC) tasks and transformations involving text matching and extraction. There are also restrictions on advanced sources and destinations, such as Oracle, Teradata, SAP, and SSAS.

One of the most common reasons that I hear for brownfield applications requiring Enterprise edition is "It might need some database-level Enterprise features, but I don't know and I don't want to risk it." This argument can be easily countered, however, as it is easily checked. The script in the following listing creates a database with a table that uses table partitioning, which is a feature that is only available in Enterprise edition.

Listing 8.3 Creating a database that requires Enterprise edition

```
CREATE DATABASE EnterpriseDatabase ;
GO

USE EnterpriseDatabase ;
GO
```

```
CREATE PARTITION FUNCTION PartFunc (INT)
   AS RANGE LEFT FOR VALUES (100, 200, 300) ;

CREATE PARTITION SCHEME PartScheme
   AS PARTITION PartFunc
   ALL TO ('PRIMARY') ;

CREATE TABLE VeryLargeTable (
   KeyColumn       INT     PRIMARY KEY    IDENTITY,
   OtherColumn     VARCHAR(50)
) ON PartScheme(KeyColumn) ;
```

We can now simply query the sys.dm_db_persisted_sku_features dynamic management view (DMV) to return a list of enterprise features. As demonstrated in listing 8.4, if we query this DMV from the database created previously, it will return a single row for partitioning. If the database was not using any Enterprise-only features, then it would return an empty result set.

Listing 8.4 Discovering Enterprise-only features

```
USE EnterpriseDatabase ;
GO

SELECT feature_name
FROM sys.dm_db_persisted_sku_features ;
```

To summarize, we should never use Enterprise edition as a default option. It is far more expensive than Standard edition and should be reserved for occasions where Enterprise-only features are required. In development environments, Developer edition should be used, as it is a fully featured edition, with the only limitation being that we cannot use it in production.

8.6 #38 Installing an instance when DBaaS or PaaS will suffice

The three major public cloud providers—GCP, AWS, and Azure—all offer SQL Server Database as a Service (DBaaS) functionality and Azure also offers SQL Server instances as a Platform as a Service (PaaS). These products can offer a large number of business benefits for some (but not all) workloads.

Let's think about MagicChoc and a new application that it is building in cloud, which will provide process automation to reduce clerical overhead. The application is to be built in Azure and will use various cloud-native components, including *Azure Event Grid*, which is a cloud-native publisher/subscriber-based message distribution service; *Azure Functions*, which is a serverless option to execute event-driven code; and *Azure Kubernetes Service*, which is a managed container service. Because the application is greenfield, nobody really knows how much compute capacity is required to run the database.

MagicChoc's DBA team is stretched. They are a small team, and in addition to the large number of projects happening at MagicChoc at the moment, they have multiple operational issues to fix, predominantly around performance tuning. The lead DBA can see the benefits of having an entirely cloud-native application, but instead of recommending using Azure SQL Database, they recommend a SQL Server VM be built in Azure. This is a mistake, and still a fairly common one. The trouble is that many DBAs are still reluctant to embrace cloud offerings. I have noticed two common reasons for this stance. The first is a lack, or perceived lack, of cloud skills, combined with a reluctance to learn a whole new technology stack. The second reason is a fear that SQL cloud offerings will make them redundant.

The first of these fears is somewhat down to the individual. Learning a new technology stack is always a daunting task, but cloud is not going anywhere and as database professionals, we can choose to adapt or we can follow the dodo into fables. The second of these fears, however, is certainly not true. Cloud will change the skill set required of the DBA, but it will certainly not make the DBA redundant.

> **TIP** DBAs should also be reassured that despite SQL Azure being quite the leap from an instance running in a data center, the fundamental Database Engine is very similar to the database engine that they are familiar with.

In our specific scenario, the DBA team is under a lot of pressure. They have high-value, high-skilled work to attend to, such as diagnosing and resolving performance issues and helping the business with projects that require new databases. By avoiding DBaaS, the DBAs have simply given themselves yet another instance to manage, configure, resolve failed patches, organize downtime, and all of the other mundane parts of the job. If they had chosen a DBaaS offering instead, then they would have had more time to focus on the higher-value work.

An additional benefit of choosing Azure SQL Database in this scenario is autoscaling. The compute capacity in our scenario is not known. Provided we build our Azure SQL Database using the serverless compute tier, we can implement autoscaling. This will free up even more time, as we will have far less concern about right-sizing. We can avoid costs getting out of control by specifying the maximum number of vCores to use. We can also avoid the database scaling in too far, with a minimum number of vCores. The script in listing 8.5 uses PowerShell to create a new Azure SQL Database that will automatically scale between 2 and 16 vCores. The code uses a technique called *splatting*, which makes the code more readable by passing parameters to a command from a hash table.

Listing 8.5 Creating an autoscaling Azure SQL Database

```
$sqlAdminName = 'MagicChocAdmin'
$sqlAdminPassword = 'Passw0rd!'

$credentials = $(New-Object -TypeName System.Management.Automation.
     PSCredential -ArgumentList $sqlAdminName,
$(ConvertTo-SecureString -String $sqlAdminPassword -AsPlainText -Force))

$serverParameters = @{
```

```
    ServerName = 'processautomationsql'
    Location = 'eastus2'
    SqlAdministratorCredentials = $credentials
    ResourceGroupName = 'MagicChocApps'
}

New-AzSqlServer @serverParameters

$databaseParameters = @{
    ResourceGroupName = 'MagicChocApps'
    ServerName = 'processautomationsql'
    DatabaseName = 'AutoPro'
    Edition = 'GeneralPurpose'
    ComputeModel = 'Serverless'
    ComputeGeneration = 'Gen5'
    MinimumCapacity = 2
    Vcore = 16
}

New-AzSqlDatabase @databaseParameters
```

While DBaaS is not suitable for every database requirement, it is a powerful tool in a DBA's arsenal. It should not be dismissed on the grounds of fear, and database professionals who plan to stay in the profession over the coming years and decades should take the time to learn and embrace cloud-native offerings.

8.7 #39 Installing all features

When installing SQL Server through the GUI, it is very easy and very tempting to perform what I call a "next, next, install" installation. This is where someone clicks next on every page of the installation wizard, accepting the default settings (we will talk more about this in the next section), and then selects all features on the Features to Install page.

When we are installing SQL Server from the command line, it is also very easy and very tempting to specify the `/ROLE` parameter as `AllFeatures_WithDefaults`. This will have the same effect as selecting all features from the list in a GUI installation.

Of course, I have not come across many people who perform a "next, next, install" installation in a professional setting, but I have encountered a lot of teams whose standard is to install all features. Let's take a look at why this might be.

A development team at MagicChoc reaches out to the DBA team and asks for a new VM with SQL Server installed. The DBA team asks what features they require, and the developers say they are not sure. "Can we have everything to start with, as we have not designed the whole system yet?"

A few months later, the project is finishing up, and the team asks for a production server to be built. "We would like it exactly the same as the development server, because we know that works."

It is typical for a DBA team to follow the path of least resistance and just wave this kind of request through. After all, what harm can it do, right? In some cases, DBA teams simply build a SQL Server instance with all features in all cases as their corporate standard. This is because it reduces effort if any new features are required in the future. This approach is a mistake, however—especially in production.

The SQL Server product stack is a large suite of applications, with each of these applications running as its own service. A service is an application that runs in the background. If we install all features, then we end up with the following services installed:

- SQL Server Database Engine
- SQL Server Agent
- PolyBase Engine
- PolyBase Data Movement
- Analysis Services
- SQL Browser
- SQL Server Full Text
- Integration Services

We will also have the Master Data Services and Data Quality Client applications installed. If we are installing older versions of SQL Server, we will also be installing all of the tools suite (2019 and below) and maybe even the Reporting Services Service (2016 and below).

That's a lot of services and applications. This poses two problems. The first problem is that services consume resources when they are running, even if they are not being used. Therefore, by running services that are not required we are consuming resources that could be used by the features that we are using.

> **TIP** We can, of course, work around this issue, by keeping the services that are not required in a stopped state, but why would we want the extra work? It also doesn't resolve the issue of using additional disk capacity. Although this isn't a massive amount of space and isn't usually a big problem, it could, in some cases, make the difference between needing to resize a disk or not.

The second, much bigger issue with running this number of services is related to security. The more services that are installed on a server, the higher the attack surface of the server. If a bad actor finds a way to exploit a service that is running on our server, they may be able to gain lateral access to other servers. Therefore, it is always good practice to only install features that we require.

> **TIP** An additional consideration relating to security is patching. If you install additional SQL Server features that run under their own service when they are not required, then they will still need to be patched. This adds additional work to support services that are not required.

A full list of features that can be installed from the SQL Server 2022 setup wizard can be found in table 8.1.

Table 8.1 List of SQL Server features

Feature	Parent feature	Feature type	Description
Database Engine Services	N/A	Instance level	Provides core relational database functionality
SQL Server Replication	Database Engine Services	Instance level	Allows data to be disbursed between disparate instances using a publisher/subscriber model
Machine Learning Services and Language Extensions	Database Engine Services	Instance level	Supports distributed machine learning solutions with support for R and Python
Full-Text and Semantic Extractions for Search	Database Engine Services	Instance level	Provides advanced searching and matching functionality inside binary data, as well as textual columns with features such as fuzzy matching and thesaurus
Data Quality Services	Database Engine Services	Instance level	Core DQS functionality, including data quality functionality and storage
PolyBase Query Service for External Data	Database Engine Services	Instance level	Allows for multiple heterogeneous data sources to be queried
Analysis Services	N/A	Instance level	Provides multidimensional and tabular data modeling and querying functionality
Data Quality Client	N/A	Shared between all instances on server	A standalone application used to interact with DQS Services and both prepare and clean data
Integration Services	N/A	Shared between all instances on server	An extract, transform, and load tool used to orchestrate data ingestion and transformation, as well as exports to other systems. Further details can be found in chapter 6.
Scale Out Master	Integration Services	Shared between all instances on server	SSIS Scale Out can reduce bottlenecks by horizontally scaling the execution of packages. The Scale Out Master is responsible for the management of this scale out.
Scale Out Worker	Integration Services	Shared between all instances on server	The Scale Out Workers execute tasks that they have retrieved from the Scale Out Master.
Master Data Services	N/A	Shared between all instances on server	Allows you to create models that allow your data to be mastered across the enterprise. This is very useful in sprawling organizations, where different departments have different terminology for the same data item, as it allows you to map these terms to a single source of truth.

Those of you familiar with extreme programming philosophy will be familiar with the *YAGNI principle.* YAGNI is an acronym for "You Aren't Going to Need It" and is designed to remove inefficiencies in development. The same principle should be applied to SQL Server installations.

8.8 #40 Not scripting SQL Server installation

Installing SQL Server manually and then configuring the instance to meet best-practice guidelines is tedious. It is also prone to human error. Even if the DBA team has a detailed runbook of how to install and configure SQL Server instances, if there are multiple people manually installing multiple instances, mistakes will happen over time and our estate will end up inconsistent, which makes it harder to look after.

Let's take MagicChoc as an example. Its DBA team manages 120 SQL Server instances, split across 100 VMs. Some of these are on-premises, and others are in the cloud. They have a build standard and a detailed build runbook, but each instance is built and configured manually. The high-level aspects of the build standard are as follows:

- Install a default instance using an appropriate edition, but the default instance can be overridden with an instance name if the server is to have multiple instances.
- Harden the instance.
- Install only the Database Engine unless other features are specifically required.

> **TIP** In your environment, I would strongly recommend that you also consider performance optimizations. These will be at both the operating system and SQL Server levels. We will discuss many of these options in chapter 10.

Unfortunately, a recent audit of instances shows that none of these areas have been consistently applied across all servers. This is because, over the years, multiple DBAs have failed to follow the runbook thoroughly when building instances in a rush. The mistake was expecting DBAs to install and configure instances manually.

Instead of installing and configuring an instance manually, the DBA team could have applied a scripted approach. Using this methodology, a script, often written in PowerShell, will install and configure instances. This means that when a new SQL Server instance is required, a DBA can simply run a reusable script, and that's it. Job done. This not only improves consistency, but it also removes much of the time and effort of building instances, freeing up DBAs for higher-value work.

> **Gold images**
>
> Some people still use the "gold image" approach to SQL installation. In this approach, a Windows Server image will be created with SQL Server preinstalled. The scripted approach is much more flexible, however.
>
> Gold images certainly improve consistency but maybe a little too much. They often lead to all SQL instances being installed as Enterprise edition and all instances being configured for online transaction processing (OLTP), even when a company has many data warehouses.
>
> The workaround for this is to have multiple gold images, but that generates a lot of work—when an update is required to an image, for example, to upgrade it to use the latest service pack.

> ***(continued)***
>
> Therefore, I recommend favoring favor a scripted approach over a gold image. It is much easier to get the right balance of consistency and flexibility by using parameters that can be passed to your script.

Let's see how we could improve the process by creating a PowerShell script that will install a SQL Server instance, run some basic smoke tests, and then configure the instance. First, though, let's think about what our build standards might be to ensure that our instances are hardened:

- Disable remote access
- Rename the `sa` account

WARNING In this example, we will make just two hardening configurations. This is for the sake of a clear and concise example. In your environment, there are many hardening configurations that you should consider. I recommend consulting the SQL Server 2022 Center for Internet Security (CIS) benchmark, which is available from CIS at https://mng.bz/eV0Q.

In addition to hardening the instance, we will also need to think about the edition that we require. We will want to install Developer edition for development machines, and we will want to be able to choose between Enterprise and Standard edition for production instances.

So let's first think about the parameters that we will want to pass to our script. Given our configuration options, we will want to be able to pass the username and passwords of the service accounts that we will use to run the Database Engine and SQL Server Agent. We will want to pass the edition, and we will also want to pass our chosen name and password for the `sa` account. Therefore, we will need a `param` block at the top of our script, so that it knows what parameters to expect. We also need to accept a parameter for instance name, but because the standard behavior, in line with our requirements, should be to install a default instance and a named instance should be by exception, we will give the parameter a default value of `MSSQLSERVER`. This means that a default instance will be installed unless we specifically override this value by manually supplying a value for the parameter at execution time.

The first task that our script will perform is to install the `sqlserver` PowerShell module. This will enable us to run `Invoke-SqlCmd` later in the script. We can run this with the `Install-Module` cmdlet.

Our second task is to determine the value of the `$pid` variable based on the edition parameter. The SQL Server installation determines which edition of SQL Server to install based on a product key. Therefore, a product key must be passed to the `/PID` parameter. If no product key is passed, the installation will default to Evaluation edition, which will stop working after the trial period if it isn't upgraded.

WARNING In a real environment, product keys, also known as product IDs (PIDs) should ideally be stored in a password vault and read out of the vault by the script. This avoids company-specific details being stored in source control.

Many organizations have volume license keys. This means that they will use the same key for all of their SQL Server installations. Therefore, we can simplify the installation by mapping a product key to an edition. Then, for each install, DBAs can simply pass a value for the edition that they want to install, rather than having to dig out a volume license key each time.

WARNING The product key 00000-00000-00000-00000-00000 used in the sample script for Enterprise and Standard editions is actually the product key for Evaluation edition. The expectation is that you will replace this key with your organization's appropriate product keys before execution.

Next, we will install SQL Server by calling `setup.exe`. The script assumes you have downloaded the installation media and that it is available and that the script is being called from the folder where the installation media is stored. This command takes most of the parameters that we pass to our scripts: the instance name, the service account names, and passwords as well as the edition. We also pass the `/IACCEPTSQLSERVERLICENSETERMS` and `/Q` parameters, which are required to accept the license terms and to perform a quiet installation. Both are required for an unattended installation. The command also uses the `$pid` parameter, which we calculated from the `$edition` parameter, and we will pass the value `SQL` to the `/SECURITYMODE` parameter to enable mixed-mode authentication. This means that we also have to pass the password for the `sa` account.

NOTE Immediately after the installation, the `sa` account will have its default name. We will change it later in the script.

Once the instance is installed, we should run some simple smoke tests to validate the installation. Finally, we will use the `Invoke-SqlCmd` tool to configure the hardening of our instance. The first `sqlcmd` command disables remote access. This disables the deprecated feature that allows local stored procedures to be run from remote servers over a linked server and vice versa. The second command changes the name of the `sa` account to a name that we will pass to the script as a parameter. The rationale behind this is that `sa` is a well-known name for the administrator account. Because `sa` is used during second-tier authentication, changing it to a novel name reduces the risk of a bad actor performing a brute-force attack against the instance to gain administrative privileges.

The script in listing 8.6 brings all of these components together into a single script that the DBA team can execute every time they need to install and configure a new instance of SQL Server.

TIP Don't forget to change the PIDs to reflect your organization's product keys.

Listing 8.6 Creating a scripted installation of SQL Server

```
[CmdletBinding()]
param(
[string] $SQLServiceAccount,
[string] $SQLServiceAccountPassword,
[string] $AgentServiceAccount,
[string] $AgentServiceAccountPassword,
[string] $SaName,
[string] $SaPassword,
[string] $edition,
[string] $InstanceName = 'MSSQLSERVER'
)

if ($edition -eq 'Developer') {
    $sqlPid = '22222-00000-00000-00000-00000'
} elseif ($edition -eq 'Standard') {
    $sqlPid = '00000-00000-00000-00000-00000'
} elseif ($edition -eq 'Enterprise') {
    $sqlPid = '00000-00000-00000-00000-00000'
}

If(-not(Get-Module NuGet -ErrorAction silentlycontinue)){
    Install-Module NuGet -Confirm:$False -Force
}

If(-not(Get-Module SQLServer -ErrorAction silentlycontinue)){
    Install-Module SQLServer -Confirm:$False -Force -AllowClobber
}

./setup.exe /ACTION=Install /FEATURES=SQLENGINE /
     INSTANCENAME=$InstanceName /SQLSVCACCOUNT=$SQLServiceAccount
     /SQLSVCPASSWORD=$SQLServiceAccountPassword /
     AGTSVCACCOUNT=$AgentServiceAccount /
     AGTSVCPASSWORD=$AgentServiceAccountPassword /PID=$sqlPid /
     IACCEPTSQLSERVERLICENSETERMS /Q /SECURITYMODE=SQL /SAPWD=$SaPassword
/SQLSYSADMINACCOUNTS=Administrator

if ($InstanceName -ne 'MSSQLSERVER') {
    $ServiceName = 'MSSQL$' + $InstanceName
    $ServerInstance = 'localhost\' + $InstanceName
} else {
    $ServiceName = $InstanceName
    $ServerInstance = 'localhost'
}

$ServiceStatus = Get-Service -servicename $ServiceName

if ($ServiceStatus.Status -eq 'Running') {
    $output = "The service for SQL Server instance: {0} is Running" -f
$InstanceName
    Write-Output $output
} else {
    $output = "The service for SQL Server instance: {0} is NOT Running.
```

Silently installs NuGet, a prerequisite to install the SQL Server module

Silently installs the SQL Server PowerShell module

Installs SQL Server instance

Start of smoke tests

```
Script terminating" -f $InstanceName
    Write-Output $output
    exit
}

$ServerName = Invoke-Sqlcmd -ServerInstance $ServerInstance -query 'SELECT
@@SERVERNAME ;' -Username 'sa' -Password $SaPassword

if ($ServerName -ne $null) {
    $output = "The SQL Server instance: {0} is accessible" -f $InstanceName
    Write-Output $output
} else {
    $output = "The SQL Server instance: {0} is NOT accessible. Script
terminating" -f $InstanceName
    Write-Output $output
    exit
}                                            <-- End of smoke tests

Invoke-Sqlcmd -ServerInstance $ServerInstance -Query "EXEC sp_configure 'show
     advanced options', 1 ; RECONFIGURE ; EXEC sp_configure 'remote
access', 0 ; RECONFIGURE ; EXEC sp_configure 'show advanced options', 0 ;
RECONFIGURE ;" -Username 'sa' -Password $SaPassword    <-- Disables remote access

$Query = "ALTER LOGIN sa WITH NAME = {0}" -f $SaName

Invoke-Sqlcmd -ServerInstance $ServerInstance -Query $Query -Username 'sa'
-Password $SaPassword                                  <-- Renames sa account
```

If the script is saved as `InstallSQLServer.ps1` into the root of the folder that contains the installation media, then it can be executed using the command in listing 8.7.

TIP The script will need to be run as Administrator.

Listing 8.7 Executing the scripted installation of SQL Server

```
./InstallSQLServer.ps1 -SqlServiceAccount 'sqlServiceAccount' -
SqlServiceAccountPassword 'Pa$$w0rd' -AgentServiceAccount
'sqlServiceAccount' -AgentServiceAccountPassword 'Pa$$w0rd' -SaName
'SQLAdmin' -SaPassword 'Pa££w0rd' -Edition 'Developer'
```

Automating SQL Server installation should be at the top of any DBA's to-do list. It reduces manual effort and promotes standardization. It also brings other advantages, such as being able to store the build in GitHub, providing version control and a simple change mechanism.

8.9 #41 Thinking configuration management doesn't apply to SQL Server

One of the main reasons for automating SQL Server installation is to promote consistency. This is important to make our enterprise supportable and to ensure that our security baseline is in place. The trouble is that, after our build has finished, anyone with an appropriate level of access can simply change it.

For example, imagine that we have just built a SQL Server instance. It is correctly configured and adheres to CIS level 1. Unfortunately, a few days after building the instance, a junior DBA enables `xp_cmdshell`. We will discuss this extended stored procedure in more detail in chapter 14, but for now you only need to know two things about it. First, it allows operating system commands to be executed from within a SQL Server instance. Second, it is a big security hole and should not be enabled.

So just a few days after being built, the instance is no longer in the desired state and there is a live security vulnerability. We could deal with this issue, in part, by correctly limiting permissions and by auditing activity. Neither of these methods fully resolves the problem, however.

A full solution is to apply a technique called *configuration management*. This is a technique where configuration is fully applied when a server is first built, but it is then periodically evaluated. If an evaluation determines that drift has occurred, then the drift is automatically fixed. Therefore, if configuration management evaluated the state of our server every 30 minutes, then a misconfiguration such as a security vulnerability would be automatically resolved between 0 and 30 minutes after it occurred.

Configuration management has been popular on Linux for more than a decade and is key to many DevOps environments. Its usage has been increasing in Windows environments for a number of years, but it is still not as commonly used as it is in Linux environments. There are multiple configuration management tools available, with some of the most popular including Puppet, Ansible, and PowerShell Desired State Configuration (DSC).

At the most basic level, these tools use the following concepts:

- A resource is a unit of code that evaluates and configures the current state of a specific server configuration. This configuration could be anything from a registry key to a folder, or even the installation of software. Each resource will have the following methods:
  - A test method, which determines if the current configuration is correct. A test method is usually executed every time a resource is evaluated.
  - A set method, which updates the configuration if it is not in the desired state. This method is usually only run if a test method discovers drift.
- A manifest, which lays out the resources that must be run to configure the server, along with the values that should be passed to the resources.

The diagram in figure 8.3 demonstrates this. It illustrates a single DSC configuration being applied to multiple servers that host SQL Server instances. It shows the process that happens on each of these servers to enforce best practices for disabling `xp_cmdshell`. Every 30 minutes, the DSC test function runs and checks if `xp_cmdshell` is enabled. If the desired state (disabled) is discovered, then it exits the process and moves on to the next configuration in the manifest. If the configuration is not in the desired state, however, it runs a set function to disable the feature.

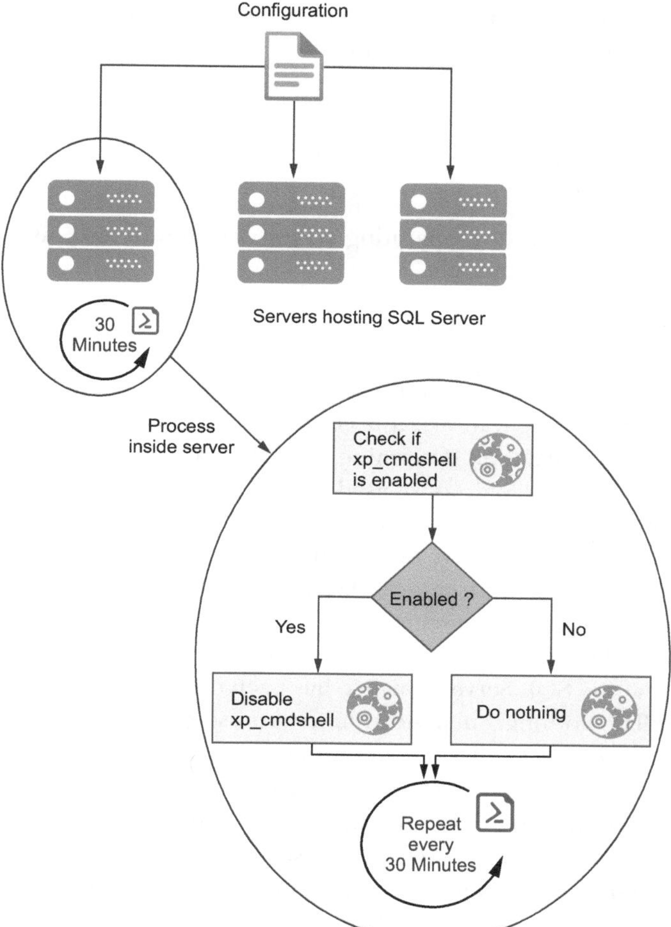

Figure 8.3 Configuration management process

Configuration management is a great approach to installing and configuring SQL Server instances. The trouble is, however, that many DBAs are either not familiar with it or fail to use it because they are not familiar with the concepts. This is a mistake. Using configuration management can not only reduce effort and make the enterprise easier and more consistent to manage, but it can also help with facets such as compliance and security.

While a full discussion of PowerShell DSC is beyond the scope of this book, as it is worthy of a book in its own right, let's explore how we could create a simple *DSC Managed Object Format (MOF)* document, which is the DSC implementation of a manifest. The MOF we create will ensure that a SQL instance is created. It will then disable remote access and create a SQL login for a local Windows user called `Pete`. We will then explore how to compile and apply the configuration.

Before we get started, however, let's get set up. We will need to install the SqlServerDsc PowerShell module, which we can achieve using the script in the following listing.

Listing 8.8 Installing DSC PowerShell modules

```
Install-Module SqlServerDsc
```

> **TIP** If we want to configure the operating system, we should also install the PSDscResources PowerShell module.

The configuration that we will create is called InstallSql and accepts parameters for the instance name (which defaults to the default instance) and the edition that we want to install. The first statement in the configuration imports the SqlServerDsc module. When creating configurations, it is considered good practice to import the modules that will be used. We then determine the PID that should be used based on the edition. This uses the same logic as we used in the previous section.

We will then define a node. This is the name of the server on which we want to run the configuration. In our case, we have only defined a node for localhost, but in more complex examples we could create a central DSC push service, which will push the configuration to multiple servers. In that scenario, we can define multiple nodes.

Inside the node definition, we will define three DSC resources. The first of these resources ensures that the SQL Server instance has been created. If the instance exists, then the resource will do nothing, but if the instance is missing, the resource will create it.

The following two resources disable remote access and create a login for Pete, respectively. If these resources were executed before the instance was created, then they would, of course, throw an error, as the resources would not be able to connect to the instance. Therefore, the DependsOn property is used to ensure that they are not executed before the instance exists. The configuration can be reviewed in the following listing.

Listing 8.9 Creating a DSC configuration

```
Configuration InstallSql {
  param (
      $SqlInstanceName = 'MSSQLSERVER',
      $Edition
  )

   Import-DscResource -ModuleName SqlServerDsc

   if ($Edition -eq 'Developer') {
       $ProductKey = '22222-00000-00000-00000-00000'
   } elseif ($edition -eq 'Standard') {
       $ProductKey = '00000-00000-00000-00000-00000'
   } elseif ($edition -eq 'Enterprise') {
       $ProductKey = '00000-00000-00000-00000-00000'
   }
```

```
    node localhost {
        SqlSetup 'InstallInstance' {
            InstanceName         = $SqlInstanceName
            Features             = 'SQLENGINE'
            SourcePath           = 'C:\SQL Media'
            SQLSysAdminAccounts = @('Administrator')
            ProductKey           = $ProductKey
        }

        SqlConfiguration 'RemoteAccess' {
            InstanceName = $SqlInstanceName
            OptionName   = 'remote access'
            OptionValue  = 1

            DependsOn    = '[SqlSetup]InstallInstance'
        }

        SqlLogin 'AddSqlAdmin' {
            Ensure        = 'Present'
            Name          = 'Pete'
            InstanceName = $SqlInstanceName
            LoginType     = 'WindowsUser'

            DependsOn     = '[SqlSetup]InstallInstance'
        }
    }
}
```

Now that we have defined the configuration, we need to compile it, which will create the MOF file. To compile the configuration, we will first need to dot source the file, which loads it within the current context. We will then run the `InstallSql` configuration, passing the parameter values as we would for a cmdlet. Therefore, assuming we save our configuration as `SqlInstallDsc.ps1` in the folder `c:\DSC`, the script in listing 8.10 will compile the MOF.

> **TIP** If you have been following along with the examples in this chapter and have already created a default instance of SQL Server, you may wish to amend the code samples in this section to create a named instance. This will avoid either uninstalling the existing instance or using a different VM. You will, of course, need to supply your own file paths.

Listing 8.10 Compiling the configuration

```
. c:\DSC\SqlInstallDsc.ps1

InstallSql -Edition Developer
```

A folder named after the configuration will be created in the working directory. Inside this folder we can find the compiled MOF file. The MOF file created from our compilation is

```
/*
@TargetNode='localhost'
@GeneratedBy=Administrator
@GenerationDate=11/05/2023 11:49:28
@GenerationHost=EC2AMAZ-43B3PBE
*/

instance of DSC_SqlSetup as $DSC_SqlSetup1ref
{
SourcePath = "C:\\SQL Media";
 InstanceName = "MSSQLSERVER";
 ProductKey = "22222-00000-00000-00000-00000";
 SourceInfo = "C:\\dsc\\SqlInstallDsc.ps1::18::11::SqlSetup";
 ResourceID = "[SqlSetup]InstallInstance";
 ModuleName = "SqlServerDsc";
 SQLSysAdminAccounts = {
    "Administrator"
};
 ModuleVersion = "16.5.0";
 Features = "SQLENGINE";

 ConfigurationName = "InstallSql";

};
instance of DSC_SqlConfiguration as $DSC_SqlConfiguration1ref
{
ResourceID = "[SqlConfiguration]RemoteAccess";
 InstanceName = "MSSQLSERVER";
 SourceInfo = "C:\\dsc\\SqlInstallDsc2.ps1::26::11::SqlConfiguration";
 OptionValue = 1;
 ModuleName = "SqlServerDsc";
 OptionName = "remote access";
 ModuleVersion = "16.5.0";

DependsOn = {

    "[SqlSetup]InstallInstance"};

 ConfigurationName = "InstallSql";
};
instance of DSC_SqlLogin as $DSC_SqlLogin1ref
{
ResourceID = "[SqlLogin]AddSqlAdmin";
 InstanceName = "MSSQLSERVER";
 Ensure = "Present";
 SourceInfo = "C:\\dsc\\SqlInstallDsc2.ps1::34::11::SqlLogin";
 Name = "Pete";
 ModuleName = "SqlServerDsc";
 LoginType = "WindowsUser";
 ModuleVersion = "16.5.0";

DependsOn = {

    "[SqlSetup]InstallInstance"};
```

```
 ConfigurationName = "InstallSql";

};
instance of OMI_ConfigurationDocument

                    {
 Version="2.0.0";

                        MinimumCompatibleVersion = "1.0.0";

                        CompatibleVersionAdditionalProperties=
{"Omi_BaseResource:ConfigurationName"};

                        Author="Administrator";

                        GenerationDate="11/05/2023 11:49:28";

                        GenerationHost="EC2AMAZ-42B3QBE";

                        Name="InstallSql";

                    };
```

The catalog can be applied to the server by using the command in listing 8.11. This command can then be added to a scheduled task that will run on a schedule and ensure that the server is always configured as required.

Listing 8.11 Applying the configuration

```
Start-DscConfiguration -Path 'C:\dsc\InstallSql' -Verbose
```

> **TIP** We are not limited to the DSC resources available in the `SqlServerDsc` module. DSC is fully extensible, and we can create our own, custom DSC resources. While beyond the scope of this book, it is something that I encourage you to explore. As a starting point, there is a chapter dedicated to DSC in the book *Windows PowerShell in Action*, 3rd ed., which can be found at https://mng.bz/px5z, or see a very basic walk-through provided by Microsoft, which can be found at https://mng.bz/OmNE.

Configuration management is a powerful tool, and DBAs should consider it as a means of reducing administrative overhead by ensuring that the SQL estate is consistent. It is the modern approach to automation and is fully extensible, regardless of the framework that we adopt.

TIP If your organization uses Azure, then DSC can be applied to Azure Arc–enabled servers using Azure Automanage Machine Configuration (formally known as Azure Policy Guest Configuration).

8.10 #42 Using SQL Server cloud images without modifying them

All major cloud providers supply images with SQL Server preinstalled. This makes spinning up SQL Server VMs in cloud very easy. Using cloud-provided images is also important if we want to use the license-included model of paying for SQL Server. In this model, instead of bringing our own SQL Server license, the license cost is included in the hourly rate of the VM. To use the license-included model, we must use a cloud provider's SQL Server image, as this is what triggers the license inclusion.

Figure 8.4 Fresh EC2 instance with SQL Server AMI

It is very common for organizations to use this image, as provided, to simply spin up a new VM in their chosen cloud whenever a new SQL Server VM is required. This, however, is a mistake.

To explain why this is a mistake, let's think about some of the things we have already discussed in this chapter. For example, we have discussed why it is not a good idea to install all SQL Server features but to limit the installation to just those features that are required. We have also discussed the use of configuration management to keep the desired configuration of the server and SQL Server instance. In chapter 10, we will also discuss why we should avoid using trace flags 1117 and 1118.

Despite these good practices, if we were to build a new SQL Server EC2 instance in AWS, we would notice that all features have been installed. This includes SSMS, which should really be used as a client tool rather than being installed on a server. The image in figure 8.4 is taken from a freshly built EC2 instance using the AWS-provided SQL Server AMI.

In Azure, the situation is even worse. Not only will all features and tools be installed, but trace flags T1117 and T1118 will also be configured on the SQL Server instance. The image in figure 8.5 was taken from a freshly built Azure VM using the Azure-provided virtual machine image. The image shows SQL Server configuration manager with all SQL services running and the startup parameters of the Database Engine service expanded to show the configured trace flags.

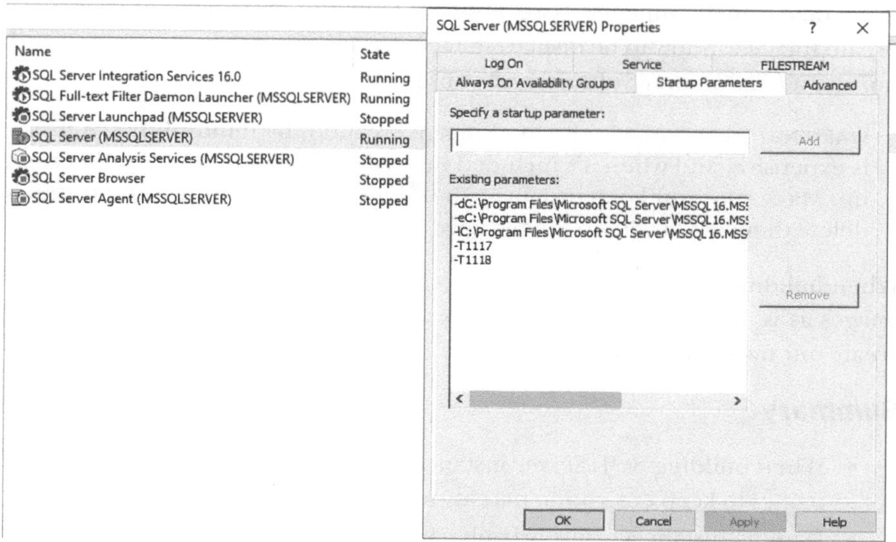

Figure 8.5 Freshly built Azure VM with SQL Server image

Why do cloud providers do this? The answer is that it's an attempt to make everything easy for all customers regardless of their requirements. This comes with the drawbacks that we discussed earlier in this chapter, however. What's more, because the SQL Server instance is baked into the image, it is fully subject to drift.

This means that using a cloud provider's SQL Server image as is can be considered a mistake—and a very common one. The way to avoid this mistake while still remaining license compliant is to create our own custom image but to base that image on the cloud provider's SQL Server image.

To do this, we can create a new VM based on the cloud provider's SQL Server image and then customize it to meet our requirements. For example, we might uninstall components such as Analysis Services and Integration Services if we do not need them. We might also configure the instance to be CIS compliant. We could even create a DSC MOF to ensure the instance remains configured to our requirements.

Once we have finished modifying the VM, we can create a new image based on our VM. The process for doing this varies between cloud providers but is always quite straightforward. For example, in Azure, we can navigate to the VM in Azure Portal and select the Capture option from the top menu. This will cause the Create an Image page to be displayed, where we can configure properties for the image, such as the resource group, and decide if we want the image to be shared to the Azure compute gallery, which will make them public, or if we want to keep it as a (private) managed image (which is almost certainly the option you will select).

Alternatively, to create an image from an AWS EC2 instance, we can simply navigate to EC2 instances in the AWS Console. From there, right-click on the EC2 instance and select Image and Templates > Create Image from the context menu. This will cause the Create Image window to be displayed. Here we can give the image a name and tags. We can also add additional volumes and configure volume sizes.

> **WARNING** If you play with cloud image creation, be mindful that SQL Server is expensive, and when it's included in the hourly cost of a VM, prices can add up. Make sure you keep instances shut down when not in use and terminate/delete them when you no longer need them.

When building SQL Server VMs in the cloud, we should not use the cloud provider's images as is. Instead, we should modify a server to meet our requirements and then create our own image.

Summary

- When building SQL Server instances, it is important to use meaningful instance names to keep environments easy to identify and avoid confusion.
- Naming instances appropriately can be something of an art over science.
- When planning a deployment, consider Linux as a viable operating system.
- SQL Server 2022 is supported on Red Hat, SUSE, and Ubuntu.
- Consider SQL Server containers, rather than assuming that SQL Server should always be installed on a VM or bare metal—especially for large development environments.
- When using SQL Server inside a container, use a Docker volume to store that data outside of the container. This allows data to be persisted even after a container is removed.
- SQL Server is fully supported on Linux containers. It is not currently supported on Windows containers, but Windows containers can still be used for SQL Server in nonproduction environments if we create our own container image.
- Server Core should be considered when planning an installation of SQL Server. Installing SQL Server on Windows Server with Desktop Experience should not be the default. Server Core is a good choice, unless there is a specific reason that the GUI is required.
- With no GUI, Server Core can be more performant and more secure than Windows Server with Desktop Experience.
- SQL Server Enterprise edition is expensive and should be reserved for cases where Enterprise-level features are required in production.
- Use Standard edition where appropriate in production.
- Use Developer edition in nonproduction environments.
- When planning SQL Server deployments, DBaaS offerings from cloud providers should be considered. They reduce overhead, as we do not need to manage the operating system or SQL Server instance.

- While cloud-native SQL Server offerings have the potential to change the required skillset of a DBA, they do not have the potential to remove the need for DBAs. Therefore, DBAs should not fear cloud.
- Only install the features that are required, rather than all features. This will reduce the security footprint and avoid unnecessary consumption of resources.
- Installing SQL Server manually is time-consuming and leads to human error.
- Automating SQL Server installation saves administrative overhead and leads to an estate that is easier to manage.
- Scripting a deployment only ensures consistency and good practice at build time. Drift can occur after the deployment.
- Using configuration management techniques allows us to keep a server and SQL Server instance correctly configured for the lifecycle of the application.
- SQL Server can be configured with configuration management tools such as PowerShell DSC and Puppet.
- Using configuration management helps us remain compliant with security requirements and reduces administrative overhead of the SQL Server estate.
- Configuration management tools include Ansible and Puppet. Microsoft also offers configuration management inside PowerShell. This is called PowerShell DSC.
- PowerShell DSC is fully extensible, and custom DSC resources can be created if required.
- Cloud images that are preloaded with SQL Server have all features installed, which consumes additional resources and increases the attack surface of the SQL Server instance.
- Create custom cloud images based on a vendor-supplied image and use the custom image instead of the vendor-supplied image.
- Custom images must be based on a vendor-supplied image when the "license included" licensing model is required. This ensures that the cost of the SQL Server license is included in the hourly cost of the VM.

9 Instance and database management

This chapter covers

- Common maintenance mistakes and misconceptions
- Capacity planning
- Database corruption
- Administrative scripting
- Patching

In this chapter, we will discuss common maintenance and configuration mistakes made by accidental database administrators (DBAs). As part of this topic, we will discuss the impact of autoshrinking databases before looking at some misconceptions around transaction log files, which lead to issues such as degraded performance.

Next, we will discuss capacity planning. This is a task that many DBAs fail to perform, and we will look at the potential consequences. We will then explore some common mistakes around scripting and automation, including the use of cursors, and a complete lack of maintenance automation.

Finally, we will explore the failure to patch our servers. We will think about the reasons for not patching and the consequences of doing so. We will also discuss how to avoid making this mistake.

Many of the topics in this chapter focus on the day-to-day work of a DBA. Therefore, not all topics have a direct impact on the business. It is important to remember, however, that there is most certainly an indirect impact on the business. For example, if we fail to patch, then there is an increased risk of the servers being attacked by bad actors, leading to massive disruption and reputational damage for the business.

What changes is our interactions with business teams. Until now, most activities that we have discussed will have been led by the business. On the contrary, many of the topics in this chapter will be led by the DBA team to avoid or resolve operations impacts on the business. For example, an issue such as log fragmentation is not something that a business team will be familiar with or ask us to resolve. Instead, we keep on top of these kinds of issues, because if we don't, then the business will be indirectly impacted by performance issues.

For examples in this chapter that require a database, we will use the `MarketingArchive` database. To create this database, you will need the `Marketing` database that we created in chapter 4. For the examples that use a SQL Server instance, I would suggest using the instance that hosts the `Marketing` database, although this is not essential.

9.1 #43 Autoshrinking databases

Most IT professionals have been in a position where a volume has been running out of disk space and they have to perform manual housekeeping to clean up old data and avoid the volume becoming full. Many database professionals have been in a position where they have asked their storage area network (SAN) administrator to extend the size of a volume, just to hear the sound of air being sucked through teeth, because the SAN is running low on capacity.

Additionally, most database professionals are aware that when a VM running SQL Server is built in a cloud environment, such as AWS or Azure, the underlying infrastructure is not owned by your organization, which means that there is a direct cost of expanding the volume.

Therefore, when a person who is new to a SQL Server administration role realizes that there is a feature that will autoshrink databases, reclaiming unused space, they can be forgiven for thinking that this sounds like a great idea. I have seen multiple occasions where an accidental DBA has enabled this feature for all of their databases, without understanding the consequences.

So let's imagine that MagicChoc has a SQL Server instance that is hosted in Azure. The instance hosts four databases, specifically:

- `Marketing`
- `SalesManagerPlus`
- `TargetManager`
- `MarketingArchive`

Disk utilization on the data volume is hovering around 75%, which is the threshold for the disk space warning in the monitoring tool. An inexperienced DBA responds to the warning and during their investigation discovers the option to autoshrink databases and turns it on. Within an hour, however, multiple application teams start raising tickets, complaining that the performance of their applications has fallen through the floor. This was because enabling autoshrink was a mistake. To understand why, it's important to understand how autoshrink works.

A background task in SQL Server will wake up periodically and assess if any databases are enabled for autoshrink. If there are, then it finds the first database that is configured for autoshrink and checks to see if there is free space that can be reclaimed. If there is, then it will perform a shrink operation on that database. The task will then go back to sleep. When it wakes up again, a few minutes later, it will check and shrink (if required) the next database that is configured to autoshrink. It will continue like this permanently, moving around the databases in a round-robin pattern.

When an autoshrink operation occurs for a database, it will acquire locks that can cause blocking for applications, which also need to acquire locks. This can cause performance issues or even timeouts if a lock timeout has been configured.

Shrink operations are also resource intensive. While the shrink is in progress, there will likely be a substantial increase in CPU usage, which could impact other operations, especially where other CPU-intensive features such as encryption or compression are used. The disk subsystem will also become very busy, and you will likely see a large spike in disk activity, which could cause additional performance issues for applications. This is exacerbated by the shrink operation being fully logged, which means that there will be heavy throughput to the transaction log file, as well as to the data files.

After the shrink operation has completed, it is likely that general database performance will also be negatively impacted by an issue called *index fragmentation.* This fragmentation is caused by how the shrink operation reorganizes the pages within the data files. We will not dwell on this here, however, as we will discuss it in much more detail in the next section.

While automatically shrinking databases sounds like a tempting idea, to keep disk space under control, it is a far better idea to perform capacity planning to ensure that data volumes are appropriately sized. We will discuss capacity planning later in this chapter.

The query in the following listing can be used to check if you have any databases with autoshrink turned on.

Listing 9.1 Checking if autoshrink is turned on

```
SELECT
      name
    , is_auto_shrink_on
FROM sys.databases ;
```

Autoshrink can be turned off using an `ALTER DATABASE` statement. The query in the following listing turns off autoshrink for the `Marketing` database.

Listing 9.2 Disabling autoshrink

```
ALTER DATABASE Marketing
    SET auto_shrink OFF WITH NO_WAIT ;
```

> **TIP** In chapter 8, we discussed enforcing configuration best practices using Desired State Configuration. If you adopt a configuration management approach, then enforcing autoshrink to be off is a great contender for your automation.

9.2 #44 Failing to rebuild indexes after data file shrink

In the previous section, we discussed why it is not a good idea to enable autoshrink for a database. SQL Server administrators also have the ability to manually shrink a database or file, however. As a general rule, shrinking data files, even manually, should be avoided. There are some occasions when shrinking a database manually can be helpful, however.

> **TIP** Shrinking log files has different considerations, which we will discuss later in this chapter.

Consider the SQL Server instance discussed in the previous section. It hosts four databases and resides on an Azure VM. One of the databases is called `MarketingArchive` and is used to store historical marketing data. The database has been in operation for a long time and now stores nine years of historical data. The business requirement is only to store the last three years of data. The data volume is at 75% capacity, so there are two options. Either the volume could be expanded or six years of data could be reclaimed from the `MarketingArchive` database. If the volume was expanded, there would be additional Azure storage charges, and the data being stored is no longer needed. Therefore, in this circumstance, it makes sense to purge the data that is no longer required and perform a one-time shrink operation on the database to reclaim space.

In this scenario, the DBA removes the data and shrinks the data files. They know that there will be a performance overhead while the shrink operation takes place, so they perform the activity during a maintenance window.

Unfortunately, after the operation completes, users start to complain that there is a drop in performance and that many of their queries are taking longer than usual to complete. The reason for this is that the indexes within the database have become fragmented. To understand this, let's follow the path that the DBA took to shrink the data files and explore what happened during the operation. But let's first remind ourselves of the core concepts of page splits and index fragmentation.

Data is stored on a series of 8 KB pages, and a series of eight continuous 8 KB pages is known as an *extent*. The data pages that make up an index are stored in a double-linked list. This means that each page stores a pointer to both the next page and the previous page. When a data page becomes full, the next time SQL Server needs to add data to that page, then a new page must be created. This is known as a *page split*. There are two types of page split, known as "good page splits" and "bad page splits."

To understand a good page split, consider the diagram in figure 9.1. This diagram illustrates an index that has become full. SQL Server needs to insert a new row into the last page, but there is no free space. Therefore, the next page from the extent is allocated and the new row is inserted onto the new page.

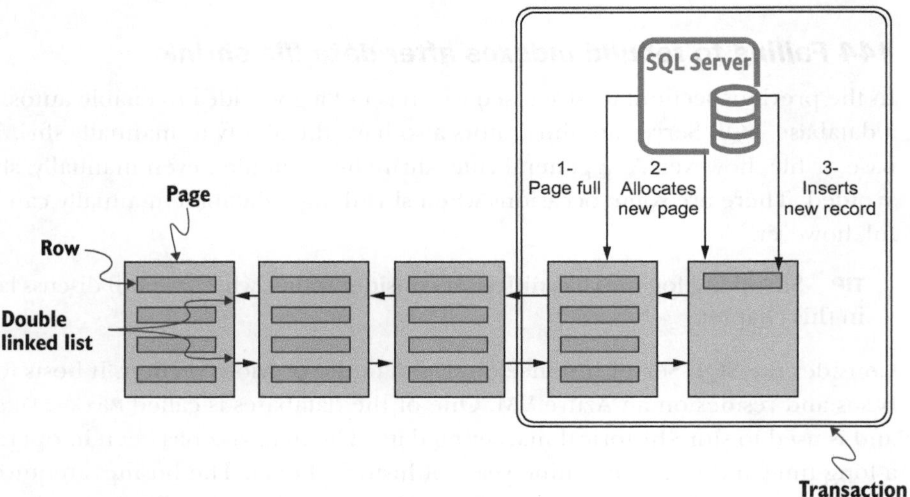

Figure 9.1 Good page splits

A bad page split occurs when an insert or expansive update happens when SQL Server needs to split a page that is in the middle of an index. When this occurs, then the page that SQL Server must create will be out of order. When pages are out of order, this is known as *external fragmentation*. Additionally, half of the rows from the original page will be moved to the new page to make space on the original page. This is known as *internal fragmentation* and can lead to SQL Server having to read more pages to return the same amount of data. A bad page split is illustrated in figure 9.2.

Before we explore this scenario any further, please use the script in listing 9.3 to build and populate the `MarketingArchive` database if you would like to follow along with the examples in this section.

NOTE The script in listing 9.3 relies on the `Marketing` database, which we created in chapter 6.

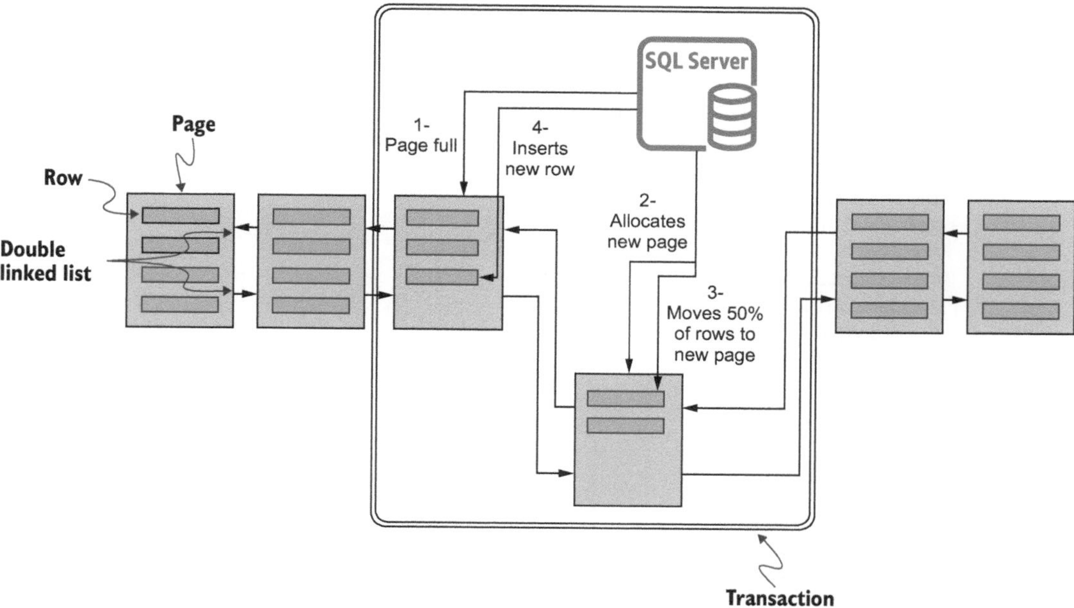

Figure 9.2 Bad page split

Listing 9.3 Creating the `MarketingArchive` database

```
CREATE DATABASE MarketingArchive ;
GO

USE MarketingArchive ;
GO

CREATE TABLE dbo.ImpressionsArchive (
    ImpressionID          BIGINT              NOT NULL IDENTITY PRIMARY KEY,
    ImpressionUID         UNIQUEIDENTIFIER    NOT NULL,
    ReferralURL           VARCHAR(512)        NOT NULL,
    CookieID              UNIQUEIDENTIFIER    NOT NULL,
    CampaignID            BIGINT              NOT NULL,
    RenderingID           BIGINT              NOT NULL,
    CountryCode           TINYINT             NULL,
    StateID               TINYINT             NULL,
    BrowserVersion        BIGINT              NOT NULL,
    OperatingSystemID     BIGINT              NOT NULL,
    BidPrice              MONEY               NOT NULL,
    CostPerMille          MONEY               NOT NULL,
    EventTime             DATETIME            NOT NULL,
) ;

DECLARE @Numbers TABLE (
```

```
    Number     INT
) ;

INSERT INTO @Numbers
VALUES (-1),(-2),(-3),(-4),(-5),(-6),(-7),(-8),(-9) ;

INSERT INTO MarketingArchive.dbo.ImpressionsArchive (
    ImpressionUID,
    ReferralURL,
    CookieID,
    CampaignID,
    RenderingID,
    CountryCode,
    StateID,
    BrowserVersion,
    OperatingSystemID,
    BidPrice,
    CostPerMille,
    EventTime
)
SELECT
    ImpressionUID,
    ReferralURL,
    CookieID,
    CampaignID,
    RenderingID,
    CountryCode,
    StateID,
    BrowserVersion,
    OperatingSystemID,
    BidPrice,
    CostPerMille,
    DATEADD(YEAR, n.Number, i.EventTime)
FROM Marketing.Marketing.Impressions i
CROSS JOIN @Numbers n ;

CREATE NONCLUSTERED INDEX EventTimeNCI
    ON dbo.ImpressionsArchive(EventTime) ;

CREATE NONCLUSTERED INDEX ImpressionUIDNCI
    ON dbo.ImpressionsArchive(ImpressionUID) ;
```

Let's first use the `sys.dm_db_index_physical_stats` *dynamic management function (DMF)*. This object returns details of index fragmentation and accepts the following parameters, in the defined order:

- Database ID
- Object ID of the table
- Index ID of the index within the table
- Partition number
- Mode

When NULL values are passed to the object_id, index_id, and partition_number, then results for all objects, indexes, and partitions will be returned, respectively. The mode parameter specifies the level of accuracy of the results, with a tradeoff against execution time. LIMITED is the fastest but least accurate mode. This mode will generate the statistics by looking at nonleaf levels of the B-tree only. SAMPLED mode will generate statistics based on 1% of the pages in the index, and DETAILED mode will scan all pages of the B-tree to generate the statistics.

The DMF returns one row for every level of the B-tree of every index in scope. This is true for both clustered and nonclustered indexes.

We can take a baseline of the amount of external fragmentation by executing the query in listing 9.4. This query uses the sys.dm_db_index_physical_stats DMF to return the fragmentation statistics of each index. It also joins to the sys.indexes system view to capture the name of the index. The index_level_size_MB column is generated by dividing the number of pages in the index level by 128. This is because 1 MB can store 128 8 KB pages. The avg_fragmentation_in_percent column returns the amount of external fragmentation. We also filter out levels greater than 0. This means that we will only return the leaf level of each index.

TIP There is a column in the DMF called avg_page_space_used_in_percent that can tell us the amount of internal fragmentation. This is not of interest within this section, but we will explore internal fragmentation in chapter 11.

Listing 9.4 Taking a baseline of fragmentation

```
SELECT
      OBJECT_NAME(ips.object_id) AS table_name
    , i.name AS index_name
    , ips.index_type_desc
    , ips.index_level
    , ips.page_count
    , ips.page_count /128 AS index_level_size_MB
    , ips.avg_fragmentation_in_percent
FROM sys.dm_db_index_physical_stats(DB_ID('MarketingArchive'), NULL, NULL,
NULL, 'Detailed') ips
INNER JOIN sys.indexes i
    ON i.object_id = ips.object_id
    AND i.index_id = ips.index_id
WHERE index_level = 0 ;
```

You will notice that the value for avg_fragmentation_in_percent is very low for every index. In my results, the clustered index and the EventTimeNCI index were both 0.01%, and the ImplessionUIDNCI index was 0.12%. Your mileage may vary, however, depending on the number of cores available to the SQL Server instance, as well as other factors, such as if you have any other transactions running within the database.

Now that we are all prepared, let's follow the same steps as the MagicChoc DBA would have taken. First, we will delete the nine years' worth of data that we do not need;

then we will perform a shrink operation on the data files. A query to purge the old data can be found in the following listing.

Listing 9.5 Purging old data

```
DELETE
FROM dbo.ImpressionsArchive
WHERE EventTime < '20200101' ;
```

Now let's use the query in the following listing to see how much free space we can clean up.

Listing 9.6 Checking free space to clean up

```
USE MarketingArchive ;
GO

SELECT
    name
    , AvailableSpaceMB
    , CurrentSizeMB
    , (CurrentSizeMB - AvailableSpaceMB) * 1.2 AS TargetSizeMB
FROM (
    SELECT
        name
        , size / 128 - CAST(FILEPROPERTY(name, 'SpaceUsed') AS INT) / 128
AS AvailableSpaceMB
        , size / 128 AS CurrentSizeMB
    FROM sys.database_files
    WHERE type = 0
) df ;
```

While your mileage may vary a little, when I run this, I see that my target space, which includes 20% for natural growth, is 838.8 MB. Armed with this information, we will now shrink the data file of the database using the `DBCC SHRINKFILE` command. In listing 9.7, we pass this command the logical name of the data file and the target size. We also use the `WAIT_AT_LOW_PRIORITY` option. This will cause the shrink operation to time out after 1 minute, if a long-running query is preventing the command from acquiring a schema lock. This option is new in SQL Server 2022 and helps mitigate the risk of adverse impact on the application.

Listing 9.7 Shrinking the data file

```
DBCC SHRINKFILE ('MarketingArchive' , 838) WITH WAIT_AT_LOW_PRIORITY ;
GO
```

If we were to now rerun the query in listing 9.6, we would see that our database is approximately the target size. So everything appears to have worked as expected, but the mistake is not understanding the impact that this will have on the fragmentation of our indexes.

If we were to rerun the query in listing 9.4, we would see that some or all of our indexes are at close to 100% fragmentation, meaning that the pages of the index are completely out of order, which will cause performance problems for queries that make sequential reads, such as index scans.

> **TIP** A common misconception is that fragmented indexes cause performance issues for all queries. This is not true. A seek operation that returns a single row will not be impacted. The performance degradation will be seen on queries that perform index scan operations or index lookup operations across multiple pages.

To understand why this is, let's discuss the diagram in figure 9.3. This diagram illustrates the shrink operation that occurred. The process started at the back of the file, and every time it encountered a page, it moved it to the first available space within the file. For many objects, this involved completely reversing the page order, leading to massive fragmentation.

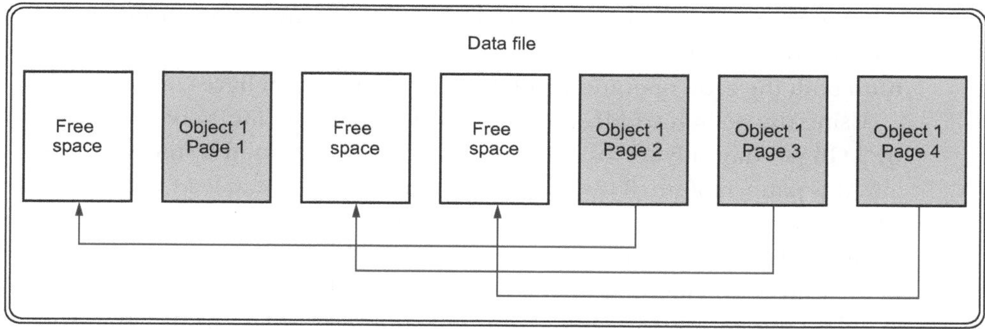

Figure 9.3 File shrink operation

Therefore, in a situation where you must shrink a data file, you should always rebuild all indexes after the shrink operation completes. The simplest way to achieve this can be seen in listing 9.8, although we will be looking at an alternative approach in chapter 11. The command executes a built-in stored procedure, which loops around every table within the database. It passes a statement to rebuild all indexes on the table using `?` as a wildcard value for the table name.

Listing 9.8 Rebuilding all indexes in a database

```
EXEC sp_msforeachtable 'ALTER INDEX ALL ON ? REBUILD' ;
```

Shrinking data files should not be done on a regular basis. It should only be done as a one-time activity, if there is a genuine need. If you do need to shrink a data file, it is important to rebuild all indexes following the operation. This will avoid performance issues relating to heavy index fragmentation.

9.3 #45 Relying on autogrow

By default, if SQL Server runs out of space in a file, it will automatically grow the file in 64 MB chunks. By default, data files can grow until the volume on which they reside is full, while log files can grow to either 2 TB or until the volume becomes full. Using these default settings can cause issues for both data files and log files.

MagicChoc's `MarketingArchive` database is a large database that grows by around 5 GB per day when an extract, transform, and load (ETL) process runs and pulls in historical data from the `Marketing` database. Some of the transactions are very large, and transactions run in parallel. This results in autogrow events occurring for both data and log files. The DBA team has used the default autogrowth settings.

The ETL processes are taking a long time to complete, and analysis shows that random processes, some of them very small, are taking a long time to complete and are blocking other transactions from completing. This is because relying on autogrow to manage file size is a mistake.

Under any circumstances, relying on autogrow to manage file sizes can be problematic. Growing files uses both disk and processor resources. In addition, if a transaction has to grow a log file, then it will block other transactions from writing to the log file until both the grow operation and the data modification have completed.

Using the default 64 MB growth setting on the data file(s) of a database that grows by 5 GB per day only serves to compound the issues caused by the overhead. Additionally, this pattern of small file growth increments in files can lead to disk fragmentation, which can also cause performance issues for sequential read operations on traditional spinning disks. Allowing log files to grow in small increments can lead to fragmentation of the transaction log, and we will explore this in depth later in this chapter.

When a file grows, it has to "zero out" the new space within the file. This consists of literally writing zeros to the file until the file is full. This accounts for much of the overhead of file growth and can be partially mitigated by using instant file initialization, which will be discussed in chapter 10.

Am I recommending that autogrowth be turned off? No, absolutely not. I am a firm believer that autogrowth should be turned on but that it should be used as a safety catch if a database suddenly grows unexpectedly rather than being used to manage file size on a day-to-day basis.

TIP For routine management, we should presize data files and log files based on their expected growth. We should then use autogrow to catch any unexpected events. We should also tune the increment that the files will grow by based on the size of the database. For example, we expect the `MarketingArchive` database to grow by 5 GB per day. Therefore, if we set the growth increment to be 5 GB, then the ETL process that runs overnight can grow the file once and once only each day. Then, provided we are monitoring for file growth, we will notice any anomalies the following morning and investigate. This approach prevents the ETL process from falling over due to a full file while giving us the opportunity to implement a strategic fix.

The statement in the following listing will configure the data file in the `MarketingArchive` database to grow in 5 GB chunks.

Listing 9.9 Changing the autogrowth increment

```
ALTER DATABASE MarketingArchive
    MODIFY FILE ( NAME = 'MarketingArchive', FILEGROWTH = 5GB ) ;
```

If we were to change the growth increment of files in the `model` system database, then this would become the default growth increment for new databases that are created on the instance. Of course, we could still override this when creating a database by specifying `WITH FILEGROWTH` in the `CREATE DATABASE` statement. In fact, I would strongly recommend making it a practice to always include file size and file growth settings whenever you create a database, especially in production.

We should not allow autogrow to manage the size of our data and log files on a day-to-day basis. Autogrowth should be enabled, but the files should be presized based on capacity planning. Autogrowth should be merely a contingency.

9.4 #46 Using multiple log files

SQL Server allows a database to have multiple data files and multiple log files. In some scenarios, splitting data into multiple files can be advantageous. Specifically, it can benefit parallelism, reduce contention on system pages, and make the database easier to migrate. It can also assist with advanced restore strategies.

So what about log files? Let's think about a `MagicChoc` example. The `MarketingArchive` database receives data from multiple parallel transactions during the nightly ETL run. The ETL run has been quite slow, and examining the wait statistics, the DBA notices that there are significant waits on `WRITELOG` wait type, indicating a performance issue when writing to the transaction log. Therefore, the DBA decides to add an additional log file to alleviate the pressure on the log and improve performance. This is a mistake, however. Let's discuss why.

Unlike data files, splitting the transaction log into multiple files offers no advantages. Log records are always written sequentially. This means that if we add an additional log file to a transaction log, then SQL Server will still write all transactions to the first log file. It will only use the second log file if the first log file becomes full. Therefore, there are no performance advantages to using multiple log files; however, there are also no performance penalties for using multiple log files. So is the practice really that bad?

The issue occurs when you need to restore the database. If the transaction log does not exist, then SQL Server will need to create it. As discussed in the previous section, it will usually also have to zero out the file. If you have two transaction log files, then it needs to zero out two files instead of one. This leads to an increased restore time.

The only time we should consider using multiple log files is as a temporary fix if we find ourselves in a situation where a transaction log has consumed all available space on a volume. In this scenario, it is acceptable to create a second log file on a different volume so that database operations can continue.

If we take this approach, we should only use it as a short-term measure while we implement a more strategic fix. This could involve expanding the volume on which the original log file resides; moving the log to a new, larger volume; or in some cases, exploring why the log is growing so large. There could be an underlying issue, such as backups not working.

What should the MagicChoc DBA have done differently to improve the performance of the ETL run? There is no hard and fast rule here, but in our scenario, where we have the pattern of a data warehouse being populated by an ETL run, there is a high chance that bulk inserts will be occurring. This is because data warehouses are often bulk loaded from online transaction processing (OLTP)–style databases or other sources on a scheduled basis, often nightly.

If this is the case, we could consider changing the recovery model of the database to bulk logged at the start of the ETL run. This will cause bulk operations to be minimally logged. This will reduce the number of log records that are written to the transaction log. The results are that less log space will be used, and there will be less I/O throughput required for the transaction log, easing the pressure on the disk subsystem. At the end of the ETL run, we would set the recovery mode back to `Full` and take a transaction log backup.

Switching back to full recovery and taking a log backup is important, because the bulk-logged recovery model does not support point-in-time recovery. This means that in a restore scenario, we would only be able to recover to the end of the transaction log backup. We would not be able to recover to a point in the middle.

The recovery model of the `MarketingArchive` database can be changed to `Bulk-Logged` using the statement in the following listing.

Listing 9.10 Setting the database recovery model to bulk logged

```
ALTER DATABASE MarketingArchive SET RECOVERY BULK_LOGGED WITH NO_WAIT ;
```

Another option for improving the I/O performance could be moving the log to a faster disk. Many SAN administrators use a blanket policy of RAID-5 or RAID-6 for all volumes. Because of the sequential nature of writes to a transaction log, however, the optimal RAID level is RAID-1.

NOTE It is not always possible for SAN administrators to support multiple RAID levels.

In summary, databases should only ever have a single transaction log file. Having multiple transaction logs does not improve performance, and it may increase recovery times. If a log volume runs out of space, we can create a second log file on a different volume, but this should only be a temporary workaround, not a permanent fix.

9.5 #47 Allowing logs to become fragmented

While most DBAs are aware of index fragmentation, far fewer are aware of transaction log fragmentation and the issues that this can cause. Let's think about the

`MarketingArchive` database. We created this database using the default size and growth settings. Therefore, the log file was initially created at 8 MB, and if the file runs out of space, it will grow in 64 GB increments, up to a maximum of 2 TB. The MagicChoc DBAs have left these default settings in place. We discussed earlier in this chapter how, in some circumstances, growing a log file can lead to an increase in I/O and the blocking of other transactions.

In this specific scenario, provided we are running SQL Server 2022 or higher, and provided that instant file initialization (to be discussed in chapter 11) is enabled, the log file will not need to be zeroed out, as it is growing in small, 64 MB chunks. In this scenario, however, allowing the log to grow using the default settings is a mistake, as it will cause log fragmentation. This, in turn, can lead to performance issues. To understand why, we need to understand a little about the architecture of the transaction log.

Inside a transaction log file, SQL Server creates several *virtual log files (VLFs)*. Inside a VLF, you have a number of *log blocks*, which are containers for log records and the unit in which transaction log records are flushed to disk. These *log records* provide a log of every data manipulation language (DML) and data definition language (DDL) statement that has been executed against a database. In `Full` recovery model, all allocated and deallocated pages and extents are also logged. Each log record is given a *log sequence number (LSN)*. The LSN consists of three parts: VLF sequence number, followed by the log block ID, and finally the log record ID.

When a transaction log is truncated, it's not the log file itself that is truncated—it is the VLFs that the log file contains. Any VLFs that do not contain any active transactions will be truncated. A transaction may be marked as active for multiple reasons, including

- The VLF contains transactions that are not yet complete.
- The VLF contains transactions that have not yet been streamed to replicas in an availability group topology.
- The VLF contains transactions that have not yet been harvested by change data capture.

A transaction log file is never fully truncated; there is always at least one active VLF, but there could be many active VLFs at any given time.

A transaction log file has a cyclical nature. When the last VLF inside the log file becomes full, SQL Server will cycle to the front of the transaction log and start using the first VLF that has been truncated. This is illustrated in figure 9.4.

If there are no truncated VLFs within a log file, when the last VLF becomes full, then SQL Server will attempt to grow the log file, based on the autogrowth settings for that file. If it is unable to grow the file because the growth settings do not permit it or because the underlying storage is full, then a 9002 error will be thrown, indicating that the transaction log is full.

When a log file grows, the number of VLFs that are created will depend on the current size of the transaction log and the size increment that it is growing. The rules used

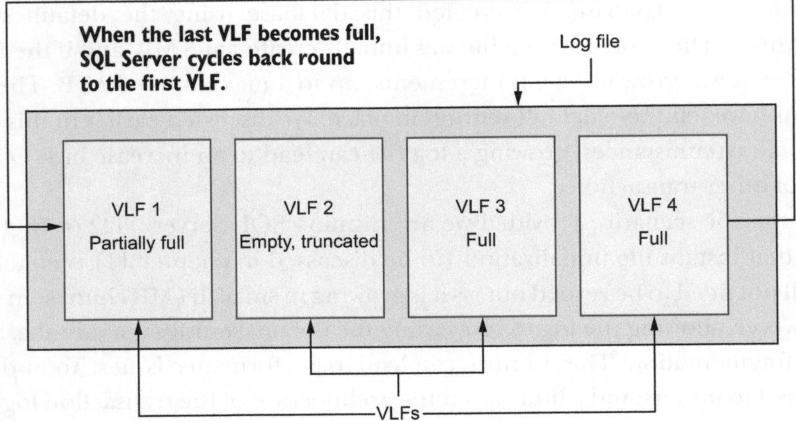

Figure 9.4 Transaction log cycle

to determine how many VLFs will be created state that, if the growth increment is less than 1/8 of the current log size, one VLF will be created. Otherwise:

- If the increment is less than 64 MB, four VLFs will be created.
- If the increment is between 64 MB and 1 GB, eight VLFs will be created.
- If the increment is more than 1 GB, 16 VLFs will be created.

This formula can lead to a log file containing a very large number of VLFs. *Log fragmentation* is where a transaction log has a disproportionate number of VLFs inside it. This can lead to performance issues when restoring a database, attaching a database, and recovering the database when the SQL Server instance starts up. It can also cause performance issues for technologies like AlwaysOn availability groups.

There is no set number for how many VLFs a log file should contain, but they can often start causing issues if there are more than 1,000. Each database must be considered on its own merits, but I generally aim for around two to four VLFs per GB of the total size of the log file. We should also avoid growing a large log file in more than 8 GB chunks, as having too few VLFs can also lead to problems.

The query in listing 9.11 can be used to determine if the `MarketingArchive` database has a fragmented log file. The subquery counts the number of VLFs for the specified database by querying the `sys.dm_db_log_info` DMF. The outer query joins these results to the `sys.master_files` system view and performs some simple calculations to convert the file size from KB to GB and calculate the minimum and maximum ideal number of VLFs.

Listing 9.11 Checking for log fragmentation

```
SELECT
      li.database_id
    , li.ActualVLFs
    , mf.size/1024/1024 AS SizeInGB
```

```
    , mf.size/1024/1024*2. AS MinIdealVLFs
    , mf.size/1024/1024*4. AS MaxIdealVLFs
FROM (
    SELECT database_id, COUNT(*) AS ActualVLFs
    FROM sys.dm_db_log_info(DB_ID('MarketingArchive'))
    GROUP BY database_id
) li
INNER JOIN sys.master_files mf
    ON li.database_id = mf.database_id
WHERE mf.type = 1 ;
```

If you discover that you need to resolve log file fragmentation, the log file should be cleared down by either backing it up (if the database is in FULL recovery model) or truncating it (if the database is using SIMPLE recovery model). We will then need to shrink the file to as small as possible using `DBCC SHRINKFILE`. Finally, we can set the growth increment to an appropriate value, depending on the target size of the transaction log.

We should always try to prevent our logs from becoming fragmented. If this does happen, we can experience performance issues during activities such as restore operations or when we are using features such as availability groups. We can remove existing fragmentation by shrinking the log file and then allowing it to grow using an appropriate increment.

9.6 #48 Failing to capacity plan

Capacity planning is the process of estimating the amount of resources that an application will need after a defined period of time. The period of time is usually in line with an organization's hardware refresh cycle. For example, let's assume that `MagicChoc` has a hardware refresh cycle of three years. Two years into the cycle, a new application is developed, which will run on VMs in the company's data center. During the capacity-planning phase of this project, the task would be to estimate how much compute, memory, and storage the application will require after one year. This will inform the organization if it has sufficient resources on the SAN and within the virtualization cluster to run the application until the next hardware refresh or if new hardware will need to be procured.

One year later, at the end of the hardware refresh cycle, another capacity-planning operation will need to take place. This time, the task will be to determine the amount of resources the application will require in three years' time. This will inform the organization how much additional compute and SAN capacity it needs to purchase in the refresh.

Let's run with the scenario that we have just been discussing to see why failing to undertake capacity planning is a mistake. We are two years into the hardware lifecycle, and we have just launched the Historical Marketing Analysis application. The `MarketingArchive` database in development is promoted to production, with data files sized at 200 GB. We notice that there are 50 GB of free space in the data files, and therefore we feel that there is plenty of free space for natural growth, and because we are busy and capacity planning is hard, we decide not to engage in the process.

What we fail to realize is that the database pulls in 5 GB of data every day and has a data retention policy of three years. This means that, after one year, by the end of the hardware lifecycle, the data files in the database will be a total of 1.78 TB. We have additionally failed to consider how large the `TempDB` system database and the transaction log will need to be. With enough space for the transaction log and `TempDB`, plus factoring in enough headroom for unexpected growth, in a large data warehouse profile such as this, it is perfectly possible that you will need in the region of 3.2 TB. The much bigger problem is that there is only 2 TB of usable capacity left on the corporate SAN, and this has been earmarked for applications that have submitted their capacity requirements.

This scenario is likely to lead to a very difficult conversation with the business. It will potentially also lead to a long period of downtime while the storage team order and install additional SAN capacity. It is clear that failing to plan for capacity is a mistake, but it is a scenario that I see frighteningly often.

To avoid this mistake, the DBA team should have worked in conjunction with the development team to estimate future requirements. Calculating the storage capacity requirements of the data files for this application is quite straightforward. The application consumes a flat rate of around 5 GB of data per day. This is what we call a *linear growth pattern* and is illustrated in figure 9.5.

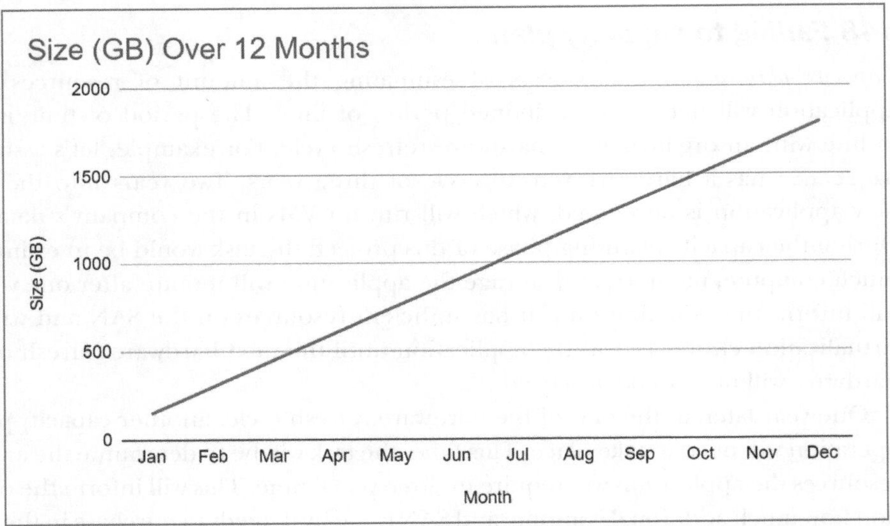

Figure 9.5 Linear growth pattern

However, imagine that, instead of growing at a flat rate, the amount of data being consumed was doubling every month. Instead of a linear growth pattern, we would instead see an exponential growth pattern, which is characterized by a "dog-leg curve." This is illustrated in figure 9.6.

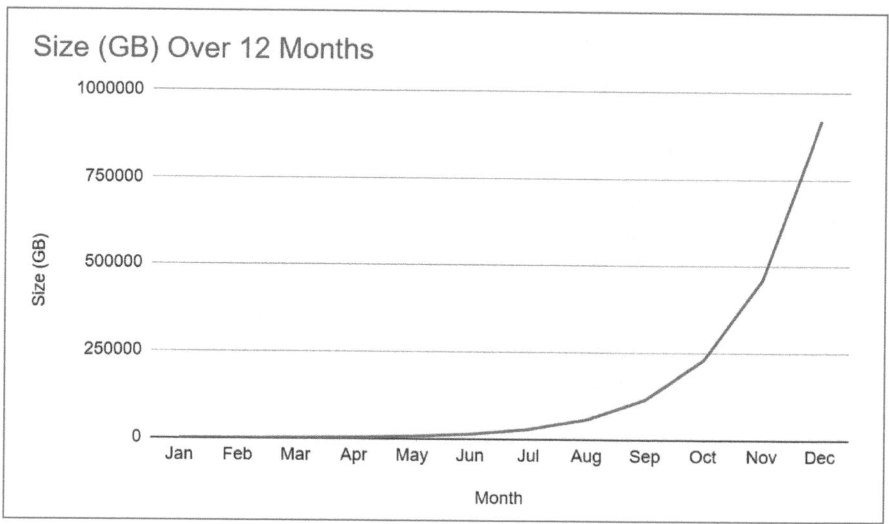

Figure 9.6 Exponential growth pattern

The method of capacity planning we have used for the data files is typically associated with existing systems that have been running for some time. We will have a series of historical data points that we can chart and project forward into the future. Unfortunately, this is not always the case with new (greenfield) applications. In many scenarios, we will not have an even rate of data landing each day.

In these greenfield scenarios, we will typically need to speak to the application owner in the business and assess the amount of business growth that is expected. For example, if the solution is a sales application, we could ask what the sales projections are for the first year of the application.

Once we have as much information as we can harvest from the business, we can define rules and explode the data in the database. For example, in a new sales database, we could manually insert the data for 10 customers, with an average number of delivery addresses determined from interviewing the business. We could then manually insert one sales order for each customer.

We can then explode the data aligned with business expectations. For example, if the sales forecast suggested that in the first year 5,000 customers would be onboarded, and each would be placing an average of 10 orders, then we can use `CROSS JOINS` and numbers tables to duplicate the customer data by a factor of 500 and the order data by a factor of 5,000. This will give us a rough estimate of the expected size of the database.

Performing typical operations against the database once the data has been exploded will also allow us to assess the size requirements of the `TempDB` database and the transaction log file. This is an important consideration, especially in data warehouse scenarios, as the amount of space required for these files may be more than you expect. In my experience, it is not uncommon for each to require in the region of 25% of the size of the database's data files.

It is also important to remember that we need headroom. For example, if we expect our combined data files, log file, and `TempDB` to be 1 TB, we should add an additional 20% for unplanned growth. Therefore, our estimate would be 1.2 TB.

> **TIP** Capacity planning is always a finger in the air, and this is especially true for greenfield systems. It is never a waste of time, however. It is far better to have a best guess on growth than to have no idea whatsoever.

In cloud scenarios, the considerations for capacity planning are slightly different, but they are still equally valid. We need to remember that while we can easily scale an instance up to a larger size, with more memory and compute capacity, this involves a restart of the VM. This means that for 24/7 workloads there will need to be an outage to increase capacity.

> **Finite cloud**
>
> The elastic nature of cloud storage means there is a tendency to think that the cloud has "infinite capacity," but this is not true. In fact, during the COVID-19 pandemic, at least one major cloud provider experienced capacity issues in some regions due to the explosion of cloud computing caused by the exodus from the office.

An even bigger consideration is cloud financial management. Contrary to an organization's data centers, which tend to fall under a capital expenditure model, in cloud we move to an operational expenditure model. This means that there is a tangible cost associated with oversized instances and that you will likely have regular conversations with your procurement team, or cloud financial management team, asking for workloads to be right-sized (made smaller). Luckily, we can be proactive about this by reviewing sizing recommendations made by cloud-native tooling, such as Azure Advisor and AWS Trusted Advisor.

This is a perfectly legitimate consideration and contravenes what we have just discussed. The answer needs to be determined by the organization on a case-by-case basis, factoring in cloud capacity reservations, savings plans and discounts, committed spend, and ultimately the tradeoff between cost and potential short outages.

For example, it may be decided that a mission critical system with a five-9s availability requirement (which we will discuss in chapter 13) is hosted on a VM that is initially oversized based on the results of capacity planning. At the same time, it may be decided that less important applications are hosted on VMs that are right-sized and the downtime is acceptable when they need to grow.

To summarize, we should always consider capacity planning for our databases. On premises, we should look at this through a capital expenditure lens, but in cloud we should look at it through an operational expenditure lens and factor cost management into our planning and decisions.

9.7 #49 Always placing TempDB and log files on dedicated drives

It has long been recommended that data files, log files, and `TempDB` should always be split onto different volumes, as this provides a performance improvement. But is this still always the correct advice? Let's return to MagicChoc to examine this question in a little more detail.

All of MagicChoc's on-premises servers are VMs, with their storage hosted on a SAN. A new server has been built to host the `MarketingArchive` database, and we have built a SQL Server instance. Following official guidance, we have asked the storage team to present three data volumes and the system volume, and we place the `MarketingArchive` data files on one of the data volumes, the `MarketingArchive` log file on another, and `TempDB` on a third.

First, let's think about this in terms of performance. All three volumes reside on a SAN. To access the data for all three volumes, we will be passing through the same network interface card, traversing the same network path, and using the same SAN fabric; then it transpires that all three volumes have been created on the same RAID array. In this scenario, we are going to see no performance improvement.

But are there any negative consequences? Usually, the answer is no, but I have seen some SAN software that requires the data files and log files to be on the same volume to perform an Application Consistent Snapshot, which can be very useful when upgrading a system to give a quick and easy restore point.

Application Consistent Snapshots

A snapshot is a special type of backup, taken at the storage layer, which uses copy-on-write technology to very quickly take a point-in-time snapshot of a volume. These normal snapshots are called Crash Consistent snapshots. They are not suitable for use with SQL Server, because if transactions are in-flight at the start of the snapshot, they are likely to have corrupted databases when they are restored.

Unlike normal snapshots, an Application Consistent Snapshot integrates with the Volume Shadow Copy Service to flush the memory to disk before the snapshot is taken. This means that, unlike normal snapshots, it can be used to recover SQL Server databases even if there were in-flight transactions at the point the snapshot started.

This, of course, does not mean that `TempDB` and log files should never be separated out. For example, the organizational standard may be to store all databases on a SAN; however, for a specific application, `TempDB` may have very high throughput requirements. In this scenario, it may be beneficial to place `TempDB` on a local M.2 drive.

In summary, if your databases are hosted on a SAN, there is no performance benefit in separating the data files, log files, and `TempDB` onto different volumes. It doesn't usually cause a problem to do so, but in a small number of scenarios it may remove the ability to take Application Consistent Snapshots. There may be other valid reasons to move logs and `TempDB` to other volumes, however.

9.8 #50 Not regularly checking for corruption

Databases can become corrupted. It's a fact. Corruption can be caused by multiple issues, including abrupt system shutdown, faulty storage, or even malicious activity. Database corruption is a nightmare. The only thing worse than database corruption is not knowing that there is database corruption.

It's Friday night, and MagicChoc's on-call DBA is just drifting off to sleep when the phone rings. It's a P1 issue. While using a mission-critical database, a user has just received an error, and they can't access the required data.

This is the last thing any DBA needs, as they are settling down on a Friday night, and it could have been so easily avoided by regularly checking for database corruption. It would also have been much better service to the business if the DBA team had noticed before the business experienced an issue.

We can simulate the issue that the user is experiencing by running the script in listing 9.12 to cause corruption in the `MarketingArchive` database. The first thing the script does is back up the `MarketingArchive` database. It is important to run this step so that you can restore from the backup. The script then dynamically creates a SQL statement, which runs the `DBCC WRITEPAGE` command to write a random value to a data page in the `ImpressionsArchive` table. Before we go any further, it very important to understand that `DBCC WRITEPAGE` is an undocumented, unsupported, and *incredibly dangerous feature*, which will write directly to a data page, bypassing the buffer cache. It is great for testing failure scenarios, but it should never be used unless you are 100% comfortable doing so and you have a backup of the database. It should also never be used in a production environment.

> **WARNING** `DBCC WRITEPAGE` *is dangerous.* Do not use it unless you are 100% comfortable and are prepared to lose data. Never use it in a production environment.

Listing 9.12 Simulating data corruption

```
USE master ;
GO

BACKUP DATABASE MarketingArchive
TO  DISK = 'D:\Backups\MarketingArchive.bak' ;
GO

ALTER DATABASE MarketingArchive SET SINGLE_USER WITH NO_WAIT ;
GO

DECLARE @SQL NVARCHAR(MAX) ;

SELECT @SQL = 'DBCC WRITEPAGE(' +
(
        SELECT CAST(DB_ID('MarketingArchive') AS NVARCHAR)
) +
```

```
', ' +
(
       SELECT TOP 1 CAST(file_id AS NVARCHAR)
       FROM MarketingArchive.dbo.ImpressionsArchive
       CROSS APPLY sys.fn_PhysLocCracker(%%physloc%%)
) +
 ', ' +
(
       SELECT TOP 1 CAST(page_id AS NVARCHAR)
       FROM MarketingArchive.dbo.ImpressionsArchive
       CROSS APPLY sys.fn_PhysLocCracker(%%physloc%%)
) +
', 2000, 1, 0x61, 1)' ;

EXEC(@SQL) ;

ALTER DATABASE MarketingArchive SET MULTI_USER ;
GO
```

If we now run a `SELECT` statement against the `ImpressionsArchive` table, we will see an error, similar to the following:

```
SQL Server detected a logical consistency-based I/O error: incorrect
checksum (expected: 0x968b1542; actual: 0x96845542). It occurred during a
 read of page (1:71224) in database ID 11 at offset 0x00000022c70000 in
file 'C:\Program Files\Microsoft SQL
Server\MSSQL16.MSSQLSERVER\MSSQL\DATA\MarketingArchive.mdf'.
```

Of course, it is possible that the error occurred just before the data was accessed, in which case we would have stood no chance of catching it, but it is not unusual for corruption to go unnoticed for an extended period. This makes it much harder to find out exactly when it happened and much harder to fix.

Checking for database corruption is as easy as running the command in listing 9.13, and if we automate the check and schedule it to run periodically, we can configure our monitoring tooling to alert if corruption is found. If corruption is found, the command will return an error.

Listing 9.13 Checking for database corruption

```
DBCC CHECKDB('MarketingArchive') ;
```

It is important to check for database corruption on a regular basis. It is much easier to resolve the issue if the corruption is found quickly. It is also a much better service to the business if DBAs notice the problem before the business notices it. If you do discover database corruption, then the best way to fix it is to perform a page restore. This minimizes, and usually completely avoids, data loss. If this is not possible, then `DBCC CHECKDB` can be used to resolve corruption, but if the corruption is in data page(s), this will result in losing the data that was stored on those pages.

9.9 #51 Failing to automate

I have heard it said that "Good developers are lazy." This is not meant as an insult. Instead, it is meant to imply that a good developer will spend twice as long coding something that can be reused to avoid having to write similar code over and over again. The same applies to DBAs. A good DBA will spend time automating as much as possible in an attempt to avoid performing manual tasks. We have already discussed automating SQL Server installations in chapter 8, but in this section I would like us to focus on automating SQL Server maintenance.

Let's imagine that our MagicChoc DBA performs the majority of SQL Server maintenance manually. Backups are automated, because these are taken by the corporate backup tool (such as Commvault or NetBackup), but all SQL Server–level maintenance, such as index rebuilds, statistics updates, and consistency checks, are performed by DBAs as part of their daily routine. I have seen more than one accidental DBA fall into this trap, but it's a big mistake, for multiple reasons.

First, performing mundane, repetitive tasks is really quite dull. This can lead to issues such as increasing staff turnover. Second, there is the opportunity cost. If the maintenance is automated, then DBAs can spend their time performing higher-value activities, such as diagnosing complex performance problems. Third, it often simply doesn't happen. An urgent operational task will come in, and the DBA will drop the routine maintenance to deal with it. Finally, it can lead to human error, caused by people performing repetitive tasks on autopilot.

An even more common mistake that I see—so common in fact, that it is probably in the majority of environments that I have come across—is decentralized automation. To understand this approach, let's imagine that our MagicChoc DBA is sick and tired of performing manual maintenance every day. Therefore, they decide to introduce some automation. They work through every single SQL Server instance and lovingly handcraft SQL Server Agent jobs, which perform the routine maintenance on each server. Why is this a mistake?

The answer is because now, every morning, our DBA must wade through every single SQL Server instance and look at the SQL Server Agent job history for every single maintenance job that has been created. While this is somewhat quicker than actually performing the maintenance, it is still subject to the same problems. Specifically, it consists of mundane, time-consuming, manual effort, which is sometimes missed because urgent operational issues arise.

How could we do this better? The answer is to centralize maintenance. If an organization's SQL Server estate is on-premises, this may involve having a centralized management server, which loops around each SQL Server instance in the estate and runs maintenance tasks.

This configuration works best when we include a registration step in the script or Desired State Configuration manifest that is used to install new SQL Server instances. It does have its complexities, however. When I implemented this in the past, I needed to build a simple scheduling engine, using tables, views, and stored procedures, to ensure that the correct jobs were performed against the correct instances on the correct schedule.

If an organization's SQL Server estate is in the cloud, there are much more elegant ways of centralizing maintenance. For example, if our SQL server estate is hosted in Azure, we could use Azure runbooks, Azure functions, or a logic app to perform maintenance against Azure SQL Server VMs. If our estate was based around SQL Database, an elastic job would be a good option for configuring the maintenance.

Whatever tool we decide to use, it is important to have centralized, automated maintenance for SQL Server. This reduces manual effort and can mitigate multiple issues. These issues include high staff turnover, missed maintenance, and opportunity cost against higher-value work.

9.10 #52 Using cursors for administrative purposes

In chapter 5, we discussed cursors from a development point of view and why we should avoid using them. I have seen several DBAs sensibly enforce the standard of not allowing cursors but then use cursors themselves for their administrative scripts. The excuse for this is normally that the script does not iterate over many objects, so it doesn't matter.

Imagine that our MagicChoc DBA team enforces a standard that disallows cursors in their environment. They are perfectly entitled to do so, because they are the ones who must troubleshoot performance issues in the production environment—sometimes at unsociable hours. They decide, however, to use cursors for their own administrative scripts.

One of the developers notices that the DBAs are using cursors and raises concern. He is a little annoyed and wants to know why DBAs can use cursors when his team cannot. The DBAs explain to the developer that their scripts are different because they only iterate over a few objects, so the performance impact is not noticeable.

The developer queries this, with the valid point that some of his queries only need to iterate over a handful of rows, so what is the difference? Faced with this, the DBAs reluctantly decide to grant an exception, allowing the developer to use cursors, providing that they do not iterate around many rows.

This starts a snowball effect, where exceptions are coming in from every angle. It becomes impossible to enforce the no-cursor policy. MagicChoc ends up with multiple cursors processing variable quantities of rows. Additionally, the application grows organically over time, and the handful of rows becomes a significant volume.

All of these issues could have been avoided by the DBAs simply following their own coding standards. Providing you understand the alternative techniques, there is never a good reason to use a cursor. For example, the query in listing 9.14 demonstrates how a DBA might use a cursor to iterate over each index in a database and rebuild it.

> **TIP** DBAs will often use conditional logic when rebuilding indexes. The examples in this section simply rebuild all indexes. We will discuss conditional logic for index rebuilds in chapter 11.

Listing 9.14 Using a cursor to rebuild all indexes

```
DECLARE @Command NVARCHAR(MAX) ;
DECLARE @Table NVARCHAR(256) ;

DECLARE Tables CURSOR READ_ONLY FOR
SELECT name
FROM sys.tables ;

OPEN Tables ;

FETCH NEXT FROM Tables INTO @Table
WHILE @@FETCH_STATUS = 0
BEGIN
    SET @Command = 'ALTER INDEX ALL ON ' + QUOTENAME(@Table) + ' REBUILD ; '
    ;
    EXEC(@Command) ;

    FETCH NEXT FROM Tables INTO @Table ;
END

CLOSE Tables ;
DEALLOCATE Tables ;
```

> **NOTE** It is worth noting that earlier in this chapter we used the `sp_msforeachdb` stored procedure to iterate over tables, rebuilding indexes. This stored procedure also uses a cursor under the covers.

So how could we rewrite this script to use a more efficient method that avoids cursors? The answer is to use a trick with the XML data type, as shown in listing 9.15. The subquery generates a list of commands that we want to run and the `FOR XML` clause turns this list into XML format. Because we are using `PATH` mode with no XPath expressions, however, it becomes one single, continuous node with no markup. Because the outer query is expecting `NVARCHAR`, the XML is implicitly converted back to this data type so that it can be executed as dynamic SQL.

Listing 9.15 Rewriting the cursor to use a more efficient approach

```
DECLARE @SQL NVARCHAR(MAX) ;

SET @SQL = (
    SELECT 'ALTER INDEX ALL ON ' + QUOTENAME(name) + ' REBUILD ; '
    FROM sys.tables
    FOR XML PATH('')
) ;

EXEC(@SQL) ;
```

Not only is this query more efficient, but it is also less than half the lines of code. With small datasets, however, the main benefit is setting a good example for the development team and leading by example.

There is never a sound technical reason to use cursors. There is always a better approach. Although DBAs sometimes use cursors for administrative scripts, this sets a bad example for developers and can lead to political challenges that can snowball. Instead, DBAs should use more efficient techniques, such as the XML trick shown in this chapter.

9.11 #53 Failing to patch

Patching is a pain. Any DBA will tell you this, and I am not going to argue. There is always a customer-facing 24/7 system that the business does not want to bring down or a data warehousing application that has an ETL run that goes on for 12 hours and must be completed before the start of the business day.

This results in a mistake that is made by many DBAs, application teams, and application owners, which is to avoid patching of their "golden" systems. So what are the consequences of this mistake? Let's look at this through the eyes of a MagicChoc DBA.

MagicChoc has two database systems, which it does not patch. It does not patch anything—operating system, middleware, or SQL Server. One of the servers is the database that supports the online sales database, which needs to be available 24/7. The other is the marketing data warehouse. This system processes a huge volume of data, and the ETL processes run all night and must be ready before the start of the next business day.

It is 3 a.m. on a cold night when the on-call DBA is awakened by the service delivery manager. There is a problem—a big problem. Nobody can access any database in the whole company. An attacker has exploited the unpatched servers and gained lateral movement, allowing them to perform a ransomware attack across the whole estate.

I am writing this text just after patch Tuesday in November 2023. In this month alone, the Cumulative Update (CU) for Windows Server fixed over 50 security flaws. Therefore, not patching on a monthly basis is a huge security risk and exposes organizations to all forms of cybercrime.

When we fail to patch, this also exposes our organizations to other risks that are not security related. Vendors such as Microsoft use CUs to fix bugs and provide stability improvements. Therefore, if we do not patch our systems, there is more chance of outages that could have been avoided. Sometimes, even minor new features are released via CU, which we will not be able to take advantage of if we have not patched.

So how can we ensure that all of our servers are patched while still meeting the business requirements? Let's look at each of the scenarios in turn. First, we will discuss the requirement for the 24/7 system, which cannot be taken down for patching.

If a database has a 24/7 availability requirement, then it must have highly available infrastructure. This means using technology such as *AlwaysOn availability groups*, which uses log streams to synchronize replica databases across multiple servers and can be used to provide disaster recovery or high availability. When used for high availability, it will offer automatic failover of the databases in the event of an outage to the primary server. When used for disaster recovery, the failover will require manual intervention. This technology can also be used to resolve the patching issue.

In this scenario, we can patch the secondary node(s) in the cluster. Once they have been patched, we can perform a controlled failover from the primary replica to a secondary replica before patching the server that was originally hosting the databases. This does technically cause an outage, but the outage will only last a few seconds, rather than potentially lasting a couple of hours for a patching window. The outage is so short from the end user perspective that it is normally no more than a blip.

The second case is that of a data warehouse with an ETL run that takes all night and needs to be completed by morning. A data warehouse may not be suitable for availability groups, which we will discuss further in chapter 13, but it may be hosted on a clustered instance. A *failover clustered instance (FCI)* hosts databases on storage that is shared between multiple nodes in a cluster. This means that if one node fails, another can automatically take ownership of the database, providing automatic failover. Even if an FCI is used, however, even a short outage of around 30 seconds, which is the average time it takes an FCI to failover, may cause serious issues with an ETL run.

Therefore, the resolution to the patching issue is simply down to scheduling. It may be acceptable for a data warehouse to have a 30-second outage during the working day. If this is the case, then a similar method of rolling updates that we described for availability groups can be used. The difference is that the outage would be scheduled during the working day, rather than during a period where there is the least activity.

If this isn't an option, there will often be a period on weekends where systems such as data warehouses are either not in use or used by far fewer consecutive users. In this scenario, we would simply schedule the outage to happen on a weekend.

To summarize, it is always important that we allow our servers to be patched, even the golden systems that are mission critical. The risks of not patching far outweigh the inconvenience of regular, monthly patching cycles.

Summary

- Shrinking a database will result in near 100% fragmentation of indexes.
- Never autoshrink databases, as it will cause an endless loop of poor performance and increased resource utilization.
- If we must manually shrink a database, then we must remember to rebuild all indexes after the operation has completed.
- Never rely on autogrow as a means of managing database size, as this may lead to performance issues.
- Do not use multiple log files as that provides no benefit. If there are multiple transaction log files, the first file will fill up before the second file is used.
- Each transaction stored within the transaction log is given an LSN. The LSN identifies a transaction and consists of the VLF, log block, and transaction IDs.
- Transaction log files contain multiple VLFs. Additional VLFs are created automatically when a log file grows.
- Having too many VLFs is known as log fragmentation and can lead to performance issues.

- Internal index fragmentation refers to how full each page of an index is.
- External index fragmentation refers to how many pages of the index are out of sequence.
- To remove log fragmentation, we must shrink the transaction log and then allow it to grow in larger increments.
- Index metadata can be found in DMVs and DMFs.
- When examining index fragmentation, there is a particularly useful DMF called `sys.dm_db_index_physical_stats`. This DMF can return one row for every level of every index in a given database.
- Failing to capacity plan can lead to business issues such as unplanned expenditure. It can also lead to outages if there is a long lead time on new hardware.
- When capacity planning, we try to look for growth patterns, such as linear growth or exponential growth.
- It is not always necessary to place database files, transaction log files, and `TempDB` on different volumes.
- If all of our data is stored on a SAN, then it is common for multiple volumes to reside on the same physical RAID array.
- We should regularly check for database corruption, which can be caused by multiple issues, such as disk errors.
- Fixing database corruption early is easier and has less risk of data loss than not noticing the corruption for a prolonged period.
- Always look to automate wherever possible. Automation reduces manual effort and human error. It also allows DBAs to perform higher-value tasks, such as investigating performance issues.
- DBAs should not use cursors. Instead, they should lead by example and demonstrate to development teams that there is always a more efficient way of doing things.
- Even golden systems should be patched. We should not allow any servers to be excluded from regular patching.
- We can use technologies such as AlwaysOn availability groups or failover clustered instances to reduce outage times for patching.
- We can resolve many patching challenges with creative scheduling.

10 Optimization

> ***This chapter covers***
> - Instance-level optimizations
> - Query optimizations
> - Table optimizations
> - Transaction isolation levels
> - Throwing hardware at performance issues

In this chapter, we will dive into mistakes and misconceptions that relate to the optimization of SQL Server performance. We will start by looking at instance-level optimizations, where we will discuss the use of deprecated trace flags, misconceptions around instant file initialization, and memory configuration mistakes. Mistakes can come in two broad flavors: failure to optimize and incorrect optimization.

> **Failure to optimize**
>
> I witnessed a failure to optimize recently. I was asked to look at an extract, transform, and load process that was taking a significant time to load data into a data warehouse. After examination of the process, it was clear that the team had not undertaken

capacity planning (see chapter 9). While the disk had space remaining, the data files had not been sized to account for the large amount of data that was pumped into the database each night. That was causing the data file to expand in small increments, multiple times per night. Instant file initialization had not been enabled, which meant that the additional file space was being zeroed out every time, which is discussed in the second mistake in this chapter. Enabling instant file initialization immediately resolved the issue, but I also sent the team away to plan their capacity and resize the disk accordingly.

We will then move on to mistakes that are made when optimizing queries. The first of these mistakes is working against the optimizer when we should be working with it. We will then discuss query-processing feedback, which is often overlooked by database administrators (DBAs).

We will move on to look at table optimizations. Here we will discuss the common mistake of overlooking useful performance optimization techniques, including partitioning tables and compressing tables.

Next we will look at transaction isolation levels, where we will explore the mistakes and misconceptions that I see time and time again. Finally, we will discuss what happens when we decide to throw more hardware at a performance issue.

To discuss the mistakes in this chapter, we will use the `Marketing` database that we created in chapter 6 and the `MarketingArchive` database that we created in chapter 9. If you have followed along with the examples in chapter 8 and have not yet repaired the `MarketingArchive` database, please run the script in listing 10.1 before continuing.

> **WARNING** In normal operations, we should not use `REPAIR_ALLOW_DATA_LOSS` unless we have no other recovery options, such as restore from backup, etc., as this option can result in data loss.

Listing 10.1 Fixing the `MarketingArchive` database

```
USE master ;
GO

ALTER DATABASE MarketingArchive SET SINGLE_USER ;
GO

DBCC CHECKDB (MarketingArchive, REPAIR_ALLOW_DATA_LOSS) ;
GO

ALTER DATABASE MarketingArchive SET MULTI_USER ;
GO
```

For the examples that make changes to an instance, any instance will suffice, but the instance on which you are hosting the `MarketingArchive` database would be a good choice.

10.1 #54 Turning on TF1117 and TF1118

Trace flags are toggle options that allow administrators to change specific configurations. Each flag has a three- or four-digit number, and while many are either undocumented or relate to older versions of SQL Server, there are certainly some useful trace flags. For example, trace flag 3226 can be used to suppress successful backup messages. This reduces the amount of "noise" in the SQL Server logs.

Depending on the nature of the trace flag, it will be possible to apply the configuration to either the local session or globally, meaning all sessions. For example, the aforementioned 3226 flag can only be turned on globally.

Trace flags can be toggled on and off using the `DBCC TRACEON` and `DBCC TRACEOFF` commands. The trace flag number is passed to the command for session configuration. For global configuration, a second parameter of `-1` is passed. For example, the following script demonstrates how to turn on trace flag 1224 within the session and then globally. This flag disables lock escalation based on the number of locks:

```
DBCC TRACEON (1224) ;
DBCC TRACEON (1224,-1) ;
```

The challenge with global trace flags is that they do not persist a restart of the Database Engine service. Therefore, if we would like a configuration to persist a restart, we must add it as a startup parameter on the SQL Server service.

Some time ago, it was common to use two of these trace flags to help with performance issues in data warehouse–style applications and in some circumstances `TempDB` on OLTP-style workloads. Specifically, T1117 (a common abbreviation for trace flag 1117), which was used to grow all files within a filegroup whenever any file reaches its autogrow threshold. SQL Server uses a proportional fill algorithm for splitting data between files in a filegroup. Therefore, growing all of the files at the same time prevents SQL Server from "favoring" the larger file and subsequently not being able to get the full benefit from reading data from files in parallel.

T1118 was used to enforce uniform extents. This means that multiple objects cannot allocate pages to the same extent. By default, mixed extents were possible for small objects, which were less than 64 KB in size. Enforcing uniform extents helps to prevent contention in system pages such as the Global Allocation Map (GAM), Shared Global Allocation Map , and Page Free Space system pages, which reside in every data file. Uniform versus mixed extents are illustrated in figure 10.1.

Both T1117 and T1118 were deprecated in SQL Server 2016, and their functionality was moved to lower levels, meaning that they can be configured more granularly. This is a much better implementation, because the configurations can be applied to the specific databases that would benefit from it, as opposed to the trace flags, which applied the configuration to all databases.

I still see people setting T1117 and T1118 on the Database Engine service, and even the Azure SQL Server image has these flags configured. This is a mistake, however, because since SQL Server 2016, these trace flags have had no effect. Administrators

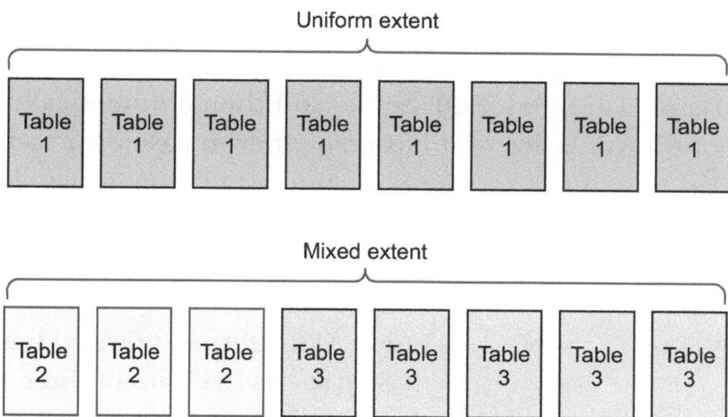

Figure 10.1 Uniform vs. mixed extents

who are unaware of this change think that they have configured these settings when in fact they haven't.

Fortunately, equal file growth is now the default behavior for `TempDB` but should still be configured for data warehouses. Uniform extents are now the default behavior for `TempDB` and user databases. But that just flips the issue around. A DBA who is unaware of these changes but wishes to use mixed extents and/or equal file growth will do nothing, unaware that the undesired behavior is default.

So what should we do instead of configuring these two trace flags if we would like to change the behavior for specific databases? The script in listing 10.2 turns on equal file growth and turns off uniform extents for the `MarketingArchive` database. The first command in the script uses `ALTER DATABASE..MODIFY FILEGROUP` to turn on `AUTOGROW_ALL_FILES`, which overrides the default of `AUTOGROW_SINGLE_FILE`. In the second statement, we use an `ALTER DATABASE SET` option to enable mixed extents.

Listing 10.2 Turning off equal file growth and uniform extents

```
ALTER DATABASE MarketingArchive
    MODIFY FILEGROUP [PRIMARY] AUTOGROW_ALL_FILES ;

ALTER DATABASE MarketingArchive
    SET MIXED_PAGE_ALLOCATION ON ;
```

TIP These commands could also be performed through Desired State Configuration (see chapter 8).

10.2 #55 Not using instant file initialization

When SQL Server creates a file or grows a file, then it has to zero out the file, which literally means filling any blank space with `0`s. As a performance optimization, it is possible to skip this process for data files, and sometimes for transaction log files, by using instant file initialization. To do this, we simply have to give the service account that runs the Database Engine service the Perform Volume Maintenance Tasks user rights assignment (`SeManageVolumePrivilege`). SQL Server will then automatically skip the zero-out on file creation or growth. Microsoft has made it even easier for us in recent versions of SQL Server by adding this as an option during installation. It has also added it as an option that can be configured on the Advanced tab of the Database Engine service in SQL Server Configuration Manager, as shown in figure 10.2.

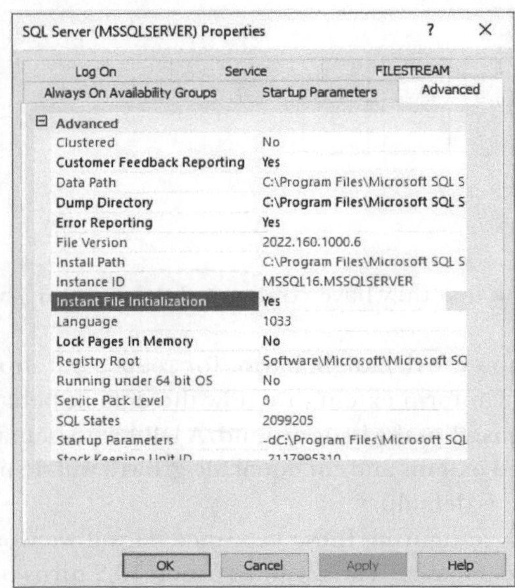

Figure 10.2 Configuring instant file initialization

So it seems like a no-brainer to enable this, right? Well, not quite, and the mistake I have seen some DBAs making is to choose not to implement it. To understand why some DBAs make this mistake, we need to understand the security implications.

Imagine that we have a database containing very sensitive information. The database is migrated to a new server and is dropped from the original server. The original server is then used to host a new database.

When data is deleted from a disk, the physical data is not deleted—only the pointers to that data. When the new data files are created in the same physical location on disk, the files are zeroed out, and hence the original data is overwritten.

In a scenario where we have used instant file initialization, however, the data is not overwritten until SQL Server allocates extents within the same physical location and writes pages to it. Therefore, there is a theoretical risk that a bad actor could retrieve the original data.

If there is a potential security risk, why am I suggesting that it is a mistake not to use instant file initialization? The answer is simply because the risk is too small to outweigh the advantages of using the feature.

For the security risk to be realized, the following criteria would all have to be met:

- Sensitive data previously existed on the disks.
- An attacker has elevated permissions to the server.
- An attacker has the specialist software and skills required to find and retrieve the data.
- An attacker has time to find and retrieve the data before
  - An administrator notices the attack.
  - The data is overwritten by new data.

Therefore, unless you have been storing the nuclear armament codes and the truth of what really happened at Roswell (and decided not to shred the disks afterward), the risk is probably too small to worry about in the context of the performance gains.

10.3 #56 Failing to leave enough memory for other applications

I imagine that many readers will have performed a double take when reading the title of this section. Surely I should be writing about how hosting other applications on the same server as a SQL Server instance is a mistake, rather than talking about memory allocation for other applications?

Well, yes, having other applications installed on the same server as SQL Server is a horrible practice, for many reasons, including security, mixing workload profiles, and troubleshooting. Therefore, I would never advocate for it. What you may not realize, however, is that other features within the SQL Server stack, such as SQL Server Integration Services (SSIS) and SQL Server Analysis Services (SSAS), are also, essentially, other applications. They have their own services, run in their own processes, and have their own memory allocations. Therefore, if we are using any of these features, then we should consider their memory requirements separately from the Database Engine.

On top of this, we should also consider agents that may be used by other teams, such as an antivirus agent, a monitoring agent, or an inventory agent, to name but a few. While they are not business facing, they are very important tools for the wider business and are often mandated to be on all servers. Of course, these tools and agents should be lightweight, but I have seen some of them use far more memory than you would expect.

We also need to consider the amount of memory that we leave available to the operating system. Microsoft recommends leaving 25% of memory available for Windows. This 25% is also used by some SQL Server components, such as extended stored procedures and executables.

By default, when you install SQL Server, the instance will allocate as much memory as it needs for the *buffer pool*, the area of memory where data and index pages are cached. A common mistake is that DBAs leave this default configuration in place on the basis that SQL Server is the only application installed on the server; therefore, it should use as much memory as it wants. This, of course, does not consider the requirements discussed earlier. The mistake is even bigger if Lock Pages In Memory has been configured, as this will stop the working set from being trimmed, as discussed in the next section.

Therefore, we should configure the maximum amount of memory that can be used by the buffer pool, using the following equation:

$$\text{Max Memory} = (\text{Server Memory} - \text{Memory Required by Other Processes}) / 100) \times 75$$

We can configure the maximum memory using the `sp_configure` stored procedure. The script in listing 10.3 configures the maximum server memory to be 48 GB, which would be appropriate for a solitary SQL Server instance, the only application running on a server that has 64 GB RAM. Of course, if the server was hosting multiple instances, then we should split the 48 GB appropriately between them, depending on their requirements.

TIP The value in listing 10.3 is specified in MB.

Listing 10.3 Configuring maximum memory

```
sp_configure 'show advanced options', 1 ;
RECONFIGURE ;
GO

sp_configure 'max server memory', 49152 ;
RECONFIGURE ;
GO
```

We should always configure the maximum memory setting to ensure that we leave enough memory for the operating system. Although we should always avoid other applications being installed on a server hosting a SQL Server instance, when configuring the maximum memory, we should consider the memory requirements of other features within the SQL Server stack, such as SSIS and SSAS. We should also consider the requirements of mandatory tools and agents that must run on the server.

10.4 #57 Failing to lock pages in memory

If Windows is running low on memory, it can become unstable, and out-of-memory errors can be thrown. In this case, Windows will try to protect itself by trimming the working set of user processes. In other words, it will cause processes to page data out to disk and reclaim the memory for itself.

Imagine that we have a resource-constrained SQL Server instance and users start complaining of severe performance degradation, including query timeouts. The DBAs investigate the issue and discover the following message in the SQL Server log:

```
A significant part of SQL Server process memory has been paged out. This
may result in a performance degradation. Duration: 0 seconds. Working set
(KB): 6081740, committed (KB): 17175674, memory utilization: 35%.
```

This error indicates that part of the buffer cache has been flushed to disk and the memory has been reclaimed by the operating system. So is locking pages in memory a no-brainer? Well, there has actually been a significant amount of debate in the community, which has led to many DBAs not configuring this setting. Why is it debated?

In earlier versions of Windows Server, the operating system was very aggressive when trimming working sets. As time moved on, this behavior became less aggressive while memory management improved in general. This meant that there was less chance of the issue occurring.

At the same time, virtualization platforms became the default environment for hosting SQL Server. One of the main benefits of a virtualization platform, such as VMware or Hyper-V, is the ability to overcommit physical resources. This means that, for example, a virtualization host with 8 CPUs and 64 GB RAM could host VMs with a total requirement of 16 vCPUs and 96 GB RAM.

The hypervisor manages this by allocating resources to VMs when they are required. When they are not being used, it reclaims those resources and assigns them to other

VMs that need them more. This process is known as *ballooning* and is illustrated in figure 10.3.

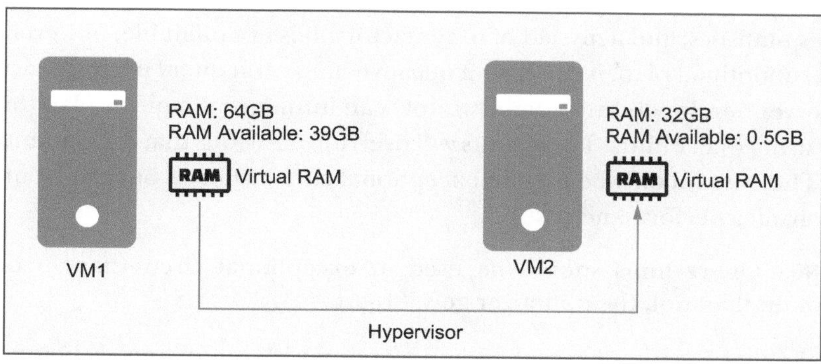

Figure 10.3 Memory ballooning

If VMs are hosting SQL Server instances that are locking pages in memory, then the memory cannot be reclaimed, and this can cause a performance issue across the whole virtualization estate.

The argument regarding VMs is perfectly valid, and when we run SQL Server in a virtual environment, we should work closely with our VMware administrators to ensure that we can offer a reliable service to our users without impacting the entire estate. The argument regarding the less aggressive trimming of the working set, however, is simply not strong enough to justify not configuring Lock Pages In Memory as a default installation option. The fact that it happens less often does not mean that it never happens, and I have seen occurrences where it has happened. We should try to avoid this, as these are perfectly preventable outages.

As cloud becomes the standard for hosting SQL Server workloads, it is also worth mentioning that major cloud providers, such as AWS, recommend configuring Lock Pages In Memory as a best practice in their environment. This is because, despite it being a virtual environment, the cloud providers do not overcommit resources. Therefore, ballooning is not a consideration.

Lock Pages In Memory is configured by granting the `SeLockMemoryPrivilege` User Rights Assignment to the service account that runs the Database Engine service. It can also be configured during SQL Server installation, or from the Advanced tab of the Database Engine service in SQL Server Configuration Manager.

10.5 #58 Working against the optimizer

T-SQL is a descriptive language. This means that when a developer writes a query, they describe the results that they want SQL Server to return, as opposed to giving SQL Server step-by-step instructions on how to perform the task at hand. The Query

Optimizer then calculates the most efficient way to return the data that the developer is looking for.

The Query Optimizer is very sophisticated and makes a lot of good decisions, based on indexes, statistics, and a myriad of other factors. It is not infallible, however, and if it chooses a suboptimal plan, it can have a negative impact on query performance.

SQL Server developers and administrators can influence the query plan that is generated by using query hints. These hints will override decisions that the optimizer wants to make. They should only be used in exceptional circumstances but can be invaluable when resolving a performance issue.

> **WARNING** Query hints should be used in exceptional circumstances only. More often than not, the optimizer gets it right.

The mistake that I see people make when working with query hints is being overprescriptive or, as I like to say, working against the optimizer when we should be working with it. The best example of this is a hint that can be used to specify the physical join operation that should happen between tables.

If we perform a join operation, such as an `INNER JOIN` or `OUTER JOIN` between two tables, then there are four physical operators that the Query Optimizer can use to perform the logical operation. Each is the most efficient choice in different scenarios. Each operator is summarized in table 10.1.

Table 10.1 Physical join operators

Operator	Description	Most efficient use
Nested Loops	Choose one table as the outer input table and the other table becomes the inner input table. For each key in the outer input table, it searches every row in the inner input table for matching key values.	Small tables
Hash Join	Builds a hash table in memory, with each row of the first table placed in a hash bucket, dependent on the key value. The keys of the second table are then hashed and compared to the first table on a row-by-row basis. If there is not enough memory for every row in the first table, then the operation will be performed in multiple steps.	Large tables not sorted by join key or where inputs have a big difference in row count
Merge Join	Checks the equality of the first key in both tables. It then compares the next row in the second table to the first row in the first table. This is similar to nested loops, but because the inputs are sorted by the join key, it can stop as soon as it finds a row in the second table that is not matched and move to the next row in the first table.	Large tables sorted by join key, where each table is a similar size
Adaptive Join	The query starts by using a hash join but can change to nested loops during execution if the table that populates the hash table is small enough for nested loops to be more efficient.	Queries where the input rows wildly swing and Batch Mode execution is used

Imagine a scenario where the query in the following listing is performing poorly.

Listing 10.4 Poorly performing query

```
SELECT
    i.ImpressionUID
FROM Marketing.marketing.Impressions i
INNER JOIN MarketingArchive.dbo.ImpressionsArchive ia
    ON i.ImpressionUID = ia.ImpressionUID ;
```

We investigate the issue and on examining the query plan, we discover that the optimizer is choosing to use Nested Loops as the join operator, as shown in figure 10.4. On my test machine, the query takes 19 seconds to run with this operator.

> **TIP** If you are following along with the examples in this chapter, then please note that the plan SQL Server chooses may differ from the plan it chose in my environment.

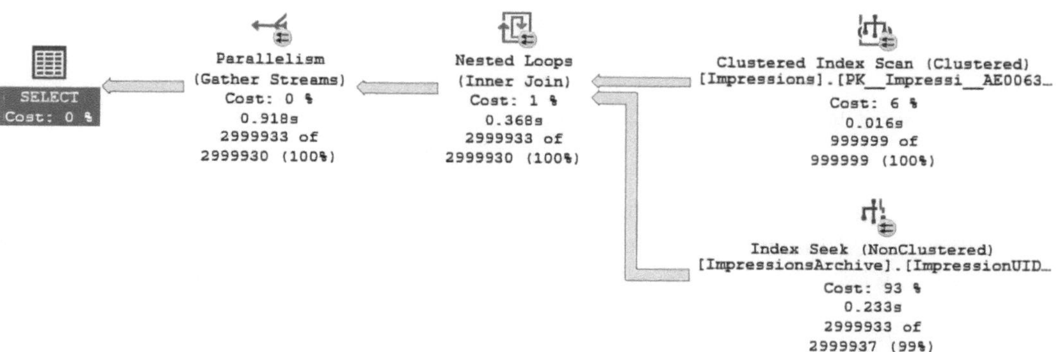

Figure 10.4 Plan using Nested Loops

> **WARNING** Before we go on, it is important to note that using query hints should be the last option. This type of issue can usually be resolved by other means, such as ensuring statistics are up to date. Query hints are a last resort.

The mistake that many DBAs would make in this scenario is forcing the optimizer to use a Hash Join, as that would likely be the most efficient option at this moment in time. There are various ways that this could be achieved, including plan freezing, Query Store hints, a `USE PLAN` query hint, a `HASH MATCH` query hint, or a join hint. For this example, we will use a join hint, as shown in the following listing.

Listing 10.5 Forcing a Hash Join with a join hint

```
SELECT
    i.ImpressionUID
FROM Marketing.marketing.Impressions i
```

```
INNER HASH JOIN MarketingArchive.dbo.ImpressionsArchive ia
    ON i.ImpressionUID = ia.ImpressionUID ;
```

This query used the plan illustrated in figure 10.5 and took 5 seconds to run on my test rig.

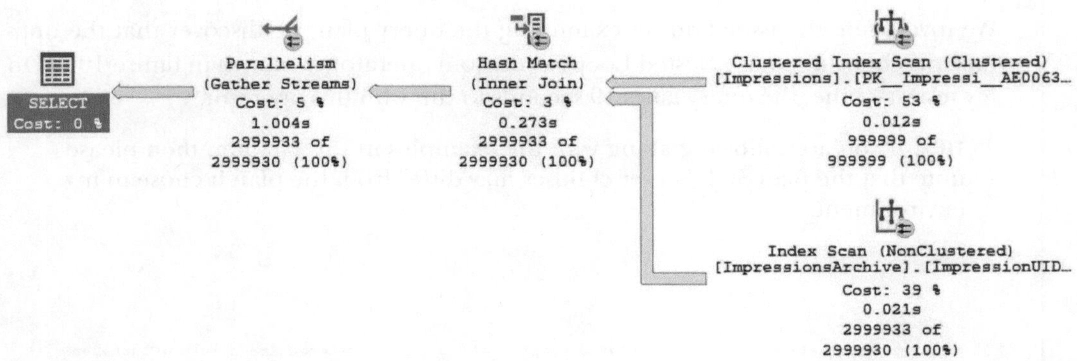

Figure 10.5 Plan using Hash Join because of a join hint

That's a great result! So why is this a mistake? Well, let's consider that, after this incident, nonclustered indexes are added to the `ImpressionUID` column of the `Impressions` table in `Marketing` database tables, which can be achieved with the script in listing 10.6.

> **TIP** There is no need to create this index for the `MarketingArchive` database because we created a suitable index in chapter 9.

Listing 10.6 Creating indexes on join columns

```
USE Marketing ;
GO

CREATE NONCLUSTERED INDEX ImpressionUID
    ON marketing.Impressions(ImpressionUID) ;
GO
```

Now the optimizer would ideally choose a Merge Join, which uses the new index, and on my test rig, takes 3 seconds to execute. Unfortunately, our hint is forcing the optimizer to use a Hash Join instead, which on my test rig takes 4 seconds with the new index. Therefore, a much better approach would have been to use a query hint where we can specify multiple options for the optimizer to choose from. Consider the query in the following listing.

Listing 10.7 Using a query hint instead of a join hint

```
SELECT
    i.ImpressionUID
FROM Marketing.marketing.Impressions i
INNER JOIN MarketingArchive.dbo.ImpressionsArchive ia
    ON i.ImpressionUID = ia.ImpressionUID OPTION (MERGE JOIN, HASH JOIN) ;
```

This hint still eliminates the possibility of using Nested Loops, which we know will never be a good idea because of the size of the tables, but it gives the optimizer the choice of using either a Merge Join or a Hash Join, depending on which it determines will be most efficient.

Although an option of last resort, query hints can be a useful tool for resolving performance issues. If you do decide to use query hints, always try to work with the optimizer, rather than against it. Where possible, give it multiple options to choose from rather than forcing a single option, which may become outdated.

10.6 #59 Not taking advantage of DOP feedback

In the previous section, we explored ensuring that we work with, rather than against, the optimizer when we think we have no choice but to use query hints. Wouldn't life be much easier if SQL Server could learn what works best and adapt plans as required?

SQL Server 2022 expands the intelligent query-processing feature set to expand the possibilities of SQL Server adapting plans, based on previous inefficiencies, by bringing query feedback features into the main product. They had already been available in Azure SQL Database, in preview, and memory grant feedback has been slowly introduced to the core product over the last three releases.

These query feedback features utilize the Query Store to allow for comparison between different plans and the associated performance. Therefore, to follow the examples in this section, Query Store will need to be enabled for the `MarketingArchive` database. This can be achieved using the command in listing 10.8.

TIP Beginning in SQL Server 2022, the Query Store is enabled by default. It is also enabled by default in Azure SQL Database and Azure Managed Instances.

Listing 10.8 Enabling Query Store for the `MarketingArchive` database

```
ALTER DATABASE MarketingArchive
    SET QUERY_STORE = ON (OPERATION_MODE = READ_WRITE) ;
```

TIP A full discussion of Query Store is beyond the scope of this book, but Microsoft has a walk-through at https://mng.bz/YVmA.

Imagine that we have periods where queries on our instance start to run slowly. We investigate by examining the wait statistics and discover that there are very high values for the `CX_PACKET` and `SOS_SCHEDULER_YEILD` wait types. We also notice that the issue is happening whenever a large reporting query is being executed. We check out the query plan and discover that the query is executing with a maximum degree of parallelism (`MAXDOP`) of 16.

> **TIP** Prior to SQL Server 2016 Service Pack 2 and SQL Server 2017 Cumulative Update 4, `CX_PACKET` provided inconsistent results. Since this bug was fixed, it has become very useful.

All of the symptoms suggest that the issue is being caused by the big reporting query, running at a degree of parallelism that is actually detrimental to its own execution time and other queries that run simultaneously.

We have already changed the instance-wide `MAXDOP` setting to 16 to benefit some other queries, so we decide to add a `MAXDOP 8` query hint to the problematic query. This is a mistake, however. Why? Because we are running SQL Server 2022, which means that we could enable DOP feedback and let SQL Server continuously evaluate and change the DOP used in the query plan based on the execution statistics. Why do DBAs make this mistake? There are two reasons: (1) because DOP feedback is the only one of the three query feedback features not to be enabled by default and (2) because in the busy life of a DBA, it's not always possible to stay up to date with all of the new features of SQL Server when they are released. This is a great example of why keeping up to date with and implementing new features is important, as it can save DBAs a lot of time and free them up to work on higher-value tasks.

SQL Server 2022 provides the following query feedback options, which are part of the intelligent query-processing suite.

- DOP feedback
- Cardinality estimation feedback
- Memory grant feedback

We have already discussed DOP feedback. It allows SQL Server to optimize the DOP of a query based on historical executions.

Cardinality estimate (CE) helps SQL Server to select the most appropriate plan based on estimating how many rows will be processed in each step of query execution. The estimates, which are based on column and index statistics and passed through a sophisticated algorithm, can sometimes be incorrect. This is because it is not possible to develop an algorithm to account for every single user's requirements and usage patterns. Poor estimates can lead to suboptimal query plans and ultimately to poor query performance. CE feedback can help SQL Server identify poor estimates and make better choices.

Memory grant feedback adapts a query's memory grant based on historical information. This can help avoid a memory grant that is too small, resulting in data spooling to disk. It can also help avoid a memory grant that is too high and results in suboptimal parallelization.

Unlike DOP feedback and CE feedback, which are both new in SQL Server 2022, memory grant feedback has been implemented in stages over the last three major releases of SQL Server. Batch-mode memory grant feedback was implemented in SQL Server 2017, with row-mode memory grant feedback implemented in SQL Server 2019. SQL Server 2022 saw the implementation of percentile and persistence modes. This brings the implementation into the Query Store, so that the statistics used to make the decisions are not lost when the instance restarts.

If Query Store is enabled for a database, memory grant feedback and CE feedback will be enabled by default, providing that the compatibility level of the database is 140 or higher for memory grant feedback and 160 or higher for CE feedback. DOP feedback is off by default, however. It can be turned on by using the command in the following listing.

Listing 10.9 Turning on DOP feedback

```
ALTER DATABASE SCOPED CONFIGURATION
    SET DOP_FEEDBACK = ON ;
```

The query in the following listing can be used to determine which query feedback features are enabled for the database in scope.

Listing 10.10 Reviewing enabled query feedback options

```
SELECT
      name
    , CASE
          WHEN value = 1 THEN 'Enabled'
          ELSE 'Disabled'
      END as Enabled
FROM sys.database_scoped_configurations
WHERE name LIKE '%feedback%' ;
```

It is good practice to enable DOP feedback in databases with a compatibility level of 160 or higher. This removes the need for the DBA to manually assess and optimize MAXDOP settings for a query.

10.7 #60 Not partitioning large tables

SQL Server is often I/O bound. This means that the disk subsystem is the bottleneck that impacts the performance of a query. This is especially true for very large databases that run reporting-style queries against very large tables.

Let's consider the `MarketingArchive` database. Imagine that our instance is struggling for IOPS and the query in listing 10.11 is frequently being run. The first command in the script turns on I/O statistics for the session.

Listing 10.11 Query against a large table

```
SET STATISTICS IO ON ;
GO

SELECT *
```

```
FROM dbo.ImpressionsArchive
WHERE EventTime >= '20210101' AND EventTime <= '20211231' ;
```

If we look at the query plan, shown in figure 10.6, we will notice that a clustered index scan is being performed. This means that every row in the table is being read.

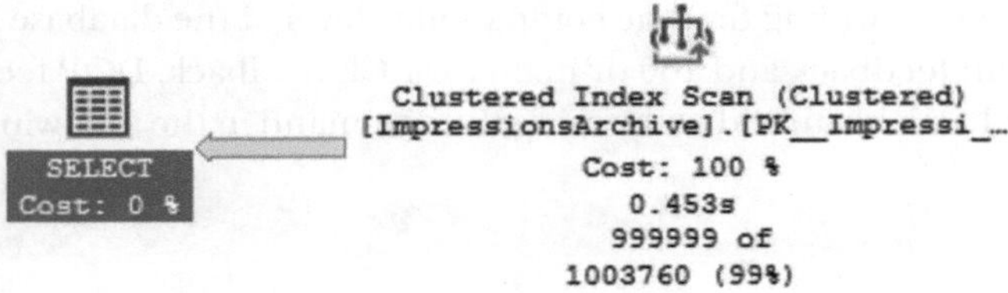

Figure 10.6 Query plan from reporting query

Let's look at the I/O statistics for this query. They will be displayed in the Messages tab, due to I/O statistics being turned on for the session:

```
Table 'ImpressionsArchive'. Scan count 1, logical reads 46979,
physical reads 1, page server reads 0, read-ahead reads 46981,
page server read-ahead reads 0, lob logical reads 0, lob physical reads 0,
lob page server reads 0, lob read-ahead reads 0,
lob page server read-ahead reads 0.
```

The buffer cache was cold, so SQL Server performed a physical read of all required pages (1 physical read and 46,981 read-ahead reads). The read-ahead reads placed the remaining pages required into the buffer cache, which is why the statistics show 46,979 logical reads.

> **Clearing the cache**
>
> For testing purposes, it is sometimes helpful to clear the buffer cache so that pages need to be read from disk. If you fail to do this, the second time you run a query the pages will already be in cache, meaning that the test is not valid.
>
> You can clear the pages from the buffer cache by running the following commands:
>
> ```
> CHECKPOINT
> DBCC DROPCLEANBUFFERS
> ```
>
> The first command causes *dirty pages*, those that have been modified, to be flushed to disk. The second command removes *clean pages*, those that have not been modified, from the cache.
>
> If you plan to run repeated tests, then it is good practice to run these commands at the start of your script. Remember, however, that you should only ever do this on a development or test server. Running these commands on a production server is likely to impact performance.

A mistake that I often see DBAs make is to investigate this far, check for missing indexes, and then stop and either say "Sorry, it is what it is!" or contact the storage team to see if they can coax any more performance out of the SAN. What they should be doing instead is investigating a greatly underutilized feature called *table partitioning*.

Table partitioning is a longstanding feature in SQL Server that splits a table into multiple smaller tables based on a partitioning key. This split is entirely seamless to the developer, as the table still appears as a single table and no code changes are required.

There are two big advantages to partitioning a large table that has reporting-style queries run against it. The first is that it is possible to place each partition on a different filegroup. If the files within those filegroups are stored on different disks, partitions can be read in parallel.

The second, in my opinion more important, advantage is the ability to eliminate partitions. In other words, SQL Server can read data just from the partitions it requires and ignore partitions that do not hold relevant data. This can result in a drastic reduction of reads, easing pressure on the I/O subsystem. It can also improve the performance of the query directly, by reading less data.

So why don't DBAs take advantage of this functionality? There are three reasons that I have come across. The first is that they are simply unaware of the feature. I always find this surprising, as the feature was introduced in SQL Server 2005—almost 20 years ago! The second reason is political wrangling. I have seen situations where the DBA team insists that it's a developer's responsibility to write the partitioning objects, as they don't have the application knowledge. At the same time, the developers refuse to implement the feature because they are not DBAs and don't understand partitioning. This is easily solved with collaboration. If both teams can pull together, then implementation will be straightforward.

The final reason is a lack of understanding of how the technology works or how to implement it. Let's address this reason in the remainder of this section.

To create a partitioned table or partition an existing table, a partition function and partition scheme must be created. To understand these concepts, I like to use the analogy of a farm with multiple fields. The fields are separated by fences, and that allows different crops to be grown in each field.

Using this analogy, the partition function is the fences. It defines the boundary points: where one field ends and the next begins. When we create a partition function, we specify the datatype of the boundary points, the specific boundary point values, and if the range is left or right.

The range left or right is used to determine if values that land on the boundary point are placed to the left of the boundary point or the right of the boundary point. This difference is illustrated in figure 10.7. In this example, a partition function has created boundary points for the integer values 10, 20, and 30.

The partition scheme defines which filegroup each partition is placed on. We have a choice of specifying a different (precreated) filegroup for each partition or specifying the `ALL` keyword, to denote that we wish to store all partitions on the same filegroup.

Finally, when we create a table, we replace the `ON <FILEGROUP>` clause with an `ON <PARTITION SCHEME>(<PARTITIONING KEY>)` clause. This architecture means that multiple partitions can be created on a single partition scheme and multiple partition schemes can be created on a single partition function.

Figure 10.7 Partition function ranges left and right

The script in listing 10.12 creates a partition function called `ImpressionDatesPF`, which uses range right and a `DATETIME` data type. It creates boundary points at the first of January in 2020, 2021, 2022, and 2023. It then creates a partition scheme called `ImpressionDatesPS`, which maps all partitions to the `PRIMARY` filegroup. Next, the script creates a new table, called `ImpressionArchivePartitioned`, on the `ImpressionDatesPS` partition scheme using the `EventTime` column as the primary key, before creating a `PRIMARY KEY` on the `ImpressionID` and `EventTime` columns. It is important to understand that, when dealing with partitioned tables, the partitioning key must be a subset of any unique key of the table. We are creating a new table, rather than partitioning the existing table, for two reasons. First, it allows for comparisons to be run against the two approaches and second, we will be using the `ImpressionArchive` table in later examples.

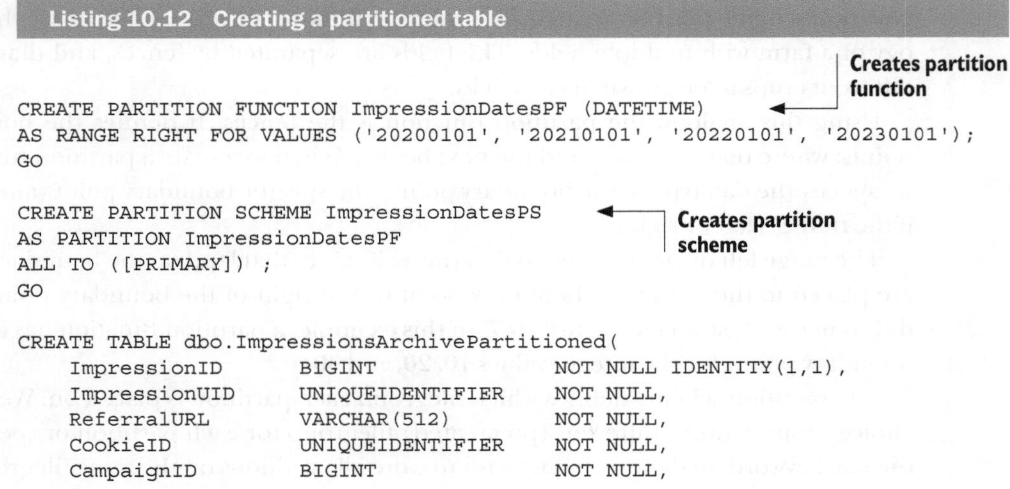

Listing 10.12 Creating a partitioned table

```
CREATE PARTITION FUNCTION ImpressionDatesPF (DATETIME)        ◄ Creates partition function
AS RANGE RIGHT FOR VALUES ('20200101', '20210101', '20220101', '20230101');
GO

CREATE PARTITION SCHEME ImpressionDatesPS                      ◄ Creates partition scheme
AS PARTITION ImpressionDatesPF
ALL TO ([PRIMARY]) ;
GO

CREATE TABLE dbo.ImpressionsArchivePartitioned(
      ImpressionID        BIGINT                NOT NULL IDENTITY(1,1),
      ImpressionUID       UNIQUEIDENTIFIER      NOT NULL,
      ReferralURL         VARCHAR(512)          NOT NULL,
      CookieID            UNIQUEIDENTIFIER      NOT NULL,
      CampaignID          BIGINT                NOT NULL,
```

```
    RenderingID        BIGINT              NOT NULL,
    CountryCode        TINYINT             NULL,
    StateID            TINYINT             NULL,
    BrowserVersion     BIGINT              NOT NULL,
    OperatingSystemID  BIGINT              NOT NULL,
    BidPrice           MONEY               NOT NULL,
    CostPerMille       MONEY               NOT NULL,
    EventTime          DATETIME            NOT NULL,
) ON ImpressionDatesPS(EventTime) ;        ◄── Creates table on partition scheme
GO
                                           ◄── Creates primary key
ALTER TABLE dbo.ImpressionsArchivePartitioned ADD CONSTRAINT
   PK_ImpressionsArchivePartitioned PRIMARY KEY (ImpressionID, EventTime) ;
GO

INSERT INTO dbo.ImpressionsArchivePartitioned (   ◄── Inserts data into new table
    ImpressionUID,
    ReferralURL,
    CookieID,
    CampaignID,
    RenderingID,
    CountryCode,
    StateID,
    BrowserVersion,
    OperatingSystemID,
    BidPrice,
    CostPerMille,
    EventTime
)
SELECT
      ImpressionUID
    , ReferralURL
    , CookieID
    , CampaignID
    , RenderingID
    , CountryCode
    , StateID
    , BrowserVersion
    , OperatingSystemID
    , BidPrice
    , CostPerMille
    , EventTime
FROM dbo.ImpressionsArchive ;
```

Now let's see what that has done to the I/O requirements by running the query in listing 10.13.

Listing 10.13 Query against a partitioned table

```
SELECT *
FROM dbo.ImpressionsArchivePartitioned
WHERE EventTime >= '20210101' AND EventTime <= '20211231' ;
```

The I/O statistics for this query are

```
Table 'ImpressionsArchivePartitioned'. Scan count 1, logical reads 15732,
physical reads 2, page server reads 0, read-ahead reads 15736,
page server read-ahead reads 0, lob logical reads 0, lob physical reads 0,
lob page server reads 0, lob read-ahead reads 0,
lob page server read-ahead reads 0.
```

Despite the query returning exactly the same rows, instead of reading 46,982 pages from disk, it has only read 15,738 pages from disk. If we examine the query plan, shown in figure 10.8, the reason is apparent. Although a clustered index scan has still been performed, all but one of the partitions have been eliminated, meaning that only a third of the data needed to be read.

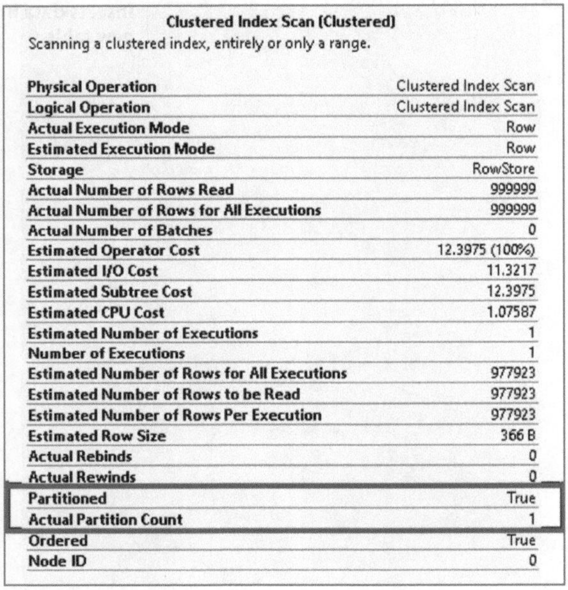

Clustered Index Scan (Clustered)
Scanning a clustered index, entirely or only a range.

Physical Operation	Clustered Index Scan
Logical Operation	Clustered Index Scan
Actual Execution Mode	Row
Estimated Execution Mode	Row
Storage	RowStore
Actual Number of Rows Read	999999
Actual Number of Rows for All Executions	999999
Actual Number of Batches	0
Estimated Operator Cost	12.3975 (100%)
Estimated I/O Cost	11.3217
Estimated Subtree Cost	12.3975
Estimated CPU Cost	1.07587
Estimated Number of Executions	1
Number of Executions	1
Estimated Number of Rows for All Executions	977923
Estimated Number of Rows to be Read	977923
Estimated Number of Rows Per Execution	977923
Estimated Row Size	366 B
Actual Rebinds	0
Actual Rewinds	0
Partitioned	True
Actual Partition Count	1
Ordered	True
Node ID	0

Figure 10.8 Partitioned table query plan

If you have very large tables with a typical usage pattern for reporting queries, you should consider partitioning the table. This approach allows partitions to be eliminated if they are not required, which can significantly relieve pressure on the I/O subsystem and improve query performance.

10.8 #61 Not understanding the limitations of partition elimination

In the previous section, we discussed how helpful partitioning can be when we have very large tables. The benefits come from partition elimination; SQL Server can choose to read the data from only the partitions that it requires. Because each partition is stored as a separate B-tree, however, if our queries are not able to take advantage of partition elimination, then queries can actually be slower than they would be against a nonpartitioned table. Therefore, it is a mistake to implement partitioning without thinking about the queries that will be using it.

I cannot emphasize enough that the partitioning key is vital to achieving partition elimination. One of the most common reasons for partition elimination not working is developers writing queries that do not use the partitioning key. For example, if we filter on the partitioning key AND another column, then partition elimination will work. If we filter on the partitioning key OR another column, however, then all partitions would need to be read. This is illustrated in listing 10.14. The first query in the script will access only a single partition. The second query, however, uses OR logic and will need to read all partitions in the table.

Listing 10.14 AND logic versus OR logic

```
SELECT *
FROM dbo.ImpressionsArchivePartitioned
WHERE CampaignID = 44538
AND EventTime >= '20210101' AND EventTime <= '20211231' ;

SELECT *
FROM dbo.ImpressionsArchivePartitioned
WHERE CampaignID = 44538
OR EventTime >= '20210101' AND EventTime <= '20211231' ;
```

Another common cause of issues is cases in which SQL Server needs to perform a conversion. For example, our `ImpressionsArchivePartitioned` table uses the `DATETIME` data type for the `EventTime` column. In the examples so far, SQL Server has been able to compare our literal value against the column, even though it is formatted as a `DATE`, because `DATETIME` is above `DATE` in the order of precedence. If we explicitly typed our value as `DATE` however, then SQL Server would need to convert it, which would stop partition elimination from working. For example, the first query in the following listing would read all of the table's partitions, whereas the second query would be able to eliminate all but one partition.

Listing 10.15 Converting data types

```
DECLARE @StartDate DATE ;
SET @StartDate = '20210101' ;

DECLARE @EndDate DATE ;
SET @Enddate = '20211231' ;

SELECT *
FROM dbo.ImpressionsArchivePartitioned
WHERE EventTime >= @StartDate AND EventTime <= @EndDate ;
GO


DECLARE @StartDate DATETIME ;
SET @StartDate = '20210101' ;
```

```
DECLARE @EndDate DATETIME ;
SET @Enddate = '20211231' ;

SELECT *
FROM dbo.ImpressionsArchivePartitioned
WHERE EventTime >= @StartDate AND EventTime <= @EndDate ;
```

The final common cause of problems is simple parameterization. If SQL Server thinks that it can reuse the plan, it will promote reuse by parameterizing the values in the filter. This will stop partition elimination from working.

We can work around this issue in two different ways. The first workaround is to specify the `RECOMPILE` option. This will prevent simple parameterization, because the plan will not even be cached. This has the obvious disadvantage that the plan will have to be recompiled every time the query is run.

The second workaround is to add a static nonequality operator to the query, such as `1 <> 2`. This will prevent simple parameterization, but the plan will still be cached so that some degree of reuse is possible.

Listing 10.16 has three queries. The first query will read all partitions of the table. The second and third queries will only read a single partition.

Listing 10.16 Simple parameterization

```
SELECT COUNT(*)
FROM dbo.ImpressionsArchivePartitioned
WHERE EventTime >= '20210101' AND EventTime <= '20211231' ;
GO

SELECT COUNT(*)
FROM dbo.ImpressionsArchivePartitioned
WHERE EventTime >= '20210101' AND EventTime <= '20211231'
OPTION(RECOMPILE) ;
GO


SELECT COUNT(*)
FROM dbo.ImpressionsArchivePartitioned
WHERE EventTime >= '20210101' AND EventTime <= '20211231'
AND 1<>2 ;
GO
```

Both of these workarounds will result in dynamic partition elimination. This means that SQL Server decides to eliminate partitions at execution time, as opposed to compile time. Figure 10.9 illustrates the seek predicates from the query plan of the third query in listing 10.16. You will notice that a single scalar operator of `3` is used to determine the partition that needs to be accessed.

Partitioning large tables can offer very worthwhile performance benefits. Partitioning rashly and not developing code to ensure partition elimination occurs, however, is a mistake. It is important that we understand the limitations of partition elimination and that performance may degrade if partition elimination does not occur.

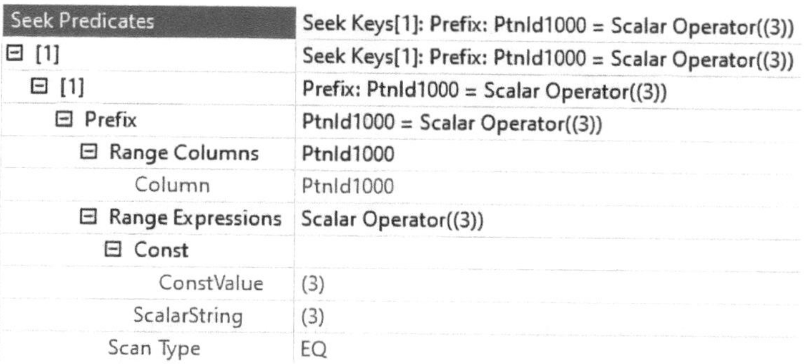

Seek Predicates	Seek Keys[1]: Prefix: PtnId1000 = Scalar Operator((3))
⊟ [1]	Seek Keys[1]: Prefix: PtnId1000 = Scalar Operator((3))
⊟ [1]	Prefix: PtnId1000 = Scalar Operator((3))
⊟ Prefix	PtnId1000 = Scalar Operator((3))
⊟ Range Columns	PtnId1000
Column	PtnId1000
⊟ Range Expressions	Scalar Operator((3))
⊟ Const	
ConstValue	(3)
ScalarString	(3)
Scan Type	EQ

Figure 10.9 Query plan seek predicates

We can work around many issues with partition elimination by avoiding simple parameterization, avoiding SQL Server having to convert values, and ensuring that developers write code that filters or joins using the partitioning key. If the code is not compatible with partition elimination, however, then we should avoid using partitioning, as it may actually have a negative impact on performance.

10.9 #62 Not compressing large tables

In the previous section, we discussed using partitioning as a way of relieving pressure on the I/O subsystem to improve query performance. Another method of doing this is to consider compression. When most DBAs think of compression, they think of reducing the size of data at the expense of performance, but this is a misconception and leads to underutilization of compression within SQL Server, which can improve query performance for some workloads.

If SQL Server is I/O bound, with spare processor capacity, then row compression and page compression can reduce the number of pages that SQL Server needs to read from disk, alleviating pressure on the I/O subsystem at the expense of additional processor cycles.

To understand how compression works, it is helpful to understand how a normal, uncompressed data page structures data within a row. This is illustrated in figure 10.10. The left of the diagram shows the high-level page structure, where a slot is a physical row container. The right side of the diagram shows how data within a slot is structured.

Let's think about the `ImpressionArchive` table. We already know from the previous section that to read all rows within this table, we would have to read 46,982 pages. But what about if we implemented row compression? Let's use the command in listing 10.17 to implement row compression.

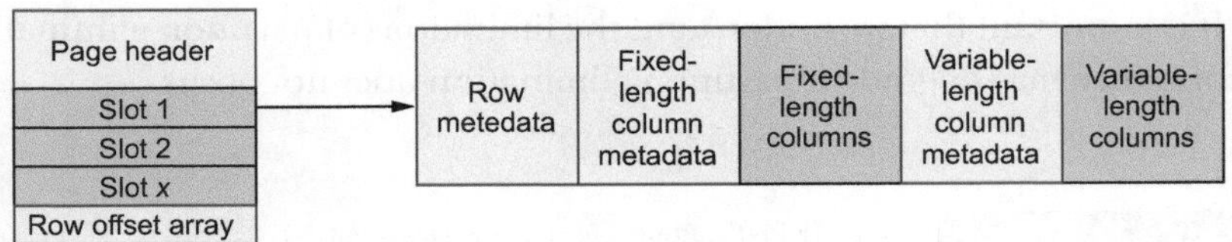

Figure 10.10 Structure of a data page

Listing 10.17 Implementing row compression

```
ALTER TABLE ImpressionsArchive
    REBUILD WITH (DATA_COMPRESSION = ROW) ;
```

The compressed table now uses 33,687 pages to store the data—an approximate 28% reduction. We can identify the number of pages used by a table either by running a query with no `WHERE` clause and looking at the I/O statistics or by running the query in listing 10.18, which pulls the page count from metadata. Filtering by `index_id = 1` ensures that we are only counting pages from the clustered index.

Listing 10.18 Determining the number of pages in a table

```
SELECT
    in_row_used_page_count
FROM sys.dm_db_partition_stats
WHERE object_id = OBJECT_ID('ImpressionsArchive')
    AND index_id = 1 ;
```

Row compression works by implementing a `VARDECIMAL` system. This means that instead of `VARCHAR`, `NVARCHAR`, and `VARBINARY` being the only variable-length data types, decimal values also become variable length. For example, in a `BIGINT` column, the value `10` will only consume 1 byte of space, as it will be stored as a `TINYINT`, and the value `50,000` will only consume 4 bytes, as it will be stored as an `INT`. A `NULL` value would not consume any space at all. Row compression also removes padded white space from fixed-length-character columns and compresses Unicode values to 1 byte per character where possible.

With this in mind, let's consider how data is stored on a data page that has row compression implemented. Compare this structure, shown in figure 10.11, with the structure of an uncompressed page.

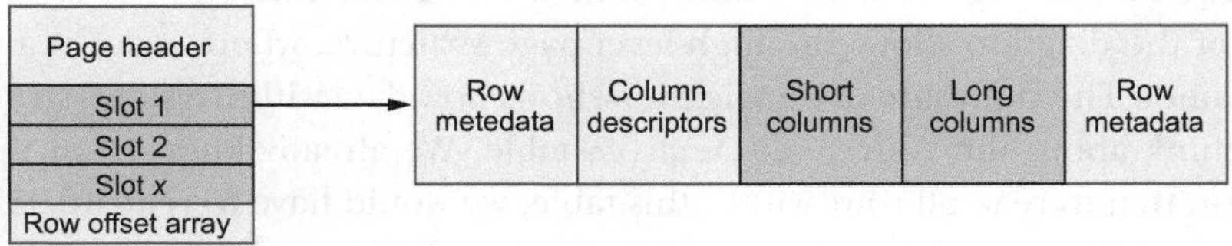

Figure 10.11 Structure of a page with row compression

What if we used page compression? The command in the following listing implements page compression for the ImpressionArchive table.

Listing 10.19 Implementing page compression

```
ALTER TABLE ImpressionsArchive
    REBUILD WITH (DATA_COMPRESSION = PAGE) ;
```

When you implement page compression, the row-compression techniques described previously are implemented. This is followed by the implementation of prefix compression and dictionary compression.

Prefix compression looks at the value stored in multiple rows of the same column within a page and tries to identify a common prefix for those rows. It selects the longest value that contains the full prefix as an anchor. All other values within that column are stored as the differential of the anchor.

After prefix compression has been implemented, dictionary compression is the final step in the page-compression process. This step looks across all values stored within a page and looks for duplicate values. What is really clever is that these values are assessed using their binary representation, which makes the process data type agnostic and improves compression rates. Matching values are stored in a dictionary at the top of the page, and the rows just store a pointer to the value's location in the dictionary.

Figure 10.12 illustrates the structure of a data page with page compression implemented. You will notice that the slot structure is the same as with row compression. You will also notice, however, the addition of a CI record. This is inserted immediately after the page header and acts as an anchor for prefix compression and a dictionary for dictionary compression. The change count is used to track how many times the pages has been updated, as this may impact the effectiveness of the CI record. SQL Server uses this to decide if a page needs to be rebuilt.

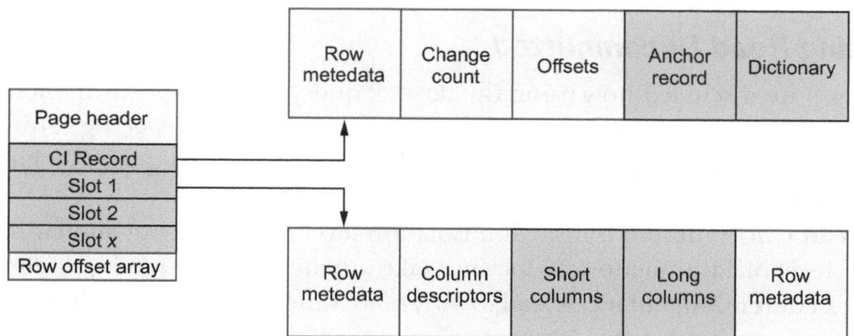

Figure 10.12 Page structure with page compression implemented

What has page compression done to the size of our ImpressionArchive table? Nothing! The table still consumes 33,687 pages. Why would this be? Well, in our case, the table has been built using random values, such as Globally Unique Identifiers and randomly generated character strings, meaning that there is so little commonality that nothing could be compressed.

We can use the `sp_estimate_data_compression_savings` stored procedure to estimate the size of a table with different compression levels before implementing a change. In our case, that would have helped us decide to use row compression instead of page compression. This would have been a good choice, as page compression did not reduce the size of the table further than row compression even though it requires more processor cycles than row compression to decompress a page.

The following listing shows how we can use the `sp_estimate_data_compression_savings` stored procedure to estimate the size of the table if we were to remove all compression compared to the size of the table with the current page compression implemented.

Listing 10.20 Estimating table size with compression

```
EXEC sp_estimate_data_compression_savings
    @schema_name = 'dbo',
    @object_name = 'ImpressionsArchive',
    @index_id = 1,
    @partition_number = NULL,
    @data_compression = 'none' ;
```

When we have large tables on I/O-bound SQL Server instances, we should evaluate data compression as a performance optimization technique. For data compression to be viable, the instance must be I/O bound, and there must be spare processor capacity. We should evaluate the impact of both row and page compression before implementing compression. This is because each technique will have varying compression rates based on the nature of the data in the table. Page compression usually achieves a better compression rate, at the expense of additional pressure on the CPU for decompression.

10.10 #63 Using Read Uncommitted

In chapter 5 we discussed how using the `NOLOCK` query hint as a performance tweak is a mistake, as the lack of locks can lead to nondeterministic results being returned, but many SQL Server professionals also make mistakes when working with locking at the level of transactions.

The Read Uncommitted transaction isolation level works in a way similar to `NOLOCK` but at the level of a transaction. It does not take out any locks for read operations. This avoids lock contention, but it can lead to *dirty reads,* which refer to reads that return data that is never committed to the database.

This means that Read Uncommitted is only an appropriate option when it's used against tables that are stored in read-only filegroups, meaning that data cannot be written to them. Unfortunately, it is not uncommon to see SQL Server professionals using this isolation level as a performance optimization when dealing with tables that accept updates.

To understand the dirty read phenomenon, let's consider the following example. A data steward is busy resolving some data issues in the `MarketingArchive` database. At the same time, a user is running a report.

> **TIP** To follow along with this example, you should have two query windows open. The first query window should be used to execute the queries in listings 10.21 and 10.23. The second query window should be used to execute the script in listing 10.22.

The query in the following listing simulates the data steward updating the `BidPrice` within the `ImpressionsArchive` table for the impression with an `ImpressionID` of `100`.

Listing 10.21 Simulating a data steward update

```
BEGIN TRANSACTION                                  ← Run in the first
                                                     query window.
    UPDATE dbo.ImpressionsArchive
    SET BidPrice = 1.812
    WHERE ImpressionID = 100 ;
```

The query in the following listing simulates the database user running a report that returns the `SUM` of all `BidPrice` values associated with a campaign.

Listing 10.22 Simulating a reporting query

```
SET TRANSACTION ISOLATION LEVEL READ UNCOMMITTED     ← Run in the second
                                                       query window.
BEGIN TRANSACTION

    SELECT SUM(BidPrice)
    FROM dbo.ImpressionsArchive
    WHERE CampaignID = (
        SELECT
            CampaignID
        FROM dbo.ImpressionsArchive
        WHERE ImpressionID = 100
) ;

COMMIT
```

The command in the following listing rolls back the data steward's transaction, as they have realized that they have made a mistake.

Listing 10.23 Rolling back the data steward's transaction

```
ROLLBACK ;
```

Unfortunately, this sequence of events means that the query returned by the reporting user is "incorrect" in the sense that it was based on data that was never committed to the database and that the query will return a different result if it is run again.

Do not use the Read Uncommitted transaction isolation level as a performance optimization in normal circumstances. It is only appropriate to use this isolation level when reading data from tables that are stored in a read-only filegroup, or in the very rare scenario that data accuracy does not matter.

10.11 #64 Using unnecessarily strong isolation levels

The Read Committed transaction isolation level is the default level of isolation in SQL Server and protects against dirty reads. It does, however, leave users exposed to *nonrepeatable reads*, a phenomenon where a transaction reads the same row twice but receives a different value on each occasion. It also exposes users to *phantom reads*, a phenomenon where a transaction reads a set of rows twice and receives a different number of rows each time.

I have seen occasions where database professionals have decided that their data is so important that they use the Repeatable Read isolation level, which protects against both dirty reads and nonrepeatable reads, or the Serializable isolation level, which protects against all consistency issues, including phantom reads, as a default for all transactions.

Using Repeatable Read and Serializable transaction isolation levels is perfectly valid and necessary in some situations, such as when actuarial calculations are being performed, but setting these isolation levels is often overkill. In many situations with conventional requirements, configuring these stronger isolation levels is a mistake. In the vast majority of cases, leaving the default configuration of Read Committed is the correct course of action.

To help make informed choices about the correct level of isolation to use in specific use cases, let's explore the consequences of a nonrepeatable read and a phantom read. To follow along with the next two examples, you will need to use two query windows. Each listing will call out which query window in which to run the query.

Let's first explore a nonrepeatable read. Imagine that, once again, the data steward is updating rows to fix data errors in the `ImpressionsArchive` table. This time, our reporting user will be using the default Read Committed transaction isolation level. The reporting user's transaction begins with the code in the following listing.

Listing 10.24 Starting the reporting user's transaction

```
BEGIN TRANSACTION

SELECT SUM(BidPrice)
FROM dbo.ImpressionsArchive
WHERE OperatingSystemID = (
    SELECT OperatingSystemID
    FROM dbo.ImpressionsArchive
    WHERE ImpressionID = 100
) ;
```

Run this script in the first query window.

The script in listing 10.25 simulates the data steward fixing the `BidPrice` for the impression with an `ImpressionID` of `100`. This time, the data steward commits the change right away.

Listing 10.25 Data steward fixes some data

```
BEGIN TRANSACTION

    UPDATE dbo.ImpressionsArchive
    SET BidPrice = 1.5
    WHERE ImpressionID = 100 ;

COMMIT
```

Run this script in the second query window.

Finally, the script in the following listing illustrates the end of the reporting user's transaction.

Listing 10.26 End of the reporting user's transaction

```
SELECT SUM(BidPrice)
FROM dbo.ImpressionsArchive
WHERE CountryCode = (
    SELECT CountryCode
    FROM dbo.ImpressionsArchive
    WHERE ImpressionID = 100
) ;

COMMIT
```

Run this script in the first query window.

In this sequence of events, the reporting user has read the value of the `BidPrice` for the impression with an `ImpressionID` of `100` twice in two different queries. The second time the `BidPrice` was read, it had a different value from the first time it was read. Neither value is "wrong"—they were both correct at the time they were read from the table. If the user tries to reconcile the values in the two queries, however, it is likely to be confusing and certainly inconsistent.

In many scenarios, this type of anomaly will not matter. If we are performing regulatory financial calculations, for example, then we may need to set the isolation level to Repeatable Read. If the anomaly is acceptable, however, then we should leave the default Read Committed isolation level.

Now let's explore a phantom read. Our data steward is back, but this time, incorrect data is being deleted. The script in the following listing begins our reporting user's transaction.

Listing 10.27 Beginning the reporting user's transaction

```
BEGIN TRANSACTION

SELECT COUNT(*)
FROM dbo.ImpressionsArchive
WHERE OperatingSystemID = (
    SELECT OperatingSystemID
    FROM dbo.ImpressionsArchive
    WHERE ImpressionID = 100
) ;
```

Run this script in the first query window.

Next, the script in the following listing simulates the data steward deleting rows from the table.

Listing 10.28 Data steward's transaction

```
BEGIN TRANSACTION

    DELETE
    FROM dbo.ImpressionsArchive
    WHERE ImpressionID IN (
        SELECT TOP 3 ImpressionID
        FROM dbo.ImpressionsArchive
        WHERE OperatingSystemID = (
            SELECT OperatingSystemID
            FROM dbo.ImpressionsArchive
            WHERE ImpressionID = 100
        )
        AND ImpressionID <> 100
    ) ;

COMMIT
```

Run this in the second query window.

Finally, the script in the following listing shows the end of the reporting user's transaction.

Listing 10.29 End of the reporting user's transaction

```
SELECT COUNT(DISTINCT ImpressionID)
FROM dbo.ImpressionsArchive
WHERE OperatingSystemID = (
    SELECT OperatingSystemID
    FROM dbo.ImpressionsArchive
    WHERE ImpressionID = 100
) ;

COMMIT
```

Run this script in the first query window.

In this scenario, when the reporting user ran the second query, it returned three fewer rows than the first query. This is known as a phantom read, but it would also be known as a phantom read if rows had been inserted into the table, meaning that additional rows were returned by the second query.

A phantom read is not considered a major issue in many situations. If we know that we have a scenario such as an actuarial calculation where a phantom read would be problematic, then we should consider using the Serializable transaction isolation level. Otherwise, we should use a weaker isolation level, ideally, Read Committed.

Stronger isolation levels prevent more data anomalies but can lead to performance issues caused by lock contention. They can even lead to *deadlocks*, which occur when two transactions are waiting for each other to complete and neither can proceed. A deadlock leads to the query that SQL Server deems least expensive being rolled back.

Therefore, we should only use stronger isolation levels when we have a legitimate requirement to do so.

10.12 #65 Not considering optimistic isolation levels

SQL Server supports two types of transaction isolation levels: pessimistic and optimistic. Pessimistic isolation levels use locks to prevent data from being updated by other transactions. Optimistic isolation levels store old versions of rows in `TempDB`. This avoids data anomalies while preventing the performance issues associated with readers and writers blocking each other.

In the previous two sections, we discussed pessimistic transaction isolation levels. In this section, we will explore the two optimistic isolation levels supported by SQL Server. These isolation levels are called Read Committed Snapshot and Snapshot, equivalent to Read Committed and Serializable, respectively, and they provide protection against data anomalies.

These isolation levels work by storing old row versions in `TempDB` up to the oldest row version within the oldest open transaction, meaning that transactions can reference the correct version of a row without the need for the locking and blocking associated with pessimistic isolation levels.

Unfortunately, these useful isolation levels are overlooked by the majority of DBAs. I think the main reason for this is fear of getting it wrong. That's understandable, because optimistic concurrency is not a magic bullet by any stretch of the imagination.

No magic bullets

While this section advocates for the consideration of optimistic concurrency, it is important to note that it is not a magic bullet. As with most things in SQL Server, there is a tradeoff.

Row versions are stored inside an area of `TempDB` known as the Version Store. For busy production database systems, this can mean that there is an awful lot of additional I/O associated with the optimistic isolation levels. Given that two sections of this chapter are dedicated to methods for reducing the amount of I/O, you can see that this could potentially pose a challenge. We also need to consider the amount of extra disk space that will be used.

When considering features like optimistic concurrency, we need to assess situations on a case-by-case basis. For example, if we have `TempDB` stored locally on non-volatile memory express (NVMe) drive with loads of free space, then switching to optimistic concurrency is likely to be a great idea. If, on the other hand, `TempDB` is stored on a creaking SAN and we are experiencing I/O bottlenecks, then we are likely to do more harm than good by implementing this feature.

The mistake in this section is the failure to consider optimistic concurrency, given a specific scenario. In the right situations, Read Committed Snapshot and Snapshot isolation can be very useful tools in our arsenal when fighting tricky performance problems.

If we are assessing a situation where there are performance issues caused by locking and blocking but strong isolation is a requirement, we should certainly assess the potential of implementing Read Committed Snapshot and/or Snapshot isolation. We do, however, need to be mindful of the I/O requirements and avoid implementing it in an I/O-bound environment.

We can turn on Read Committed Snapshot isolation by using the command in the following listing.

Listing 10.30 Enabling Read Committed Snapshot

```
ALTER DATABASE MarketingArchive
    SET READ_COMMITTED_SNAPSHOT ON WITH NO_WAIT ;
```

Once Read Committed Snapshot is enabled, the ability to use the pessimistic Read Committed isolation level is removed and Read Committed Snapshot becomes the default isolation level for all transactions.

The script in the following listing demonstrates how to enable Snapshot isolation for a database.

Listing 10.31 Enabling Snapshot isolation

```
ALTER DATABASE MarketingArchive
    SET ALLOW_SNAPSHOT_ISOLATION ON ;
```

Because Read Committed Snapshot is now the default isolation level, we can examine the rows in the Version Store by starting any transaction and then looking at the system metadata. The script in the following listing begins a transaction and updates a row.

Listing 10.32 Beginning a Read Committed Snapshot transaction

```
BEGIN TRANSACTION

    UPDATE dbo.ImpressionsArchive
    SET BidPrice = BidPrice + 0.1
    WHERE ImpressionID = 100 ;

    UPDATE dbo.ImpressionsArchive
    SET CostPerMille = CostPerMille + 0.1
    WHERE ImpressionID = 100 ;
```

We can now view the Version Store by executing the query in the following listing.

Listing 10.33 Examining the Version Store

```
    SELECT *
    FROM sys.dm_tran_version_store ;

COMMIT
```

You will notice that the original version of the row is stored as a binary value, with the byte length stored in an additional column.

Every situation is different, and if you are under IO pressure, then optimistic concurrency may not be the right solution. That said, not considering it if you have performance issues caused by pessimistic concurrency is a mistake. Read Committed Snapshot and Snapshot isolation levels can be useful tools for a DBA in the right situation.

10.13 #66 Throwing more hardware at the problem

This entire chapter has been dedicated to optimizing SQL Server performance, but a mistake that I see time and time again, often made by managed support partners, is failing to dig into a performance issue and instead trying to throw more hardware at it.

This approach has never been a good idea. The main problem with it is that, if you have a performance issue, scaling the hardware is unlikely to solve the problem; and even if it does solve it, the effects are likely to be temporary, and you will have to upgrade again.

Let's examine an incredibly badly written query, shown in the following listing, which simply updates the `BidPrice` column in all rows of the `MarketingArchive` table but does so using a cursor.

NOTE This script may take a long time to run.

Listing 10.34 A very slow cursor

```
DECLARE @ImpressionID BIGINT

DECLARE Impressions CURSOR FAST_FORWARD FOR
SELECT ImpressionID
FROM dbo.ImpressionsArchive ;

OPEN Impressions ;

FETCH NEXT FROM Impressions INTO @ImpressionID
WHILE @@FETCH_STATUS = 0
BEGIN
    UPDATE dbo.ImpressionsArchive
    SET BidPrice = BidPrice + 0.1
    WHERE ImpressionID = @ImpressionID ;

    FETCH NEXT FROM Impressions INTO @ImpressionID ;
END

CLOSE Impressions ;
DEALLOCATE Impressions ;
```

On my test rig, this query took a whopping 10 minutes 15 seconds to run. Figure 10.13 shows the machine's resource utilization while the query was running.

While this may be an exaggerated scenario, I frequently have conversations with junior DBAs who will argue that a performance issue like this was caused by processor utilization because there was a spike to 100%, even though it has settled at 8% usage.

Instead of investigating the cause of the problem, they simply want to throw more processors at the situation.

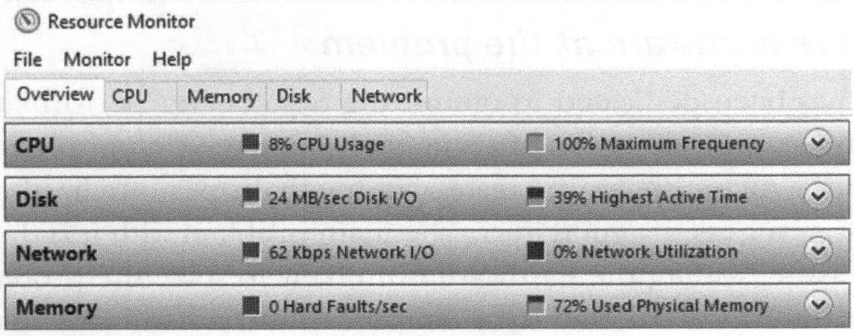

Figure 10.13 Resource utilization during query execution

Now you probably realize that it doesn't matter how much hardware you throw at this issue; the only way to fix it is to rewrite the query, as shown in the following listing, which takes 3 seconds to run on my test rig.

Listing 10.35 Updating `BidPrice` using relational technique

```
UPDATE dbo.MarketingArchive
SET BidPrice = BidPrice + 0.1 ;
```

Even though this diagnostic approach was never helpful in the age of the VM, it is now also a cost consideration in the age of cloud. Throwing more hardware at a performance issue means needlessly spending more money by increasing the size of the cloud VM or purchasing faster storage.

Of course, there will be times when a workload outgrows the available capacity of a server and an upgrade is required, but hopefully we will have noticed and planned for this during our capacity planning, which is discussed in chapter 9.

We should always try to resolve a performance issue rather than defaulting to a hardware upgrade. Upgrading hardware doesn't necessarily resolve the issue or may only alleviate the symptoms for a short time. Instead, we should try to get to the root cause of the issue. We can use performance optimizations discussed in this chapter, ensure coding best practices discussed in chapter 5 are being adhered to, or use any of SQL Server's vast array of features and diagnostic tools to address the issue.

Summary

- Trace flags are used to toggle SQL Server functionality on and off.
- Trace flags T1117 and T1118 have been deprecated and no longer have any effect on a SQL Server instance. More granular alternatives such as `AUTOGROW_ALL_FILES` and `UNIFORM_PAGE_ALLOCATION` should be used instead.

- Instance file initialization should be used in the vast majority of situations. It should only be avoided in the most secure of environments.
- Lock Pages In Memory should be used in many situations. There are times when it should be disabled in private clouds, but public cloud providers recommend it.
- Always leave enough RAM for the operating system and any other applications that are running on the server. This is especially important if Lock Pages In Memory is used.
- Use the Max Server Memory setting to configure the maximum amount of RAM that can be allocated to the SQL Server buffer pool.
- Always try to work with the optimizer, rather than against it. In rare situations when query hints are required, try to leave the optimizer with multiple options.
- Remember to take advantage of DOP query feedback.
- DOP feedback is disabled by default, unlike other query feedback mechanisms.
- Consider partitioning large tables to improve performance and reduce load on the I/O subsystem.
- Partitioning tables allows for partition elimination, meaning that partitions are not read if they do not store relevant data.
- Consider using data compression as a performance enhancement for large tables.
- Data compression is best suited to workloads that are I/O bound and have spare processor capacity.
- The compression rate achieved will be dependent on the data stored within the table. Use the `sp_estimate_data_compression_savings` stored procedure to evaluate the impact of row compression and page compression before implementing either option.
- Avoid the Read Uncommitted transaction isolation level unless you are working with tables stored in read-only filegroups.
- The Read Uncommitted isolation level can result in dirty reads just as the use of the `NOLOCK` query hint can.
- Avoid using strong isolation levels such as Repeatable Read or Serializable unless they are absolutely required, as they can lead to lock contention and deadlocks.
- Consider using optimistic isolation levels in situations when you face performance issues caused by lock contention.
- The optimistic isolation levels are Read Committed Snapshot and Snapshot.
- Optimistic isolation levels are best suited to environments where `TempDB` is not I/O bound and there is plenty of free space on the `TempDB` volume.
- Avoid throwing extra hardware at performance issues. Try to diagnose the root cause of the issue and resolve it instead.

11 Indexes

This chapter covers

- Index fragmentation
- Index maintenance
- How indexes interact with extract, transform, load processes
- Database Engine Tuning Advisor
- Columnstore indexes

In this chapter, we will first explore some common mistakes and misconceptions around fragmentation. Understanding index fragmentation can be crucial to a well-performing database. For example, index fragmentation is often considered universally bad, but we will explore how too little internal fragmentation can lead to bad page splits.

We will then turn our attention to index maintenance and look at various mistakes that can lead to an increase in index fragmentation and suboptimal performance. These mistakes range from not rebuilding indexes at all to rebuilding them indiscriminately. We will also assess how index maintenance interacts with updating statistics.

We will explore how indexes impact extract, transform, load (ETL) operations. Specifically, we will explore bulk load operations and discuss how our index strategies are crucial to a performant ETL run. After this, we will take a look at Database Tuning Advisor and think about why it might not be a good idea to rely too heavily on this feature.

Finally, we will look at columnstore indexes, which can add incredible performance improvements to analytical and data warehouse–style workloads. Despite being introduced to SQL Server over a decade ago, they're still not used by many people. We will discuss why this is and why it is a mistake.

In this chapter, code examples will use the `Marketing` and `MarketingArchive` databases that we created in previous chapters. Therefore, I recommend using these databases if you would like to follow along. Before starting, however, I provide a quick refresher on index concepts that we introduced in chapter 4.

If we create a table with no clustered index, this is known as a *heap*. In a heap, data is stored in no particular order. Instead of an index root, there is a simple Index Allocation Map that stores a list of all pages allocated to the heap. For larger tables, this means that SQL Server has to work hard to find any given value. Specifically, almost any query `SELECT` statement issued against a heap will require SQL Server to read every single data page that makes up the table. A heap is illustrated in figure 11.1.

TIP Queries that include keywords such as `TOP` may not require a read of all pages in the table.

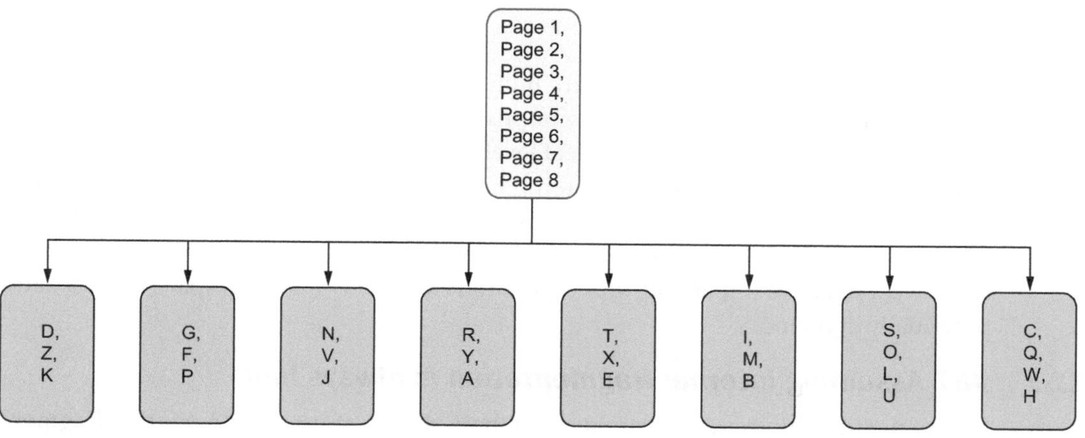

Figure 11.1 A heap stores pages in no particular order

If we create a clustered index on a table, then SQL Server builds a B-tree structure, such as the structure illustrated in figure 11.2. This operation orders the pages in a table using the clustered key. The clustered key is usually built on the primary key of the table. If you have a wide primary key, however, it is possible to build it on a different, unique column.

A clustered index allows for read operations to be performed more efficiently, and we will discuss the different index operations that are available later in this chapter. The leaf level of the B-tree structure is the actual data pages of the table. This means that the data pages of the table are stored in the order of the clustered key. For this reason, we can only have a single clustered index on a table.

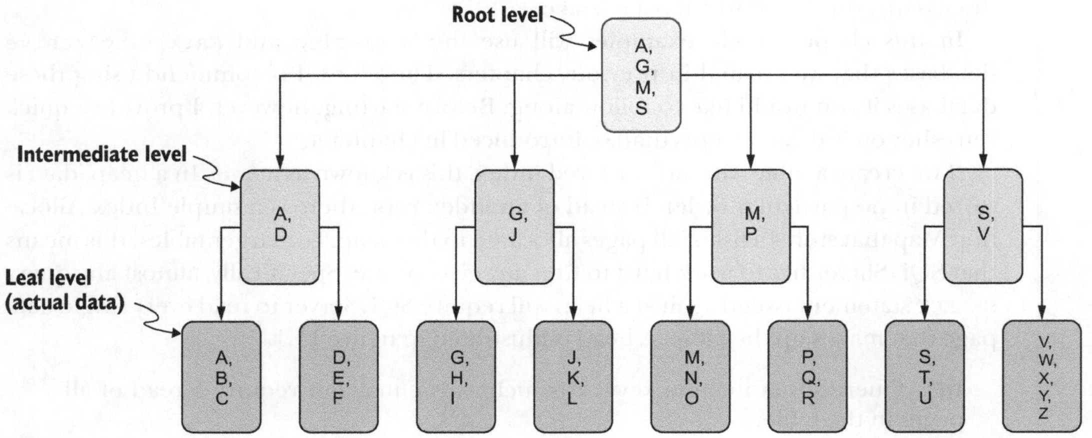

Figure 11.2 A clustered index creates a B-tree and orders data pages

A *nonclustered index* is a B-tree structure built on a different column(s) within the table. SQL Server can use these indexes to improve the performance of operations such as joins, filters, and aggregations. The leaf level of a nonclustered index contains pointers to the data pages of the heap or clustered index. Because it does not impact the order of the actual data pages, we can have multiple nonclustered indexes on a table. In fact, a table can support up to 256 nonclustered indexes, although having too many can have a negative impact on write operations and also consumes space on disk, and potentially in memory.

11.1 #67 Assuming internal fragmentation is always bad

One of the first things we are taught as database administrators (DBAs) is that fragmentation is bad: don't allow our indexes to become fragmented, or performance will suffer. This is not quite the full story, however, and can lead to problems. To understand why, we need to remember the two types of fragmentation that can occur. *External fragmentation* refers to index pages becoming out of physical order. *Internal fragmentation* describes the amount of free space on index pages. In this section, we will focus on why internal fragmentation can be problematic.

Imagine that we have a database that supports transactional workloads. That is, there are frequent `INSERT`, `UPDATE`, and `DELETE` statements being issued against the database, and this includes inserts to a table that contains customer information. To improve performance, we have created a nonclustered index on the `LastName` column, and this index has the default settings, which means that, when the index was built, SQL Server had a target to completely fill every index page, only leaving enough space for a single row.

A user runs an `INSERT` statement to add a new customer and a new row, including a new `LastName`, is inserted into the table. Because there is an index on the `LastName` column, a new row also needs to be inserted into the index page of a nonclustered index.

The diagram in figure 11.3 depicts the process that needs to happen for the new row to be inserted. First, SQL Server tries to insert the value, in this case `Crane`, to the page, but discovers there is no room. It then creates a new page, which will cause external fragmentation and moves half of the data from the original page to the new page. There is now enough space in the page for SQL Server to insert the row. The pointers between the pages also need to be updated.

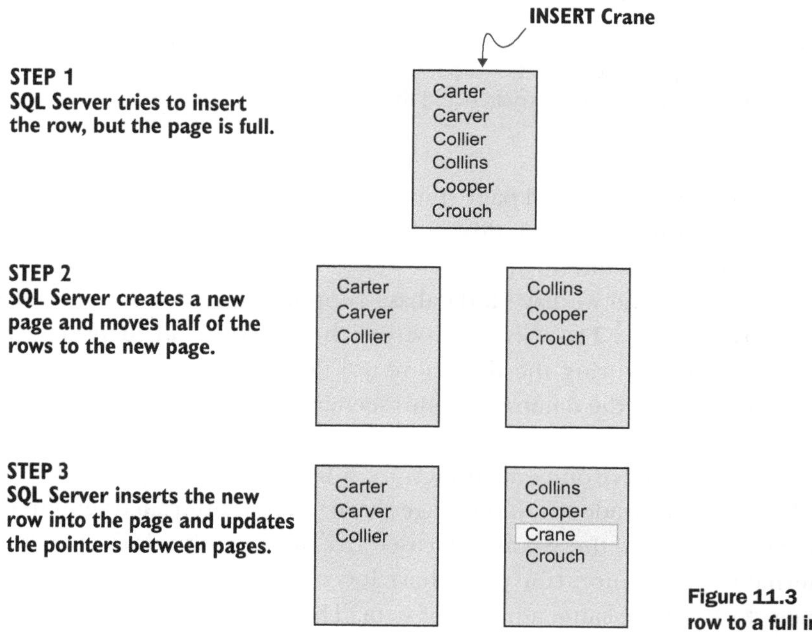

Figure 11.3 Adding a new row to a full index page

This process is known as a *page split*, and it's a bad type of page split. It generates additional I/O and causes external fragmentation in the process. We should try to minimize this type of page split occurring whenever possible.

TIP Page splits can be caused by updates as well as inserts. If, for example, a `VARCHAR(60)` column held a value that was 5 characters long and was updated to hold a value 60 characters long, then the increase in the size of the data could result in a page split. This is known as an *expansive update.*

In the preceding example, the bad page split occurred on a nonclustered index, but page splits can also occur on clustered indexes. This tends to happen when the clustered key is not sequential, but it can also be caused by expansive updates when the clustered key is sequential.

Mini-mistake—page splits are not always bad

Just as many people believe that fragmentation is always bad, many people think page splits are always bad. In fact, a page split is a perfectly normal operation in SQL Server. If page splits never occurred, then it would not be possible to add new rows to a table or index.

The difference between good and bad page splits depends on which page in the index is split. If the last page in the index is split because we have added a new row to an index that is full, then a new page is allocated at the end of the index, and new rows can be inserted. In this instance, data is not moved to the new page. A new page is simply allocated to the table. This is regarded as a good page split.

In the preceding example, however, the split happened in the middle of the index, resulting in external fragmentation (out-of-order pages) and avoidable I/O. This is regarded as a bad page split, and we should try to avoid this scenario.

So if having full pages causes bad page splits, should we just accept a high level of internal fragmentation on all of our indexes? Well, no. It is very much dependent on the particulars of our environment.

For example, imagine we have a database supporting data warehouse–style workloads. There is a nightly ETL process that drops the indexes, bulk loads data, and then rebuilds the indexes. During the day, there are no `INSERT`, `UPDATE`, or `DELETE` statements executed against the database. In this scenario, there is no opportunity for page splits to occur, so we will probably want our pages to be as full as possible.

In a transactional environment, things are a little more complicated, and we are going to have to make tradeoffs. If our pages have very low internal fragmentation (the pages are very full), then there is an increased risk of page splits. If the pages have very high internal fragmentation (the pages have lots of free space), however, then it takes more pages to store the same amount of data. This means that SQL Server needs to read more pages from disk, which means more I/O and that data pages will not stay in the cache for so long. This in turn means that the *buffer cache hit ratio* will drop. This means that pages will need to be read from the disk more often.

Therefore, it is not possible to give a firm recommendation for target internal fragmentation levels. The correct level will depend on many factors, ranging from read and write performance of the disk subsystem to the number and type of transactions that are performed against the database. As a starting point, however, for data warehouse–style workloads, pages as full as 95% to 100% full may be appropriate. For busy transactional systems, the ideal level may be as low as 60% to 70%.

We have talked a lot about internal fragmentation and ideal levels of *page density*, which means how full the pages are. What we have not discussed is how to configure the target page density. We discuss this next.

SQL Server uses a setting called `FILLFACTOR` to determine the target page density for pages on the leaf level of an index. It also has a setting called `PAD_INDEX`, which can be used to control page density at the intermediate levels of the index. The root level always consists of exactly one page, so is not subject to either internal or external fragmentation.

The default value for `FILLFACTOR` is `0`, which means 100% full. If this is replaced with any other value, then this becomes the target page density percentage. `PAD_INDEX` can only be configured as `ON` or `OFF`; `OFF` is the default option. If we configure `PAD_INDEX` as `ON`, then it will apply the `FILLFACTOR` level to the intermediate pages. It is not possible to configure a page density that is different from the leaf level.

`PAD_INDEX` is arguably less important than `FILLFACTOR`, but for large indexes with multiple intermediate levels, a page split can propagate right up the B-tree, significantly compounding its impact. Therefore, `PAD_INDEX` is worth enabling for indexes on very large tables that have a transactional workload and are suffering from page splits.

To configure the `FILLFACTOR` for an index or enable `PAD_INDEX`, we need to rebuild the index. The command in the following listing sets the `FILLFACTOR` of the `ImpressionUID` index on the `Marketing.Impressions` table of the `Marketing` database to be 90% and enables `PAD_INDEX`.

Listing 11.1 Setting a `FILLFACTOR` and enabling `PAD_INDEX`

```
ALTER INDEX ImpressionUID ON marketing.Impressions REBUILD
WITH (
    FILLFACTOR = 90,
    PAD_INDEX = ON
) ;
```

Many DBAs are taught to believe that index fragmentation is always bad. Internal fragmentation can actually be better than having 100% full pages, however. This is because overly full pages can lead to a large number of bad page splits. We need to trade off the number of page splits against the number of pages used to store our indexes. The correct `FILLFACTOR` will be unique to the requirements of a specific workload.

11.2 #68 Believing that external fragmentation causes problems for all queries

External fragmentation causes performance degradation. There are no two ways about it. A trap that I see many DBAs fall into, however, is using index rebuilds as their very first troubleshooting step whenever a user complains of performance problems. In some cases, this can take some time, and in situations where there is no chance that index fragmentation is the root cause, we risk wasting valuable time.

For example, imagine that users are complaining that queries are taking a long time to run against a database. Many of the queries that run are returning either a scalar value or a single row. In these scenarios, as we will see shortly, the root cause of the issue is unlikely to be fragmentation, so running an emergency rebuild of all indexes in the database is unlikely to help. What's more, depending on how we rebuild the indexes, we have the potential to degrade performance even more for the duration of the maintenance.

To understand this, we need to understand the different operations that can be performed against an index. These operations are seek, scan, and lookup. A *seek* operation starts at the root page of an index and traverses each level of the B-tree structure to find the row it's looking for. This process, illustrated in figure 11.4, is the fastest operation for retrieving a small number of rows.

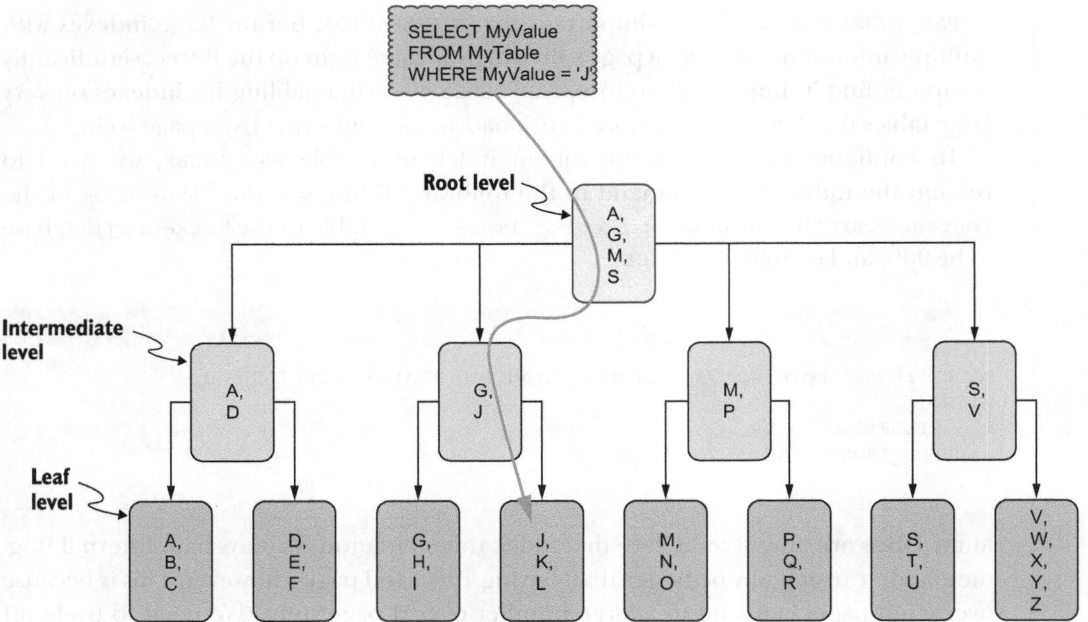

Figure 11.4 Index seek

An index *scan* comes into effect when SQL Server has to read a higher percentage of rows from an index. In this situation, a seek operation would be inefficient, so instead it scans all pages at the leaf level of the B-tree. This is illustrated in figure 11.5.

While index seeks and index scans apply to both clustered and nonclustered indexes, an index *lookup* applies only when a nonclustered index has been used to satisfy the query. SQL Server uses the nonclustered index to perform operations such as filtering data through the `WHERE` clause but then needs to perform a lookup operation to the data pages of the clustered index or heap to return additional columns. This is illustrated in figure 11.6.

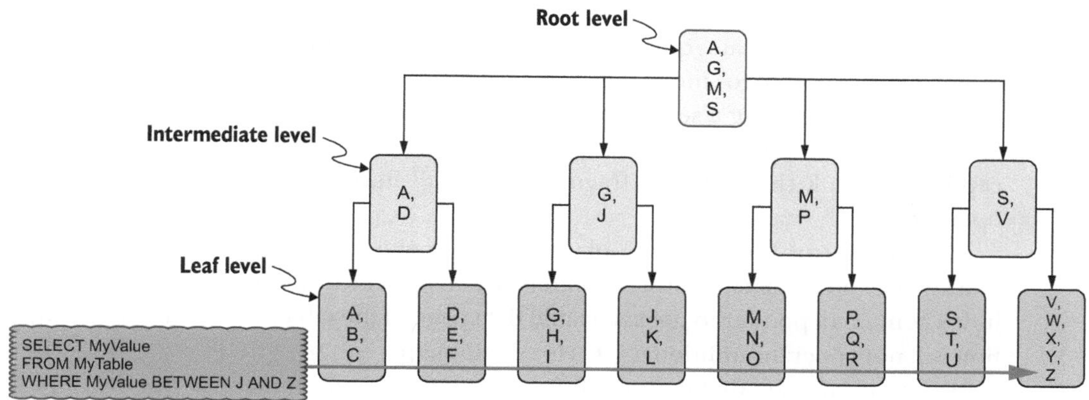

Figure 11.5 Index scan

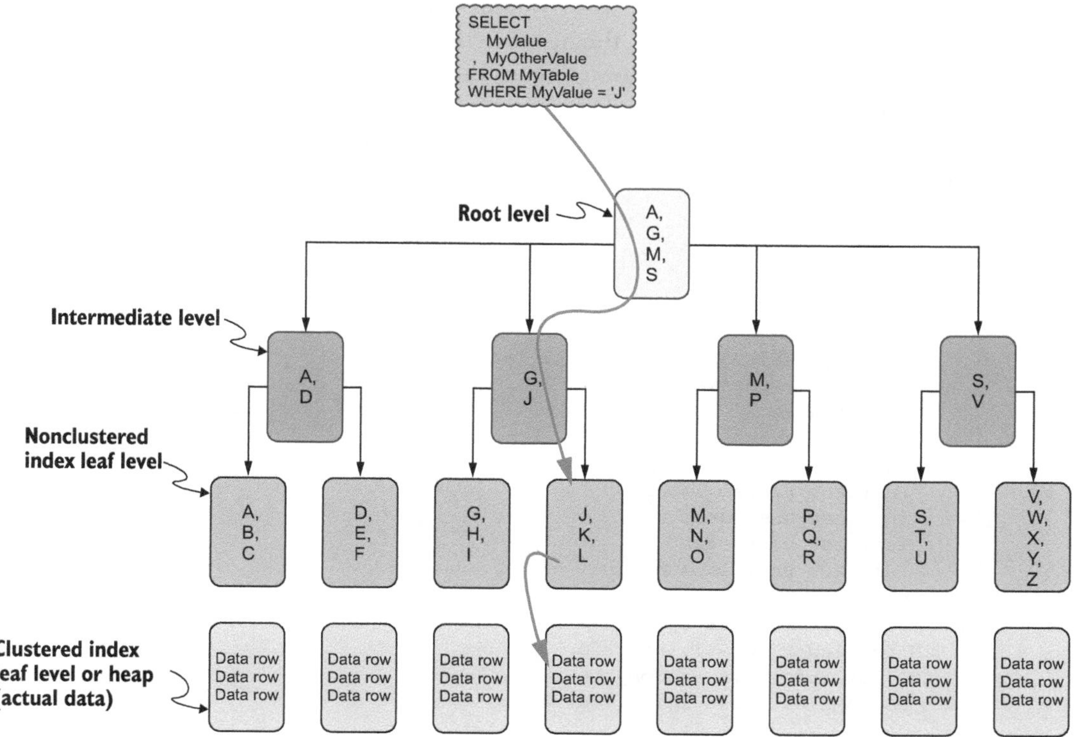

Figure 11.6 Index lookup

Clearly, if the index pages are out of order, an index scan operation will be degraded. Therefore, we can all categorically agree that external fragmentation will result in suboptimal performance for index scan operations.

If we are performing a seek operation, however, then the pages being out of order at the leaf level will have no impact on query performance. Therefore, it is a misconception to think that external fragmentation will impact the performance of seek operations.

The same is true for an index lookup from a nonclustered index to a clustered index or a key lookup from a nonclustered index to a heap. The leaf level of the nonclustered index contains a pointer to the associated data page in the table. Therefore, fragmentation will not generate additional I/Os for the lookup.

We can clearly see that external fragmentation does not impact all queries, and if SQL Server is performing a low ratio of scan operations against an index, then fragmentation is unlikely to be the root cause, and our attention is best spent investigating other possible causes.

We can quickly assess the ratio of index scans against other index operations by using the `sys.dm_db_index_usage_stats` dynamic management view (DMV). This object returns a row for every index in the instance that has been used since the last time the Database Engine cycled. Each row contains the number of index operations, as well as the last time they were performed.

The query in listing 11.2 returns information for indexes within the `Marketing` database. It joins these results to the `sys.indexes` catalog view to return the name and type of the index.

Listing 11.2 Discovering index usage by index operation

```
SELECT
      OBJECT_NAME(ius.object_id) AS TableName
    , i.name AS IndexName
    , i.type_desc
    , ius.user_seeks
    , ius.user_scans
    , ius.last_system_lookup
    , ius.last_user_seek
    , ius.last_user_scan
    , ius.last_user_lookup
FROM sys.dm_db_index_usage_stats ius
INNER JOIN sys.indexes i
    ON ius.index_id = i.index_id
    AND ius.object_id = i.object_id
WHERE DB_NAME(database_id) = 'Marketing' ;
```

TIP `sys.dm_db_index_usage_stats` does not include information about memory-optimized indexes. While this type of index is beyond the scope of the book, it is worth noting that their usage statistics can be found in `sys.dm_db_xtp_index_stats`.

Don't think that fragmentation impacts all index operations. It will have a negative impact on index scans but will not affect seek operations. Therefore, if an index has a high ratio of seek operations, fragmentation is unlikely to be the root cause of the issue. Our time is best spent investigating other possible causes.

11.3 #69 Reorganizing indexes to fix page density

We have two options for maintaining indexes in SQL Server: reorganizing indexes and rebuilding indexes. When we rebuild an index, SQL Server creates a new B-tree structure and removes the original. This allows for near-perfect removal of fragmentation but has quite a high resource cost. Reorganizing an index, on the other hand, has a much lower cost but is limited in what it can achieve. Instead of creating a new B-tree structure, it condenses leaf-level pages up to the level of the `FILLFACTOR` in an attempt to remove internal fragmentation and attempts to reorganize the leaf-level pages to remove external fragmentation.

Imagine we have an index with an intentionally low `FILLFACTOR` of 60%. As data is inserted into the index, the pages become full. Because of the low page density, however, there is very little external fragmentation.

A mistake that I have seen many a DBA make in this scenario is to base their index maintenance on external fragmentation alone and reorganize the index. The trouble with this approach is that when we reorganize an index, it condenses pages up to the level of the `FILLFACTOR` but it does not reduce page density down to the level of the `FILLFACTOR`.

The result of this is that even though we have recently reorganized the index, it will very soon become highly externally fragmented because the pages are still full after reorganizing, and therefore bad page splits will soon start occurring.

We will then have to rebuild the index to repair the external fragmentation and reduce page splits. This means that, in a short space of time, we will end up both reorganizing and rebuilding the index when we could simply have rebuilt it in the first place.

We can check the level of internal and external fragmentation by using the `sys.dm_db_index_physical_stats` dynamic management function (DMF). This function accepts the parameters detailed in table 11.1.

Table 11.1 `sys.dm_db_index_physical_stats` parameters

Parameter	Description
`database_id`	The database ID of the database for which we wish to return results. `NULL` returns details for all databases.
`object_id`	The object ID of the table for which we wish to return results. `NULL` will return information for all tables.
`index_id`	The index ID for which we wish to return results. `NULL` will return results for all indexes.
`partition_number`	The partition number for which we wish to return results. `NULL` will return information for all partitions.

Table 11.1 `sys.dm_db_index_physical_stats` **parameters (*continued*)**

Parameter	Description
mode	Can be specified as LIMITED, SAMPLED, or DETAILED. LIMITED will only scan the root and intermediate levels of the B-tree. SAMPLED will scan 1% of the pages within a table* and DETAILED will scan every page of the index.

* If the table has fewer than 10,000 pages, then DETAILED mode will be used.

The function returns one row for every level of every index in scope. The key columns of interest for determining the level of fragmentation are avg_fragmentation_in_percent, which details the level of external fragmentation, and avg_page_space_used_in_percent, which details the page density.

> **TIP** While avg_fragmentation_in_percent and avg_page_space_used_in_percent are the key columns for determining fragmentation, other columns are also important to help us interpret the data. We will discuss this more in the next mistake.

The query in listing 11.3 illustrates how to return the internal and external fragmentation for all indexes in the Marketing.Impressions table of the Marketing database. The index_level column refers to the level of the B-tree, where 0 is the leaf level.

Listing 11.3 Determining index fragmentation

```
DECLARE @object_id BIGINT
SET @object_id = (
    SELECT object_id
    FROM sys.objects
    WHERE name = 'Impressions'
) ;
```

Populates a variable with the object_id of the Impressions table

```
SELECT
      OBJECT_NAME(ips.Object_id) AS TableName
    , i.name AS IndexName
    , ips.avg_fragmentation_in_percent
    , ips.avg_page_space_used_in_percent
    , index_level
FROM sys.dm_db_index_physical_stats(
    DB_ID('Marketing'),
    @object_id,
    NULL,
    NULL,
    'DETAILED'
) ips
```

Returns the fragmentation levels from sys.dm_db_index_physical_stats

```
INNER JOIN sys.indexes i
    ON ips.index_id = i.index_id
    AND ips.object_id = i.object_id
ORDER BY
```

Joins to the sys.indexes system view to return the name of the index. The join must be on both the object_id and the index_id (unique within the table).

```
    ips.object_id
  , ips.index_id
  , index_level DESC ;
```

Reorganizing an index can be a useful means of reducing small amounts of external fragmentation, as well as internal fragmentation in a lightweight manner. Where a low page density is required to avoid page splits, however, it is important to consider page density as well as external fragmentation when planning index maintenance. We can check the fragmentation of an index using the `sys.dm_db_index_physical_stats` dynamic management view.

11.4 #70 Misinterpreting fragmentation statistics

A common complaint that I hear from DBAs is that "rebuilding my index doesn't remove the fragmentation." Even worse, I have heard this used as a reason for not rebuilding indexes. In fact, rebuilding indexes certainly does remove fragmentation, and the reason for believing otherwise is driven by a misunderstanding of how to interpret the results of `sys.dm_db_index_physical_stats`. Take the query in listing 11.4 as an example of the mistake I have seen DBAs make. The query pulls data for the `Impressions` table from `sys.dm_db_index_physical_stats`. Because the output returns a row for each level of the B-tree, the query calculates the average internal fragmentation for each index on the table.

Listing 11.4 Mistakenly aggregating internal fragmentation statistics

```
SELECT
      i.name AS IndexName
    , AVG(ips.avg_page_space_used_in_percent)
        AS AveragePageDensity
FROM sys.dm_db_index_physical_stats(
                DB_ID('Marketing')
              , OBJECT_ID('marketing.Impressions')
              , NULL
              , NULL
              , 'DETAILED'
    ) ips
INNER JOIN sys.indexes i
    ON ips.index_id = i.index_id
    AND ips.object_id = i.object_id
GROUP BY i.name
ORDER BY IndexName ;
```

Averages the data across root, intermediate, and leaf levels of the B-tree

If we assume that the indexes have just been rebuilt and the `FILLFACTOR` of the indexes is set to `0` (100% full—enough free space for one row) then you might be surprised by the results. My results are shown in figure 11.7, but your results may vary.

You will notice that the average page density of indexes 1 and 2 is 66% and 58%, respectively. This is against a target of 100%. Therefore, at first glance, it looks as if the internal fragmentation has not been removed, but this is because we are asking the "wrong question."

	IndexName	AveragePageDensity
1	ImpressionUID	66.2356972242814
2	PK__Impressi__AE00637B967C6A3E	58.5592661230541

Figure 11.7 Average internal fragmentation when aggregated across all levels of the B-tree

Let's examine this in more detail by homing in on the `ImpressionUID` index and running the query shown in listing 11.5. This query does not aggregate the data. It returns one row for each level of the index, and this time we have added the index name to the join to limit the number of rows returned (we could also use a `WHERE` clause). You will also notice that we have included the `index_level`, `page_count`, and `record_count` columns from `sys.dm_db_index_physical_stats`. This will give us a lot more context.

Listing 11.5 Returning granular details with contextual information

```
SELECT
    i.name AS IndexName
  , ips.avg_page_space_used_in_percent
      AS PageDensity
  , ips.index_level
  , ips.page_count
  , ips.record_count
FROM sys.dm_db_index_physical_stats(
            DB_ID('Marketing')
          , OBJECT_ID('marketing.Impressions')
          , NULL
          , NULL
          , 'DETAILED'
    ) ips
INNER JOIN sys.indexes i
    ON ips.index_id = i.index_id
    AND ips.object_id = i.object_id
    AND i.name = 'ImpressionUID' ;
```

Pulls raw data with no aggregation. This results in one row being returned for each level of the index.

While your results may differ, the results I received are shown in figure 11.8.

	IndexName	PageDensity	index_level	page_count	record_count
1	ImpressionUID	99.922942920682	0	3832	999999
2	ImpressionUID	91.8777983691623	1	17	3832
3	ImpressionUID	6.90635038299975	2	1	17

Figure 11.8 Results of detailed internal fragmentation showing fragmentation at each level

You will notice that level 0 (which is the leaf level) has the target page density. It also has 3,832 pages. Level 1 (the intermediate level) has a 91% page density but only has 17 pages. Level 2 (the root level) only has a page density of 6% but consists of a single page.

The root level has such a low page density because it does not contain enough rows to fill more than 6% of the page. The average page density for the intermediate level is also impacted by the low number of pages. One page that is not full is a much higher percentage when aggregated as an average than when 1 page out of 3,832 is not full.

This means that, if we aggregate the averages for each index level, the results are skewed, and it appears as if the average page density has dropped to 66% when in fact the meaningful average density is 99%, which is perfectly acceptable.

We should be careful when interpreting the results of `sys.dm_db_index_physical_stats`. Double-aggregating results will lead, in many cases, to false results, which can lead us to incorrect assumptions about our indexes. This could in turn lead to issues such as unnecessarily maintaining indexes or even thinking we can neglect index maintenance altogether. In most cases, we should only be concerned about fragmentation at level 0, which is always the leaf level of the index.

11.5 #71 Not rebuilding indexes

The most common reason I hear for failing to rebuild indexes is that a database is used 24/7 and there is no maintenance window. Therefore, index maintenance is not possible, as SQL Server will hold object locks for the duration of the rebuild, stopping users from accessing the table. In some scenarios where DBAs have this philosophy, index reorganization is relied upon as a substitute. In other scenarios, index maintenance is simply not performed.

This approach is a mistake and will almost always lead to degraded performance due to both internal and external fragmentation, which in turn will lead to suboptimal performance whenever index scans are required. A far more appropriate approach would be to use online index rebuilds. This feature was introduced as far back as 2005, but many DBAs just aren't aware of it.

When an online index operation is performed, instead of holding restrictive locks for the duration of the operation, a schema stability lock is acquired at the start of the operation, and a schema modification lock is acquired at the end of the operation. Both of these locks are only held for a short period. It is noteworthy, however, that if the schema lock is blocked by other transactions, it will itself block other transactions that are behind it in the queue. During the main phase of the index operation, the only lock held is an `intent shared` lock on the table, which does not block other transactions.

It is also worthy of note that, when using online index rebuilds, we should ensure that we use a `MAXDOP` of `1`. `MAXDOP` determines how many cores will be used for an operation. Setting `MAXDOP` to `1` means that only a single core will be used. The way index fragments are allocated to processors in an online rebuild means that, if `ALLOW_PAGE_LOCKS` is turned on and this is the default option, then we actually have a risk of increasing, rather than removing, external fragmentation. If we were to turn `ALLOW_PAGE_LOCKS` off, then users of the index would not be able to escalate from row to page locks, meaning many more object locks will be acquired.

NOTE An online index rebuild takes longer than an equivalent offline index rebuild.

The command in the following listing demonstrates how to rebuild the `ImpressionUID` index as an online operation.

Listing 11.6 Rebuilding an index online

```
ALTER INDEX ImpressionUID
ON marketing.Impressions REBUILD
WITH(
    ONLINE = ON,
    MAXDOP = 1
) ;
```

NOTE For the rest of this section, I will use the term *maintenance window* to refer to a period of lower user activity, as opposed to an offline window.

Since the release of SQL Server 2017, it has also been possible to pause and resume online index rebuilds if they exceed a maintenance window. The command in the following listing will pause the operation if it takes longer than 1 minute to complete.

Listing 11.7 Resumable online index rebuild

```
ALTER INDEX ImpressionUID
ON marketing.Impressions REBUILD
WITH(
    ONLINE = ON,
    RESUMABLE = ON,
    MAX_DURATION = 1,
    MAXDOP = 1
) ;
```

This would allow us to restart the index rebuild in the next maintenance window, using the command shown in the following listing.

Listing 11.8 Resuming an online index rebuild

```
ALTER INDEX ImpressionUID
ON marketing.Impressions RESUME
WITH(
    MAXDOP = 1
) ;
```

If there is no paused rebuild waiting to be restarted, the command will fail. Therefore, I would recommend that you use a `TRY..CATCH` block in this process, as shown in listing 11.9. This script will attempt to resume an index rebuild. If no paused rebuild is available; then it will start a new rebuild operation.

Listing 11.9 Resuming or starting a new rebuild

```
BEGIN TRY
    ALTER INDEX ImpressionUID
    ON marketing.Impressions RESUME
    WITH(
        MAXDOP = 1
    ) ;
END TRY
BEGIN CATCH
    ALTER INDEX ImpressionUID
    ON marketing.Impressions REBUILD
    WITH(
        ONLINE = ON,
        RESUMABLE = ON,
        MAX_DURATION = 1,
        MAXDOP = 1
    ) ;
END CATCH
```

Not performing index rebuilds will lead to external fragmentation. It will also lead to pages that have a higher-than-target page density. Both of these issues can negatively impact the performance of queries. To work around this, consider online index rebuilds. These rebuilds take longer than offline operations but do not block user transactions for the duration of the operation. They can also be paused at the end of a maintenance window and then resumed in the next window.

11.6 #72 Rebuilding all indexes indiscriminately

It is important to maintain our indexes. Doing so, however, results in increased resource utilization. Therefore, to keep this utilization to a minimum, we should only rebuild indexes that require it. The mistake that I see some DBAs make is to simply rebuild all indexes, regardless of the level of fragmentation. An example of this approach would be the simple script in listing 11.10, which could be scheduled to run in a SQL Server Agent job. The script constructs a list of `ALTER INDEX..REBUILD` statements as XML and then converts it into a single script in `NVARCHAR(MAX)` before executing the script.

> **TIP** Further details on avoiding the use of cursors for DBA activity can be found in chapter 9.

Listing 11.10 Rebuilding all indexes indiscriminately

```
DECLARE @SQL NVARCHAR(MAX) ;

SET @SQL = (
    SELECT ' ALTER INDEX ' +
        i.name +
        ' ON ' + s.name +
        '.' +
        o.name +
```

```
        ' REBUILD ;'
    FROM sys.indexes i
    INNER JOIN sys.objects o
        ON i.object_id = o.object_id
    INNER JOIN sys.schemas s
        ON s.schema_id = o.schema_id
    WHERE i.type_desc <> 'HEAP'
        AND o.type_desc = 'USER_TABLE'
    FOR XML PATH('')
) ;

EXEC(@SQL) ;
```

The only filters are HEAP and USER_TABLE, meaning that all indexes on all user tables will be rebuilt.

This approach will be particularly problematic for large databases with many indexes due to the prolonged period of intense resource utilization that it will cause. Instead of taking this approach, it is advisable to only rebuild indexes with a high level of fragmentation.

The script in listing 11.11 builds on the previous example, adding `sys.dm_db_index_physical_stats` into the query, which allows us to examine index fragmentation levels as well as the number of pages that make up the index. This means we can add additional filters for `page_count` and both external fragmentation and page density. The page density filter is looking for an average page density greater than the index target fill factor, as this cannot be fixed by reorganizing an index.

Listing 11.11 Rebuilding indexes based on fragmentation

```
DECLARE @SQL NVARCHAR(MAX) ;

SET @SQL = (
    SELECT
        ' ALTER INDEX ' +
            i.name +
            ' ON ' +
            s.name +
            '.' + o.name +
            ' REBUILD ; '
    FROM sys.dm_db_index_physical_stats(
        DB_ID(),
        NULL,
        NULL,
        NULL,
        'DETAILED'
    ) ips
    INNER JOIN sys.indexes i
        ON i.object_id = ips.object_id
        AND i.index_id = ips.index_id
    INNER JOIN sys.objects o
        ON i.object_id = o.object_id
    INNER JOIN sys.schemas s
        ON s.schema_id = o.schema_id
    WHERE i.type_desc <> 'HEAP'
        AND o.type_desc = 'USER_TABLE'
        AND (
```

We still filter out system tables and heaps.

```
            ips.avg_fragmentation_in_percent > 20 OR
            ips.avg_page_space_used_in_percent >
            CASE
                WHEN i.fill_factor = 0
                    THEN 100
                ELSE i.fill_factor
            END    #B
        )
        AND ips.page_count > 1000
        AND ips.index_level = 0
    FOR XML PATH('')
) ;

EXEC(@SQL) ;
```

We filter out any indexes that do not have fragmentation issues

We filter out tiny indexes and nonleaf levels.

> **NOTE** The level of external fragmentation that should trigger a rebuild should be dependent on the workload profile of the specific application. The 20% that I have used here is illustrative only and not meant as a best practice recommendation.

We should not rebuild all indexes, as this unnecessarily consumes server resources. Instead, we should look to rebuild only those indexes that require it based on fragmentation levels and page density.

11.7 #73 Updating statistics after rebuilding indexes

Many years ago, I wrote a blog post about the world's worst maintenance routine. It was based on a maintenance routine I had just found in a company I was working with at the time. It ran on a nightly basis and performed the following tasks:

1. Rebuild all indexes
2. Update all statistics
3. Shrink the database

We have already discussed why shrinking databases as a matter of course is not a good idea, as it causes near-perfect fragmentation. Therefore, it is easy to see why performing this operation just after rebuilding all of our indexes would be a really bad idea. In this section, however, we will dive into why updating all statistics just after rebuilding all indexes is also a bad practice.

To understand why, we need to understand how statistics are updated. By default, if we were to run `UPDATE STATISTICS` against a table, it would update all statistics that have been created against columns and indexes on that table. It would update these statistics by using the default sample size. This default sample is based on the following rules:

- If the table is < 8 MB: scan 100% of rows.
- If the table > 8 MB: sample between 10% and 30% of rows, based on the number of rows.

If we want to execute all statistics in the database, we would use the system-stored procedure called `sp_updatestats`. If we run `sp_updatestats` without parameters, it will execute a cursor that loops around every table and issues UPDATE STATISTICS using the default values. The result of this will be that all column and index statistics on all tables larger than 8 MB are updated using a sample rate of between 10% and 30%.

We then need to consider that, when we rebuild an index, it automatically updates the index statistics using a full 100% sample size. Therefore, if we rebuild an index, it has statistics based on 100% of rows in the index. If we then update the statistics on that index using default values, we actually reduce the quality of those statistics while unnecessarily consuming resources.

What should we do differently? Well, in the vast majority of cases, automatically updating statistics is acceptable. There is an option to automatically update statistics as required, and an additional option to update them asynchronously, which will prevent the process from blocking the query that triggered the statistics update. Although the asynchronous option does mean that the query that triggered the update will not benefit from the updated statistics, subsequent queries will. It will also prevent the query that triggered the update from being blocked until the statistics finish updating.

Automatically updating statistics is on by default, but if it has been turned off, then we can toggle it back on, using the command in the following listing.

Listing 11.12 Enabling AUTO_UPDATE_STATISTICS

```
ALTER DATABASE Marketing
    SET AUTO_UPDATE_STATISTICS ON ;
```

If we need statistics to update asynchronously, which of course has the limitation that the query that triggered the update will not benefit from them, then we can do so using the command in listing 11.13. Note, however, that this option requires AUTO_UPDATE_STATISTICS to also be turned on. Otherwise, it will have no effect.

Listing 11.13 Enabling AUTO_UPDATE_STATISTICS_ASYNC

```
ALTER DATABASE Marketing
    SET AUTO_UPDATE_STATISTICS_ASYNC ON ;
```

If we are dealing with a specific performance issue, where we need to ensure that queries always have the very latest statistics, we can use UPDATE STATISTICS against a specific set of tables. If this needs to happen on the same schedule as index rebuilds, we can use the COLUMNS keyword to limit the update to the column statistics and ignore index statistics. This is demonstrated for the marketing.Impressions table in listing 11.14. The FULLSCAN keyword will use a 100% sample rate.

Listing 11.14 Updating column statistics only for a given table

```
UPDATE STATISTICS marketing.Impressions
WITH
      FULLSCAN
    , COLUMNS ;
```

WARNING When updating statistics manually, consider the tradeoff of performance enhancements that up-to-date statistics provide against the cost of recompiling the query.

If we did find ourselves in a position where we had to update the column statistics for all tables in a database, then we could use the same approach as we took to rebuilding indexes. This is demonstrated in the following listing.

Listing 11.15 Updating all column statistics in a database

```
DECLARE @SQL NVARCHAR(MAX) ;

SET @SQL = (
    SELECT
        ' UPDATE STATISTICS ' +
        s.name +
        '.' +
        t.name +
        ' WITH FULLSCAN, COLUMNS ; '
    FROM sys.tables t
    INNER JOIN sys.schemas s
        ON t.schema_id = s.schema_id
    FOR XML PATH('')
) ;

EXEC(@SQL) ;
```

TIP For a large subset of tables, this query could be enhanced to filter by a schema or table name pattern.

We should avoid updating statistics manually unless we have a specific use case that requires it. If we must update statistics manually, we should avoid updating index statistics after performing index rebuilds, as this may leave us with worse statistics.

11.8 #74 Not optimizing index maintenance for our needs

As SQL Server has evolved, a raft of index enhancements has been added to the product that allows us to customize our index maintenance for our specific environment. Despite this, however, it is quite rare to see DBAs taking advantage of these enhancements. Almost invariably, less seasoned DBAs and accidental DBAs continue to use the most basic syntax for index rebuilds. This is a mistake, however, as they are often missing out on performance optimizations that could impact maintenance or index usage.

We have discussed some of these enhancements already, such as online index rebuilds and resumable index operations. There are still more, even less commonly used enhancements, however, that we should consider. In this section, we will explore the considerations for `MAXDOP`, which is rarely specified for index rebuilds. We will also consider the use of `SORT_IN_TEMPDB`. Finally, we will look at `OPTIMIZE_FOR_SEQUENTIAL_KEY`.

11.8.1 Considerations for MAXDOP

Many DBAs are familiar with `MAXDOP`, which controls the maximum number of processors that can be used to execute a query that SQL Server has algorithmically calculated meets the parallelization cost threshold. Many DBAs, however, do not understand the implications of this setting in the context of index rebuilds.

If we do not specify `MAXDOP` for an index rebuild, SQL Server will use the default `MAXDOP` setting of the database. Not considering the `MAXDOP` for index rebuilds is a mistake, because there are performance tradeoffs that we should take into account.

To understand this, consider the diagram in figure 11.9. The diagram assumes a `MAXDOP` of 4 and illustrates that the index is broken into fragments, with one fragment assigned to each of the four processors. The fragments are then stitched back together to form the new index.

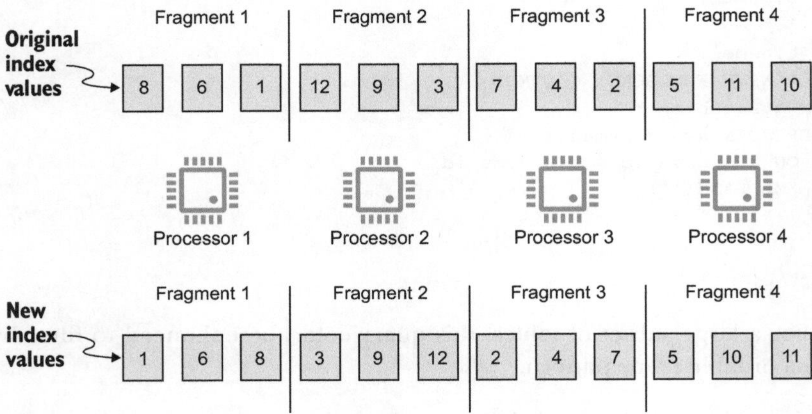

Figure 11.9 Parallel index rebuild creates an index fragment for each processor.

You will notice that while values have been correctly ordered within each fragment, there is still fragmentation within the index because consideration has not been given to the order of values between fragments. Therefore, it is important that we consciously consider the optimum `MAXDOP` to use during our index rebuilds based on the needs of our environment. If we have a very short maintenance window and our indexes fragment quickly, throwing multiple processors at the rebuild will mean we can reduce the time it takes for the rebuild to complete. If we have no time constraints, however, performing the rebuilds as a single threaded operation will reduce the final fragmentation levels and therefore improve performance for index scan operations.

11.8.2 Considerations for SORT_IN_TEMPDB

`SORT_IN_TEMPDB` is an index rebuild option that I have never seen used to its full potential. When the option is used, the intermediate sorting is performed in `TempDB` as opposed to the user database, which is where the sorting will happen by default. On the rare occasions when I have seen it being used, it has been because DBAs have been using it to work around an issue where they are short on disk space on their data volume and do not have enough free space to rebuild their larger indexes. In this scenario, when TempDB is stored on a different volume, DBAs push the intermediate storage requirement to a different volume. This workaround may have some validity if we have SQL Server running on a physical server, but for virtual or cloud machines, we really should just allocate more space to the struggling volume.

The benefit of SORT_IN_TEMPDB, which I have seen almost universally missed, is actually in relation to the performance of the maintenance operation. In environments where TempDB is stored on fast storage, such as local M.2 and data files that are stored on slower SSD disks, we can reduce the time of an index rebuild operation by using the SORT_IN_TEMPDB option for large indexes. The process is illustrated in figure 11.10.

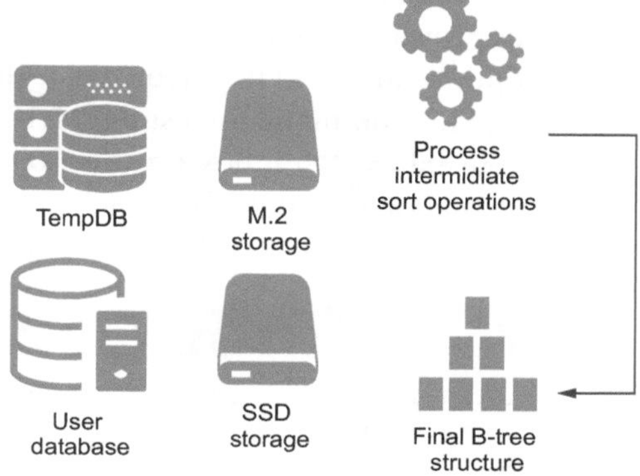

Figure 11.10 Optimizing performance of intermediate sorts by performing them on faster storage

The tradeoff that we need to consider here is disk space. While we are reducing the space requirements for the user database, we are increasing the storage requirement overall. When we perform the intermediate sort operations in the user database, the extents used for the sort operation are released at roughly the same rate as they are allocated to the new index structure. When we sort the results in TempDB, however, we need enough space in TempDB to store the entire intermediate sorting while also requiring enough space in the user database to store the final B-tree structure.

11.8.3 Understanding OPTIMIZE_FOR_SEQUENTIAL_KEY

Index keys will sometimes be sequential and sometimes nonsequential. An example of a sequential index key would be a clustered key that is built on an IDENTITY column. The values (unless we reseed the column) will be ever increasing. An example of a nonsequential key would be a clustered index key built on a GUID column. New values that are inserted may need to be inserted anywhere within the index to keep the index in order.

When we have a sequential index that has a high volume of inserts, we can suffer from performance issues caused by page latch contention on the final page of the index. We can have so many inserts that a queue of page latches forms, with all of them moving at the speed of the slowest request. For example, if one insert operation is delayed because it needs to perform a page split, all of the operations lined up behind it will need to sit and wait for their page latch to be granted. This is known as *last page insert contention*.

Unbeknown to many DBAs, SQL Server 2019 introduced a new feature into indexes, known as `OPTIMIZE_FOR_SEQUENTAL_KEY`. If we build an index specifying this option, SQL Server will apply optimizations that are intended to alleviate this issue.

When we turn this option on, SQL Server uses a flow-control mechanism, which assesses threads before the point where they request a page latch. It assesses the state of the thread and the processor on which the thread is running. It uses this information to prioritize threads that are likely to complete in a single processor cycle, which increases throughput.

It is really important that we only use this option when we have a specific use case that requires it, however. For the use case that it was designed for—indexes that have a sequential key and the throughput of threads requiring latches is far greater than the available number of processors—the option can yield a substantial performance improvement. For indexes that are not suffering from throughput issues, however, the option can result in performance degradation—even if the key is sequential.

The command in listing 11.16 demonstrates how to enable the option for the `ImpressionUID` index on the `marketing.Impressions` table. You will notice that the `ALTER INDEX` statement uses the `SET` clause. The `SET` option is applied immediately, and there is no need to rebuild the index.

Listing 11.16 Enabling `OPTIMIZE_FOR_SEQUENTIAL_KEY`

```
ALTER INDEX ImpressionUID
ON marketing.Impressions
SET (
    OPTIMIZE_FOR_SEQUENTIAL_KEY = ON
) ;
```

11.9 #75 Not disabling indexes for bulk load

Well-maintained indexes and a good indexing strategy are vital to ensuring optimal read performance. There is a downside, however, and that is the negative performance implication on write operations. A common mistake is to perform bulk loads into a table that has multiple nonclustered indexes.

Consider the `ImpressionArchive` table in the `MarketingArchive` database. This table could potentially be subject to a bulk insert of millions of rows on a single load. This load will require thousands of I/O operations to allocate new pages to the table and write the data.

But now consider that two nonclustered indexes have been created to support reporting requirements. Not only do the data pages of the table need to be updated, but each of the nonclustered indexes must be updated. The row size in a nonclustered index is smaller than the row size of a clustered index because it only contains the nonclustered index key, any included columns, and a pointer to the clustered index. This is opposed to the full row of data contained in the clustered index. Despite this, for a large insert, page splits are inevitable, and they are far more likely to be bad page splits. This process is illustrated in figure 11.11.

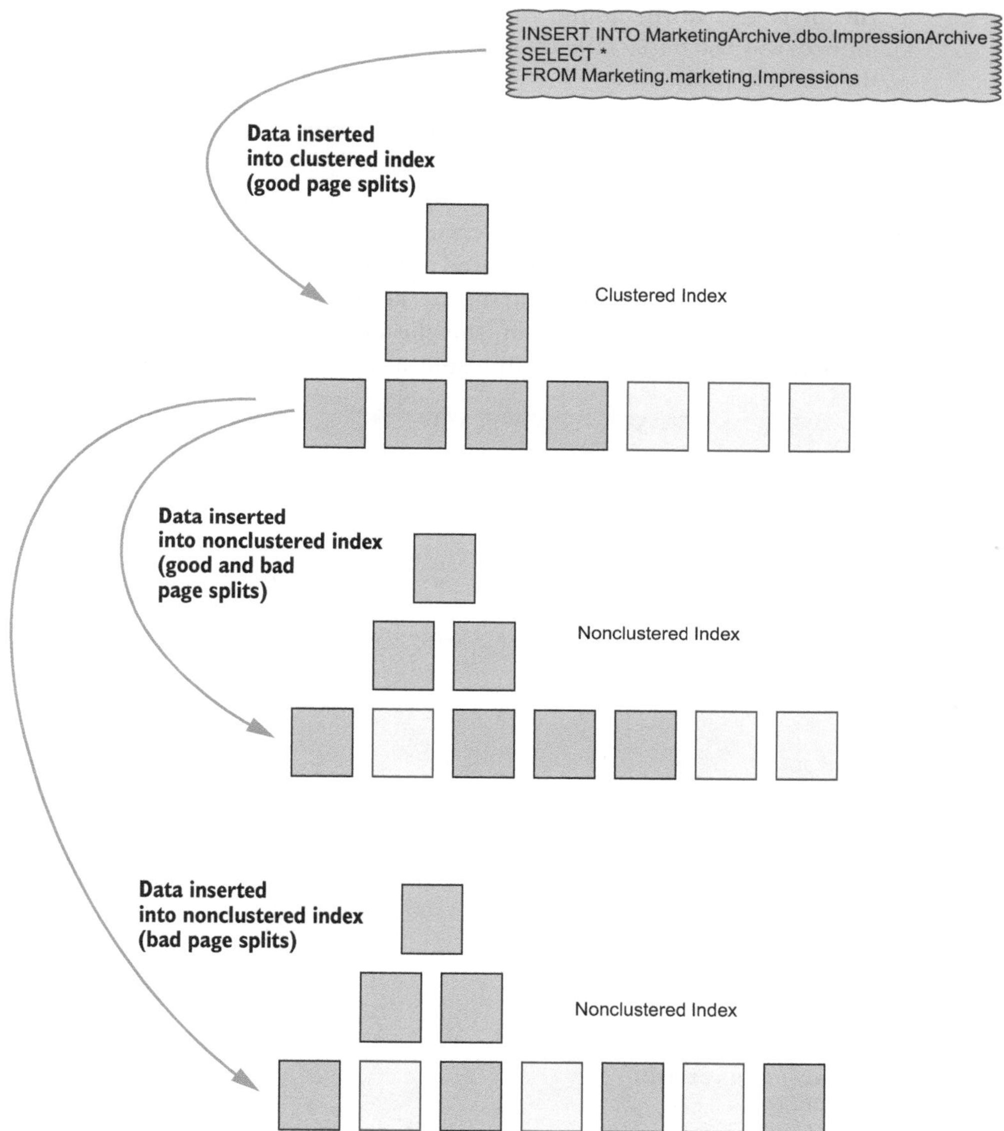

Figure 11.11 Inserting new rows into a table with nonclustered indexes

We can imagine the amount of additional I/O (and time) required for the updates to the nonclustered indexes. Instead of using this approach, which is also likely to add external fragmentation to the nonclustered indexes, it is often more performant to disable the indexes and then rebuild them when the load is complete.

TIP It is also worth noting that the updates required to the nonclustered indexes will also impact the I/O required to write to the transaction log during the `INSERT` operation.

The script in listing 11.17 demonstrates how to disable all nonclustered indexes on the `ImpressionsArchive` table, perform the `INSERT` operation, and then rebuild all of the nonclustered indexes. Note that disabling the clustered index will result in the table becoming inaccessible. Therefore, we will use a dynamic script based on metadata in `sys.indexes` to disable the nonclustered indexes instead of using the `ALL` keyword. For the rebuilds, however, we are using the `ALL` keyword, which means the clustered index will be included. If we did not want the clustered index to be rebuilt, we would have to script the index rebuilds using the same approach as the disable indexes operation.

Listing 11.17 Disabling and reenabling indexes

```
DECLARE @SQL NVARCHAR(MAX) ;

SET @SQL = (
    SELECT
        ' ALTER INDEX ' + name + ' ON ImpressionsArchive DISABLE ; '
    FROM sys.indexes
    WHERE object_id = OBJECT_ID('ImpressionsArchive')
        AND type > 1
    FOR XML PATH ('')
) ;

EXEC(@SQL) ;
GO

INSERT INTO MarketingArchive.dbo.ImpressionsArchive (
    ImpressionUID,
    ReferralURL,
    CookieID,
    CampaignID,
    RenderingID,
    CountryCode,
    StateID,
    BrowserVersion,
    OperatingSystemID,
    BidPrice,
    CostPerMille,
    EventTime
)
SELECT
      ImpressionUID
    , ReferralURL
    , CookieID
    , CampaignID
    , RenderingID
    , CountryCode
    , StateID
    , BrowserVersion
```

```
    , OperatingSystemID
    , BidPrice
    , CostPerMille
    , EventTime
FROM Marketing.marketing.Impressions ;
GO

ALTER INDEX ALL ON dbo.ImpressionsArchive REBUILD ;
GO
```

Although nonclustered indexes improve performance for read operations, they can have a negative impact on the performance of `INSERT` and `UPDATE` statements. For bulk load operations, it can be beneficial to disable and reenable indexes, instead of performing the required index updates during the bulk load process.

11.10 #76 Relying too heavily on Database Engine Tuning Advisor

Database Engine Tuning Advisor (DTA) is a graphical tool, accessible from the Tools menu of SQL Server Management Studio, which can offer DBAs guidance on the creation and removal of indexes, indexed views, partitioning strategies, and potential changes to the physical design of a database. In this section, we will focus on its guidance around indexing strategies.

A common mistake that I see less experienced DBAs make is to run DTA against a workload and then implement all recommendations without further consideration. The trouble with this approach is that it does not take into consideration workloads that are not included in the sample provided, and, more importantly, it does not reflect any business knowledge.

When we run DTA, we select the database(s) for which we want to receive a recommendation and then provide it with a workload to analyze. This workload can be in the form of a SQL trace file (or table) or we can point it at the plan cache, or, if Query Store is implemented, we can run it against that. Any queries that are not contained in the workload provided will not be considered, of course. This means that it is easy for business-critical queries to be missed.

In addition, tools of this nature can simply never have the business knowledge that a skilled DBA or developer will have. For example, imagine that we have a critical month-end process that takes a long time to run and has a short ETL window to run in. If we have provided a SQL trace file that does not cover the night when the month-end process ran, then DTA may recommend we drop an index, which will cause the process to overrun its next window.

Real-life example

The most telling example I have seen of this mistake dates back around 10 years. A new DBA at a company I was working with ran DTA and then implemented all recommendations without reviewing or truly understanding them.

> ***(continued)***
>
> The problem was that he provided the plan cache as a workload a couple of hours after the Database Engine service had been restarted. He was unaware that the plan cache is cleared on an instance restart.
>
> The end result was that he dropped around 90% of the indexes across all databases on the instance. To make matters worse, this was before the days when SQL Server objects were routinely stored in source control. All in all, it was a very long weekend fixing the issue!

DTA can be a very useful tool for getting ideas about how we can improve our index strategy. It has limitations, however, and its recommendations should never be implemented blindly. We should always assess the results and use our business knowledge to determine how its implementation may impact processes that were not captured in the workload that was analyzed.

11.11 #77 Not using columnstore indexes

Up until now, we have focused on traditional indexes, which use a B-tree structure to organize data, but what if I told you that there was another type of index called a *columnstore* and that this type of index could provide a 100× performance improvement for data warehouse–style queries? Wow. But what if I then told you that adoption of columnstore indexes is really low among data warehouse developers and DBAs who manage those systems? What's going on? Surely we would all like our queries to complete 100× faster, right? Well, yes, and that's why not using them can be a big mistake. Before we dive into why, let's take a moment to explore what a columnstore index is.

> **Data storage complexities**
>
> SQL Server storage optimizations mean that certain data items may be stored outside of a row. For example, a string more than 8,000 bytes long will be moved to a different allocation unit for overflow values. Also, if features such as filestream are implemented, then data items could even be stored outside of the Database Engine. For the purposes of this illustration, however, we will keep things simple and work with the grossly simplified assumption that all data items are stored within the data pages of a table.
>
> With this rather large caveat in mind, we can say that, in a traditional index, data is organized by storing rows on pages. Therefore, the minimum content of a single data page is an entire row of data. Therefore, the leaf level of a clustered index is rows of data. In the root and intermediate levels of a clustered index and also in all levels of a nonclustered index, the data pages still contain rows of data, but these rows of data simply point to other data pages.

In a *columnstore index*, the organization of data is pivoted. Instead of organizing data into rows, data is organized into columns. Pages are then used to store collections of column values, as opposed to collections of rows.

A columnstore index is split into segments, each containing between 102,400 and 1,048,576 rows. Each segment contains metadata about the data it contains, and this means that the query engine can eliminate (skip) any segments that are not relevant. Within each segment, data is then split into columns, with each column stored on a different set of pages. The index is then compressed quite substantially, which further reduces the number of pages that need to be read to satisfy a query. The difference in how data is organized is illustrated in figure 11.12.

The way columnstore indexes are structured makes them incredibly powerful for data warehouse–style queries. If we create columnstore indexes on fact tables, then queries that require fact aggregation can see a large performance enhancement.

So that brings me back to the question of why adoption is low, and frankly it is a case of first impressions count. When the first version of columnstore indexes was introduced, in SQL Server 2012, they were limited to say the least. Only nonclustered columnstore indexes were supported, and we could only create one per table. They were not supported on indexed views, and we could not use them in combination with change tracking or change data capture.

The biggest limitation, however, was that, once we created a columnstore index on a table, the table became read-only. This meant that we had to drop the index before we could perform any `INSERT`, `UPDATE`, or `DELETE` statements. To compound this issue, columnstore indexes take longer to build than B-tree indexes.

Overall, the first version of columnstore indexes did not work for the vast majority of use cases. The problem is that, despite drastic improvements over the last 12+ years, their reputation has stuck, and as soon as many DBAs think of a columnstore index, their instant reaction is, "They won't work for me!" This is simply a mistake.

In the modern world of columnstore indexes, there are still some awkward limitations. Advanced data types, such as `HIERARCHYID`, `GEOGRAPHY`, and `GEOMETRY`, are not supported, nor are large data types such as `(N)VARCHAR(MAX)` or `XML`.

> **TIP** We are still limited to having a single columnstore index on a table, but because of the nature of columnstore indexes, this makes sense. We can simply include all relevant columns in the single index.

With that said, however, both clustered and nonclustered columnstore indexes are now supported, and if we create a clustered columnstore index, we can still create nonclustered B-tree indexes on the table as well. This means that they have become genuinely useful for analytical and data warehouse workloads, and we should consider using them when we have large fact tables that are subject to large aggregations.

To see what difference a columnstore index can make, let's compare the performance of an aggregate query with a traditional B-tree clustered index versus a clustered cloumnstore index. The script in the following listing runs a query that calculates the average `BidPrice` and average `CostPerMille` from the `ImpressionsArchive` table in the `MarketingArchive` database.

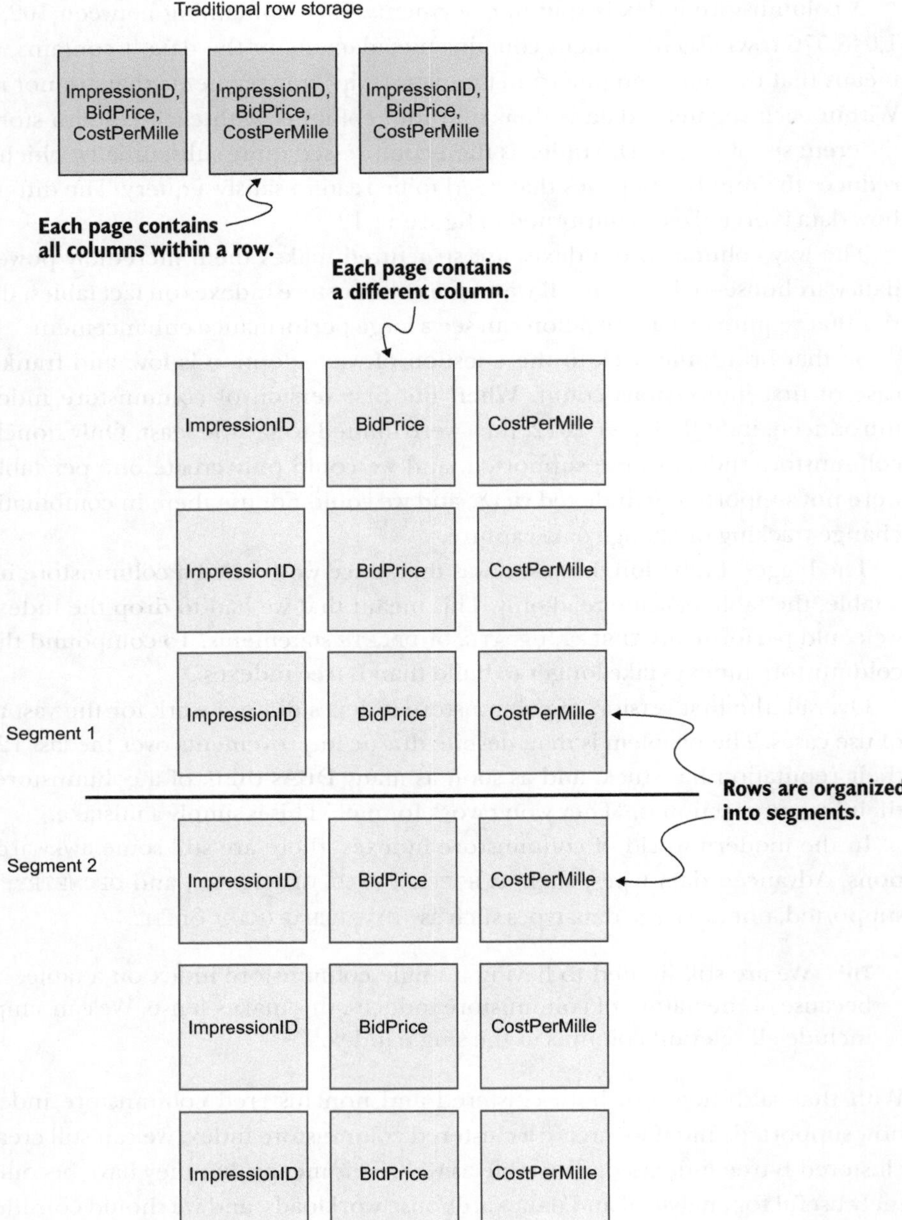

Figure 11.12 How data is organized in a columnstore index

Listing 11.18 Running an aggregate query

```
SET STATISTICS TIME ON ;

SELECT
      AVG(BidPrice)
    , AVG(CostPerMille)
FROM dbo.ImpressionsArchive ;
```

If we examine the execution statistics in the Messages tab of the query results, we can see how long it took for the query to run. On my test rig, the total elapsed time was 1,067 ms. This is fast, but remember that the table is relatively small, for demonstration purposes. In a production table, we may have billions of wide rows.

> **TIP** Remember, if you run the query yourself, the speed will vary, based on multiple factors such as the specification of the computer and any other processes that are consuming resources.

The script in the following listing demonstrates how to create a clustered columnstore index on the `ImpressionsArchive` table of the `MarketingArchive` database.

Listing 11.19 Creating a clustered columnstore index with a nonclustered B-tree index

```
CREATE CLUSTERED COLUMNSTORE INDEX ImpressionsArchiveCCSI
ON dbo.ImpressionsArchive ;
GO
```

Now let's rerun the query in listing 11.18 and review the execution time statistics. On my test rig, the total elapsed time was 45 ms. This means that the query completed in just 4% of the time that it took to execute the query against the traditional B-tree clustered index. If you scale this up to queries against very large production tables, it's easy to see how massive performance gains can be achieved.

The command in the following listing demonstrates how to create a nonclustered B-tree index, which will support queries that filter by `CampaignID` and `CostCode` but also return `BidPrice` in the `SELECT` list.

Listing 11.20 Creating a nonclustered B-tree index

```
CREATE NONCLUSTERED INDEX CampaignIDCountryCodeWithBidPrice
ON dbo.ImpressionsArchive(CampaignID, CountryCode)
INCLUDE (BidPrice) ;
GO
```

Summary

- A B-tree structure is the structure that indexes are organized into. They have a root level consisting of a single page, zero or more intermediate levels, and a single leaf level.

- The leaf level of a clustered index is the actual data pages of the table whereas the leaf level of a nonclustered index contains pointers to the data pages of the table.
- Internal fragmentation refers to a low page density, which causes more pages than necessary to be read.
- Low page density needs to be traded off against the risk of page splits caused by updates to very dense pages.
- Good page splits occur when pages are allocated at the end of an index.
- Bad page splits occur when pages are allocated in the middle of the index and data needs to be moved to the new page. These page splits cause increased I/O and performance penalties.
- External fragmentation refers to pages being out of order, which can damage performance.
- External fragmentation only causes a performance issue for index scans. Index seeks are not impacted.
- An index seek starts at the root level of the B-tree and traverses all levels until it finds the required row.
- An index scan reads the leaf level of an index until it reaches the end of the data it is searching for.
- An index loop uses a nonclustered index to perform a filter or aggregation and then looks up further data from the clustered index or heap.
- Seek, scan, and lookup ratios can be determined by using the `sys.dm_db_index_usage_stats` dynamic management view (DMV).
- Do not reorganize indexes to fix page density. Reorganizing indexes only fills pages up to the level of `FILLFACTOR`. It does not reduce density to the level of `FILLFACTOR`. We should rebuild indexes instead.
- Avoid aggregating fragmentation statistics from `sys.dm_db_index_physical_stats`. Instead, focus on the leaf-level data.
- Not rebuilding indexes will have an impact on index scans and therefore query performance. If a database is 24/7, use online index rebuilds.
- Do not rebuild all indexes indiscriminately. Only rebuild indexes that require it based on fragmentation statistics.
- Do not update statistics after rebuilding indexes, as this can result in worse statistics.
- In the majority of cases, automatically updating statistics is good enough.
- If you decide to update statistics, consider the tradeoff against plan recompilation.
- Depending on the query performance tradeoff against a maintenance window, consider `MAXDOP` for index rebuilds.
- If you are suffering from last page insert contention, consider using `OPTIMIZE_FOR_SEQUENTIAL_KEY`.

- If you need to perform bulk load operations, consider disabling nonclustered indexes on the target table to improve write performance.
- Do not rely too heavily on tools such as Database Engine Tuning Advisor. You can use them as a guide, but you must layer them with your own business knowledge.
- Columnstore indexes organize pages around columns instead of rows.
- Consider using columnstore indexes on large fact tables to improve the performance of analytical queries.

12 Backups

This chapter covers

- How to align backup strategies with organizational requirements
- The importance of testing backups and how to do this in a practical way
- How database snapshots and storage snapshots can complement a backup strategy
- The importance of considering extract, transform, and load processes when scheduling backups
- SQL Server's three recovery models and when each is most appropriate
- Security considerations for database backups

In this chapter, we will discuss common mistakes that database administrators (DBAs) make when planning and implementing backups. Over the years, I have seen a tendency for backup strategies to be treated as something of an afterthought. The value of backups can be difficult to quantify—until such a point when we urgently need to recover a database, of course.

Real-life example

Some years ago, when working as a solution architect and lead developer on a project, I asked the DBA team to back up a production database and restore it over the top of the development database to refresh the environment. Unfortunately, the DBA took a backup of the development database and restored it over the top of production.

I therefore asked the DBA to urgently restore the previous night's backup of the production database, only to be told that the backup had been failing and the most recent backup available was from three weeks prior.

Fortunately, I was able to rebuild the last three weeks of data from the source data, although this took a horribly long time. In some cases, the lack of backups can cause a company serious issues, including lost revenue, reputational harm, or regulatory noncompliance. There are even examples of organizations going out of business due to lack of backups.

We will begin this chapter by discussing backup strategies and ensuring that we have factored in the business requirements for recovery point objective (RPO) and recovery time objective (RTO). We will then move on to discuss mistakes that DBAs make when relying on snapshots as restore strategies.

There is an old adage that you do not have a backup until you have restored it, and we will explore the impacts of not testing backups. We will then move on to considering backup schedules. Here we will look specifically at the conflicts of scheduling maintenance windows around extract, transform, load (ETL) windows.

We will then look at the different recovery models that can be implemented in SQL Server and the impacts that using the wrong recovery model can have on performance and disk space, as well as the impact of not taking a backup after changing recovery models. We will discuss how we should take ad hoc backups in a way that avoids breaking the restore sequence before finally looking at the security implications of our backup strategy.

12.1 #78 Not considering RPO and RTO

RPO refers to how much data it is acceptable to lose in the event of a failure. *RTO* refers to how much time it will take to recover from a failure. These are both critical considerations when planning a backup strategy for a database.

If we ask the business how much data they can afford to lose in the event of a failure, their answer will inevitably be "None." Similarly, if we ask the business the acceptable duration of an outage in the event of failure, their answer will usually be "I need instant recovery."

If these assertions are true, then we should configure high availability and disaster recovery for the applications, which will be discussed in chapter 13. If, however, we dig a little deeper with the application owner and explain the costs involved in hosting the redundant, geographically dispersed servers required for such a topology, we will often find that the requirements are not as they first appeared. For example, if an application is considered P4 (where P1 is a mission-critical application), then it is unlikely that building a highly available topology would make good business sense, and, in fact, they can rely on a backup–restore strategy.

These conversations can be a little arduous sometimes, depending on the skills and personality of the application owner. Because of this, a mistake that I see many DBAs fall into is simply putting all databases on the same default schedule and avoiding the tricky conversations with application owners.

This is a mistake that we should avoid, however. If we simply use a default schedule, without understanding the RPO and RTO requirements, we can cause issues. For example, if our default schedule allows for 1 hour of data loss but it would cause serious business impact if they lost more than 30 minutes of data, then we are storing up problems for later down the line.

If, on the other hand, we had a default schedule that allowed for 30 minutes of data loss, but only a very small percentage of applications had an RPO of less than 4 hours, then we will be unnecessarily using resources to take backups that are not required. We will also be using more storage than we need. This has a cost associated with it, and if the storage is in cloud, it is a directly addressable cost.

If we fail to consider RTO, we could land in a situation where we have significant business disruption caused by not being able to recover the databases in an acceptable amount of time.

To understand how we can impact the RPO of a database, let's remind ourselves of the different types of backup that we can take in SQL Server. The backup types at our disposal are detailed in table 12.1.

Table 12.1 Backup types

Backup Type	Description
Full	Backs up all data within the database*
Differential	Backs up data pages within the database that have changed since the last full backup*
Transaction log	Backs up the transaction log, which includes a record of all transactions since the last transaction log backup

*It is possible to limit a backup to specific data files or filegroups.

A full backup has the most impact on resources and can cause a performance problem on a busy system. Therefore, full backups are usually taken in a maintenance window. The impact of a differential backup is variable. It depends on how many pages within the data files have changed since the last full backup. Therefore, while they are usually far more lightweight than a full backup, there can still be an impact on busy online transaction processing (OLTP) systems.

A transaction log backup does not touch the data files and simply backs up the transaction log. Because the transaction log records all transactions since the last log backup, it is the equivalent of an incremental backup in some systems. During a restore operation, these transactions are replayed into the database, meaning that we can perform a *point-in-time recovery*, which is where we can stop the restore at a specific point in time, in the middle of the transaction log backup file. This is very useful in situations where there has been user error leading to some data being mistakenly updated or deleted. We can stop the recovery immediately before the erroneous operation. This is not possible from a full or differential backup, as they are backing up data pages. Figure 12.1 illustrates a *restore chain*, which is the order in which we restore backups to recover a database.

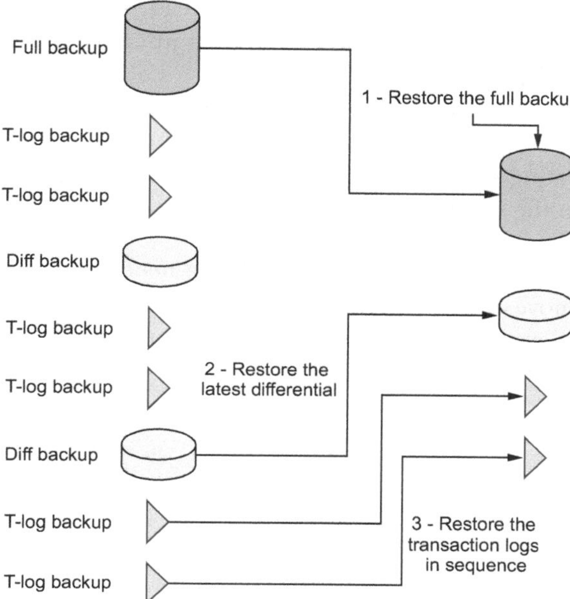

Figure 12.1 Restore chain

In a typical backup schedule, we may schedule a full backup to occur overnight when an application is not being used. We might also schedule a differential backup to occur at lunchtime, when there is minimal usage. To meet the required RPO, however, the key is transaction log backups. We will schedule these to be taken in line with the RPO. For example, if we have an RPO of 1 hour, we will schedule transaction log backups to happen on an hourly basis.

The biggest consideration with RTO is where the backups are stored and how quickly we can retrieve them. In the worst example I have seen, database backups were taken by an enterprise backup tool, which compressed and deduped them before sending them directly to tape. There was then a 6-hour service level agreement (SLA) to retrieve them from the tape robot.

A more common scenario is that an enterprise backup tool caches backups on disk for a period of time, usually a few days, before sending the disks to tape. In a cloud environment, the equivalent is an orchestration where the backup tool stores backups on instant access storage, such as S3 in AWS or Blob Storage in Azure for a few days.

The data is then moved into archive storage, such as Azure Deep Archive or Azure Storage Archive Access Tier. This storage is not instant access. In the case of Deep Archive, for example, the SLA for retrieval is 24 hours, although in reality it is usually returned much faster.

We may also face situations where we have a backup team that is slow to respond. I have witnessed a request for the previous night's backup being delayed by multiple hours, just waiting for someone in the backup team to pick the request off their queue.

In situations like these, if we have a short RTO, we may choose to avoid the enterprise tool taking database backups using a SQL Server Agent. Instead, it may be appropriate to schedule our own, native SQL Server backups and then just have the enterprise backup tool offload the backup files.

If we take this approach, however, we must be mindful that it becomes our responsibility to ensure that backups are successful and to remediate where required. We also need to be mindful of duplicating storage costs. If we do this for many large databases, the extra storage required on the database servers can mount up. If our servers are in cloud, this can result in a substantial, direct cost increase.

Therefore, if we do need to cache our backups locally, we need to ensure that we have processes in place to remove old backup files. The PowerShell script in listing 12.1 demonstrates how we can remove backup files that are older than three days, assuming a backup location of `D:\Backups`. We could schedule this to run with SQL Agent or with Windows Scheduled task.

Listing 12.1 Deleting old backups

```
$Path = 'D:\Backups\'
$Days = 3
$CutoffDate = (Get-Date).AddDays(-$Days)

Get-ChildItem -Path $Path -Recurse | Where-Object {$_.CreationTime -lt
$CutoffDate} | Remove-Item -Force -Recurse -Verbose -Confirm:$false
```

We should always consider the business requirements when planning a backup strategy for a given database. While it might seem easy to have a single backup schedule for all of our databases, we are simply storing up problems for the future. Instead, we should ensure that we understand the RPO and RTO of a database and plan the backup strategy for each database such that the requirements are met and without unnecessarily using resources.

12.2 #79 Using database snapshots as a recovery strategy

Database *snapshots* use copy-on-write technology to take a read-only, point-in-time snapshot of a database. These snapshots can be incredibly useful for a number of use cases. For example, snapshots are a great choice for generating reports of data at a given point in time. They are also great if we need to generate reports that compare current data to a point in time. What's more, they can be used to protect data from human error. If someone accidentally deletes data, it is easier and quicker to copy data back in from a snapshot, or even revert the whole database to the snapshot, than it is to perform a restore to a different location and copy the missing data back in. They can also be used to roll back a failed deployment, providing the source database is still healthy.

It is clear that snapshots can complement a backup strategy. A mistake I have seen made, however, is to use snapshots as a replacement for a backup strategy. This is a situation that we must absolutely avoid. To understand why, we need to understand how database snapshots work.

The image in figure 12.2 illustrates the snapshot process. When a database snapshot is first created, it is entirely empty. This is known as a *sparse file*, and the technology is implemented using New Technology File System (NTFS) sparse files. Every time a page is modified in the source database, that page is copied over to the snapshot database, before the update is made. When a user queries the snapshot, SQL Server will see if the required data pages exist in the snapshot. If they do, they will be returned from the snapshot. If they do not, they will be returned from the source database.

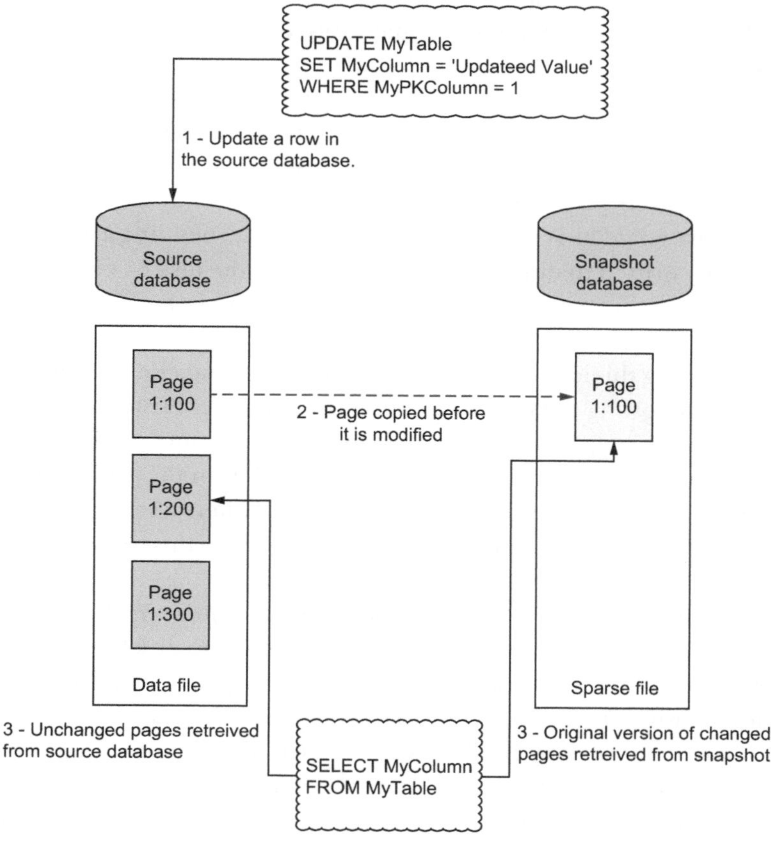

Figure 12.2 Snapshot process

You can see that the snapshot is entirely dependent on the source database. If the database were to be corrupted or deleted, the snapshot would also become unavailable. What's more, even if the snapshot was available, its dependence on the source database means that it cannot be moved to a different instance. Therefore, if the instance or server were unavailable, we would not be able to recover from the snapshot.

While database snapshots are very useful for several use cases, including complementing a backup strategy, they cannot replace a backup strategy. A decision to implement database snapshots should have no bearing on our backup strategy.

12.3 #80 Using crash-consistent snapshots as a recovery strategy

Most enterprise-class storage solutions provide a snapshot solution, allowing us to perform a backup of a disk or a whole VM. The implementation of snapshot technology varies from vendor to vendor, so we will not dwell on that here. There are, however, some common concepts that we need to understand.

First, snapshots are *block-level backups*, which means that the blocks on the physical disk are being backed up, as opposed to files that are accessible at an operating system level. Second, there are different types of snapshots, each of which provides a different level of consistency.

The most basic level of consistency is a *crash-consistent snapshot*. With this model, the write order of data is preserved, and all blocks on the disk are backed up based on a specific, identical timestamp. This leaves files in a consistent state.

The problem is that SQL Server does not work in the same way as a filesystem. During a transaction, there could be some data in the buffer cache, pending a write to disk, and other data already written to disk. This means that when the disk or VM is restored, the database may be in an inconsistent state if transactions were in flight at the point of the backup.

Not understanding this leads to a mistake when storage and cloud teams can provide protection to VMs hosting databases by configuring crash-consistent snapshots. They do not realize that the snapshots may be causing corruption until the VM is restored.

Snapshots are often used for the quick recovery of a VM in the event of bad change. Therefore, many change plans will have a rollback plan, where a server is restored from a snapshot. If crash-consistent snapshots are being used, then this rollback plan may not suffice.

Another level of protection is an *application-consistent snapshot*. With this type of snapshot, databases are quiesced and data in memory is flushed to disk before the snapshot occurs. This ensures database consistency and makes this type of snapshot a safe option.

Application-consistent snapshots of disks hosting Windows servers are performed by using Volume Shadow Copy Service (VSS) to deal with the pending I/O. Support for application-consistent snapshots in Linux is patchy, however. For example, at the time of writing, VMware only supports Linux application-consistent snapshots with the implementation of pre-freeze and post-thaw scripts, which must be written manually. There is a similar limitation in Azure, but Microsoft provides a template configuration file on GitHub that we can populate. This configuration file can be found at https://mng.bz/GNzO.

> **Reversing the mistake**
>
> I have also seen this mistake flipped. In some organizations, teams do not use snapshots for protecting database servers at all. This is because they are aware of the corruption that can be caused by crash-consistent snapshots and therefore shy away from snapshots entirely.
>
> In reality, application-consistent snapshots can provide a very useful mechanism by which to quickly recover from a failed deployment. Of course, they should only supplement a proper database backup strategy, as opposed to replacing it, but they still have value.

While it is unlikely to be the responsibility of a DBA to configure storage snapshots, it is very important for DBAs to understand the implications of snapshots and how they should be configured. This allows the DBA to provide input and advice to the storage or cloud team that is tasked with configuring snapshots.

Snapshots can provide a quick recovery and can be a good supplement to a database backup strategy. We should advise storage teams to only configure application-consistent snapshots for database servers, however. Crash-consistent snapshots should not be used, as they may lead to restoring corrupt databases.

12.4 #81 Not testing backups

Let's go back to that old adage: "You do not have a backup until you have restored it." There is certainly some truth in this. When we are performing a backup, we are performing a heavy I/O operation to a disk, and this is often over a network. There is every possibility that there could be a blip on the network, a blip on the storage, or a bad sector. Any of these could cause a bad write, and we would not know that our backup was corrupt until we tried to restore it and find that we are unable to.

I can imagine you rolling your eyes as you read the paragraph above and thinking "But I can't restore all of my backups. I don't have the time or the disk capacity to do so!" You would be right, and I would never evangelize for an unrealistic expectation. There is a middle ground where we can increase confidence in our backups without costing a fortune in time and disk resources, but it is an approach that is commonly missed by DBAs. Not finding a middle ground is a mistake that can come back and bite very hard.

So what is this middle ground? Well, there are multiple aspects to it. First, we need to check that our backups have been completed successfully. I know this sounds obvious, but it is surprisingly common for DBAs to either not check at all or simply to ignore any failures. Second, we should verify the integrity of our backups. We will discuss each of these points in the following sections.

12.4.1 Checking that backups completed successfully

If database backups are taken through an enterprise backup tool, then it is likely that a report will be sent out each day, detailing any failed backups. As DBAs, we should ask to be included in the distribution list of that report. We should review it with our first cup of coffee each morning and chase the backup team to remediate any backup failures by rerunning the job in an appropriate window. Of course, the longer a database has been without being backed up, the greater the risk exposure. If a backup fails multiple times, we should work with the backup team to investigate the cause.

If backups are taken using native SQL Server backups, we should check that the backups are successful and remediate any failures ourselves. This can sound like an impossible task, however, especially in large estates. Therefore, it is important that we add some alerting or reporting around it.

If we have a monitoring tool that is used to monitor our SQL Server instances, we can write a custom check that checks for the success of the backup jobs. If we do not have this option, however, there are multiple ways to achieve the same outcome using SQL Server–native features.

The first way would be to add SQL Agent alerts on the SQL Agent jobs that perform the backups. The trouble with this approach is that we would also need to enable Database Mail on every SQL Server instance. This is rather cumbersome to manage and is not in line with the CIS Level 1 security benchmark for SQL Server.

The second method would be to configure a Central Management Server. This can be achieved in SQL Server Management Studio by navigating to the View menu and selecting Registered Servers. This causes the Registered Servers window to be displayed. Here, we can create a Central Management Server. Under this newly created node, we can create a Server Group that contains all of the instances in the estate. Finally, in this group, we can register all of our instances. The Registered Servers window with Central Management Server is shown in figure 12.3.

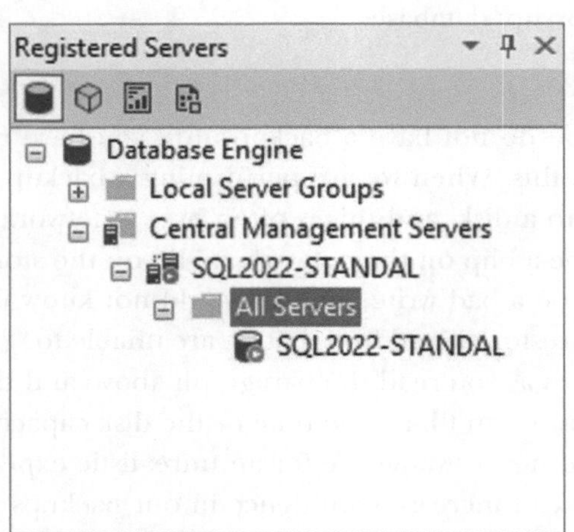

Figure 12.3 Registered Servers window

This allows us to run a query against a group of instances. When we do this, a column called `Server` will be added to the output of a query to let us know which instance the row has been returned from. Each morning, we can then run the query in listing 12.2 against the server group to see a list of any failed backups on the last run. The query uses the `ROW_NUMBER()` function to assign an incrementing number to each row. The `PARTITION BY` clause ensures that row numbers will be calculated for each individual server, and the `ORDER BY` clause will ensure that the latest execution receives the value of `1`. The outer query then filters all rows that do not have a row number of `1` (the latest execution).

> **WARNING** To use this script, ensure that you replace the job name with your own. The script assumes you have used a consistent job name for your backup jobs across all instances.

Listing 12.2 Retrieving failed backup jobs for all servers

```
SELECT
      Server
    , name
    , message
    , run_status
FROM (
    SELECT
          Server
        , j.name
        , jh.message
        , jh.run_status
        , ROW_NUMBER() OVER(PARTITION BY Server ORDER BY run_date, run_time
     DESC) AS RowNumber
    FROM msdb.dbo.sysjobhistory jh
    INNER JOIN msdb.dbo.sysjobs j
        ON j.job_id = jh.job_id
    WHERE jh.run_status = 0
    AND j.name = 'Backups'
) Results
WHERE RowNumber = 1 ;
```

The third and most complex method is to create an inventory database that stores details of all SQL Server instances within the estate. This database will ideally be populated as part of our automated instance provisioning process. It can be used for many purposes; hence the possible data items that can be stored in it are endless. For this specific purpose, however, we would need to record the server and instance name, the name and encrypted password of a login with appropriate permissions, the databases hosted on the instance, and the backup schedule required for each database.

This will allow us to write a scheduling engine that can work out which databases are due to be backed up on which servers at any given time. We can then schedule a PowerShell script to run every minute using SQL Agent. This PowerShell script will pull a list of databases that need to be backed up from the scheduling engine. The script can then pull the user and password details for the relevant instance and iterate over each to back up relevant databases. The script can then write the results back to the database. This allows us to easily manage backups from a single location, including changing backup schedules. It also allows us to easily report on backup failures from a single location.

My personal preference is to use an inventory database with a scheduling engine. I have created this in a few roles over the years, and it has worked well. I tend to use it for scheduling all common database maintenance, not just backups. It is worth considering, however, that the first time I created this it took nearly three months of effort to get everything written and set up as per the requirements of the company I was working with. While subsequent implementations have been much quicker because I now have the base code, it still takes a considerable amount of time to get everything configured and tested. Therefore, it is not an appropriate option for many organizations.

If a custom scheduling engine is not appropriate for your environment, I would recommend using a Central Management Server. This option is not ideal, because it relies on features of SQL Server Management Studio, rather than just core SQL Server features. It is still preferable to trying to manage Database Mail on every instance, however.

12.4.2 Verifying backup integrity

SQL Server provides the possibility for us to verify that a backup is valid without actually restoring it. The process reads the entire backup set to ensure that it is complete and accessible. It also performs limited data checking in an attempt to highlight as many issues as possible. If the backup has been taken with a checksum, it will validate this. It will also ensure there is enough space on disk to perform the restore.

When taking a backup, it is possible to enable page checksums. This causes a checksum of each page to be calculated and stored in the page header before it is written to disk. When the page is read from disk, the checksum can be recalculated to ensure it matches. The command in the following listing demonstrates how to turn this option on for the `Marketing` database.

Listing 12.3 Turning on page checksums

```
ALTER DATABASE Marketing
SET PAGE_VERIFY CHECKSUM ;
```

If this option is turned on, these checksums will be validated when reading pages from disk. If we then use the `WITH CHECKSUM` option when taking the backup, SQL Server will generate a database-wide checksum. When we restore a backup, or in this use case, perform a backup verification, SQL Server will ensure that the database checksum is valid.

> **NOTE** Using the `WITH CHECKSUM` option is the best option to ensure backup integrity, but it will have an impact on backup throughput. You will likely see a degradation in backup performance, especially for large databases.

The command in listing 12.4 takes a backup of the `Marketing` database using the `WITH CHECKSUM` clause to generate a checksum. We will then be able to validate the checksum when we verify our backup.

> **TIP** When following examples in this chapter, be sure to change the backup location to match your own.

Listing 12.4 Backing up a database with `checksum`

```
BACKUP DATABASE Marketing
TO  DISK = 'D:\Backup\MarketingFull27122023.bak'
WITH
      NAME = 'Marketing-Full Database Backup'
    , CHECKSUM ;
```

We can verify our backup using the `RESTORE VERIFYONLY` command. This is demonstrated for the `Marketing` database in the followng listing.

Listing 12.5 Verifying a backup

```
RESTORE VERIFYONLY
FROM DISK = 'D:\Backup\MarketingFull27122023.bak'
WITH CHECKSUM ;
```

If we take backups using native SQL Server backups, we can add a job step after the step that performs the backup to run the `RESTORE VERIFYONLY` command. We should then ensure that this job step completes successfully using one of the techniques discussed in the previous section.

If backups are being taken using an enterprise backup tool, things get a little more complicated. Most market-leading tools support the `RESTORE VERIFYONLY` feature when using their SQL Server Backup Agent, but they don't necessarily make it easy to run for all databases across the whole estate. In this instance, we will need to work with the backup team to create a scripted approach that uses the backup tool's API.

It is unlikely to be practical to fully restore every single database backup that is taken. We can find a middle ground, however, by checking that backup jobs are successful and by verifying backup integrity. If you do have the infrastructure capacity to configure an automated restore, you should consider taking it. Even with `CHECKSUM` and `RESTORE VERIFY ONLY`, it is still possible to have a corrupt backup.

12.5 #82 Taking backups during an ETL window

A well-written ETL process will be rerunnable, or, to put it another way, it will support eventual convergence. This means that, if the process were to fail part of the way through, the process can be rerun and all data processed with no data duplication occurring. For an ETL process to be rerunnable, several conditions must be met. First, the source data must be available in its original form. This can be achieved through data retention, if the source data comes from flat files, or from a configurable API. It is more complicated if the source data comes from a transactional database and will usually involve caching the data. The second condition is that the ETL process must have parameterized dates. If a process is scheduled to run at 10 p.m. and has `WHERE DataDate = GETDATE()` hardcoded, it is not rerunnable. Technically, the code could be modified and the process manually run, but the spirit of rerunnable processes means that they can be rerun without any code changes. Finally, and arguably most importantly, the process must merge data into tables as opposed to inserting it. If a process uses `INSERT` statements, there is a good chance that rerunning the process will result in some form of data duplication in a complex ETL run. This is because even though a failure will result in a transaction being completed or rolled back, large, complex ETL processes require many transactions. Therefore, even though the data will be transactionally consistent, it may not be consistent through the lens of business logic.

Unfortunately, we must accept that not all ETL processes are well written. Imagine that we have an ETL process that is not rerunnable. It uses `INSERT` statements across multiple transactions, generating new rows in multiple tables. The tables have `IDENTITY` columns, so each row is unique to SQL Server but allows for duplicate business keys. This scenario is fairly common. Let's assume that the process is configured to run at 1 a.m. and runs for 5 hours. Let us also assume that our backup schedule for this server runs a full backup at 2 a.m.

Within the first hour of running, the ETL process has extracted all of the data from various disparate sources and loaded staging tables in a data warehouse. It has also started populating tables within the star schema of the database, some of which require multiple layers of complex transformation. At 2 a.m. the backup begins, and the read phase of the backup completes 10 minutes later; this is the point of consistency for the backup—the point in time that we would restore to if we restore from this backup. The backup finishes at 2:18 a.m. and the ETL process completes at 5:56 a.m. But then disaster strikes. At just after 6 a.m., the storage fails completely and corrupts the database. We have no choice but to restore it from a backup. This issue is illustrated in figure 12.4.

We restore the database from the backup that we took at 2 a.m., and the application support team reruns the ETL process. Unfortunately, when the business performs its checks on the recovered system, it finds that the data is inconsistent. Some but not all data has been duplicated. We restore the previous night's backup, and the application support team reruns the last two nightly ETL runs. The business checks the data and finds that there are now duplicates for the previous day.

Note that, given the ETL process takes around 5 hours to complete and assuming the restores take 30 minutes and the data checks also take 30 minutes, we are now 18 hours into a P1 incident, and we have still not restored service. Everybody is very tired and very stressed, and the next day's ETL run is due to start in 1 hour.

This situation could well be described as a nightmare. I know this because it is loosely based on a scenario that I encountered on a mission-critical system I inherited some years ago. There are only two solutions in this scenario. The first is for a developer or application support team to spend the next [insert a scarily high number] of hours manually running queries to deduplicate data in base tables and deleting data from the tables that store the complex calculations. They would then have to manually run some aspects of the ETL process to perform the complex calculations.

The second option would be to restore versions of the database from the last two backups. A developer or application support team would then spend the next [insert equally scarily high number] of hours attempting to merge data from the two databases to form a single, coherent dataset. They would likely then have to delete data from the tables that store the complex calculations. They would then have to manually run some aspects of the ETL process to perform those complex calculations again.

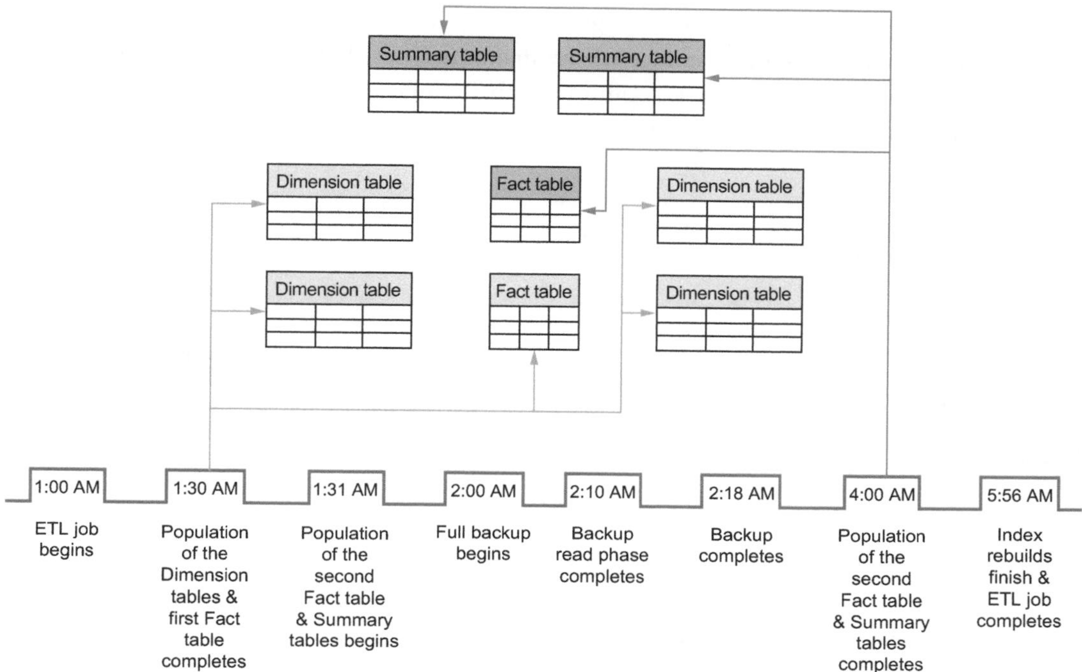

Figure 12.4 Backup during ETL

Either method is equally risky and time consuming. Both methods are likely to leave the data in an imperfect state, unless there is as much luck as there is skill involved in the fix. Depending on the type of data being fixed, this could potentially result in poor business decisions being made or even regulatory noncompliance. The simple moral of this story is that it is a mistake to take backups at the same time as an ETL process is running. DBAs should always assume the worst.

Another consideration, even if our ETL processes are well written, is performance. Complex ETL processes are often resource intensive and can require good disk performance. If we run backups at the same time as the ETL processes, then we are very likely to cause a performance impediment.

So what should we do differently? I have seen scenarios with long-running ETL processes, which means there is no time to perform a full backup of the database outside of business hours, either before or after an ETL process.

The answer depends very much on the data involved, but there are multiple possible solutions. The first possibility I tend to look for is what I call *creative scheduling*. Often a data warehouse is sized to allow for ETL processes to run efficiently within a window. This can mean the server is actually oversize for its use during the working day. If this is the case, we may be able to just take the full backup during the business day, when data is being read but not modified.

This scenario is illustrated in figure 12.5, which illustrates disk throughput over a 24-hour period, as a percentage of the maximum possible throughput. The working day has significantly lower throughput than the maximum, even when we take a full backup in the middle of the day.

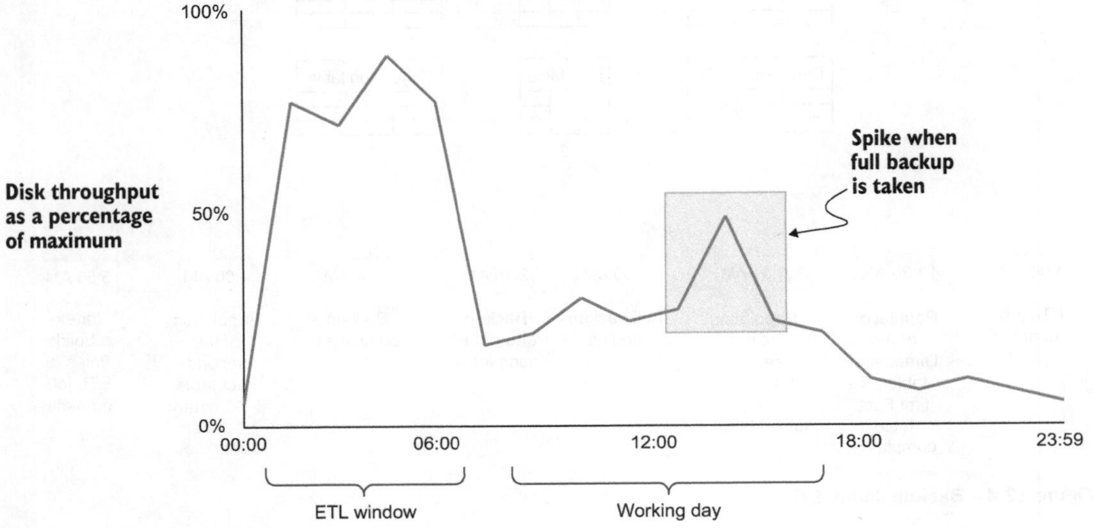

Figure 12.5 Disk throughput over 24 hours

If creative scheduling is not possible, then another option is to use differential backups. In this scenario, we would take a full database backup at weekends and a differential at the end of the ETL run each day. This can be a good, pragmatic solution but may not work in some cases. A differential backup contains all pages that have been modified since the last full backup. If we are running a large ETL process every night and also performing tasks such as index rebuilds (see chapter 11), then by the end of the week a differential backup may be so large that it also does not complete within the given window.

Finally, we could consider filegroup backups. This is my option of last resort, as it introduces both complexity and risk. In this scenario, we would back up different filegroups on different days of the week, as illustrated in figure 12.6. The complexity comes from having to piece together multiple backup files to perform the restore. The risk is that we may not be able to meet the required RPO.

CAUTION If we have an RPO of 24 hours (which is common in this kind of system), we would not meet the requirements with this approach. The business would need to accept this risk before we implemented it.

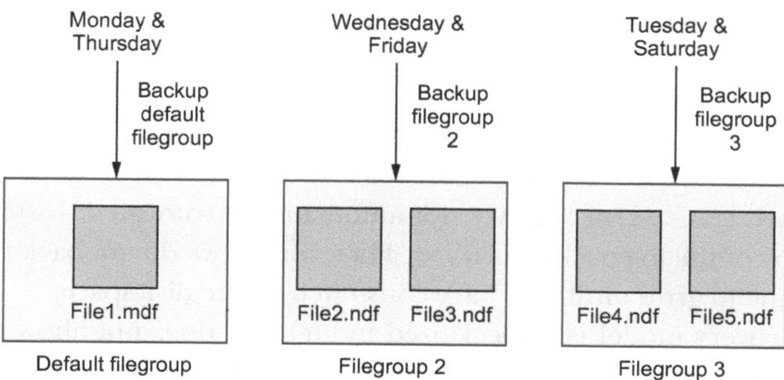

Figure 12.6 Filegroup backup strategy

We should always consider ETL processes when scheduling backups and avoid them overlapping. Sometimes we can achieve this by simply scheduling backups to occur in a different window. If this isn't possible, we could consider taking nightly differential backups and weekly full backups. As a last resort, we could consider filegroup backups, but this not only adds complexity but also has negative effects on the RPO.

12.6 #83 Always using the FULL recovery model on data warehouse and development systems

The database *recovery model* defines how a database is protected. There are three recovery models; `FULL`, `SIMPLE`, and `BULK LOGGED`. When a database is set to `SIMPLE` recovery model, we are only able to take full backups and differential backups. Transaction log backups are not possible. Full backups are mandatory to be able to restore the database, and differential backups are optional. When in `SIMPLE` recovery model, SQL Server automatically truncates the transaction log when a checkpoint occurs. This process is used to flush modified (dirty) pages from the buffer cache to disk. A checkpoint is triggered based on the specified recovery interval of the database and when certain operations, such as a backup, are performed. It can also be triggered manually by a DBA running the `CHECKPOINT ;` command. These recovery models are set out in table 12.2.

Table 12.2 Recovery models

Recovery model	Full backups	Differential backups	Transaction log backups	Log truncation	Protection level provided
`SIMPLE`	Yes	Optional	No	At checkpoint	Transactionally consistent
`BULK LOGGED`	Yes	Optional	Yes	Log backup	Recovers to end of a backup
`FULL`	Yes	Optional	Yes	Log backup	Recovers to a specific point in time within a backup

NOTE In recovery models other than `SIMPLE`, a checkpoint does not truncate the transaction log.

When we are in FULL recovery model, we must take both full and transaction log backups. Differential backups are, again, optional. The transaction log backup allows us to perform a restore to a specific point in time. This is opposed to full and differential backups, where we must restore the complete backup set. When in FULL recovery model, it is vital that we perform transaction log backups. This is because when in FULL recovery model, transaction logs are not automatically truncated. Instead, they are truncated as part of the log backup process. Therefore, if we do not back them up, they will just continue to grow until they have consumed all the disk space.

BULK LOGGED recovery model is a specialized model that does not allow point-in-time recovery. It can be used to improve the performance of bulk insert operations. We would usually only use this model for a short time, during a heavy ETL process, when the normal recovery model for the database is FULL.

There is a common misconception that FULL recovery model should be used for all databases. There is an even more common misconception that FULL recovery model should be used for all production databases but not for nonproduction databases. Following these misconceptions would be a mistake.

The choice of recovery model should be based primarily on the recovery requirements for a database. If we consider a development database, it is likely the data rarely changes. It is much more likely that the database schema changes, and if the developers are following modern development practices, these changes will frequently be checked into source control.

TIP See chapter 7 for more information on source control.

This means that the RPO for the database will be much higher than for a production database and there is unlikely to be a requirement to restore it to a specific point in time. This means there is no need to take transaction log backups. We can simply take a daily, or perhaps even a weekly, backup on the database. If we were to use FULL recovery model for such development databases, we would also need to manage the transaction log backups, which means additional effort for no benefit.

That explains why SIMPLE is often the correct recovery model for a development database, but what about data warehouses that run in production? Because they are production databases, then surely we will have a much lower RPO and a requirement to restore to a point in time, right?

Well, this is not often the case. Consider a typical data warehouse or data mart that is populated by a nightly ETL process and then is used for reporting during the day. In this scenario, the RPO of the database is actually 24 hours. The only need is to be able to restore the database to a point after the last ETL run. Therefore, SIMPLE recovery model is often the most appropriate choice.

I have seen several large data warehouses that have suffered performance problems on their nightly ETL runs because of a poor choice of recovery model. The issue is that when we are in FULL recovery model, much more information is written to the transaction log. SQL Server needs to be able to restore the database to any given point.

Therefore, the logging is verbose, even including the specific pages that have been allocated to complete a transaction.

In SIMPLE recovery model, however, SQL Server only needs the transaction log to be able to roll back a transaction and leave the database in a consistent state. Therefore, far less data needs to be written. To follow from the example of FULL recovery model recording every allocated page, SIMPLE recovery model, by contrast only needs to record the allocation of extents. Because there are eight pages in an extent, this can be as low as 1/8 of the data.

We should always make the best possible decision for a specific use case. This means that we should consider the most appropriate recovery model for any given database, as opposed to using a blanket rule.

12.7 #84 Using SIMPLE recovery model for OLTP databases

In the last section, we explored the consequences of the inappropriate use of the FULL recovery model. In this section, we will flip that mistake around and explore the consequences of inappropriate use of the SIMPLE recovery model.

I have seen some environments where DBAs have used SIMPLE as their default recovery model for all databases, including databases with OLTP-style workloads, in production. Reasons for this include problems with the transaction log filling up the disk and the system being too busy to tolerate more than one backup a day. These reasons are often erroneous, however. Let's explore them.

Regarding the transaction log filling up the disk, we explored log truncation in the previous section and the fact that, in FULL recovery model, transaction logs are truncated at the point of a transaction log backup. Therefore, we can avoid the transaction log continuously growing and consuming all disk space by ensuring we take transaction log backups. If we take a transaction log backup and the log is not truncated, then we need to investigate the reason. The query in the following listing will determine why the log was not truncated on the previous attempt.

Listing 12.6 Exploring the reason the log was not truncated

```
SELECT
      name
    , log_reuse_wait_desc
FROM sys.databases ;
```

Many of the reasons that a log fails to truncate are transient and down to unfortunate timing, such as no checkpoint occurring since the last backup, an active backup or restore process being in operation, or the creation of a database snapshot being in progress.

There are some other reasons that are usually transient but that, if they occur repeatedly and cause the transaction log to start growing wildly, should be investigated. For example, a common reason is that there was an active transaction. This is usually transient, but if our data-tier application has many long-running transactions, this can cause problems—and not just issues for log backups but also issues with lock contention or deadlocks. Developers may need to address this to avoid transactions running for extended periods of time.

If the reason for the log not being truncated is either `REPLICATION` or `AVAILABILITY_REPLICA`, this means that transactions are being applied to the secondary databases. If this persists, there may be an issue with delivering or applying these transactions. We should check our monitoring tools and dashboards to ensure that our replication or AlwaysOn availability group topology is healthy and to understand the latency in applying transactions.

A wait type of `XTP_CHECKPOINT` can occur when we use memory-optimized tables. Memory-optimized checkpoints flush the data streams of persistent memory-optimized tables to disk. A log truncation issue related to memory-optimized checkpoints can occur for several reasons that need to be dealt with. First, in older versions of SQL Server, such as 2014 or 2016, there were some bugs that caused issues with memory-optimized table checkpoints, and we should apply the latest service pack and cumulative update.

Another reason for this issue is that, when we have memory-optimized tables, automatic checkpoints only occur when the transaction log has 1.5 GB of transactions since the last checkpoint. For smaller systems, I have seen this lead to not enough data being written to the log to ever cause a checkpoint to occur, and therefore log truncation never happens. If this is the case, we may need to schedule a manual checkpoint to occur prior to the transaction log backup. If our backups are scheduled with SQL Agent, we can simply add a job step before the step that takes the log backup. If our backups are taken by an enterprise backup tool, we will have to collaborate with the backup administrators to add a prebackup step into the backup policy.

> **TIP** If a server has 16 cores and 128 GB of RAM or more, large checkpoints will be enabled. This means that the checkpoint only occurs after 12 GB has been written to the log since the last checkpoint.

It is important to understand that, although referred to as log truncation, it is actually virtual log files (VLFs) that are truncated. Truncation can only happen as far as the first active VLF. If any VLF other than the VLF currently in use fails to truncate, the `log_reuse_wait_desc` column will show the reason. The transaction log illustrated in figure 12.7 would show a `log_reuse_wait_desc` of `ACTIVE_TRANSACTION`, although two VLFs are truncated.

This means that all but one of the VLFs may have truncated and there is no issue. We can determine the number of VLFs in use by running the query in listing 12.7. This query returns the total number of VLFs, the number of VLFs in use, and the reason for the last truncation failure (which is the same as `log_reuse_wait_desc`) for the `Marketing` database from the `sys.dm_db_log_stats` DMF.

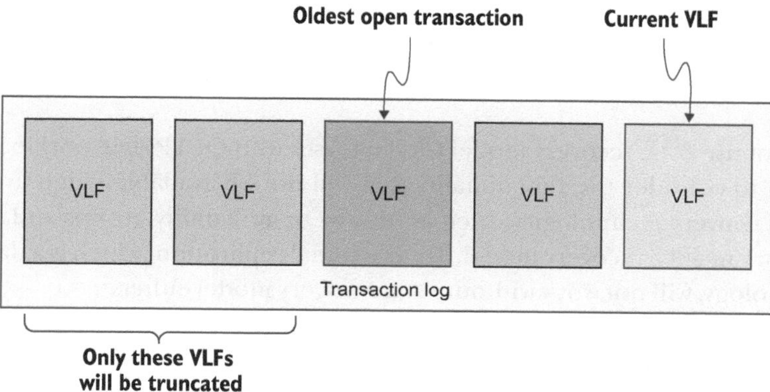

Figure 12.7 VLF truncation

Listing 12.7 Determining how many VLFs are active

```
SELECT
      total_vlf_count
    , active_vlf_count
    , log_truncation_holdup_reason
FROM sys.dm_db_log_stats(DB_ID('Marketing')) ;
```

When we think about a system being too busy to accept more than one backup a day as a reason for not using FULL recovery model, we need to take a step back and think about the implications of this. There are two main points to consider.

First, we need to consider the RPO of the database. If a database is so busy that it is difficult to schedule multiple backups, then it is likely that the database has a high rate of change. This means that the database may have a very short RPO. If this is the case, it is likely that taking a single, full backup each day will not meet our recovery requirements.

The second thing we should consider is the impact of taking the log backup. While a full backup can cause a performance impact on the database and is best scheduled during a period of low or no use, a transaction log backup has comparatively small impact. The transaction log is usually no more than 20% of the size of the database in total and will not necessarily be full at the point we take the backup. In fact, the more often we take a transaction log backup, the fewer VLFs will need to be backed up and the smaller the impact.

If a transaction log backup is causing performance issues on a data-tier application, there are several things that we can consider. We could consider taking log backups more frequently, which would reduce their duration. If we are using AlwaysOn availability groups, we could schedule our backups to occur on a secondary server, meaning that there is no performance impact on the primary. Finally, if a transaction log backup is causing performance issues, we need to ask ourselves if the server is appropriately sized. While I usually don't advocate for "throwing more hardware at the problem," a server needs to meet its use case, and that includes catering to nonfunctional requirements such as RPO.

If we do not use FULL recovery model for databases with OLTP-style workloads, then we also need to consider the functionality that will not be available. High availability and disaster recovery technologies, such as AlwaysOn availability groups and log shipping, only work in FULL recovery model. Transactional replication, which is a data distribution technology, will not work without FULL recovery model either.

It is usually a mistake to use SIMPLE recovery model for a database that supports OLTP-style workloads in a production environment. We can overcome issues with using FULL recovery model by ensuring that we have a transaction log backup strategy or by troubleshooting issues with long-running transactions and memory-optimized tables.

The most important reason for using FULL recovery model is to ensure that we have an RPO that meets the needs of the business. We should also consider, however, high availability and data distribution technologies, which rely on FULL recovery model.

12.8 #85 Not backing up after changing recovery model

A common mistake I see when a preproduction database is promoted in place to become a full production database is that the recovery model is changed from SIMPLE to FULL and transaction log backups are scheduled alongside the full backups and left to run. This sounds perfectly reasonable, doesn't it? So why is it an issue?

Let's imagine that we promote our database to production at 2 p.m. We have a full backup scheduled at midnight, and we have scheduled transaction log backups to occur every 30 minutes. This means that after the promotion there will be 19 transaction log backups before the next full backup.

Let's see this in action. The script in the following listing creates a new database called PromotionDB, with the SIMPLE recovery model, and then takes a backup of the database.

Listing 12.8 Creating a database and taking a full backup

```
CREATE DATABASE PromotionDB ;          -- Creates the database
GO

ALTER DATABASE PromotionDB SET RECOVERY SIMPLE ;     -- Ensures SIMPLE recovery model is set
GO

USE PromotionDB ;
GO

CREATE TABLE dbo.Incidental (
    ID    INT
) ;
GO
```

```
BACKUP DATABASE PromotionDB
TO  DISK = 'D:\Backups\PromotionDBSimpleBackup.bak' ;
GO
```

Performs a full backup of the database

Now let's imagine that it's time to promote the database. The script in listing 12.9 changes the recovery model to `FULL`. It then simulates user activity by inserting some data into the table.

Listing 12.9 Promoting the database

```
ALTER DATABASE PromotionDB SET RECOVERY FULL ;
GO

INSERT INTO dbo.Incidental
SELECT object_id
FROM sys.all_objects ;
```

Next, we can simulate our SQL Agent job, which runs the transaction log backups, by using the command in the following listing.

Listing 12.10 Backing up the transaction log

```
BACKUP LOG PromotionDB
TO DISK = 'D:\Backups\PromotionDBLogBackupInFull.trn' ;
```

Oh dear! Running this command to back up the transaction log fails with the following error:

```
Msg 4214, Level 16, State 1, Line 1
BACKUP LOG cannot be performed because there is no current database backup.
Msg 3013, Level 16, State 1, Line 1
BACKUP LOG is terminating abnormally.
```

But we clearly took a full database backup in listing 12.8. So what is the problem?

The trouble comes from a little-known fact: after changing a database from `SIMPLE` recovery model to `FULL` recovery model, we must initialize the new recovery model with a full backup. If we do not, then effectively the database remains in `SIMPLE` recovery model until a full backup has been taken.

Therefore, in our example, there will be 19 failed transaction log backups before the next full database backup. When the scheduled full backup runs at midnight, then the issue will sort itself out and the subsequent log backups will succeed. This does not help in the meantime, however. If we are unlucky enough to have an issue on the first day and need to perform a restore, we will not be able to.

So what should we do differently? Well, it's fairly simple. We just need to ensure that when we change the recovery model of the database, we also perform a full backup of the database. We should ensure that this is part of our deployment process when we are promoting a database.

12.9 #86 Scheduling log backups immediately after a full backup

I have seen, on more than one occasion, an accidental DBA, knowing that they need to take transaction log backups to enable point-in-time restores, create a SQL Agent job to perform backups on the schedule depicted in figure 12.8. This job will take a full database backup and then immediately take a transaction log backup.

Creating a backup schedule like this is a mistake, but let's explore why. The reason the DBA has scheduled a transaction log backup is to enable point-in-time recovery. Technically, the solution works. The transaction log holds all transactions since the last transaction log backup.

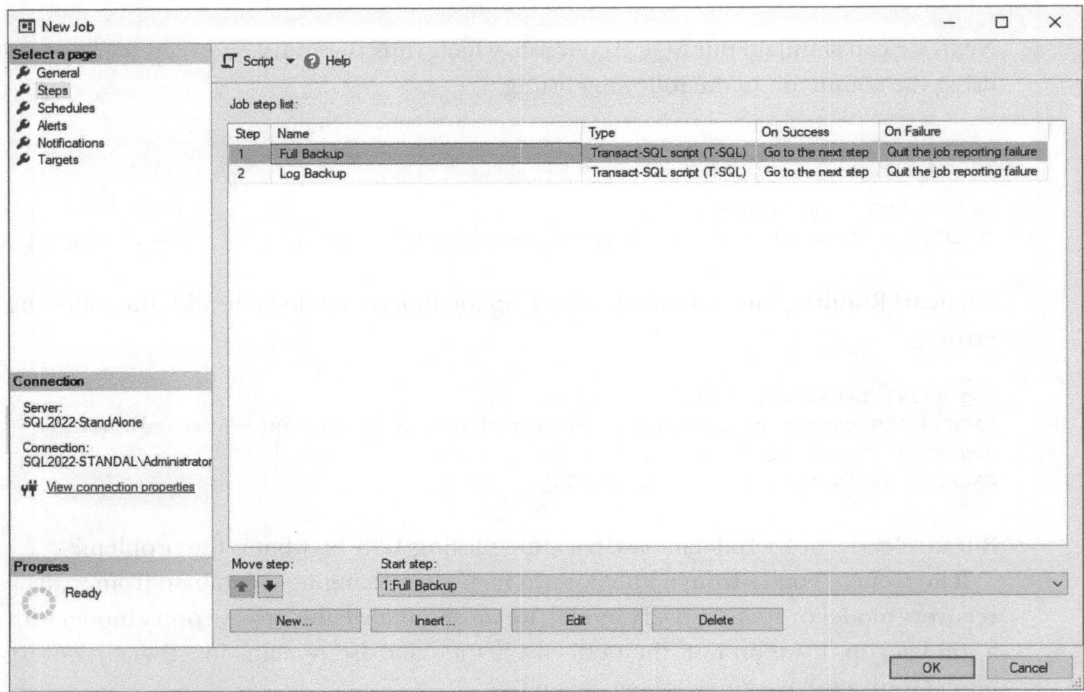

Figure 12.8 Mistaken backup schedule

Imagine that this SQL Agent job is scheduled to run at midnight every day. If there is an incident at 10 a.m. in which someone accidentally deletes some data and we are tasked with restoring the database to 9:55 a.m., then we can achieve this. We would take another transaction log backup and then restore the data to the desired point in time.

The problem occurs if there is a catastrophic failure. At 10 a.m., the disk array that the database is stored on fails, and we need to restore the database to a new server. In this scenario, we are unable to take a transaction log backup. Our only option is to restore the full backup. In this scenario, the log backup that we took immediately after the full database backup is useless.

What we should do instead is schedule our transaction log backups in line with the required RPO of the database. If the maximum acceptable data loss for a database is 1 hour, we should schedule our log backups to happen once per hour. While scheduling a log backup immediately after a full database backup will technically allow for point-in-time recovery, it does nothing to help achieve the required RPO.

12.10 #87 Not using COPY_ONLY backups for ad hoc backups

There are occasions when we will need to take a database backup that is outside of our usual backup schedule. This is often to provide a restore point immediately prior to a change or because we want to refresh a development environment with the latest cut of data from production. If we take a normal full backup, however, we can cause issues with our restore sequence. Imagine that we have the following backups scheduled:

- 1 a.m.—Full backup
- 6 a.m.—Differential backup
- 12 p.m.—Differential backup
- 6 p.m.—Differential backup
- Transaction log backups every hour

Under normal operations, in the event of a failure occurring at 1:30 p.m., our restore sequence would be as follows:

- Restore full backup from 1 a.m.
- Restore differential backup from 12 p.m.
- Restore transaction log backup from 1 p.m.

Now imagine that we performed a change at 10 a.m. and, as part of this change, we took a full database backup as our rollback strategy. The change was successful, so we discarded the full backup.

The issue is that, when we took the full backup at 10 a.m., this became the differential base for the differential backups that are taken at 12 p.m. and 6 p.m., and because we discarded it we are no longer able to restore these differential backups.

Therefore, the restore sequence in our scenario becomes

- Restore full backup from 1 a.m.
- Restore differential from 6 a.m.
- Restore seven transaction log backups, from 7 a.m. to 1 p.m.

If we are unaware that a backup was taken at 10 a.m., then we are likely to attempt the standard restore sequence and waste valuable time trying to debug why we cannot restore that differential from 12 p.m.

What should we do differently? Backups in SQL Server have a feature called `COPY_ONLY`. This is designed specifically for the use case where we need to take an ad hoc backup outside of our normal schedule. Specifically, it will not impact the differential base and therefore not impact our restore sequence.

The command in the following listing demonstrates how to take a `COPY_ONLY` backup of the `Marketing` database.

Listing 12.11 Taking a `COPY_ONLY` backup

```
BACKUP DATABASE Marketing
TO  DISK = 'D:\Backups\MarketingFullCopyOnly.bak'
WITH COPY_ONLY ;
```

If we take differential backups, then ad hoc backups should be taken using the `COPY_ONLY` option to avoid affecting the differential base and changing our restore sequence. Personally, as a good practice, I always use `COPY_ONLY` for ad hoc backups, even where no differentials are taken. There is no negative impact of doing so, and it means that I don't have to worry about checking the backup schedules.

12.11 #88 Forgetting that backups are part of our security posture

We usually consider backups from the perspective of data recovery. Unfortunately, however, we live in a world where we must also consider security risks, such as ransomware attacks. Backups are a key aspect in protecting our organizations against this form of attack but only if we consider it when we are planning our backup strategy. So what might happen if we do not take ransomware into consideration when planning our backup strategy?

Imagine that we take backups using SQL Server's native backup functionality and store them on a file share. An attacker strikes, and we suddenly find that our databases have been deleted. We attempt to restore them from the backups, only to find that the file share has been encrypted and we cannot access it. At best, this will be very costly. At worst, there will be regulatory issues and brand damage. At this point, it will become clear that our backup strategy was a mistake.

To avoid the attack being successful, we need to consider providing an air gap for our backups. If we take backups using an enterprise backup tool, then depending on our environment, it is likely that our backups will already be offloaded to a tape robot, where tapes can be ejected and are therefore not subject to attack, or that we will use a backup provider's cloud-based ransomware protection. This usually involves offloading the backups to cloud storage, which is owned and managed by the backup vendor and therefore is not subject to the attack either.

If we take our backups using SQL Server native backup, however, then we must take responsibility for ensuring that our backups are protected. The best way to achieve this is to offload our backups to cloud-native storage where we can implement storage, lifecycle policies. For example, Azure Blob Storage provides us with time-based retention policies, which include container-level write once, read many storage, which will prevent blobs within the container from being altered for the duration of the retention period.

As an additional security method, we should ensure our database backups are encrypted. To encrypt our backups, we must first ensure there is a database master key in the `master` database. We must also ensure there is a certificate created in the `master` database that can be used to encrypt our backups. The script in the following listing demonstrates how to create the prerequisite cryptographic objects in the `master` database.

Listing 12.12 Creating cryptographic objects required to encrypt backups

```
USE master ;
GO

CREATE MASTER KEY                                    <-- Creates a database master key
    ENCRYPTION BY PASSWORD = 'Pa$$w0rd' ;
GO

CREATE CERTIFICATE CertForBackupEncryption           <-- Creates the certificate
   WITH SUBJECT = 'Backup Encryption Certificate' ;
GO
```

Before we use our certificate, it is very important that we back it up to a safe location. If we lose our certificate, there will be no way to recover our encrypted backups. Essentially, we will be performing a ransomware attack on ourselves! The command in the following listing demonstrates how to back up a certificate.

Listing 12.13 Backing up a certificate

```
BACKUP CERTIFICATE CertForBackupEncryption
TO FILE = 'c:\Certs\CertForBackupEncryptionCert'
WITH PRIVATE KEY (
    FILE = 'c:\certs\CertForBackupEncryptionPK' ,
    ENCRYPTION BY PASSWORD = 'Pa$$w0rd'
) ;
```

With these objects in place, we can now use the command in listing 12.14 to perform an encrypted backup. Using the `WITH ENCRYPTION` option, we specify the desired encryption algorithm (in our scenario, that is AES 256) and the certificate that should be used to encrypt the data.

Listing 12.14 Performing an encrypted backup

```
BACKUP DATABASE Marketing
TO  DISK = 'D:\Backups\MarketingFull256.bak'
WITH ENCRYPTION (
      ALGORITHM = AES_256
    , SERVER CERTIFICATE = CertForBackupEncryption
) ;
```

A full list of supported encryption algorithms in SQL Server 2022 is as follows:

- AES 128
- AES 192
- AES 256
- Triple DES

TIP We should be mindful that the longer the algorithm, the higher the performance impact.

When we consider backups, we should consider security as well as recovering from disaster. We should ensure that our backups are stored on immutable storage; ideally this storage will be disconnected from our network. We should also limit exposure by ensuring that our backups are encrypted.

Summary

- Point-in-time restore refers to restoring a database to a specific point in time in the middle of a transaction log backup.
- A restore chain refers to the sequence of backup files that must be restored.
- RPO defines the acceptable amount of data loss in the event of a disaster.
- RTO defines the acceptable duration of downtime in the event of a disaster.
- When planning your backup strategy, ensure that you consider both the RPO and RTO and define your strategy accordingly.
- Database snapshots use copy-on-write technology to provide a point-in-time snapshot of a database.
- A database snapshot can complement a backup strategy, but it cannot replace it because the snapshot relies on data pages in the source database.
- Storage snapshots back up data at the block level and provide a means of quickly recovering a volume.
- If storage snapshots are used with SQL Server, it is important that application-consistent snapshots are used.
- Crash-consistent snapshots can cause database corruption, as they do not use VSS Writer to flush pending I/O to disk.
- It is important to validate that backups have been successful. You can do this using `RESTORE WITH VERIFY ONLY`.
- Avoid taking backups during an ETL window because not all ETL processes are rerunnable. This can lead to the backups being worthless.
- `FULL` recovery model allows for transaction log files to be backed up.
- In `FULL` recovery model, the log is only truncated during the transaction log backup process.
- `SIMPLE` recovery model only allows for full and differential backups to be taken.

- In `SIMPLE` recovery model, the transaction log is automatically truncated when a checkpoint occurs.
- A checkpoint flushes data that has been modified in memory to the disk.
- You do not always need to use a `FULL` recovery model for nonproduction databases or data warehouses, even when they are in production. The required RPO may not justify it.
- In general, use `FULL` recovery model for OLTP-style databases in production. Not doing so can impact the RPO and stop you from using high-availability features.
- After changing the recovery model of a database, always perform a full backup. If you change a database from `SIMPLE` recovery model to `FULL` recovery model, the change will not take effect until a full database backup has been taken.
- Do not schedule a single transaction log backup to happen after a full database backup. While this will allow for point-in-time recovery, it will not help achieve database RPO requirements.
- If you need to take an ad hoc backup outside of your routine backup schedule, use the `WITH COPY_ONLY` option. This will avoid impacting the differential base and therefore altering your restore sequence.
- Remember that backups play an important role in security. Specifically, they can help protect against ransomware attacks.
- Ensure that your backups are either air gapped or that they reside on immutable storage with an appropriate retention policy.
- Ensure that your backups are encrypted to offer an additional layer of protection against cyberattacks.

13 Availability

This chapter covers

- The difference between high availability and disaster recovery
- Availability requirements
- Testing disaster recovery
- When AlwaysOn availability groups are appropriate
- Overloading clusters

High availability (HA) and disaster recovery (DR) are key concepts that every database administrator (DBA) should fully understand to make the correct implementation choices and protect their environments from single points of failure. The topic is both broad and deep, and this chapter does not attempt to focus on the actual implementation of HA and DR. Instead, we will focus on some of the key mistakes that DBAs make when planning their HA and DR strategy. For guidance on how to implement HA and DR in SQL Server, I recommend my book *SQL Server 2019 AlwaysOn*, which can be found at https://mng.bz/znaQ.

As SQL Server has matured, the scope of concepts and technologies that DBAs need to understand to implement HA and DR has increased dramatically. For example, to implement AlwaysOn availability groups (which we will now refer to as just availability groups), DBAs need to have an understanding of Windows clustering. Even if the implementation is a collaboration with a Windows team, DBAs must still understand the concepts.

In this chapter, we will first focus on the concepts of HA and DR, as I still find a reasonable number of DBAs get these confused, which can lead to risk and ultimately outage of critical business applications. We will then discuss the implications of not architecting a HA/DR strategy against the business requirements.

We will explore the risks associated with not testing our DR strategy, which is a surprisingly common reality. We will then discuss why availability groups are not always the correct solution, which will prevent a common pitfall. Finally, we will discuss the consequences of overloading a cluster and how this can lead to extended downtime in the event of an incident.

13.1 #89 Confusing HA and DR

Disaster recovery (DR) refers to the mechanism used to recover a database in the event of a critical incident. This incident may range from a corrupt database to a dead server. It could even be the loss of a whole data center or cloud availability zone. The most basic form of DR is a backup–restore strategy, but many critical applications require a solution that provides faster recovery in the event of a disaster. This is achieved through redundant hardware, usually in a different geographical location, which is kept synchronized with the production system. This is known as a *warm standby*.

High availability (HA), on the other hand, refers to the mechanism used for a database to automatically fail over and recover itself in the event of an issue on the production server. This also requires redundant hardware, but that hardware is often stored in the same location as the production server. The close proximity reduces network latency during the synchronization and also any client-to-server latency after failover has occurred. The redundant infrastructure in this scenario is called *hot standby*.

The mistake that I see some DBAs make is confusing these two concepts. While they are similar and have some overlap, they serve different use cases. Therefore, I have seen DBAs configuring an HA topology and then telling the business that they have implemented DR. As long as they are taking backups of the databases involved in the HA topology and storing them off-site, what they have said is technically true, but it misleads the business.

Why does this matter? The answer is that the business is left with the misconception that it can quickly recover from a far wider range of failures than is actually the case. The perfect example is the loss of a data center. This can happen for many reasons, including loss of power, a bad network change to a core switch, or even a natural disaster.

The diagram in figure 13.1 illustrates an HA topology configured using availability groups. The topology has two servers, and each is located in a different server rack in the same data center. This means that the server, the rack, and the top of rack switch have been removed as single points of failure. This has led the DBA to believe that DR is in place.

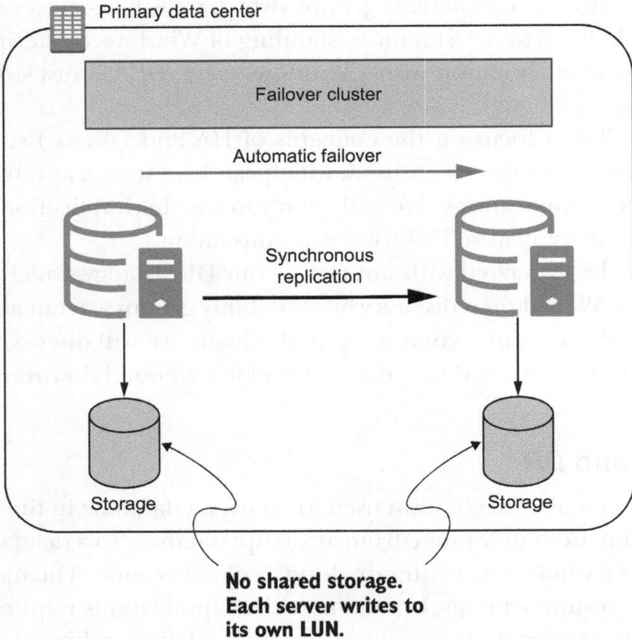

Figure 13.1 HA topology with availability groups providing automatic failover in a single site

The trouble with citing this topology as DR is that there are still many single points of failure, and it is not possible to recover from all failure scenarios. For example, imagine that there is a power outage to the data center or that the data center floods. Depending on the data center topology, the loss of a critical networking component, such as a core switch, could even bring down the whole environment, leaving the DBA with a need for a server to be spun up in a different data center or cloud environment, ready to restore from the latest backup.

Now let's consider the topology illustrated in figure 13.2. This is a DR topology that does not offer HA. In other words, the redundant server is in a second data center and allows us to quickly recover service in the event of a disaster. It is not providing HA, however. The definition of HA is there will be automatic failover, and this design relies on a manual failover process. In this configuration, the cluster is known as a *multisubnet failover cluster* because it will have virtual IPs associated with each subnet, to allow failover between the sites.

TIP A subnet is a division within a larger network. Typically, each site will have its own subnet(s). This reduces the amount of traffic sent across the WAN link, because it avoids network traffic such as broadcasts being sent between sites.

So why don't we simply configure HA across two data centers and kill two birds with one stone? In some environments, where there is a very fast low latency link between the two sites, this may be possible. Generally speaking, however, the challenge is how the redundant infrastructure is synchronized.

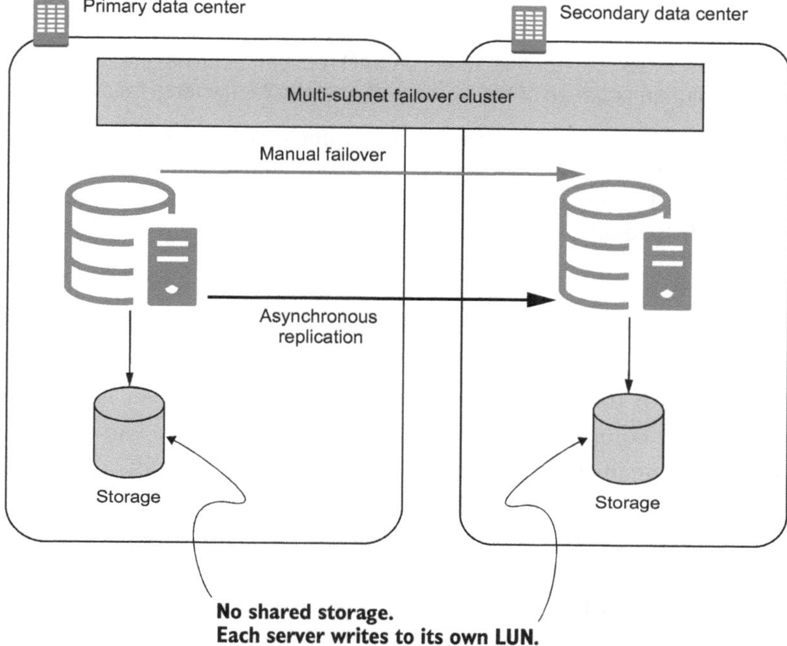

Figure 13.2 DR topology with availability groups providing manual failover between sites

Technologies like availability groups replicate data synchronously when used to provide HA. This means that no data can be lost if an unexpected failure occurs. It also means, however, that every write must complete on the secondary server before it completes on the primary server. If the servers are not close to each other, network latency will increase, and this will have a damaging effect on performance.

Availability groups vs. traditional clustering

If traditional clustering is used to provide HA, then instead of synchronizing the data, only one copy of the data is held, usually on a storage area network (SAN). This means there is no network latency involved in synchronizing the data and hence no performance issue.

This also means that the storage introduces more single points of failure into the topology, however—for example, the network connection to the SAN, the storage controller, and the storage itself. These single points of failure are usually on paper only, however. In reality, a cluster will usually have a resilient network path to the SAN. The SAN will have multiple nodes and the storage itself will be configured in a RAID array.

The real benefit of availability groups over traditional clustering is its flexibility. It can be used to implement HA, DR, and even read scaling. A traditional cluster can accommodate HA only, because it is in a single data center. While it is possible to configure a

> ***(continued)***
>
> geographically dispersed cluster that relies on SAN replication cross-site; this is often not a supportable solution because of the number of complexities when a failover is required.
>
> Availability groups also allow for a more granular implementation. Clustering is implemented at the instance level, whereas with availability groups, the implementation is at the database level. This means that it is possible to configure just the most important databases with HA to reduce the overhead.

When used to provide DR, technologies like availability groups will instead replicate the data asynchronously. This means each write is completed on the primary server and then replicated to the secondary. Because the primary server is not waiting for confirmation of write completion, we can avoid the performance issues caused by network latency. It also means there is the risk of a small amount of data loss. How much data loss occurs will depend on network performance as well as the performance of the servers. If the servers are undersized, there is the risk of a queue of transactions building up, waiting to be synchronized.

Many critical systems will require both HA and DR to be configured. This can be achieved in a variety of different ways. Technologies can be mixed, or we can simply use availability groups for the whole implementation. For example, consider the topology in figure 13.3. This illustrates a topology where availability groups have been used to implement both HA and DR.

It is important that DBAs understand the difference between HA and DR. Failure to understand these concepts can lead to a situation where the business thinks it has a higher level of protection than it actually does.

13.2 #90 Failing to architect for the requirements

To determine the correct HA/DR architecture to build for an application, we must understand the availability requirements. The trouble is that if we ask an application owner, "How long can your application be down?" the answer will invariably be "It can't!"

On the surface, this is fine. In theory, we could build a full HA/DR topology for every single application in our organization. The problem with this approach is that it quickly becomes very expensive. If we are lucky enough to have a solution architect and a business analyst involved in the project, then this is less of an issue because they will be responsible for understanding the requirements and defining the appropriate solution. As DBAs, we will simply implement their design.

Unfortunately, we are not always lucky enough to have access to architectural or analysis resources. This means that DBAs sometimes need to fill this gap. A common mistake I see DBAs make in this scenario is to simply accept what an application owner states as their availability requirements. When we rely on an application owner to make this decision in isolation, however, they often do not understand the implications of their request.

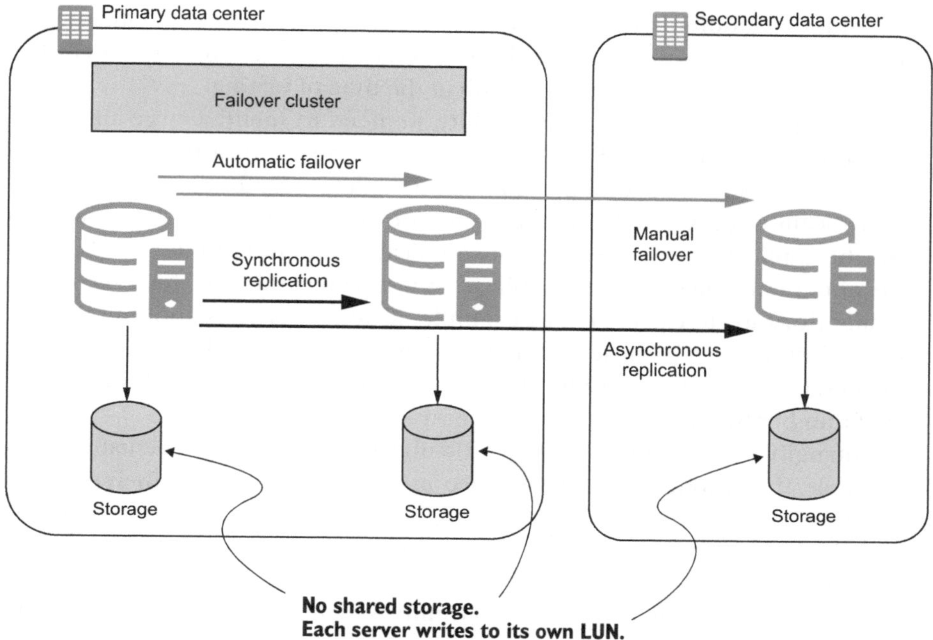

Figure 13.3 HA/DR topology using availability groups providing local automatic failover and cross-site manual failover

To understand this issue, we need to understand levels of availability. You may have heard people state that they have a requirement for four 9s or five 9s of availability, but what does this mean in practice?

The level of availability refers to the percentage of time that an application is available to users. The number of 9s in the availability requirement refers to the number of 9s in the percentage of availability. For example, four 9s means that an application is available 99.99% of the time, and five 9s means that an application is available 99.999% of the time.

The amount of acceptable downtime for each of these availability levels is detailed in table 13.1.

Table 13.1 Levels of availability

Level of availability	Downtime per week	Downtime per month
99%	1 hour, 40 minutes, 48 seconds	7 hours, 18 minutes, 17 seconds
99.9%	10 minutes, 4 seconds	43 minutes, 49 seconds
99.99%	1 minute	4 minutes, 23 seconds
99.999%	6 seconds	26 seconds

When reviewed in these literal terms, we can see that five 9s of availability is not easy to achieve. A 6-second outage could be caused by something as simple as a network blip.

To add some additional context, if we were to spin up a server in a major public cloud platform such as Azure, we would only receive a service level agreement for a standalone server of 95% uptime per month at the time of writing.

To achieve a full five 9s of availability, we need to spend a large amount of money on both local and geographically dispersed redundant infrastructure, with redundant private links between sites. This simply isn't cost effective for the majority of use cases.

To really understand the requirements, we need to understand the cost of downtime for the application. This requires the application owner to understand both the tangible and intangible costs of an application not being available. Tangible costs are quite straightforward to calculate. For example, if we have a sales application, the tangible cost is lost revenue because customers cannot place orders. The hourly cost can be calculated by taking the monthly sales figures, multiplying them by 12, and then dividing that number by 8,760 (the number of hours in a year).

Intangible costs are much more difficult to quantify but can actually be higher. For example, if a customer is unable to place an order, they may place their order with a rival company and never return. Other intangible costs may include a drop in the sales team morale, leading to higher staff turnover or even a loss of company reputation. In some situations, it could even lead to regulatory noncompliance. Because intangible costs can only be estimated, the industry rule of thumb is to multiply the tangible costs by 3.

Once an hourly cost of downtime has been calculated, this number can be expanded out to the full lifecycle of the application. This number can then be compared against the cost of the infrastructure required to meet the requirement for each level of availability. For example, imagine that an application owner has determined that the cost of downtime for an application is $1,000/hour and the application has an expected lifecycle of three years. The total cost of downtime for two 9s of availability would be $87,650. This can be calculated using the following formula.

(Downtime hours per year × Years in application lifecycle) × Downtime cost per hour

We can then compare this against the cost of the infrastructure needed to support the requirement. An example of this can be found in table 13.2. The cost of downtime assumes $1,000/hour.

NOTE The cost of the solution just has example costs. This will, of course, be different for every application.

Table 13.2 Comparing the cost of downtime

Level of availability	Total cost of downtime	Cost of HA/ DR solution	Cost of downtime + HA/DR solution
99%	$262,810	$0*	$262,810
99.9%	$26,290	$89,193	$115,483
99.99%	$2,630	$100,389	$103,019
99.999%	$259	$301,167	$301,696

* Can be achieved without resilient architecture, provided backups are available

In this example, the cost of achieving five 9s of availability is $301,696. This is more than the cost of downtime with no redundant infrastructure, which is $262,810. Therefore, it is not economical. Achieving four 9s would achieve a cost saving of $159,791 over having no redundant infrastructure ($262,810 – $103,019). Achieving three 9s would only produce a cost saving of $147,327 over having no redundant infrastructure ($262,810 – $115,483). Therefore, achieving four 9s would be the most appropriate level of availability to aim for in this scenario. When we present an application owner with the financial implications of their requirements, they are able to understand why zero downtime is not a reasonable ask.

On premises, the best design for achieving our required level of availability will depend on our organization's infrastructure, and we should discuss this with our infrastructure team. Usually, however, achieving four 9s of availability will require a cross-site HA/DR topology similar to the design shown in figure 13.3.

In cloud, each cloud provider offers different service level agreements. At the time of writing, however, in Azure, four 9s of availability requires two VMs split across two availability zones for an infrastructure as a service (IaaS) solution or an Azure SQL database configured at the Business Critical or Premium tiers.

Before configuring an HA/DR topology, it is very important we understand the requirements. We need to accept that if we do not have access to a solution architect or business analyst, we will need to support the business in understanding what the requirements are for a given application. We should always encourage application owners to base their requirements on cost versus benefit.

13.3 #91 Not testing the DR strategy

A very common mistake that accidental DBAs make is to never test their DR strategy. The rationale is that they can see the data is synchronized. What could possibly go wrong? Unfortunately, the answer to this question is that there is plenty that can go wrong, and it is always better to find this out during a controlled test, rather than at 2 a.m. when it needs to happen in a real recovery scenario.

Let's start by thinking about some of the everyday issues that can happen during failover. The most common of these is caused by the performance of the secondary node. Imagine that we fail over an availability group from a primary replica to a secondary replica in a different data center. The failover works, but users instantly start complaining that performance is so poor that they cannot work. This can be caused by a number of factors, ranging from network latency to the secondary site to the secondary replica simply being too low-spec to handle the user throughput.

Another common reason for an inability to fail over is permissions. For failover to be successful, the `SYSTEM` account must have the `VIEW SERVER STATE`, `CONNECT SQL`, and `ALTER ANY AVAILABILITY GROUP` permissions on the secondary replica. I have seen a couple of examples where security-conscious DBAs have removed permissions from the `SYSTEM` account, unaware of the implications for availability groups.

The third most common issue I have seen involves encryption. If `FORCE PROTOCOL ENCRYPTION` is configured on the secondary replica but the secondary replica is not configured for encryption, health monitoring on the secondary replica will be prevented from connecting to the local replica, which is part of the failover process.

This is just a small sample of issues that can occur when we attempt to failover availability groups, and of course, other HA/DR technologies, such as clustering and log shipping, all have their own unique set of issues that can occur. In chapter 12, we mentioned the adage that "You don't have a backup until you have restored it." There is a similar philosophy that "You don't have DR until you have failed over."

Therefore, it is important that we test our DR strategy on a regular basis. Depending on the number of applications we support and the policy of our organization, the frequency of this test will vary. It is typical, however, to assume that every application has a DR test once a year. Usually, it is sensible to run this as a rolling task, testing a small number of applications every week or month. This allows us to build it into our standard business-as-usual routines.

Organizing a DR test involves arranging a downtime window with the application owner. We should be sure to arrange a window that is longer than we are expecting the failover to take, in case there are any problems that need to be addressed. It is also important to ensure that we have one or more users available to test that they can connect to the application and that it is functioning with tolerable performance during the test. Depending on the technologies we use and the skills within the DBA team, we may also need to arrange for other teams to be on hand for support. For example, if we do not have Windows skills in the team, and we use either availability groups or failover clustering as our HA/DR technology, then we may want to have a Windows engineer on hand for support. Alternatively, if we have a geo-cluster, then we will likely need a SAN engineer on hand to perform the storage failover, as well as provide support with any required troubleshooting.

Performing DR testing may feel like a chore, both to DBAs and to the business, but it is vitally important. It is much better to discover that we cannot fail over an application during a controlled test with scheduled downtime than it is to discover we cannot fail over in the middle of a P1 incident.

13.4 #92 Assuming availability groups are always the right answer

Since their introduction, availability groups have become the go-to HA/DR technology for all DBAs. This leads to a common misconception, however, that availability groups are always the right choice of technology for all data-tier applications. This is a mistake that can cause issues if we do not understand the limitations of availability groups and the alternatives available.

Imagine that we have a large data warehouse that processes a very large volume of data every night. The reporting the data warehouse supports is business critical, and it is vital that we have high availability in place. We configure availability groups in synchronous mode with automatic failover. Unfortunately, the application team complains that the extract, transform, and load is no longer completing within the window.

After investigation, we realize that the synchronous commit between the replicas is likely the cause of the issue. The very large volume of transactions that happens during the ETL run is causing a queue of commits to build up on the secondary replica, and the primary replica cannot commit a transaction until it has been notified that the commit has succeeded on the secondary. This is the process that ensures no data loss can occur. So to resolve the issue, we change the configuration of the availability group to use asynchronous commit. Of course, this means that we must also change to manual failover. This does not meet the requirement for automatic failover, but we hope that it will be a middle ground that will be good enough.

Unfortunately, the application team reports that, while the ETL performance is significantly better, it is still not completing within the ETL window, so we have to go back and investigate what else could be causing the problem.

After further investigation, we realize that, to implement availability groups, we have had to change the recovery model of the data warehouse database from `SIMPLE` to `FULL`. This is causing significantly more I/O, because every transaction is fully logged. There is no way around this. Either we accept that the ETL process will run for significantly longer, which does not meet the needs of the business, or we accept that we don't have an HA or even a DR solution, which also does not meet the business requirements.

This is a great example of where availability groups are not the correct HA/DR technology for a database, and it is an example that I have come across on more than one occasion. In this scenario, to meet the business requirements, failover clustering is the best technology to use. This is because it only stores the data once, and in the event of a failover, it detaches the storage from the failed node and attaches it to a redundant node. This is illustrated in figure 13.4.

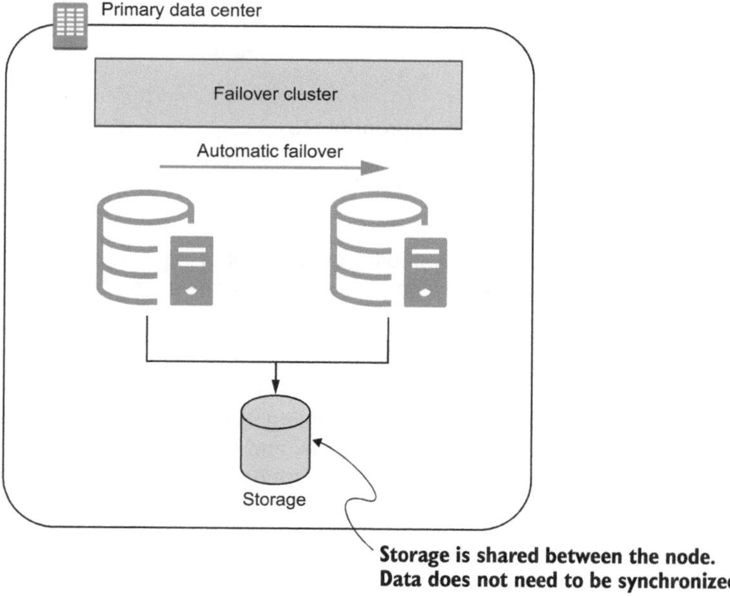

Figure 13.4 HA with failover clustering providing automatic failover in a single site

Failover clustering is not fashionable in the industry, but if you have on-premises data warehouses or other applications with a significant write volume, it may still be the best option instead of availability groups. Because the data does not need to be synchronized, there is no need to use `FULL` recovery model, and therefore we can avoid fully logging the transaction.

TIP Further discussion around the choice of recovery model can be found in chapter 12.

If we have a data warehouse that we plan to host in cloud and we need HA, a good candidate may be a dedicated SQL pool in Azure Synapse. This technology, which was previously called Parallel Data Warehouse, uses massively parallel processing technology to implement distributed queries. In this architecture, queries are run against a control node, which then distributes the query to a compute node. The data is stored in Azure storage, and there is a data-movement service that coordinates data movement between compute nodes when this is required to satisfy a query. This is illustrated in figure 13.5.

Should we ever use log shipping or replication?

Log shipping is an old method for achieving DR, which works on the premise of backing up transaction logs, shipping them to a secondary server, and restoring them to a database. Just like availability groups, it requires a database to be in `FULL` recovery model. It has very few of the benefits, however. It can only be used for DR, and the secondary database cannot be brought online until the point of failover. This means that it cannot be used for read scaling or offloading administrative tasks. Additionally, after a failover event, if we do not wish to fail back, then we have to reconfigure log shipping in the other direction. After failover, applications must also be repointed to the secondary instance, as the solution does not use clustering.

There is only one use case where it is still appropriate to use log shipping, although I have not done so myself for some time. This is a scenario where the business wants a delay before the data is applied at the secondary database so that it has a window to undo an accidental action by a user.

This use case cannot be catered for in availability groups, but in log shipping it is as easy as increasing the frequency at which the logs are reapplied at the secondary database.

Replication is a technology that can be used to disperse data. There are multiple different types of replication, such as transitional, merge, and snapshot. Many years ago, before technologies like availability groups were introduced, some people used it as a DR tool to get around some of the limitations of log shipping. Not only is this not what replication was designed for, but the tool is highly complex and often has a high operational overhead to keep it reliable. In the modern era, there are no use cases where replication is a suitable tool for DR.

When we implement an HA/DR solution, it is important that we choose the right technology for the job. There is no doubt about it: availability groups are usually the right

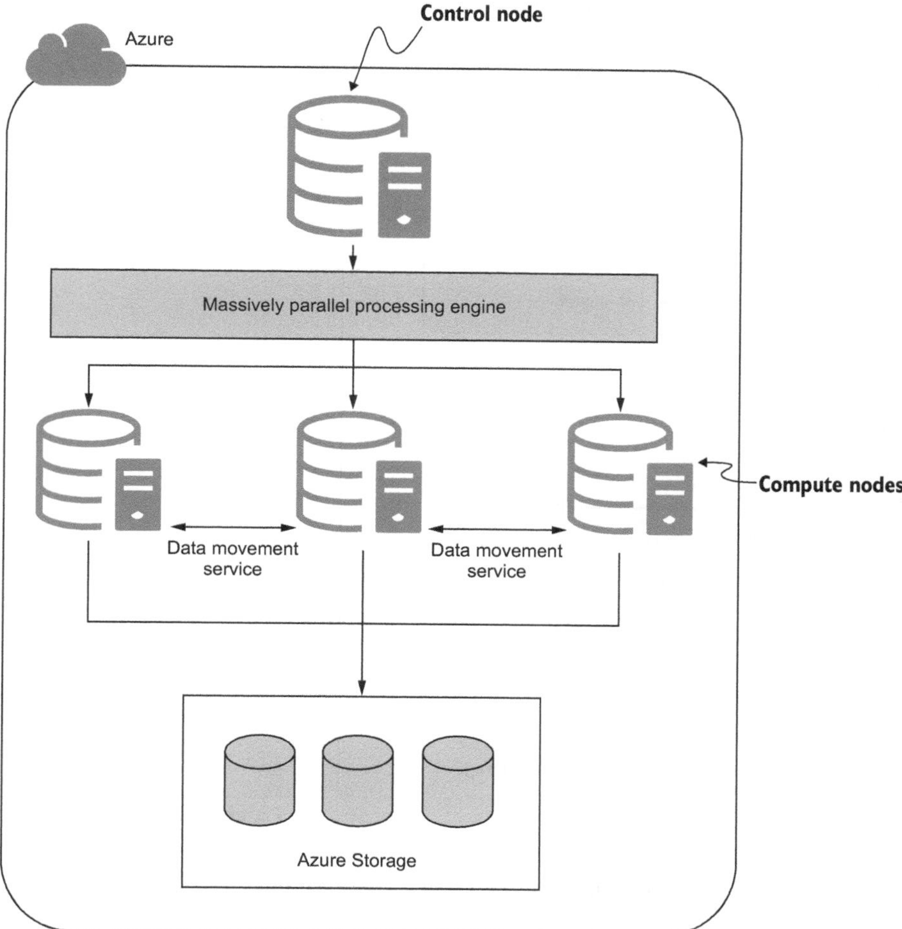

Figure 13.5 Azure Synapse dedicated SQL pool

technology. This is not true in all scenarios, however, and we must understand their limitations and when we should steer away from them. If we have a large data warehouse, or even an OLTP application with a massive volume of writes, then availability groups may not be the right choice—especially if HA is required. In this scenario, it is still appropriate to consider failover clustering. We may also decide to move to an appropriate cloud technology, such as Azure Synapse dedicated SQL pool.

13.5 #93 Overloading a cluster

Most organizations are cost conscious, and redundant hardware costs money. Therefore, it is a common practice to use an active/active cluster for failover clustering topologies and availability group topologies alike. In an active/active cluster, all nodes or replicas host production databases. If any node in the cluster fails, then the databases hosted on that node fail over to one of the other nodes. This is illustrated in figure 13.6, which depicts a two-node cluster in which each replica hosts a production availability group.

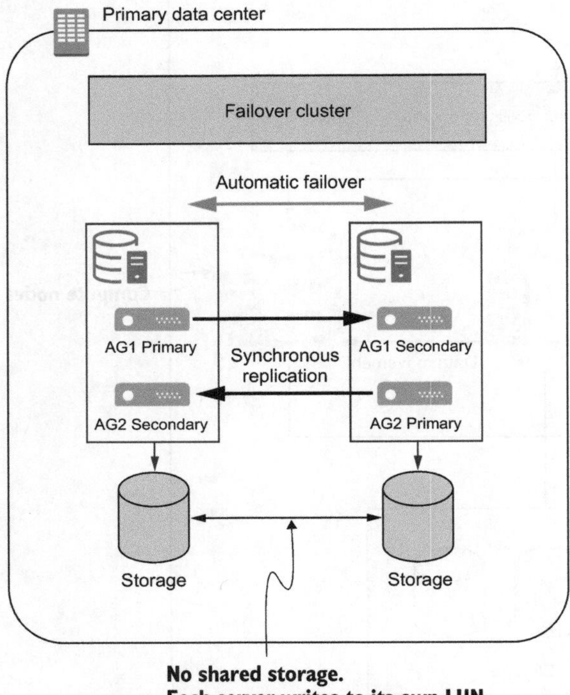

Figure 13.6 Active/active cluster using availability groups providing automatic failover in a single site

Active/active is not load balancing

It is important to understand that an active/active cluster is not a load-balancing solution. Only one copy of any given database can be active for writes at the same time. The only technology that allows us to use any form of load balancing (for write activity) is Azure Synapse dedicated SQL pool. This implements a massively parallel processing technology to coordinate transactions and synchronize data.

You may also hear that a technology called peer-to-peer replication can be used as a load-balancing solution, but this is not quite correct. Peer-to-peer replication is built on transactional replication, and multiple versions of the database can be updated.

There is no cluster or controller in front of the databases, however; an application must connect directly to one of the nodes. Additionally, conflict handling is rudimentary at best. If a conflict occurs, then the distribution agent will stop and an alert will be raised.

> A DBA must then either reinitialize the replica or manually synchronize the changes. In reality, this means that the technology can only practically be used for updating different areas of the database in most cases.

The design in figure 13.6 allows for the load to be spread across multiple nodes in the cluster. The result is that all infrastructure is utilized while still maintaining the ability to fail over. This comes with an accepted risk that performance may be impeded in the event of a failover event but that it will only be a short-term issue, as a DBA will fail the databases back to their original node as soon as the issue is addressed. It provides a good tradeoff of reliability versus cost optimization.

The mistake that I sometimes see is that the load in this topology then grows. Sometimes it is because of organic growth in an application, and other times it is because more availability groups or failover clustered instances are added to each node.

This can result in a situation where, in the event of a failover, the node that is now the primary node for all databases simply doesn't have enough capacity to deal with all the requests. This can result in poor performance, timeouts, and loss of monitoring; I even saw one instance with a failover cluster where Windows was simply not able to bring the failed-over instance online at all.

As DBAs, it is critical that we avoid this scenario, and there are a couple of methods that can work together to achieve this. The first method is simply performing capacity planning for data-tier applications. We should do this before an application goes live, but then we should also proactively monitor trends to ensure that we have enough capacity on a single node to be able to run all applications—even if they are running hot. You can find further discussion of capacity planning in chapter 9.

The second method is ensuring that DR tests are regularly carried out. This gives us the opportunity to rehearse a failover event and ensure that performance is still acceptable to the business. This is discussed in more detail in section 13.3.

Summary

- High availability (HA) refers to the automatic failover of a database in the event of a failure.
- Disaster recovery (DR) refers to the ability to recover a database in the event of a major incident.
- HA is usually configured between servers that are physically close and have low latency.
- DR is usually configured between servers that are geographically dispersed so that an application can withstand the loss of a data center.
- An application's level of availability refers to the percentage of time that it is available for use. This is often shortened to be reflected as a "number of 9s."
- Ensure that an HA/DR solution is cost effective. The cost of the redundant solution should never be more than the cost of the application downtime.

- Always test a DR strategy. Just because a database is synchronized does not mean that we can actually fail over.
- It is common practice to test the DR strategy for every application on an annual basis. This is best served through a rolling schedule of DR tests throughout the year.
- When you test DR, involve users so that they can test that they have acceptable performance after failing over.
- Availability groups are an excellent, highly flexible technology, but they are not always the correct answer.
- Failover clustering is unfashionable in today's world, but do not be afraid to use it if it is the correct technology for a use case.
- Availability groups may not be the correct technology when a database has a very high volume of writes and HA is a requirement.
- Availability groups also may not be suitable for large data warehouses, even with asynchronous replication.
- Avoid overloading a cluster, as this can lead to issues when you fail over. You can avoid this by ensuring you undertake capacity planning and DR testing.

14 Security

This chapter covers

- Working with permissions
- Service account security
- Using `xp_cmdshell`
- Auditing privileged activity
- Attacks against encryption
- SQL injection attacks

In this chapter, we will explore some of the common mistakes that are made around the security of SQL Server. We will start by looking at the principle of least privilege. This principle states that users should only have enough permission to perform their day-to-day duties, but it is often not adhered to. We will explore the reasons for this and why it is so important. We will also explore the `sa` account, which is SQL Server's built-in administrator account. Many accidental DBAs leave this account enabled, and we will discuss why this is not a good idea and how we can rectify it.

We will then turn our attention to service accounts. We will explore common mistakes that are made when defining our service account strategy. We will also discuss how to use a modern approach to implementing service accounts and how this can make our environment more secure and easier to manage.

We will look at the controversial subject of `xp_cmdshell`, which is an extended stored procedure that allows us (and bad actors) to interact with the operating system from inside a SQL Server instance. We will debunk the myths that lead database administrators (DBAs) to open their enterprise up to unnecessary attack.

Next, we will explore passive security, specifically, auditing. We will look at the very common mistake of not implementing auditing of administrative activity. We will also explore how to configure this in a way that avoids nonrepudiation.

Our next topic is whole-value substitution attacks. In these attacks, a bad actor will manipulate encrypted data to their advantage. We will discuss how they do this and how we can prevent it from happening.

Finally, we will explore SQL injection attacks. We will discuss how bad actors use SQL injection to attack our enterprise and how we can stop them. Ultimately, DBAs are the last line of defense against such attacks.

To get the most from this chapter, you must be familiar with some basic security terminology. Table 14.1 provides a glossary of some key security terminology that you should understand before moving on.

Table 14.1 Security terminology

Term	Definition
Security principal	An entity, such as a person or an application, that is granted permission to access a resource
Securable	An object that can have permissions applied to it. In SQL Server, this is often an object such as a table or a stored procedure.
Login	A security principal at the instance level that allows a person to access an instance
Database user	A security principal at the database level that (usually) maps to a login and allows a person to access resources within a database*
Server-level role	A group that contains one or more logins and can be granted permissions on instance-level securables. If a server role is "fixed," then it refers to a built-in role that is preconfigured with a set of permissions that meets a common use case.
Database level role	A group that contains one or more database users and can be granted permissions to database-level securables. If a database role is "fixed," then it refers to a built-in role that is preconfigured with a set of permissions that meets a common use case.
Active directory (AD)	A Windows-hosted directory service that allows permissions to be managed centrally.
Domain	A collection of AD objects, such as users, groups, and computers. The information is stored within a database that is synchronized between domain controllers. Domain controllers are the servers running the domain controller service, which are used to manage AD.
AD user	A Windows user that is created and managed in AD.
AD group	A group that is created and managed in AD. It will contain AD users and can be granted permissions on securables throughout the domain.

Table 14.1 Security terminology (*continued*)

Term	Definition
Service account	A user account, typically an AD user, that is intended for running Windows services only. These accounts are typically configured to disallow interactive logins and are often set for their passwords to not automatically expire.**
Kerberos authentication	A secure authentication protocol used by AD that provides a method of mutual authentication via key exchange
Service principal name	A unique identifier for an instance of a service. This is a feature of Kerberos authentication.

* A contained user is not mapped to a login. Therefore, access is only possible within a single database.

** If automatic password expiry is disabled for a service account, it should still have its password rotated.

14.1 #94 Not implementing the principle of least privilege

The bedrock of IT security strategy, the whole way through the stack, from an application down to data center security, is the *principle of least privilege*. This principle states that any security principal (such as a person or service) should only have access to the things they need to fulfill their day-to-day responsibilities. If they ever need additional privileges for a specific task, then these privileges can be granted for the duration of the task and then subsequently revoked.

Despite this being a well-understood, commonsense principle, it is often not applied at the SQL Server layer. It is scary how common it is to see a SQL Server instance with multiple members of the `sysadmin` fixed server role who are not members of the DBA team. The `sysadmin` fixed server role provides full access to a SQL Server instance—the ability to do anything.

The most common reason for this is a lack of understanding of SQL Server permissions and how to configure them. To be clear, this misunderstanding is often not with DBAs. Often the misunderstanding comes from IT professionals or organizations who do not have SQL Server as their specialist discipline. For example, it is often the case that an application team will state that they need `sysadmin` rights because they need to create and delete databases on their nonproduction server.

What is even more common is that the request comes from a third-party company that states that its software must have `sysadmin` rights on all SQL Server instances to be able to function. The most frequent offenders here are companies that provide backup tools, monitoring tools, and, ironically, sometimes even security tools.

This scenario is always particularly worrying, as complying with the request often means granting a single account `sysadmin` permission on every SQL Server instance within our enterprise. This is clearly a massive security hole. If this account is compromised, someone could gain access to all of the organization's data.

From the DBA perspective, the mistake is to say "yes" to these requests. Admittedly, it can be hard when a vendor is categorically stating that it requires `sysadmin` permission, but as the last line of defense for an organization's data, it is important that we remain steadfast.

For example, a backup tool that states it requires `sysadmin` permission certainly will not. It is likely that it will only require the `##MS_DatabaseManager##` server-level role and the `db_backupoperator` fixed database role in databases that need to be backed up.

> **NOTE** The `##MS_DatabaseManager##` role was introduced in SQL Server 2022. In prior versions of SQL Server, the `db_creator` role can be used instead. The benefit of the new role is that it is consistent with Azure SQL database.

For the vast majority of use cases, there will be a fixed server role or fixed database role that grants the permissions that a user of an application requires without exposing the organization to the security risks associated with granting `sysadmin` to multiple accounts. A full list of fixed server roles can be found at https://mng.bz/0MV6, while a full list of fixed database roles can be found at https://mng.bz/aVWX.

> **Operational support**
>
> It is important to understand that security is not the only issue with granting non-DBAs elevated permissions. There is also the problem that, as a DBA team, we are responsible for the reliable and performant running of our SQL Server environment. If we grant elevated access outside of our team, then other people are able to make changes that we are not even aware of. This can lead to performance and stability issues that we are then on the hook to resolve ourselves.

If there is not a suitable server or database role, we can create our own custom roles with the required permissions. For example, the script in listing 14.1 creates a server role called `AvailabilityGroupsFailover`. It then adds the `SYSTEM` account to this group before adding the permissions that the `SYSTEM` account requires on the secondary replica to be able to perform a failover.

Listing 14.1 Creating a custom server role

```
CREATE SERVER ROLE AvailabilityGroupsFailover ;
GO

ALTER SERVER ROLE AvailabilityGroupsFailover ADD MEMBER [NT
AUTHORITY\SYSTEM] ;

GRANT ALTER ANY AVAILABILITY GROUP TO AvailabilityGroupsFailover ;

GRANT CONNECT SQL TO AvailabilityGroupsFailover ;

GRANT CREATE AVAILABILITY GROUP TO AvailabilityGroupsFailover ;

GRANT VIEW SERVER STATE TO AvailabilityGroupsFailover ;
```

The script in listing 14.2 demonstrates how to create a custom database role that fixes a common problem that DBAs see, which is the lack of a database role that allows stored procedures to be executed without granting unnecessary permissions to a database. If this script is executed in the `model` database, it will be automatically generated in all new databases that are created on the instance.

Listing 14.2 Database role to allow stored procedure execution

```
USE model ;
GO

CREATE ROLE ExecSP ;
GO

GRANT EXECUTE TO ExecSP ;
```

> **TIP** The `model` database can be very useful, but we should be careful not to overload it with too many things, as this can become a burden to manage and maintain across the enterprise.

SQL Server makes it easy for us to manage permissions using the principle of least privilege. Unfortunately, other teams and organizations do not always make it quite so easy. It is important, however, that we stick to our guns and help consumers define exactly what permissions they require. This allows us to fulfill our role as the last line of defense for our organization's data.

14.2 #95 Not disabling the sa account

SQL Server provides two authentication modes, namely, Windows authentication and mixed-mode authentication. If Windows authentication is configured on an instance, then all security principals must use Windows authentication to access the instance. In this scenario, we must add at least one Windows user or group to the `sysadmin` fixed server role during instance installation.

If mixed-mode authentication is configured, then the instance can be accessed either by using Windows authentication or by using second-tier authentication. *Second-tier authentication* refers to SQL logins that have a password associated with them. Users can then access the instance by specifying the name and password of the login. When mixed-mode authentication is enabled, it is still possible to add users to the `sysadmin` server role, but the `sa` account will be enabled and we must specify a password for this account during instance installation.

> **TIP** In an ideal world, we would always use Windows authentication. In many cases, however, this is not possible. Many applications rely on SQL authentication to access the instance.

A very common mistake made by accidental DBAs is to leave this configuration as is. But why is this a mistake? The issue is that `sa` is a well-known account, and it has full administrative permissions to the instance. This means that if a bad actor were to attack our instance, their first port of call would likely be to try and compromise the sa account.

To make matters worse, because of the nature of SQL logins, they are vulnerable to brute-force attacks. A *brute-force attack* is where an attacker programmatically tries to log in using a known login name and a password dictionary. They try each password in turn until one works. Because the sa account is well known, the attacker will have to do no work to try to figure out the name of an account with administrative permissions; they already know it. Therefore, they can just crack on with a brute-force attack against it.

So what should we do differently? Well, there are two options. First, we could simply disable the account. In this scenario, we will ensure that we have other security principals (ideally, Windows users via an AD group) in the sysadmin server role. These administrative accounts can be used instead of relying on sa. The following listing demonstrates how to disable the sa account.

Listing 14.3 Disabling the sa account

```
ALTER LOGIN sa DISABLE ;
```

Alternatively, we could choose to keep the sa account but rename it. If we take this approach, the account will retain its administrative permissions but will no longer have a well-known name. This makes it harder for a bad actor to attack but not impossible. If they manage to discover the name of the account, it is still subject to brute force. This means that, while this improves security, it is not as effective as disabling the account and using Windows authentication for administrators.

WARNING Any SQL login is subject to brute-force attack. We should avoid granting elevated permissions to SQL logins wherever possible.

The command in the following listing demonstrates how to rename the sa account.

Listing 14.4 Renaming the sa account

```
ALTER LOGIN sa
    WITH NAME = InstanceAdmin ;
```

sa configuration

When working with SQL logins, especially sa, it is a good idea to make them as secure as possible. A nice feature of SQL Server is it can enforce the domain password policy and expiration for SQL logins. This will ensure that password complexity is adhered to and also force passwords to be rotated. The following command demonstrates how to enforce domain password policy and expiration:

```
ALTER LOGIN InstanceAdmin
    WITH CHECK_POLICY = ON
        , CHECK_EXPIRATION = ON ;
```

Because sa is a well-known account with full administrative permissions to the instance, it is likely to be the first port of call for a bad actor who wants to attack our instance. To keep our instance as secure as possible, we should disable the sa account. If this is not possible, then we should rename the account.

14.3 #96 Using the wrong granularity of a service account

Defining a strategy for service accounts has historically caused a lot of debate. From a purist security perspective, the ideal would be to have a different service account for every single service on every single SQL Server instance. Therefore, if you imagine that you have three SQL Servers, each running the Database Engine, SQL Server Integration Services, and SQL Server Analysis Services, you would have a total of nine service accounts.

The trouble with this approach, which we call a *fine-grain strategy*, is that it quickly becomes a real headache to manage. If we have a SQL Server estate with 200 instances spread across 150 servers, each running an average of two services, then we suddenly need to manage 400 accounts across 150 servers. Although automatic password expiration is usually disabled for service accounts, these are often highly privileged accounts, and we still need to rotate all the passwords on a regular basis.

To make matters worse, this can often involve synchronizing a change across AD or SQL Server resources and sometimes even other changes such as application configuration files or registry keys. When we go with this level of granularity, usually passwords never get rotated and, although the fine grain avoids lateral movement between instances and features, it still increases the security risk exposure for individual resources. Some of these will be business critical, and if our organization is subject to regulatory compliance, we may need to demonstrate that passwords are rotated.

This often leads to organizations going to the other end of the scale, where they have a single (or very few) service accounts managing vast numbers of instances and features. This is known as a *coarse-grain strategy*. This is even worse than a fine-grain strategy. It means that if the service account is compromised, the attacker has access to our entire SQL Server estate. What's more, it usually means that the password still doesn't get rotated, because it is impossible to coordinate the change across that many applications at the same time.

The mistake that DBAs make is not realizing that Microsoft solved this conundrum back in Windows Server 2012, when it introduced Group Managed Service Accounts (gMSA). These are a special kind of service account with simplified management of service principal names and automatic password rotation. The passwords are highly complex and stored inside AD. These passwords are never exposed to administrators. The accounts are entirely self-managed, and they also cannot be used interactively. These features combined make them far more secure than traditional service accounts.

An AD administrator will create a gMSA in AD, and then a script will be run on the server hosting SQL Server, which will authorize the server to use the account. The reason that DBAs do not tend to use these accounts is simply because many DBAs have not heard of them. There is simply no reason not to use them.

Holistically, the main advantage of gMSAs in our service account strategy is that they allow us to have a much coarser grain without exposing our organization to an increased security risk. Each organization will have its own standards for the exact grain that should be used for gMSAs, but as a starting point, I tend to segregate them by ecosystem and business division. There is no reason not to use gMSAs for SQL Server, and we should always use them instead of traditional service accounts.

14.4 #97 Enabling xp_cmdshell

`xp_cmdshell` is an extended stored procedure that allows administrators to execute commands in the operating system. It has long been considered a security risk, and it is disabled by default. The reason it is considered a security risk is because it allows for *lateral movement* from a SQL Server instance into the operating system. What's more, it will run in the context of the SQL Server service account, which is usually a highly privileged account. If you have a coarse grain of service account (see section 14.3), then you may also allow lateral movement to other SQL Server instances.

Lateral movement

Lateral movement is a technique used by bad actors to exploit a vulnerability on one server to gain access to other servers. For example, if an attacker has gained access to a SQL Server instance, they could gain access to other SQL Server instances, either by spoofing over privileged credentials or by using linked servers.

Alternatively, an attacker could use `xp_cmdshell` to gain access to a server's operating system from a vulnerable SQL Server instance. They could then use other attack techniques such as an SMB interception attack to expose credentials that have elevated access to other servers. This is illustrated in this sidebar figure.

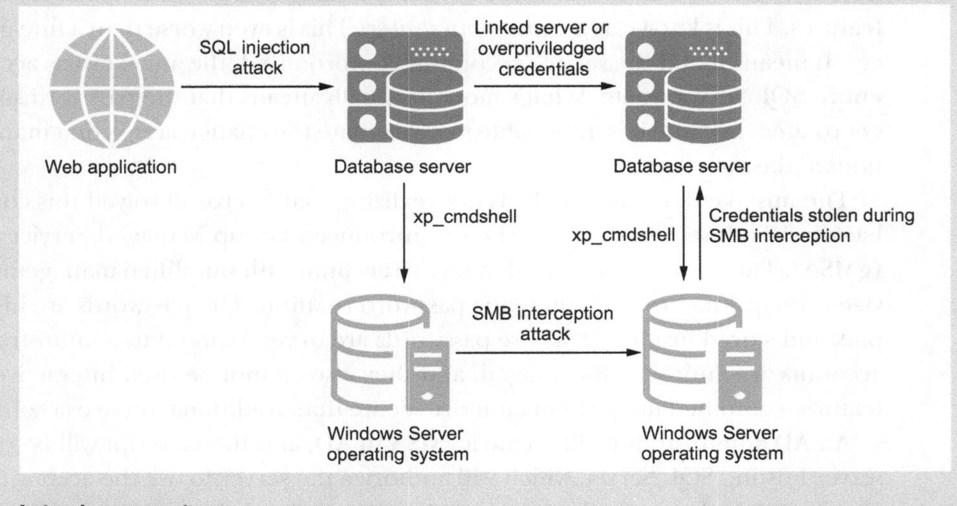

Lateral movement

Unfortunately, in recent times there has been a trend toward less experienced DBAs enabling the feature. The arguments for doing this are twofold. First, people argue that it is only members of the sysadmin server role who are permitted to use the feature, and DBAs can be trusted to use it responsibly. The second argument is that disabling xp_cmdshell does not improve security because members of the sysadmin server role can simply turn it back on. This means if a bad actor has compromised an administrative account, they can just enable it if they want to use it.

Let's tackle each of those points in detail. First, let's discuss the argument that only members of the sysadmin server role can use it and that they can be trusted to use it responsibly. The first point to make here is that it is incorrect that only members of the sysadmin role can use the feature. In reality, the requirements for running the stored procedure are as follows:

- Member of the sysadmin server role
- Granted the CONTROL SERVER permission on the SQL Server instance
- Granted EXEC permissions on xp_cmdshell (requires an xp_cmdshell proxy)
- Granted permissions to impersonate a user that meets any of the above requirements

It would be unusual for someone to gain access via any method other than sysadmin, so why does this matter? Well, it matters exactly because it would be unusual. Because it's unusual, it's also opaque. We may well be keeping a close eye on who is a member of sysadmin, but are we really keeping an eye on who has been directly granted the CONTROL SERVER permission or who has been granted the IMPERSONATE permission on another security principal?

When considering this, it is important to remember that more than 70% of attacks are internal and performed by a bad actor who works for, or previously worked for, the target organization—the very people who may have the opportunity to engineer a back door by using opaque permissions.

We must also consider why we need to use xp_cmdshell. If a DBA has permissions to the operating system, why would they not just use the operating system directly? In my experience, DBAs who advocate for the use of xp_cmdshell are usually those who, by company policy, are not allowed operating system permissions. In these cases, it is the DBAs themselves who are using xp_cmdshell as a back door to provide lateral movement to the operating system. This may not be a malicious attack, but we should consider any practice that breaks our organization's security policy as bad, no matter how benign the intentions.

So let's consider the second argument, which states that if you have permissions to use xp_cmdshell, then you have permissions to enable it. This is true in all cases, except where an xp_cmdshell proxy has been configured, and the user has been granted EXECUTE permissions on the stored procedure.

If we look at it on the surface, this sentiment is fair. Even if we make sure xp_cmdshell is disabled by using a data definition language (DDL) trigger or SQL Server policy-based management, then an administrator will have the permissions to disable that trigger or policy-based management policy prior to executing the procedure.

If we look deeper, however, we should consider layers of security. If xp_cmdshell is enabled, then it can easily be used. If it is disabled, then an attacker will first need to enable it. If we have a trigger preventing the feature from being enabled, this trigger will need to be deleted, then the procedure enabled, before damage can be done. Each of these layers takes time and increases the likelihood of the attack being spotted and stopped.

To this end, possibly the most important thing that we can do as DBAs is to ensure that alerting is in place to raise a P1 alert in the event that somebody attempts to enable xp_cmdshell.

Consider the script in listing 14.5. First, the script creates a custom error message warning that someone has tried to enable xp_cmdshell. It then creates a trigger that will catch this event. DDL triggers are created at the instance level and trigger in response to the execution of DDL commands. This trigger is set to respond to ALTER_INSTANCE events. When any ALTER_INSTANCE event fires, the trigger will be executed. The trigger reads the executed command text into a variable. It then uses the CHARINDEX() function to see if the statement contains the strings sp_configure and xp_cmdshell. If it does, then the custom error message we created at the start of the script is fired using the WITH LOG statement. This ensures the alert is sent to the SQL Server log and the Windows application event log. Finally, the script rolls back the transaction and prevents xp_cmdshell from being enabled.

Listing 14.5 Creating a trigger to prevent xp_cmdshell execution

```
EXEC sp_addmessage 50001, 16, 'Attempt to disable xp_cmdshell' ;
GO

CREATE TRIGGER prevent_xp_cmdshell
ON ALL SERVER
FOR ALTER_INSTANCE
AS
BEGIN
  DECLARE @Statement NVARCHAR(4000) ;

  SET @Statement = (SELECT EVENTDATA().value('(/EVENT_INSTANCE/TSQLCommand/
     CommandText)[1]',
'nvarchar(4000)')) ;

  IF (CHARINDEX('sp_configure', @Statement) > 0)
        AND (CHARINDEX('xp_cmdshell', @Statement) > 0)
  BEGIN
    RAISERROR(50001, 16, 1, 'Attempt to disable xp_cmdshell') WITH LOG ;
    ROLLBACK ;
  END
END ;
GO
```

We can now ask our observability team to create an alert in the event that error 50001 is raised to the event log. If our organization does not have an enterprise monitoring tool, then we can achieve the same results with SQL Agent alerts. An enterprise monitoring tool is preferable, however, to avoid having to run Database Mail.

TIP Alerting on errors is covered in chapter 7.

If we respond to this P1 security alert quickly, we will have an opportunity to catch the attack before it does any damage. It is far from perfect and certainly not risk free as an approach, but it is far better than allowing `xp_cmdshell` to be enabled and letting bad actors freely perform lateral movement and compromise other areas of our estate. As an added bonus, it will also keep the cyber security team and auditors happy, which will save us time in writing exception reports.

Each security team will have its own processes and policies for what to do if an active attack is discovered. My own personal approach, however, is to take down the instance while the incident is being investigated. This will cause an outage, but it is the best way to safeguard a company's data.

It is worrying that `xp_cmdshell` is making its way back into the consciousness of accidental DBAs. It is a highly dangerous procedure that exposes our organizations to risk. Unfortunately, there is no way to entirely eliminate this threat, but we should minimize the risk by introducing layers of security. This involves ensuring that as few people have elevated permissions on the instance as possible by using the principle of least privilege. It means disabling dangerous features that we do not (or should not) use, such as `xp_cmdshell`, and making sure that robust alerting is in place so we stand a chance of preventing an attack from succeeding. Additionally, we should use auditing to ensure that privileged accounts have nonrepudiation. That is the perfect segue to our next mistake, which discusses this very subject.

14.5 #98 Failing to audit administrative activity

As mentioned previously in this chapter, we may not like to think about it, but the majority of cyberattacks are internal. When we consider this, we must remember that in large organizations there may be many people who have administrative access to SQL Server instances. Ideally, this would just be the DBA team, but as discussed earlier in this chapter, in some environments we may have a suboptimal security stance where other individuals, such as application developers or application support teams, also have administrative access. Even if we do manage to limit `sysadmin` membership to just DBAs, in many companies this will involve a combination of staff, contractors, and third-party managed services. We must also consider that, even if we are subject to an external attack, an administrative account could be compromised and used against us.

For these reasons, it is important that we ensure nonrepudiation. Every individual with privileged access must be accountable for their actions. Also, if an account has been compromised and is being used to perform an attack, we must be able to quickly identify this and take measures (such as disabling the account) to avoid the attack from continuing.

SQL Server allows us to ensure nonrepudiation by auditing administrative activity with a lightweight auditing tool called SQL Server audit. This tool can be configured to write audit actions to the Windows security log to prevent SQL Server administrative users from tampering with it. The majority of environments I see do not have SQL Server audit configured, however, and this is a mistake that any security-conscious DBA should immediately resolve.

To capture administrative actions in a tamper-proof way, there are some prerequisite steps that need to be taken. In many organizations, DBAs will need to ask for support from the Windows team with these prerequisites:

- The audit object access setting must be configured to allow *application-generated* audit events. This can be achieved using the auditpol command-line utility.
- The SQL Server service account must be granted the *generate security audits* user rights assignment. This can be achieved in the `secpol.msc` snap-in.
- The audit policy must be configured to allow the *audit object* policy to audit success and failure. This can also be performed in the `secpol.msc` snap-in.

TIP The server should be restarted after these changes are made.

These prerequisite steps allow for SQL Server to write audit events to the Windows security log, which cannot be tampered with by members of the `sysadmin` server role. Once these steps are complete, we can create an audit in SQL Server. This audit object specifies where we want to store the audit results and the action that should be taken if there is a failure writing to the audit log. This action can be set to continue, fail operation, or shut down the server. The command in the following listing demonstrates how to create an audit that will save the logs in the Windows security log.

Listing 14.6 Creating an audit object

```
USE master ;
GO

CREATE SERVER AUDIT AdminActivityAudit
TO SECURITY_LOG WITH (
      ON_FAILURE = CONTINUE
) ;
```

We now need to create an audit object specification. This is where we define what activity we would like to audit. The list of audit action types is expansive, covering almost any action that can be performed in SQL Server. At the instance level, this covers everything from backup–restore operations, login attempts, and database creation or deletion. At the database level, everything from a batch starting to changing a schema owner can be captured. The full list of action types is too vast to include in these pages, but a full list can be found at https://mng.bz/9on1.

Table 14.2 lays out the action types that we will want to audit for our use case.

Table 14.2 Audit action types

Audit action type	Description
AUDIT_CHANGE_GROUP	The event is raised when an audit is created, dropped, or altered. Adding this will ensure nonrepudiation if an administrative user tries to shut down an audit, perform a nefarious activity, and then reenable it.
DBCC_GROUP	The event is raised when a DBCC statement is run.

Table 14.2 Audit action types (*continued*)

Audit action type	Description
SERVER_OBJECT_CHANGE_GROUP	The event is raised when an instance-level object is created, dropped, or altered.
SERVER_OBJECT_PERMISSION_CHANGE_GROUP	The event is raised when permissions are assigned to or revoked from a schema-bound object.
SERVER_OBJECT_OWNERSHIP_CHANGE_GROUP	The event is raised when the owner of an instance-level object is changed.
SERVER_OPERATION_GROUP	The event is raised when instance configuration changes are made.
SERVER_PERMISSION_CHANGE_GROUP	The event is raised when permissions are assigned to or revoked from instance-level permissions.
SERVER_PRINCIPAL_CHANGE_GROUP	The event is fired when instance-level principals are created, dropped, or altered.
SERVER_PRINCIPAL_IMPERSONATION_GROUP	The event is raised when impersonation of an instance-level principal occurs.
SERVER_ROLE_MEMBER_CHANGE_GROUP	The event is raised when the membership of a server role is changed.
SERVER_STATE_CHANGE_GROUP	The event is raised when the state of the instance is modified.

To create this audit specification, we can use the command in the next listing. Note that the `FOR SERVER AUDIT` clause links the audit specification to our audit object.

Listing 14.7 Creating an audit specification

```
CREATE SERVER AUDIT SPECIFICATION AdminActivitySpecification
FOR SERVER AUDIT AdminActivityAudit
    ADD (SERVER_ROLE_MEMBER_CHANGE_GROUP),
    ADD (AUDIT_CHANGE_GROUP),
    ADD (DBCC_GROUP),
    ADD (SERVER_OBJECT_PERMISSION_CHANGE_GROUP),
    ADD (SERVER_PERMISSION_CHANGE_GROUP),
    ADD (SERVER_PRINCIPAL_IMPERSONATION_GROUP),
    ADD (SERVER_OBJECT_CHANGE_GROUP),
    ADD (SERVER_PRINCIPAL_CHANGE_GROUP),
    ADD (SERVER_OPERATION_GROUP),
    ADD (SERVER_STATE_CHANGE_GROUP),
    ADD (SERVER_OBJECT_OWNERSHIP_CHANGE_GROUP) ;
```

Database audit specifications

As well as auditing instance-level activity with a server audit specification, we can also audit database-level activity with a database audit specification. These objects are again attached to an audit object but allow for fine-grain auditing of every activity, down to `SELECT` statements. If we have multiple databases that we wish to audit, we will need to create the database audit specification in each database.

> ***(continued)***
>
> We need to be a little careful of performance. Despite the fact that SQL Server audit is a lightweight tool, if we audit too many unnecessary events, we can have a performance impact on a busy server. Generally speaking, low-level auditing is reserved for compliance requirements or specific use cases.

Because of the nature of accounts with `sysadmin` permissions, we should always introduce an audit of administrative activity at the instance level to ensure nonrepudiation if we come under internal attack. This also helps us isolate an account that has been compromised if we come under external attack. We can audit privileged actions using SQL Server audit, and we can ensure the logs are not tampered with by saving the audit records to the Windows security log.

14.6 #99 Exposing the business to whole-value substitution attacks

SQL Server provides multiple ways to encrypt data to protect against different attack scenarios. This includes transparent data encryption, which provides protection from a bad actor "stealing" a database and trying to attach it or restore it to a different instance. It also includes Always Encrypted, which prevents even members of the `sysadmin` server role from decrypting and viewing data. This is helpful in highly secure environments with extremely sensitive data.

In this section, however, we focus on cell-level encryption and a common mistake that is made when configuring this type of encryption, which allows us to encrypt certain sensitive data such as credit card numbers. The specific mistake that we will explore is leaving our organizations open to a whole-value substitution attack. This is an attack where a bad actor replaces an encrypted value with a different encrypted value that they believe will benefit them or allow them to perform a nefarious action such as credit card fraud.

> **WARNING** Cell-level encryption should always be used sparingly. It can cause serious performance degradation as well as up to 4,000% bloat. It is usually reserved for compliance reasons or for very specific use cases.

To understand what a whole-value substitution attack is, let's use the `HumanResources` database that we created in chapter 3. This database contains a table called `Employees`, which stores all of the employee records for the fictional company MagicChoc. Let's imagine that our human resources department has decided that the `Salary` column of this table is highly sensitive and must be encrypted.

In the next section, we will prepare an encrypted environment that we can use, and in the following section we will explore what a whole-value substitution attack is and how we can prevent it.

14.6.1 Preparing an encrypted environment

To meet this requirement, we will first need to create the encryption hierarchy of objects that will be required. This starts with a Service Master Key, which is encrypted using the Windows Data Protection API and is the encryption root within the SQL Server instance. This key is used to encrypt the database master key, which is the encryption root within a specific database. The database master key is then used to encrypt asymmetric keys and certificates within the database. At the bottom of the hierarchy are symmetric keys. These symmetric keys are encrypted using a certificate or asymmetric key and are used to encrypt the data. This hierarchy is illustrated in figure 14.1.

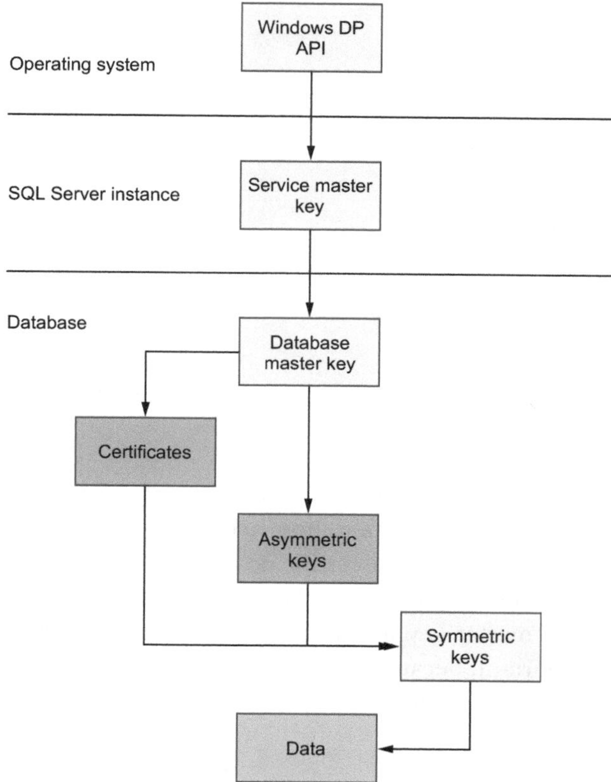

Figure 14.1 SQL server encryption hierarchy

Symmetric vs. asymmetric keys

While a full explanation of cryptography is beyond the scope of this book, it is always useful to understand the difference between a symmetric key and an asymmetric key. A symmetric key has a single key, which is secret and is used to both encrypt and decrypt data. An asymmetric key, on the other hand, has a secret key (known as a private key) that decrypts data but a different, public key that is used for data encryption.

This difference in approach, which is illustrated in the figure in this sidebar, makes asymmetric encryption more secure but also adds additional overhead. This is why a symmetric key is often used to encrypt the data.

(continued)

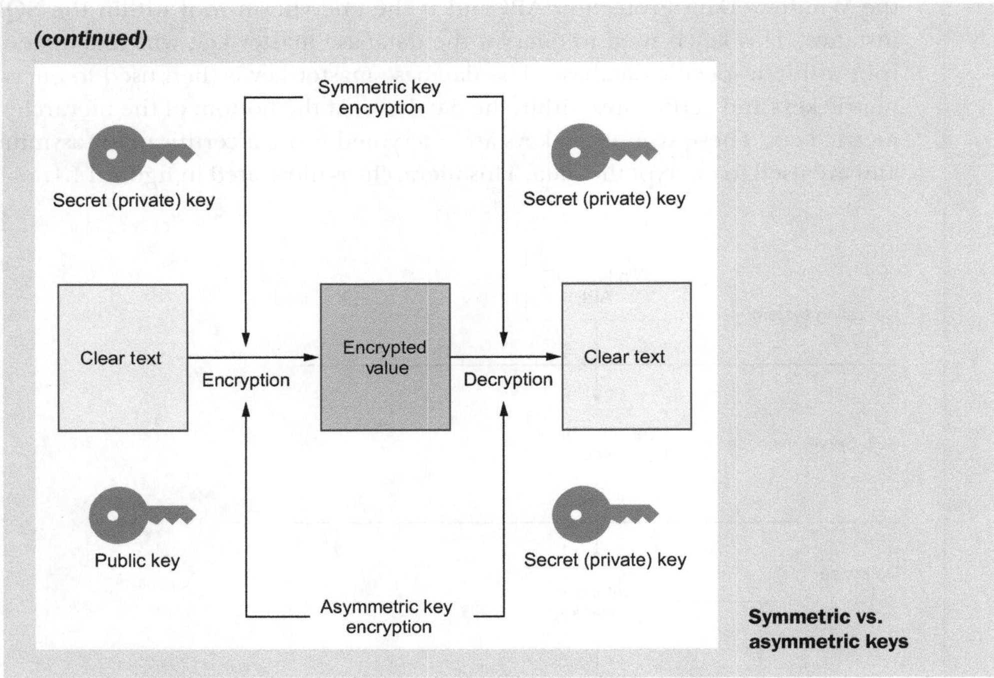

Symmetric vs. asymmetric keys

The service master key is automatically created the first time the SQL Server instance is started, but the script in listing 14.8 demonstrates how to create a database master key in the `HumanResources` database along with a certificate and symmetric key. The certificate is encrypted using the database master key. You will notice that the script also takes a backup of the database master key, and the symmetric key is encrypted using the certificate. This is very important, because if we lose this key, then we lose access to all data that is encrypted below it in the hierarchy.

Listing 14.8 Creating the encryption hierarchy

```
USE HumanResources ;
GO

CREATE MASTER KEY ENCRYPTION BY PASSWORD = 'Pa$$w0rd' ;     ← Creates database master key
GO

OPEN MASTER KEY DECRYPTION BY PASSWORD = 'Pa$$w0rd';
BACKUP MASTER KEY TO FILE = 'c:\keys\HumanResourcesMasterKey.key'     ← Backs up database master key
    ENCRYPTION BY PASSWORD = 'Pa$$w0rd' ;
GO

CREATE CERTIFICATE SalaryCert     ← Creates a certificate
WITH SUBJECT = 'Employee Saleries' ;
GO
```

```
CREATE SYMMETRIC KEY SalaryKey
WITH ALGORITHM = AES_128
ENCRYPTION BY CERTIFICATE SalaryCert ;
GO
```

Creates a symmetric key

The next step is to prepare the table by adding a column called `EncryptedSalary`, which will have a data type of `VARBINARYY(8000)`. Encrypted values are always stored as `VARBINARY`. This column will be used to store the encrypted values and can be added by using the command in the following listing.

Listing 14.9 Adding the `EncryptedSalary` column

```
ALTER TABLE dbo.Employees
    ADD EncryptedSalary VARBINARY(8000) ;
```

The script in listing 14.10 will populate the `EncryptedSalary` column by updating the column to add the encrypted version of the salary. To do this, the script first opens the symmetric key. It then uses the `ENCRYPTBYKEY()` function to encrypt the data. The first parameter passed to the function is the globally unique identifier (GUID) of the symmetric key. To avoid needing to look this up, the script embeds a function called `KEY_GUID()`. We pass this function the name of the symmetric key and it returns the key's GUID. The second parameter of the `ENCRYPTBYKEY()` function is the data that we want to encrypt. In this case, it is the `Salary` column. Finally, the script closes the symmetric key to prevent it from being used by another query.

Listing 14.10 Populating the `EncryptedSalary` column

```
OPEN SYMMETRIC KEY SalaryKey
DECRYPTION BY CERTIFICATE SalaryCert ;

UPDATE dbo.Employees
    SET EncryptedSalary =
        ENCRYPTBYKEY(KEY_GUID('SalaryKey'), CAST(Salary AS VARCHAR(10))) ;

CLOSE SYMMETRIC KEY SalaryKey ;
```

NOTE In a production environment, we would drop the `Salary` column so that the data is no longer stored in clear text.

14.6.2 Understanding and preventing whole-value substitution attacks

To understand a whole-value substitution attack, imagine that MagicChoc has unwittingly hired a dishonest person. Robin Round is the recruitment manager. He works in the human resources department, and therefore he has `SELECT` and `UPDATE` permissions on the `Employees` table. If Robin runs a `SELECT` statement against the table, he will be able to see employee details, such as their name and role. He will also be able to return the encrypted salary column, although the results will be a meaningless encrypted value.

While Robin is not able to determine what salary Bob Walford (the CEO) receives, he knows that it will be far more than his own salary. This means that if he updates his own salary to have the same encrypted value as Bob Walford's, he will simply bypass all of our encryption and give himself a very large pay raise! This is known as a whole-value substitution attack and is demonstrated in the following listing.

Listing 14.11 Performing a whole-value substitution attack

```
UPDATE dbo.Employees
SET EncryptedSalary =
(
    SELECT EncryptedSalary
    FROM dbo.Employees
    WHERE FirstName = 'Bob'
        AND LastName = 'Walford'
)
WHERE FirstName = 'Robin'
    AND LastName = 'Round' ;
```

The query in the following listing uses the `DECRYPTBYKEY()` function to decrypt the `EncryptedSalary` column and show that Robin Round and Bob Walford now have the same salary.

Listing 14.12 Assessing the impact of the attack

```
OPEN SYMMETRIC KEY SalaryKey
DECRYPTION BY CERTIFICATE SalaryCert ;


SELECT
      FirstName
    , LastName
    , Role
    , CAST(CONVERT(VARCHAR(10),DECRYPTBYKEY(EncryptedSalary)) AS MONEY)
FROM dbo.Employees
WHERE (FirstName = 'Bob' AND LastName = 'Walford') OR
      (FirstName = 'Robin' AND LastName = 'Round') ;

CLOSE SYMMETRIC KEY SalaryKey ;
```

Running this query will show that both people now have a salary of $96,000.

So what should we have done differently? Well, we can protect against this attack pattern by adding what is known as an *authenticator column*. This designates an additional value, often the primary key of the table, to be encrypted alongside the sensitive data. This authenticator is then checked when the value is updated to ensure that it matches.

To understand this better, let's use the script in listing 14.13 to add another column to the `Employees` table. It is called `EncryptedSalaryWithAuth`, and the script populates it by encrypting the `Salary` column. This time, however, we use the `EmployeeID` column as an authenticator.

Listing 14.13 Encrypting salaries with an authenticator

```
ALTER TABLE dbo.Employees
    ADD EncryptedSalaryWithAuth VARBINARY(8000) ;
GO

OPEN SYMMETRIC KEY SalaryKey
DECRYPTION BY CERTIFICATE SalaryCert ;

UPDATE dbo.Employees
        SET EncryptedSalaryWithAuth =
            ENCRYPTBYKEY(
                Key_GUID('SalaryKey'),
                CAST(Salary AS VARCHAR(10)),
                1,
                CAST(EmployeeID AS VARBINARY(8000))
            ) ;

CLOSE SYMMETRIC KEY SalaryKey ;
```

With this in place, let's use the query in the following listing to simulate the attack again—this time against the `EncryptedSalaryWithAuth` column.

Listing 14.14 Simulating the attack with an authenticator

```
UPDATE dbo.Employees
SET EncryptedSalaryWithAuth =
(
    SELECT EncryptedSalaryWithAuth
    FROM dbo.Employees
    WHERE FirstName = 'Bob'
        AND LastName = 'Walford'
)
WHERE FirstName = 'Robin'
    AND LastName = 'Round' ;
```

We can now use the query in the following listing to assess the impact of this attack.

Listing 14.15 Assessing the impact of the attack with authenticator column

```
OPEN SYMMETRIC KEY SalaryKey
DECRYPTION BY CERTIFICATE SalaryCert ;


SELECT
      FirstName
    , LastName
    , Role
    , CAST(
        CONVERT(
            VARCHAR(10),
            DECRYPTBYKEY(
                EncryptedSalaryWithAuth,
```

```
                    1 ,
                    CONVERT(VARBINARY, EmployeeID)
                )
            ) AS MONEY
    )
FROM dbo.Employees
WHERE (FirstName = 'Bob' AND LastName = 'Walford') OR
      (FirstName = 'Robin' AND LastName = 'Round') ;

CLOSE SYMMETRIC KEY SalaryKey ;
```

Executing this query will show that Robin's salary now shows as a NULL value. Although he was able to update the encrypted salary value, the decryption no longer works because the authenticator doesn't match. This means that the attack was unsuccessful.

Encryption can be a very useful tool for protecting sensitive data. It should be used sparingly, because if it's used widely it can cause significant bloat and performance issues. When it is used to encrypt very sensitive data, we should ensure that we do not leave our organization open to whole-value substitution attacks. These attacks involve a bad actor replacing an encrypted value with a different encrypted value. Adding an authenticator column can prevent this attack pattern from succeeding.

14.7 #100 Exposing the business to SQL injection attacks

SQL injection is an attack pattern in which the attacker will attempt to enter T-SQL statements in the fields of an application where standard user input is expected. This results in the application building valid but unintended and often harmful statements. These statements will be designed to cause serious damage to the SQL Server environment and often to perform lateral movement to other environments.

A mistake that I see often among accidental DBAs is a belief that this form of attack is something that they do not need to worry about. Instead, they believe that all of the responsibility lies with the application developers to ensure that their applications correctly validate all input.

To a certain extent, this is right. So to understand why this is a mistake, let's use the analogy of a museum that hires a night watchman. Just because they have hired a night watchman, does this mean that when they close up for the day, they will leave all of the doors unlocked and turn off the alarms on the cases that house priceless artifacts? No, of course not. This would dramatically increase the risk that a burglar will simply sneak in while the night watchman is doing his rounds on a different floor.

It is vitally important for DBAs to remember that they are the last line of defense for an organization's data. Yes, of course, application developers should be validating input in their applications, but we cannot guarantee that they are doing this. We certainly cannot guarantee that an application developer hasn't simply made a mistake that did not get picked up during testing.

To understand why protecting against SQL injection is so important, let's take a little time to understand how attacks are performed and the damage they can do. To this end, let's set up a very basic, insecure web page with an insecure SQL Server configuration in the backend.

The examples in this section assume that these poor practices have been followed:

- The service account is in the `Administrators` group in Windows.
- The service account is a member of the `sysadmins` server role.
- `xp_cmdshell` is enabled.
- The instance uses mixed-mode authentication but doesn't disable or rename the `sa` account.
- The SQL logins are not set to enforce domain password policy.
- The web app has no input validation.
- The web app uses the `sa` account to connect to the database.
- The web app stores the username and password in code, in clear text.
- The web app builds SQL dynamically.

TIP An additional security concern that should be noted is that user passwords are stored in plain text in the `Users` table. Passwords should usually be encrypted.

The script in listing 14.16 creates a database called `SQLInjection`, which contains a table called `Users`. This table is populated with two usernames and passwords. The website we create will assume that the database resides in the default instance. If you want to use a named instance, just update the connection string in the C# file accordingly.

Listing 14.16 Creating the `SQLInjection` database

```
CREATE DATABASE SQLInjection ;
GO

USE SQLInjection ;
GO

CREATE TABLE dbo.Users
(
    ID              INT             NOT NULL    IDENTITY    PRIMARY KEY,
    UserName        NVARCHAR(128)   NOT NULL,
    UserPassword    NVARCHAR(512)   NOT NULL
) ;
GO

INSERT INTO dbo.Users(UserName, UserPassword)
VALUES('Pete', 'Password1'),
      ('Terri', 'MyPassword') ;
GO
```

The script in listing 14.17 provides the code for a very basic login page and a basic welcome page. To follow this example, you will need to create a C#-based ASPX Web

Forms project in Visual Studio. You should then add two web forms to the project and copy the code for each.

> **TIP** If you are using Visual Studio 2022, Microsoft will steer you down the path of Razor. This demonstration uses the ASP.NET Web Application (.NET Framework), however. To access this, ensure that you have the Additional Project Templates (Previous Versions) component installed. When you create the project, use the Web Forms option.

Listing 14.17 Code for login page and welcome page

```
<%@ Page Language="C#" AutoEventWireup="true" CodeBehind="Login.aspx.cs"
Inherits="SQLInjection.Login" %>                    ← Code for Login.aspx

<!DOCTYPE html>

<html xmlns="http://www.w3.org/1999/xhtml">
<head runat="server">
    <title></title>
    <style type="text/css">
        .auto-style1 {
            width: 503px;
            height: 249px;
            margin-left: 67px;
        }
    </style>
</head>
<body>
    <form id="form1" runat="server">
    <div style="margin-left: 280px">

        <br />
        <br />
        <asp:Login ID="Login1" runat="server" Height="244px"
OnAuthenticate="Login1_Authenticate" Width="483px" BackColor="#EFF3FB"
BorderColor="#B5C7DE" BorderPadding="4" BorderStyle="Solid"
BorderWidth="1px" Font-Names="Verdana" Font-Size="0.8em"
ForeColor="#333333" style="margin-left: 64px">
            <InstructionTextStyle Font-Italic="True" ForeColor="Black" />
            <LoginButtonStyle BackColor="White" BorderColor="#507CD1"
BorderStyle="Solid" BorderWidth="1px" Font-Names="Verdana" Font-
Size="0.8em" ForeColor="#284E98" />
            <TextBoxStyle Font-Size="0.8em" />
            <TitleTextStyle BackColor="#507CD1" Font-Bold="True" Font-
Size="0.9em" ForeColor="White" />
        </asp:Login>
        <br />
        <br />
        <asp:Label ID="Label1" runat="server"></asp:Label>
        <br />

    </div>
    </form>
```

```
</body>
</html>
```

```
<%@ Page Language="C#" AutoEventWireup="true" CodeBehind="Welcome.aspx.cs"
 Inherits="SQLInjection.Welcome" %>

<!DOCTYPE html>

<html xmlns="http://www.w3.org/1999/xhtml">
<head runat="server">
    <title></title>
    <style type="text/css">
        .auto-style1 {
            width: 856px;
            height: 336px;
            margin-left: 235px;
        }
    </style>
</head>
<body>
    <form id="form1" runat="server">
    <div>
    </div>
        <br />
        <asp:Label ID="Label2" runat="server" Text="Welcome!"></asp:Label>
    </form>
</body>
</html>
```

Code for Welcome.aspx

We can then use the code in listing 14.18 to create the C# files that sit behind the ASPX files. Again, to follow along, you can just copy and paste the code.

> **NOTE** The code for Welcome.aspx.cs is just an empty placeholder. It doesn't provide any functionality.

Listing 14.18 Code for C# files behind the ASPX files

```
using System;
using System.Collections.Generic;
using System.Linq;
using System.Web;
using System.Web.UI;
using System.Web.UI.WebControls;
using System.Data;
using System.Data.SqlClient;
using System.Reflection.Emit;

namespace SQLInjection
{
    public partial class Login : System.Web.UI.Page
    {
```

```
        protected void Page_Load(object sender, EventArgs e)
        {

        }

        protected void Login1_Authenticate(object sender,
      AuthenticateEventArgs e)
        {
            SqlConnection con = new SqlConnection(@"Data Source=.;Initial
Catalog=SQLInjection;Integrated Security=False;Uid=sa;Pwd=Pa$$w0rd");
            string qry = "SELECT * FROM Users WHERE UserName='" +
Login1.UserName + "'AND UserPassword='" + Login1.Password + "' ";
            SqlDataAdapter adapter = new SqlDataAdapter(qry, con);
            DataTable datatable = new DataTable();
            adapter.Fill(datatable);
            if (datatable.Rows.Count >= 1)
            {
                Label1.Visible = false;
                Session["Parameter"] = datatable.Rows[0].Field<string>(1);

                Response.Redirect("Welcome.aspx");
            }
        }
    }
}
```

```
using System;
using System.Collections.Generic;
using System.Linq;
using System.Web;
using System.Web.UI;
using System.Web.UI.WebControls;

namespace SQLInjection
{
    public partial class Welcome : System.Web.UI.Page
    {
        protected void Page_Load(object sender, EventArgs e)
        {

        }
    }
}
```

If we were to use this website as designed, then we would enter our username and password and be directed to the welcome page. If we were a bad actor wanting to attack the organization, however, then we would perform a SQL injection attack. To understand this attack, we need to understand that if we were to log in as the user `Pete`, then the application would build the following query:

```
SELECT * FROM Users WHERE UserName='Pete' AND UserPassword='Password1' ;
```

If, however, instead of typing a username, the attacker entered `' OR 1=1--` into the username field and some random characters into the password field, then the query would become

```
SELECT * FROM Users WHERE UserName='' OR 1=1-- ' AND
UserPassword='randomchars' ;
```

Because everything to the right of `--` is a comment and not executed and because 1 always equals 1, all users in the table will be passed into the dataset and C# will use the first row to be returned. In short, the attacker has just spoofed the identity of the first user in the table.

In a more sophisticated attack, a bad actor could leak information such as the database name, instance name, or even the AD domain to give them the required information to perform further attacks. For example, if the bad actor were to use `' or 1 = db_name()--`, then the resulting error message would include the following:

```
Conversion failed when converting the nvarchar value 'SQLInjection' to data
type int
```

You will see that this has leaked the database name, `SQLInjection`. If the bad actor wanted to perform a lateral movement attack, then, because of our insecure configuration, they could simply use the command `' AND 1=1; EXEC xp_cmdshell 'net user hacker WeakPa$$w0rd /ADD'--` in the username field. The result would be that a new user called `hacker` is created on our server. This user can then be used to perform further downstream attacks against our network.

How can we protect our organization against such attacks? The primary answer to this is to follow the advice in this chapter and security recommendations in general. There is an additional protection mechanism that we can take, however, which is to enforce coding standards.

If we mandate that web applications must use stored procedures, rather than building SQL dynamically, we can prevent this form of attack. For example, consider the stored procedure in the following listing. The procedure accepts variables for username and password, which would be passed by the application.

Listing 14.19 Creating a login stored procedure

```
CREATE PROCEDURE dbo.Login
      @UserName NVARCHAR(128)
    , @Password NVARCHAR(128)
AS
BEGIN
    SELECT *
    FROM dbo.Users
    WHERE UserName = @UserName
        AND UserPassword = @Password ;
END
```

The simple procedure uses the same logic as the dynamically built SQL from the website, but let's see what happens if we run the script in listing 14.20. The script first simulates the correct use of the stored procedure, where a valid username and password are passed in. It then simulates an attack by a bad actor trying to spoof a password.

Listing 14.20 Simulating the use of a login stored procedure

```
DECLARE @UserName NVARCHAR(128) = 'Pete' ;
DECLARE @Password NVARCHAR(128) = 'Password1' ;

EXEC dbo.Login @username, @password ;          ◄── Simulates execution as a normal user


SET @UserName = ''' OR 1=1--' ;
SET @Password = 'randomchars' ;
                                               ┐ Simulates execution
EXEC dbo.Login @username, @password ;          ◄┘ as a bad actor
```

You will notice that the first invocation of the stored procedure returns the desired results. The second invocation of the stored procedure does not return any results. This will result in the attack failing.

> **TIP** An advantage of enforcing stored procedures, as opposed to having strict validation on a field in a web app, is that it prevents a poor user experience for people who have double-barreled last names without the website input validation becoming overly complicated.

SQL injection is a common form of attack in which a bad actor will attempt to use a weak security posture to perform malicious actions. These malicious actions could range from spoofing another user to destructive attacks that delete data or drop tables. Such an attack can even be used to perform lateral movement to other areas of our network. We should always implement security best practices to avoid such attacks. We should also consider enforcing coding standards, which prevent this attack pattern from succeeding.

Summary

- The principle of least privilege states that any person should only have the level of permissions they require to perform their day-to-day tasks.
- If someone needs to perform an action outside of their normal activities, then they should have their permissions increased and then revoked when the task is complete.
- Push back against third-party software providers who claim to need `sysadmin` permissions.
- The `sa` account is a well-known, highly privileged account. Therefore, it is often subject to attack.

- If your instance uses mixed-mode authentication, disable or rename the `sa` account.
- Group Managed Service Accounts (gMSAs) should be used instead of traditional service accounts.
- gMSAs are more secure than traditional service accounts and also simplify security operations.
- `xp_cmdshell` should not be enabled. SQL Server is best secured through multiple layers of protection.
- `xp_cmdshell` opens the door for attackers to perform lateral movement attacks and gain access to the server's operating system.
- Configure a P1 alert that fires if anyone attempts to enable `xp_cmdshell`. This gives an early warning that could prevent an attack from being successful.
- Audit administrative activity of your SQL Server instances. This ensures non-repudiation and also helps you stop an attack if a privileged account has been compromised.
- You can use SQL audit to provide a lightweight mechanism for auditing administrative activity.
- Use cell-level encryption sparingly, because it can cause substantial bloat and performance issues. It is a good tool for securing highly sensitive data, however.
- A whole-value substitution attack describes an attacker replacing an encrypted value with a different encrypted value that they believe will benefit them.
- Whole-value substitution attacks can be used to perform nefarious activity such as credit card fraud.
- If you use cell-level encryption, consider using an authenticator column, which will prevent whole-value substitution attacks.
- SQL injection is a common attack pattern in which a bad actor will insert malicious SQL commands into an application that builds SQL dynamically.
- SQL injection attacks can be used to spoof user identities, leak information, destroy data, and perform lateral movement to other network resources.
- You can mitigate the risk of SQL injection attacks by ensuring you have a strong security posture.
- You can also protect against SQL injection attacks by enforcing coding standards, such as insisting applications access data via stored procedures as opposed to dynamically building SQL.

index

C

D

G

H

I

J

K

L

M

RELATED MANNING TITLES

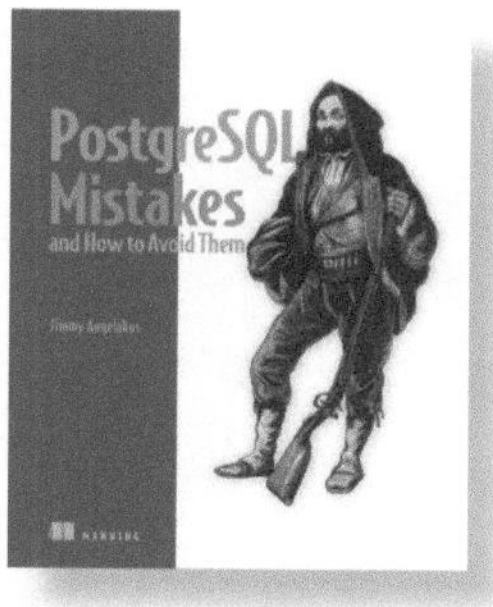

PostgreSQL Mistakes and How to Avoid Them
by Jimmy Angelakos

ISBN 9781633436879
270 pages *(estimated)*, $49.99
Spring 2025 *(estimated)*

Learn SQL in a Month of Lunches
by Jeff Iannucci

ISBN 9781633438576
336 pages *(estimated)*, $49.99
January 2025 *(estimated)*

Learn dbatools in a Month of Lunches
by Chrissy LeMaire, Rob Sewell, Jess Pomfret, Cláudio Silva
Foreword by Anna Hoffman

ISBN 9781617296703
400 pages, $59.99
May 2022

Java Persistence with Spring Data and Hibernate
by Cătălin Tudose
Forewords by Dmitry Aleksandrov and Mohamed Taman

ISBN 9781617299186
616 pages, $59.99
January 2023

For ordering information, go to www.manning.com

MANNING

liveBook

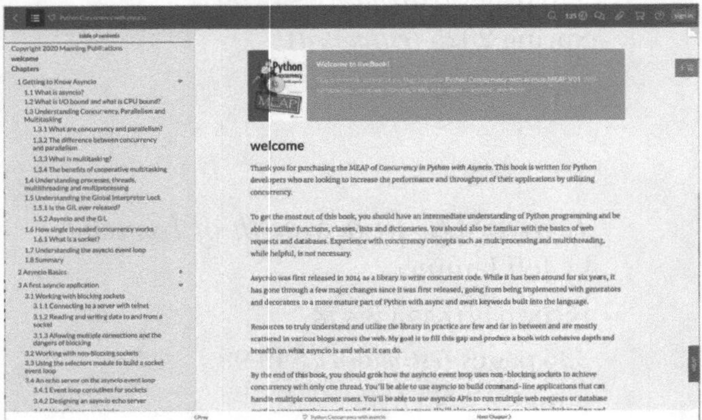